- .No previous knowledge of Java is required
- . Step-by-step skill acquiring through programs & solutions
- . Every chapter focuses on an important aspect of Java
- . Many programs and their outputs in order to demonstrate the application of programming concepts
- . A complete self-contained course for individual learning and a workshop companion for practical work in Java
- . Creating your own Java applets for the Internet

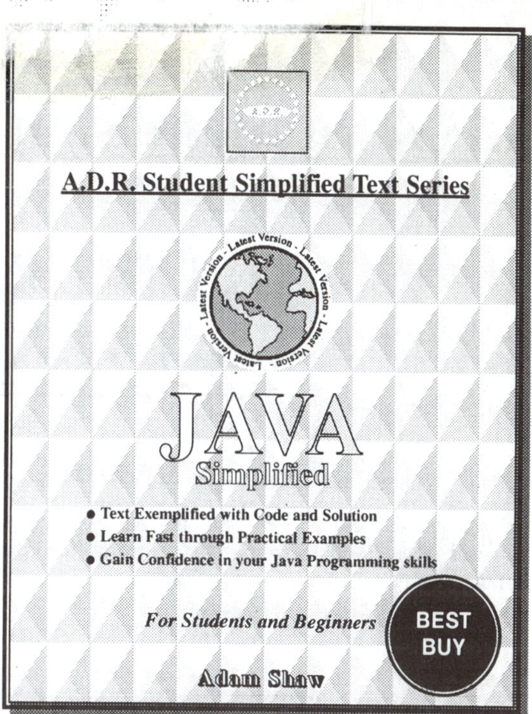

ISBN: 190 1197 883 Paperback £15.99 1999 Size: 249x190 mm Pages: 325 (Total)

- . No previous knowledge of C++ is required
- . Step-by-step skill acquiring through programs & solutions
- . Every chapter focuses on an important aspect of C++
- . Many programs and their outputs in order to demonstrate the application of programming concepts
- . A complete self-contained course for individual learning and a workshop companion for practical work in C++

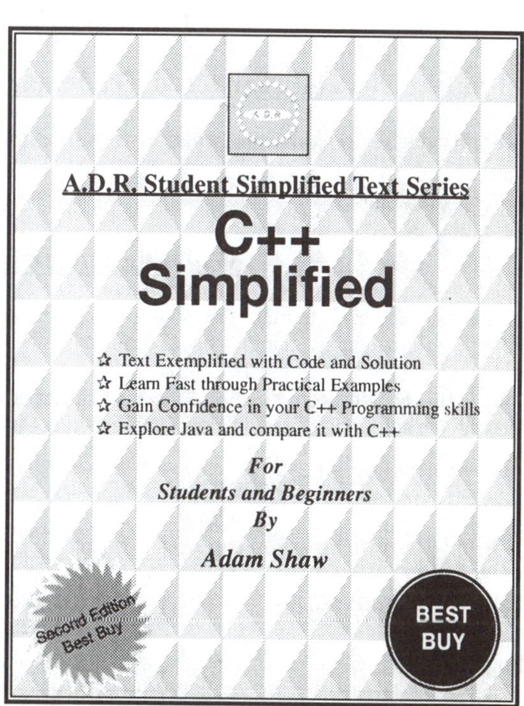

ISBN: 190 1197 999 Paperback £14.99 1998 Size: 249x190 mm Pages: 309 (Total)

A.D.R. Student Simplified Text Series

XHTML Simplified

Web Technology

Copyright

British Library Cataloguing in Publication Data

A catalogue record for this book is available from the British Library

ISBN 190 1197 700

Trademarks and registered Trademarks & Acknowledgements

Warning and Disclaimer

Direct Order

In case of difficulty, you can obtain this copy from the publisher.

A . D . R . (London) Limited
24 St. Alban Road
Bridlington
YO16 7SS
England

Tel: 01262 400323/605538
Fax: 01262 400323
E-mail: sales@ adrlonodon.ltd.uk
Web Site: http:// www.adrlondon.ltd.uk

Printed in Great Britain

A.D.R. Student Simplified Text Series

A person who searches for knowledge is a student

XHTML Simplified

- Text exemplified with code and solution
- Learn fast through practical examples
- Gain confidence in your XHTML Web page development skills
- Explore both XML and HTML and compare these with XHTML

By

Rachel Webster

A.D.R.(London)Limited

Preface

Why should you buy this book?

ADR Student Simplified Text Series is comprised of practical programming and Web books for you to acquire new knowledge and skills and apply them in order to improve your chances of success in this increasingly competitive world. The amount of positive feedback we have received from our readers confirms that self-motivated people have undoubtedly benefited from our books.

In accordance with our approach to the subject matter and readership, a person who searches for knowledge is a student. Therefore, if you buy this book with a view to learning and, applying this knowledge in order to develop your own Web site or contributing towards the development of a Web site at work, as a member of a team, you are a student. Indeed, you will find this book invaluable.

Irrespective of your current economic activity, this book is intended to guide you through scores of worked and fully illustrated examples of the application of XHTML for the development of a Web site. It also provides you with some essential information.

It is filled with numerous practical examples and their solutions, all of which are coded in XHTML and fully explained. At present, there is an acute shortage of XHTML browsers or any other user agents, which can validate XHTML documents. Indeed, there are plenty of browsers for HTML documents, but these browsers do not understand the XHTML. The W3C HTML Validation Service is the most reliable means of validating XHTML documents. Unlike some other books on the market, all practical XHTML examples in this book have been validated by this service. This is an important factor which you should consider before buying any XHTML book.

After the successful validation of each solved XHTML example, each document was previewed successfully in the Internet Explorer 5 and 5.5 versions. The screen captures for all worked examples are included so that you can see the outcome of each one. You can preview your XHTML documents in another browser. The solved practical examples may appear to be simple at first but they demonstrate the development of the Web site. The output of the document developed is an important part of an example as it will enable you to learn the features of the" markup language" introduced. You are advised to try these out on your computer as you progress through the book. A practical skill is best learnt by a hands-on approach; therefore, it is recommended that you work through these examples.

It is a practical book and thus covers those topics for which space was available to demonstrate their application. I believe that the contents of this book without the inclusion of some other XHTML topics are sufficient for the development and working of a Web site. The emphasis is on learning from experience and applying it. The book will enable you to achieve your objective to learn XHTML, and develop a Web site either individually or as a member of a group at work or on a programme of Web site development learning. It will lay the foundation for advancing your practical skills in this comparatively new technology.

I hope you derive as much pleasure and satisfaction from it as I enjoyed in its writing. Good luck!

Rachel Webster, England

June 2001

****

Chapter 11 Forms for Online Application 227

Chapter 12 Including Frames in Your Web Pages 255

Chapter 1

Towards the Understanding of XHTML

This is to congratulate Tim Berners-Lee, Director W3C, and several teams of experts who have been working laboriously towards the development and advancement of W3C technologies for the benefit of all Web users throughout the world.

(ADR)

• Learning resources

I have used Microsoft Windows 98 suite on my PC Pentium. I started using the Internet Explorer 5.0 (IE5.0), but in the middle of writing this book, I changed over to IE 5.5. In order to submit your documents to W3C HTML Validation Service, you will need to upload your documents to your Web site. Therefore, you must have installed a FTP browser for this purpose. I have made use of Terrapin FTP Browser. In addition to this book, you too must have access to these or similar learning resources. Good luck in your XHTML learning project. Be patient!

• Chapter 1

The primary aim of this chapter is to lay the foundation of understanding and applying XHTML by way of introducing you to some of the essential developments in the field of the World Wide Web.

By reading this chapter, you should be able to describe the various ideas and concepts learnt in this chapter. You should also be able to give some reasons for the invention of XHTML.

• What is XHTML?

• Why should you learn XHTML?

The **W**orld **W**ide **W**eb or **WWW or Web** or **W3** is a distributed information service. It was developed in the early 1990s, at CERN, the European Centre for Practical Physics, Geneva. CERN launched the Web in 1991. It is, in fact, the software for distributed information service, which runs on the Internet. In short, the Web is the most exciting and popular part of the **Internet** that is a computer communications network system. It was developed during the 1970's in the USA. It is now a huge collection of computer networks linked together world wide. You can even link loosely, your own PC system to the Internet.

The **W**orld **W**ide **W**eb **C**onsortium, widely known as **W3C**, was founded in 1994 at the Massachusetts Institute, Laboratory for Computer Science (MIT/LCS) in collaboration with CERN, where Tim Berners-Lee worked. At the time of writing this book, it has more than 400 member organisations all over the world. The membership includes corporate users, governments, research laboratories, vendors of technology products and the like. Its prime objective is to lead the WWW to its full potential. In order to achieve this objective, it has a number of roles to play. One such role is to standardise Web technologies by means of specifications.

> " W3C's role in making the Recommendation is to draw attention to the specification and to promote its widespread development. This enhances the functionality and interoperability of the Web."
> (Recommendation – as spelled in this quotation) (Reference: http:// www. w3. org/TR/REC-xml)

These specifications outline the building blocks of the Web. Before proceeding any further, at this stage, it is desirable to know three important terms: markup, SGML and hypertext, so that the following discussion becomes clearer.

• Markup

The word **'mark-up'** has been borrowed from the traditional publishing industry. In this industry, the hand written information for the typesetters is known as mark-up. This mark-up information is only for the typesetters, and thus it does not appear in the final version of a printed document (e.g. a book). The mark-up instructs the typesetter about the document layout. Note that 'markup' for Web technologies is spelled without the hyphen in order to distinguish it from traditional hand-written mark-up instructions for the typesetters.

In electronic processing, the markup consists of code written in a particular markup language. The code itself is embedded within the document, which is to be displayed. When the document is displayed or printed, the embedded code does not appear on the screen. In other words, the embedded code is hidden.

• SGML - Standard Generalized Markup Language

It is used for defining the syntax of textual markup languages. It can be said that it is the mother of HTML, XML and XHTML markup languages. It is possible that you have not heard of SGML before, but it was developed at IBM a long time ago. Since 1986, it has been formally standardized as ISO/IEC 8879. It has many powerful features. However, its complexity has inhibited its adoption in the Web in its own right.

• **hypertext** – the term hypertext (one word begins with small h) includes both text and pictures. It is a technique for interconnecting links between documents or Web pages and within the same document. With hypertext links, required items of information on the Web can be reached easily. The hypertext links technique is a powerful means of creating and viewing multidimensional Web pages, such as an encyclopaedia. Of course, it is also used for less complicated documents such as a Web site of a small company, which has a few hyper linked web pages. A **Web site** consists of Web pages. It is just like this book, but on-line. A collection of whatever you wish to publish on the Web with the view to communicate with Web users across the world.

Now, it is appropriate to discuss some of the W3C's specifications which are as follows:-

• **HTML** - **H**yper**T**ext **M**arkup **L**anguage based on **SGML**.

- HTML was created by Tim Berners-Lee in 1991. He combined some of the concepts of SGML with hypertext links ideas and thus created HTML in 1991.
- The format of HTML is fixed. It has three versions as listed below:-
  - First version published as **HTML 3.2** in January 1997
  - Second version published as **HTML 4** in December 1997
  - Revised in April 1998
  - Revised as **HTML 4.01** in December 1999. The revision fixes minor errors found in the HTML 4.0.

You can create and edit HTML documents by using any editing tools. You can use Microsoft WordPad for this purpose. Whenever, you access a **Web** document, follow the hyperlinks by using your mouse pointer, see animated images on your screen, and so on. All these things are created by using the HTML language. The HTML enables you :

- to create pre-formatted text.
- to format documents - you can choose numerous typeface styles, sizes...
- to create hyperlinks – the hyperlinks allow you to point to such things as multimedia files, or other Web documents. It enables you to create links to other documents on the Internet.
- to create tables, lists, frames....
- to create graphical images and link these to other documents – you can link these to other documents all over the internet

- interactive tasks – a user can perform various tasks. For example, form completion
- other features – such as downloading and running of Web pages on your system

HTML has been the backbone of the Web since it was invented. There are many millions of Web pages across the Web based on this markup language. Its popularity is so great that it is supported world wide by browser developers, editors (software for it), e-mail software and the like. HTML has also led to the development of some other technologies, such as Java, JavaScript, and so on.

A **browser** is a piece of software which enables the user to locate and view documents on the Internet. You can also test your documents locally in a browser before publishing them on the Internet. A well-known browser is Microsoft Internet Explorer 5.0 (IE5). At the time of writing, the latest version of Microsoft Internet Explorer is 5.5. You will meet it again. Another popular browser is Netscape. In fact, now-a-days, there are a growing number of user agents. More about them later on as the book progresses.

Despite its popularity, HTML has some shortcomings. These shortcomings are attributed to its growth and complexity. For instance, the portable handheld devices have become increasingly popular. HTML is just too big and complex to be used with such devices. It was intended for formatting and presenting documents on the Internet, but as the Web has been getting bigger and bigger, the HTML limitations have become more apparent. It is still here, but W3C has already developed the next generation of markup language. These are:

- **XML 1.0** - Extensible Markup Language.
  - It is a subset of SGML. It is the first step towards the next generation of languages for specific requirements. It is meant to be easy to learn and use on the Web.
  - XML 1.0 - first published in February 1998
  - XML 1.0 (Second Edition) published on 6 October 2000
  - Its format is not fixed like HTML. It has no pre-defined tags. For this reason, it is called extensible. It means that it allows the author of the document to generate some new tags for the purpose they are required. You may be wondering how it can be simple if it allows the generation of an unknown number of tags by an enormous number of authors across the world. Furthermore, an unknown number of tags may create problems for browsers and the maintenance of Web sites.
  - XML concentrates on document structure. This is particularly useful as it is not dependent on any specific media for its document delivery. On the Web, media similar to newspapers, magazines and television, has evolved and is becoming increasingly popular.
  - XML requires strict application of its rules unlike the HTML. The HTML document author can

be flexible in implementing some tags. The HTML browser can fix syntax errors, and the document can perform its task. Furthermore, there are many HTML dedicated editors software which can be used to develop error free HTML documents. The problem is that the more error fixing tasks browsers perform, the more complex and bigger in size they become. This is not desirable as large browsers cannot be handled by smaller devices such as mobile phones. Such small devices do not have sufficient memory and network bandwidth (one word) to render HTML documents.

The term **bandwidth**, generally means the rate at which information is sent through a network. A high bandwidth refers to a large amount of information. A large document will take too much bandwidth.

Another important point to note is that large and complex browsers tend to be slower. In fact, this is rather disadvantageous as many web users can confirm.

• How does XML propose to solve these problems?

XML requires strict application of its syntax rules. This requirement means that there is no need to develop large and complex browsers for handling XML based documents. Lighter and less complex browsers can process XML documents faster and more efficiently. It is worth mentioning that XML has two classes of documents namely, **well-formed** and **valid**. These classes of documents are distinguished by their characteristics. No doubt, you will learn more about XML in Chapter 3.

• Parsing

The dictionary definition says that parsing is the analysis of a sentence into its component parts and a description of them grammatically. The same principle is applied when the parser is parsing or analysing an XML document into an element tree.

• Dedicated XML parsers and browsers

The XML parser is a piece of software. The first browser to have an XML parser was Microsoft Internet Explorer 4.0. Now-a-days, there are dedicated XML parsers (or processors) as well as browsers on the world market. The parser presents the structure and content of an XML document to an application. It does so by means of an interface such as DOM.

DOM is another technology developed by the World Wide Consortium (W3C). It is an Application Programmer Interface (API) to the document structure. The DOM is not specifically tied up to any programming language or to any particular platform. You can obtain further information about DOM from the Web site at :

http://www.w3.org/DOM/Activity

Some of these parsers are free and can be downloaded from the XML software site at:

for XML parsers **http://www.xmlsoftware.com/parsers**

At the time of writing, I counted 45 different parsers at this site. These parsers were developed for a variety of platforms, including:

Windows 95/ 98, Windows NT, Linux, Solaris, SML, Unix, Perl, Python, ActiveX Java and its different versions.

Microsoft XML Parser Version 3.0 is free like some of the other parsers. For Java platform, you will find several parsers to choose one that suits your needs.

for XML browsers **http://www.xmlsoftware.com/browsers**

At this site, there were 13 dedicated XML browsers. This list included Microsoft Internet Explorer 5. Like the parsers, these browsers were developed for a variety of platforms and cover some of the above listed platforms. These browsers are for viewing XML documents. The XML browsers are either tree-based or application specific and driven by style sheets (see style sheets).

Main differences between validating and non-validating parsers

Validating parsers	Non-validating parsers
• impose the rules of XML grammar - syntax rules	• enforce the rules of XML grammar - syntax rules
• know how to validate a document against a Document Type Definition (DTD)	• check a well formed document in order to make sure it is written in accordance with XML syntax rules. It checks only the well formed requirements.
• can check well formed document to examine that syntax rules have	• can check valid documents but without validating them.
been observed correctly for validation	• do not load DTDs or entities external to the document
• load DTDs or entities external to the document	and thus a valid document may not work with a non-validating parser

Table 1

. Types of Parsers

Like the well formed and valid documents distinction, there are two types of parsers namely, validating and non-validating parsers. Their main differences are summarised in table 1 shown above.

. How is the DTD validated ?

Since the document is validated by the parser, the DTD is also validated, if it is the validating parser. It is the tree which is validated against the DTD by the validating parser. As stated already that the tree is created in memory which precisely matches with the XML file on the system (hard disk).

. XHTML 1.0 - the **E**xtensible **H**ypertext **M**arkup **L**anguage

- Based on HTML and applies the syntax of XML.

  It is a reformulation of HTML as an XML application. It simply means that it makes use of HTML tags and syntax (grammar) of XML. This way, it combines the best features of both HTML and XML markup languages.

. Why have W3C created XHTML as XML is extensible?

In short, there are two basic reasons for developing XHTML. These are:

- There are millions of HTML documents on the Web. It is inconceivable to convert so many documents to XML in order to benefit from it. It can cause many problems in a very large number of organisations who have very many Web pages.
  It is just not feasible to persuade millions of HTML users to switch over to XHTML in a short space of time.

- As discussed above that HTML based documents are too big to be handled by in creasing smaller devices (having smaller browsers), and the Internet is getting bigger and bigger.

Thus, W3C had to start thinking to reformulate HTML as an XML application.

- First recommended in January 2000. At the time of writing, this is the current W3C 'Recommendation' for the latest version of HTML 4.01.

- XHTML has three variants known as " flavours". These are:

  . Transitional
  . Strict
  . Framest

- The document has some additional information concerning how the browser should display the content of the document. This additional information is just a set of rules which is known as **Document Type Definition – DTD**. When the browser reads an XHTML document, the DTD helps the browser to interpret the tags in the document. Most of the latest browsers have built-in DTDs, and are thus capable of distinguishing which of the html version is being implemented. Some older browsers cannot display either fully or partially HTML 4.01 or XHTML. 1.0.

- There are three types of DTDs in order to let the browser know whether it is Transitional, or Strict, or Frameset variants of XHTML One of these must be in your XHTML document.

- XHTML promises richer Web pages on a variety of browsers, cell phones, pagers, television, wallet sized wireless communications, kiosks, desktops, PDA, and so on.

- Old HTML documents can be converted into XHTML using W3C's Open Source HTML Tidy utility

- XHTML is modular. It can be **modularized** for a variety of browsers and tools.

  For instance, to surf the Web page designed for HTML browser on a cell phone can create considerable problems.

  XHTML can be modularized to work with it in order to surf the Web. This way, XHTML can be used efficiently with browsers which vary greatly in their capabilities.

- Therefore, XHTML is most suited for new devices designed to surf the Web.

. Some essential terms, concepts and tools

The theme of this book is XHTML. Before proceeding any further, it is highly desirable that you have some understanding of the topics discussed in the remainder of this chapter. Your knowledge of these terms, concepts and tools will enable you to follow the book with some ease, instil confidence and help you to learn faster.

. What is meant by the structure of a document in general?

The dictionary definition of the word **structure** is the way something is put together, organised, or built. Therefore, you can say that anything, which has some parts, has a structure. For instance, a page has a number of paragraphs, each of which has several sentences and each sentence is composed of some words and punctuation marks put together in accordance with the rules of English grammar.

In fact, one can even further analyse the page in order to find out the total number of words, characters and punctuation marks. The content of a page gives information about something which makes the page a document as it meets a dictionary definition of the **document** which states that a document is a paper affording information, proof or evidence of anything.

You can think of countless documents that surround you in any busy office. For instance, a reference manual of your PC is a document as it has several parts **(structure)**, and it also provides you with some technical guidance (**information)** concerning your PC.

An example of a document

Medical Fact Sheet

The Human Brain

The human brain is as big as a coconut, and the shape of a walnut. It has two hemispheres, which are covered in a thin skin of deeply wrinkled grey tissue called the cerebral cortex.

Each infold on this surface is known as sulcus, and each bulge is known as gyrus. The surface landscape of each individual's brain is slightly different, but the main wrinkles - like nose - mouth grooves and crow's feet on an ageing face - are common to all and are used as landmarks.

For further Information: TheBrainSurgeon @home.com

Document: Medical Fact Sheet

For instance, the above document called Medical Fact Sheet has a **structure** which is analysed as consisting of:

- the title of the document: Medical Fact Sheet
- the topic name: The Human Brain
- three paragraphs: information on the topic itself making up the body of the document
- last paragraph: directing the reader where to obtain further information from

This decomposition of the document identifies only the main components of the document. Indeed, you can go beyond this analysis in order to identify the smallest elements in the entire structure of this document. In addition, the purpose of this document is to give some **information** on the human brain. Thus, the actual **content** of each paragraph is the information which you can read.

This idea of a document is applied in markup languages. Similarly, the XHTML document also has both **structure** and **content** (information). In diagram 1, the XHTML document is viewed as consisting of **structure** (markup) and **information**. For ease of learning, the **information** component is further decomposed as shown in this diagram 1 below.

Diagram 1

Information

The Web Page contains this information for displaying in the browser window as a Web Page for the viewer. Consider it as data for distinguishing it from the script below

Markup

The structural information which is not displayed when the Web Page is viewed in the browser window. It describes the structure of the document in **XHTML**

Script

The code written in a programming language such as **JavaScript**. The code is required for manipulating the content of the document

XHTML Document

Not all Web pages require a script. This is just an illustration.

- The document Medical Fact Sheet is written in Times New Roman font, size 10-point. It has no other fonts of another size or type in order to make its appearance more appealing. Of course, by applying some formatting techniques, I can make this document not only attractive but also very different in its appearance. For instance, I can use **bold font** font, or *italics* type Arial font for the heading and also underline it. I can also change the background by using a colour for the background. Similarly, the rest of the document can also be transformed into a different appearance.

The changes in a document's appearance are made through the process of **formatting**. You can specify a number of formatting features. Collectively, these formatting features are called **style.** A word processor lets you create a variety of appearances for the same document. Different word processors apply different standards for formatting and styles.

• The style

The style concerns the way the document is displayed on your screen. Here, the word 'displayed' also includes other formats such as printed document and spoken document. Thus, a document is displayed either to be read or heard. Before a document can be displayed, it should be formatted and styled. The W3C have already published the following two recommendations for **Style Sheets**:

- **Cascading Style Sheets (or css or CSS)** – originally developed for HTML
  It has two levels. CSS1 and CSS2.
- **XSL** – it stands for XML Stylesheet Language. It has two parts. These are:
  - **XSLT** – it is short for **XSL** Transformation
  - **XSLFO** – it is short for **XSL** Formatting Objects

The Cascading Style Sheets have been in use for some time. They are supported by major browsers including the Microsoft Internet Explorer 5 **(IE5).** In addition, it also supports XSL.

• What are structural objects of a document?

In the above examples, the whole document is divided into three paragraphs, title, and topic name components. Each of these components of the document also has its own content (information). Therefore, each division or component of the document is, in its own right, considered as **structural object** which has its own structure and content/information. A document can have many such **structural objects.**

For further Information: TheBrainSurgeon @home.com

The component shown above in the shaded area is a **structural object**, because it meets both requirements for a structural object, namely, the structure and the information or content.

• What about the appearance or style of the document?

The appearance or style is the way the document is displayed, say, in the browser window. Of course, to the human eye, the good appearance of a document helps you to read it. For instance, you can format the information content of the document to make it look very nice by using different size fonts for both title and topic name. You can also use a different type and size of font for the last paragraph.

Furthermore, the use of a colour scheme can also make its appearance not only attractive but very different to what is shown above. The style tools control the formatting elements such as fonts sizes, types, background colour and the like. The process of formatting the document by means of variety of style tools generates some new objects, which are known as **flow objects**.

• What are these flow objects?

When the browser displays a Web page on your computer screen, it is termed as the document flows. If it is written in English, its content in the form of characters, words, paragraphs, symbols, etc. It flows from top to bottom, and from left to right. Thus, the flow object is anything in the flow which is displayed or printed.

The human brain is as big as a coconut, and the shape of a walnut. It has two hemispheres, which are covered in a thin skin of deeply wrinkled grey tissue called the cerebral cortex.

For instance, the above paragraph is formatted in 10 point Times New Roman font, and styled with a grey background. When it is output and displayed on your screen, its content, in the form of characters, words, punctuation marks and the background colour, flows as a discrete unit of **flow object** of text on a grey background. A document will have a number of such flow objects. In theory, a character can be the smallest flow object, but in practice, it is often a bigger unit, such as a word.

• Does the formatting and various style tools (software) alter the document structure?

No. The style tools and formatting do not alter the structure at all. In fact, the well thought out formatting exposes the structure of a document as well as helps its reader. You can think of structure as the basis of the document from which appearance is derived by means of formatting techniques. Indeed, there is a relationship between the structure of the document and its appearance to the extent that appearance is derived from it, and that the structure is not dependent on the appearance. It is the style of the document changes by applying various style tools, but the information and structure remains the same.

• What is a network?

The word network features in this chapter and elsewhere in this book. It is essential to establish its meaning in the context of the Internet, prior to discussing the Internet. It will help you to understand the Internet and the Web.

In simplest terms, the network means computers linked to each other by cables in order to share and exchange data or information. The network also enables its users to share other devices such as printers, and other resources. Historically, there were just two types of networks namely, **Local Area Network (LAN)** and **Wide Area Network (WAN)**. A local area network exists in many organisations in both private and public sectors of the economy. For instance, you can find **LAN** in schools and companies. Some commercial firms have local area networks if they do not have to cover a large geographical area, to exchange and share data and other computing resources with colleagues.

The **Wide Area Network (WAN)** exists mainly in large organisations, as they can handle a large volume of data and cover a large geographical area at a very fast speed. Since it covers a wide area, it can have a number of LANs at different places within the organisation at remote locations. Thus, a WAN comprises of several LANs at different places. A WAN is connected by high speed and high volume cables (optical fibre cables). In order to operate the WAN over a wide geographical area, radio or satellite links are required. WANs are rather complicated and expensive, and require the services of specialist telecommunication organisations. In the UK, BT, Mercury , AT & T are three such WAN connections service providers.

The invention of the network has led to the development of the Internet. Now, it is the right time and place in this book to discuss the Internet.

. What is the Internet?

In order to answer this question, firstly, I must briefly trace the history below that has led to the development of today's Internet.

Yes, indeed, it is a network of interconnected computers **(nodes)**. It is a computer communications network system. Its historical development goes back to the year 1969, when in the USA, the Advanced Research Projects Agency, abbreviated as **ARPA**, was established by the United States Department of Defence. The ARPA established a network known as Advanced Research Projects Agency Network, abbreviated as **ARPAnet**. The ARPAnet connected a number of military and research sites, developed a communication protocol, and methods for routing data through communication paths. In the 1970's, still in the USA, some other networks developed, using the technology developed by **ARPAnet**. These networks were used by universities and some commercial enterprises.

Again, in the USA, in the 1980's, some more networks developed. Among these networks, the National Science Foundation **(NSF)** developed **NSFNET**, which was used by universities. The NSFNET provided very high speed connections, and thus became popular.

Some more networks developed and interconnected, and were used by universities, researchers and some commercial enterprises. In Britain, in 1984, the Joint Academic Network (Janet) developed from a number of separate networks. Similar developments took place in some other parts of the world. Thus, the beginning of ARPANET and its various developments led to the growth of a number of other networks world wide.

This growth of interconnected networks collectively is known as the Internet (or Net for short). With the aid of diagram 2, you can visualise the Internet as a huge (estimated over 80 000 networks) network of networks of interconnected computers world wide.

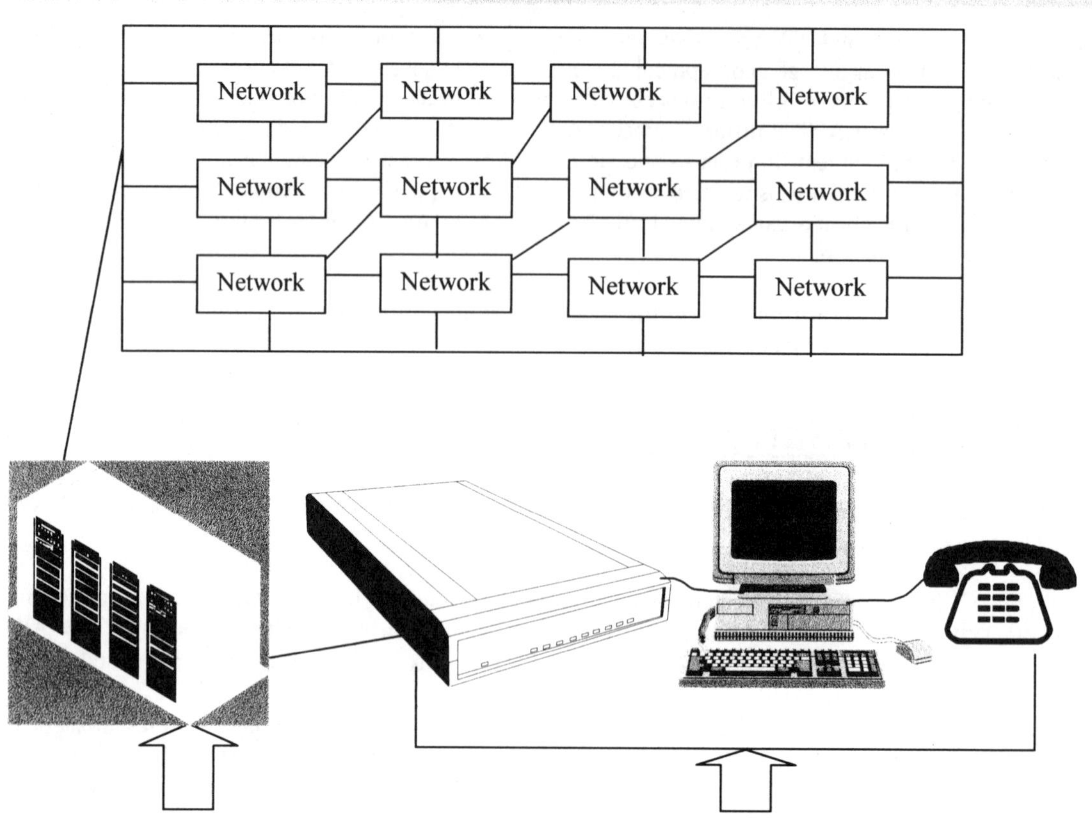

Internet Service Provider (ISP)

. Hub - computer system commercial service provider such as Global Internet

User of the Net

. Modem internal or external - here it is shown as external. It can also be fitted to your PC internally. You can have either an **analogue** or **isdn** modem.

. Telephone line is attached to the modem which is attached to the computer externally or fitted internally. For an **Isdn** modem, in the UK, BT can install for you either home highway or business highway for faster speed, if you can afford the extra costs of installing and running it. Your phone bill will be higher, if you use the home or business highway. First carry out cost and benefit analysis!

Diagram 2

At the beginning of the third millennium, the Internet is not just a network of computers for some universities or government agencies. On the contrary, it is increasingly used by all kinds of small and large organisations in both private and public sectors. It is also increasingly used by people from all walks of life all over the world through services provided by commercial organisations. These commercial organisations have made it possible for personal computer users to loosely link their PC's to the Internet by means of the modem and telephone line. It can bring a vast amount of information into your home or office in the form of words, numbers, pictures, visual, and audio. Its major features are listed below:

- **connects a myriad of computers all over the world** - tens of thousands of computers, which are known as servers are connected to the Net to make up the Net itself. Each year, the Net is getting bigger and bigger.

- **has databases** - information held within a computer system. There are an enormous number of databases on the Net for all kinds of purposes one can imagine. For instance, databases for library resources, travel information, entertainment information, and weather information. You can think of any other topic, and it is highly likely that you will find some information on it on the Net.

- **facilitates e-commerce** - the new buzz word invented in the late 1990's. It is another way of doing business which relies on the Net. You can do all kinds of business on the Net. For instance, a shopkeeper can place an order for goods. A housewife can buy groceries from a store, and so on. You can set up your own shop, accountancy, estate agency or any other type of business on the Internet, and hope to sell your products or services to your prospective customers anywhere in the world.

- **facilitates e-mail** - you can send and receive post or messages instantly anywhere in the world by means of the Net.

- **has newsgroups** - There are very many newsgroups for topical discussion with like-minded people across the world. It is highly likely that on the Internet you will find more than one news group dedicated to the subject area of your interest on which you wish to exchange, information, views or whatever. It could be baking bread, or looking for a brain surgeon for a friend. Newsgroups are often used for 'chat' . If you are interested in entertaining yourself , or debating a topic and the like, you can try newsgroup.

- **has FTP - File Transfer Protocol** - On the Internet, you can transfer a file across the Internet from one computer to another. It is often used by companies for things such as software delivery instantly and directly to the computer where it is needed.

. Is it a single entity?

It does not exist as an entity in its own right. Therefore, it is not owned by any one organisation or a group of companies. Thus, there is no single centre or an organisation to manage the Internet world wide. It is managed and owned by thousands of individual organisations who own and manage these individual networks throughout the world, which constitute the Internet.

Some writers show the Internet by an uneven circle or by a cloud form figure surrounded by computers, which are linked to it making a network together. These representations give the wrong impression that the internet is some sort of co-ordinating body. It is not so. In reality, the Internet does not exist as such.

• The Web

Founder of Web: Tim Berners-Lee

At the beginning, it is stated,

"the Web is the most exciting and popular part of the Internet."

By now you know that when someone says the Internet, it implies interconnected computers across the world. Of course, these interconnected computers store masses of information. The Web is a software concerning distributed information service over the Net. One can say, it is a method of accessing this stored information by anyone anywhere in the world by means of a computer system. The computer system can be a PC, which is equipped with some relevant software, a modem and a telephone line. Of course, the PC user has to have an account with the Internet service provider.

The Web has made it possible to ensure that the information stored on the Internet can be accessed by anyone. In general, the Web's appeal is that most people find it easy to make use of it. On the other hand, other parts of the Internet are not so easy to use, and require some technical skills and experience.

• What is a Web site?

It is an interactive document. It is an electronic version of a document or photo, illustration or any other thing you can think of. For instance, a leaflet on this book can be a Web site used for selling this book. If it is a Web site, then it is in the electronic format, and on-line, where prospective customers can see it. In fact, on-line, the leaflet is just like a shop, where a customer can place an order, by filling in the order form. The order form is a part of this leaflet. You can find all kinds of information on the Web. For example, you can make an airline booking from London to Moscow. In fact, it is highly likely that you will find some good bargains to travel across the world.

One of the differences between Web pages and traditional types of publishing is that Web sites can contain hyperlinks (links for simplicity). A link is an underlined word or phrase, or an image. When you click it with a mouse it opens the required page. In fact, this required page can be anywhere on the Web. A great advantage of a Web site is that it usually has forms for visitors to fill in. Many large organisations have built their web sites with a search facility in order to assist the visitor to find the required information.

• How are the interconnections and communication links between a myriad of computers all over the world organised/managed?

The voluntary agreements between the owners of a myriad of computers all over the world concerning the technical aspects such as the Internet Protocols and addressing methods have led to certain rules which are observed by the owners of networks. There a number of organisations such as:

- **The Internet Society**
- **Internet Engineering Task Force**
- **The Internet Assigned Number Authority**

who are able to communicate among themselves in the interest of devising voluntary acceptable rules concerning technical aspects. There are no international political pressures on the Internet, though in any individual country across the world, there may be some local legal restrictions concerning the storage, retrieval, manipulation and transfer of information in all forms on the Internet.

In order to transmit the information around the Internet, the Internet uses the **TCP/IP -Transmission Control Protocol/ Internet Protocol**. A protocol is a set of rules and standards for the communication of information (data).

TCP/IP was developed in the USA, by the Defence Advanced research Projects Agency (DARPA) in the 1970's. Now, the TCP/IP is a family of a number of protocols, which together dictate how the Net functions. The TCP/IP family of protocols is often described as "glue" which holds the Internet together. In brief, it transmits the required information in packets to its destination. It also makes sure that the delivered information is unpacked and assembled together correctly.

There are other TCP/IP compatible protocols. One such protocol is called **Hypertext Transfer Protocol – HTTP (or http)**. The WWW uses a communication protocol, which is similar to http. This is a public domain protocol. It is used with a specific **URL**. URL is the acronym for Uniform Resources Locators.

• What is the purpose of the URL?

Its purpose is to take you to a particular Web site and then let you connect to the required document on the Net. It creates a link. It is simply the full address of a page or document you are interested in on WWW. The general format of URL is as follows:

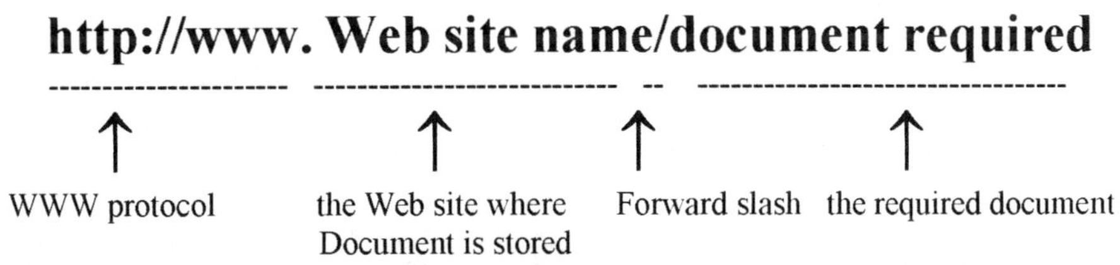

For instance: **http://www.microsoft.com/ie**. This address will take you to the Microsoft Web site where you will find Microsoft Internet Explorer.

. Web server & Web browser

Generally speaking, a server is a computer which serves other computers on the Internet. It can only do so through the web server software. The computer, on which a particular web page is located, is the server. This is its simplest meaning. It is worth mentioning that in the context of the Internet and the Web, you may hear that there are many commercial Web Server service providers to allow you to use the Internet. It simply means the Internet service provider **(ISP)**. **Why?**

It is due to the fact that these service providers have their computers interconnected, and hold Web pages. These interconnected computers communicate with each other on the Internet. They serve each other on the Internet. A server runs most of the time, except when it requires servicing. A server communicates on the internet with the client program, which you know by now is called the **browser** (software). Thus, in order to access a vast amount of information world wide, you have to install a browser software on your computer. Sometimes, it is also called a **graphical Web browser**, because it operates by means of a mouse input device. The mouse moves a pointer to a required icon, menu or some graphics. Modern computers are graphical based, as you use the mouse, they have colours, pictures, sounds and a graphical display. For older computers, you can have a text-based browser. This book is concerned with modern computers. Thus, the graphical browser is simply called browser.

. What exactly does a browser do?

For the user, the browser performs two specific **major** tasks. These are as follows:

- to decode the markup code in the Web page; and
- to display the decoded page (document) for you.

Once, the document has been decoded and the decoded page is currently displayed on the user's computer screen, then the browser interacts with the user, and **performs further tasks** described below:

- The user clicks the **hyperlink**, which is in the web page.

. What is this hyperlink?

Its purpose is to enable the user to link the current document to another required document on the Web or on the local system. It responds directly to the user's interest. The user clicks it with a mouse to go to another page. The link to a page anywhere on the Web requires the full URL for the page. The link to another page on the same system requires a path to the file in which the page is stored. The hyperlinks are shown in colours. Sometimes, due to background colours, a hyperlink may not be visible, but you can make hyperlinks stand out. Hyperlinks have different colours to represent their current state. For instance, a visited link is usually in purple. If your window has a purple background, it will not be visible. Without hyperlinks in documents, there will not be any connections to pages on the Web. The text you get when the link is made is called hypertext.

•How does it happen?

In response to the user's click, the **browser** communicates via the **HTTP (Hyper Text Transfer Protocol) network protocol** with the Web server, where the required document is stored. The required document can be anywhere on the Web. The link may take you to a page which is published by another publisher and kept on another computer on the Internet anywhere in the world. **Why?**

This is because a publisher of a document is not restricted to creating links only to his/her document. The hyperlink is like a jump to another related page of information. The browser requests for the specified document to be called up.

• How does the Web server respond?

In response to the browser's request for the specified document, the Web server via the HTTP protocol presents the required document to the browser.

• What happens next?

The browser now is able to interpret or decode the document, and presents it to the user in the required format. Now, the user is able to read the document. If the user wants to link this document to other pages, he can do so by clicking the hyperlink accordingly. The process can be repeated as long as the user is searching for the required information or service.

• Is it possible to trace all links which the user has tried ?

The hyperlinks can be traced back to the beginning of the hyperlinking process by the user. The browser keeps a record of all links the user made as he/she visited some documents.

• What is the advantage of keeping a record of hyperlinks by the browser?

This backtracking record can enable the user to know how he/she has been able to link to some documents in order to find the required information or service. It may be that the user has to visit a large number of pages kept on different servers in different countries. The user can return to a page several stages further back, if he/she wants.

This backtracking record can enable the user to know how he/she has been able to link to some documents in order to find the required information or service. It may be that the user has to visit a large number of pages kept on different servers in different countries. The user can return to a page several stages further back, if he/she wants.

• Which browser should you install on your computer?

There are a number of browser software packages on the market. You can obtain a browser software free of charge with some computer magazines, as **Freeware software**. If you do not pay for a piece of software, it is termed as freeware. When it costs you a nominal charge, it is called **shareware software**. The most commonly used browsers are Microsoft Internet Explorer and Netscape Communicator (originally known as Netscape's Navigator) from Netscape Communications Corporation. These two browsers dominate the market. There are many other browsers which are freeware or shareware. This book is not about browsers. It is highly likely that your Internet Service Provider (ISP) will supply you with one browser as part of the service (ask for it). For instance, on my computer, there is Microsoft Internet Explorer supplied by AOL. I also have Internet Explorer 5 as part of Microsoft Windows 98. Recently, I have acquired the latest version on Internet Explorer 5.5 If you have Windows 95 or Windows 98, you already have on your computer Microsoft Internet Explorer. For whatever personal reasons, you may be enthusiastic about browsers. In a super bookstore, you can find a number of books on browsers, especially on Microsoft Internet Explorer 5.

• User agents

Recently, the Web browser was the only means for viewing Web pages. This is not the case any more. Now-a-days, Web pages can be viewed by a variety of devices. These devices come under the term user agents. Some examples of user agents are cell phones, handheld devices, voice browsers and Web TV. User agents also mean the Web browser (just browser).

• How can you view a Web page?

Two different types of software are needed at two different places to view a Web page on the Internet.

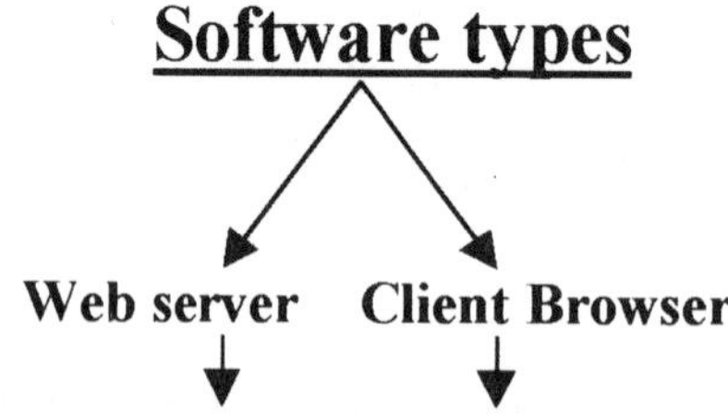

Software being used by the computer holding (ISP) the Web page

Software being used by you in order access the Web page and some other pages which may be linked to it

• Summary

This chapter has given you sufficient information to follow the next chapter and beyond.

Chapter 2

HTML Leading to XHTML

The prime aim of this chapter is:-

- to enable you to acquire some fundamental understanding of HTML in relation to XHTML

By reading and practising techniques that are demonstrated in this chapter, you should be able:-

- to explain the basic structure of HTML document
- to create a simple HTML document, save it, and view it locally
- to be aware that HTML and XHTML are two different standards as HTML browsers cannot validate XHTML documents to prove that the document meets XHTML language requirements.

This will help you to compare HTML with XHTML and XML as you progress through the book.

• Introduction

HTML is not a computer programming language. It is a markup language, and as such, it does not have the complexity of a programming language. For instance, to learn C++ or Java or any other programming language, one has to learn how to analyse a given situation, analyse requirements, and code a set of instructions in a particular programming language. The coding of a program can involve a complex program structure and decision making, in order to design a program that will do a job satisfactorily. A programmer has to learn programming language which is more demanding than HTML or any other markup language. This makes HTML comparatively easy to learn. The HTML language has its own set of symbols and rules that are part of HyperText Transfer Protocol (HTTP or http).

The HTML is a standard method of presenting textual material on the Web. It has features for controlling the appearance of the document. In addition, it allows you to include hyperlinks in your documents. To achieve all this, one has to learn its tags and their application. The good news is that the Web page designer can be flexible in the use of tags and can afford to violate some HTML syntax rules. Usually, the HTML browser is capable of matching tags in its own tags dictionary and thus edits the document. If it cannot match the tag, it just ignores it. One must learn the use of the following basic tags(elements).

• Creating HTML document

The HTML documents contain plain text, **ASCII code.** These documents use special **markup codes**, which are embedded in the text. I have used Windows 98 NotePad (tool) for my HTML documents. If I wanted to use, say Microsoft Word or WordPad for producing the HTML document, I could have done so. Thus, you can use whatever word processing tool is available on your computer. Some essential tags are described below:

• HTML tags

HTML tags (see elements) are typed into the document. These markup codes are surrounded by special markers which are the **angle brackets**, < and >. All HTML documents have four sections. Therefore, the following tags must be included in all HTML documents in order to create it.

• The <html > tag

Your document must begin with the **declaration or opening** tag **< html>**, and it should end with the **closing** tag **</ html>**. It should be noted that the closing tag has a forward slash within the < >. These tags signal to the browser that the document has been written in HTML.

• The <head> and <title > tags

An HTML document must have a **head** and **body**. These divisions of the document enable the browsers to interpret the document correctly. The <title> tag is written within the <head> section of an HTML document. Each document that is displayed by the Web browser should have its title shown in the top border (title bar) of the browser window. Like other tags, <head> and <title> tags have their own closing tags, as demonstrated by the following example:-

```
<head>
        <title>
            My First Attempt
        < / title>
</head>
```

Here, **My First Attempt** is the title of the document. This information is about the document itself. This is known as **meta-information**. This meta- information is additional information that will appear on the title bar of the browser.

• <BODY> tags

The **body** of the HTML document can have the bulk of the information that makes up your Web page. It produces the actual look of the Web page. The simplest example is shown below:-

```
<BODY>
            This is my first HTML document towards the design of my own Web site.
< / BODY>
```

To summarise, each of these tags is in a pair. The HTML markup codes are **not case-sensitive**. A case-sensitive standard or language distinguishes between upper and lower case letters. You can use either lowercase or uppercase letters. Now, is the right time to put theory into practice by preparing a workable HTML page.

• How do we create an HTML document?

You can use any **editor** in order to create an HTML document. Yes, there are also numerous specialised editors for this purpose. Some specialised editors can be obtained almost free. These editors can:

- enable you to create an HTML document
- check spellings of HTML words (keywords) automatically
- speed up the process of document creation
- provide you with some additional features such as templates , or codes. Codes you you can insert in your document by using function keys or pull down menus, and thus no keying manually is necessary.
- let you see what you create on the screen providing it is a full blown editor. Such an editor formats a document as you create and lets you see it on the screen, almost as it will appear in a Web browser and so on.

• Do you really need such a specialised HTML editor?

The frank answer is **no** for the following reasons:-

- restricts learning due to graphical design tools controlling code creation
- may not be able to support all HTML tags, despite great promises
- may be too complex for your needs, and thus an unwise investment in a costly product
- HTML document can be created successfully by means of any standard text editor such as **NotePad**, **WordPad**, and similar plain text editors. These text editors can easily facilitate the learning of HTML in a short space of time and at the same time save you money. It is advisable to start learning

with a simple text editor which is already available on your own PC - free of charge. Be wise with your resources!

• Example 1

In order to make a good start, just enter the simple html code shown in Diagram 1, in the NotePad or WordPad or any other text editor of your choice.

HTML code for Example 1 – MyFirstAttempt.html

```
<html>
<head>
<Title>My First Attempt
</title>
</head>
<body>
    This is my first attempt towards the design of my own Web site.
</body>
</html>
```

Diagram 1

The above HTML document is simple but complete for a basic Web page.

• Saving your document

Having keyed in your HTML code in a text editor, you must save it as text file, and store it in the same folder in which you keep all your Web documents. Both NotedPad, and WordPad will allow you to save your Web page/document or file by applying the following method shown in the shaded box:-

If you select:-

Save As from the menu
Save in : select your own folder for Web documents
File name: any suitable name ending with **.html**
Save as type: Text Document ⇐ to save your file in plain ASCII code is essential.

You must select it from the list of document types which will be shown in a menu

A Method for Saving HTML file as text file by using Microsoft NotePad or WordPad

By applying this method, I have saved this document as MyFirstAttempt.html

- This code will create your simple Web page or document with the following text to be displayed on screen:- This is my first attempt towards the design of my own Web site.

• Explanation

- In Diagram 1, the HTML code starts with an **<HTML> tag**. It declares that it is HTML document.
- <**HEAD**> tag - it has no other information about the document, except to include the title tag.
- <**TITLE**> tag - it is followed by the title of your document –meta-information (see meta-data and meta-information). The title is followed by the closing tag **</TITLE>**.
- </**HEAD**> tag - There is no other information to go into the **head section** of this HTML document, and thus the next line contains nothing except the closing tag for this section.
- <**BODY**> tag - it begins the body section.
- There is only one line of text in this <body> section of this document. This is the text that is displayed on the Web page. The body section contains the actual information which constitutes the document.
- </**BODY**> is used to close this section. It is then followed by the HTML closing tag: </**HTML**>.

For this example, you do not need to code anything else. Indeed, it is a complete executable file which can be viewed in Microsoft Internet Explorer or any other browser locally. By locally, it means off-line. This is prior to placing the document on a Web site for public viewing.

• Previewing your document locally

You can preview your html document by means of a Web browser. On my machine I have Microsoft Internet Explorer 5. I use it to preview documents locally prior to public viewing on the Web.

The advantage of previewing locally is that you can check your Web page before its publication on the Net. In order to preview your html file in the Microsoft Internet Explorer 5, the following steps are required:

- open the Internet Explorer (assuming this is on your machine)
- pull down the **File menu**
- select **Open** your folder in which you are storing your html files. In my case, it is **Examples**.
- locate the file required. In my case, it is **MyFirstAttempt.html**.

- select the required file. In my case, it is MyFirstAttempt.html.

- click **Open**, and click **OK**.

- Diagram 2 shows the html document. This document contains only one line of text. This diagram shows exactly what your html file in diagram 2 contains, except the html mark up tags. The title, " My First Attempt" is displayed in the title bar of the browser. The file name together with the full path is listed in the address box. The content of this document is just one line of text.

My First Attempt previewed in Internet Explorer

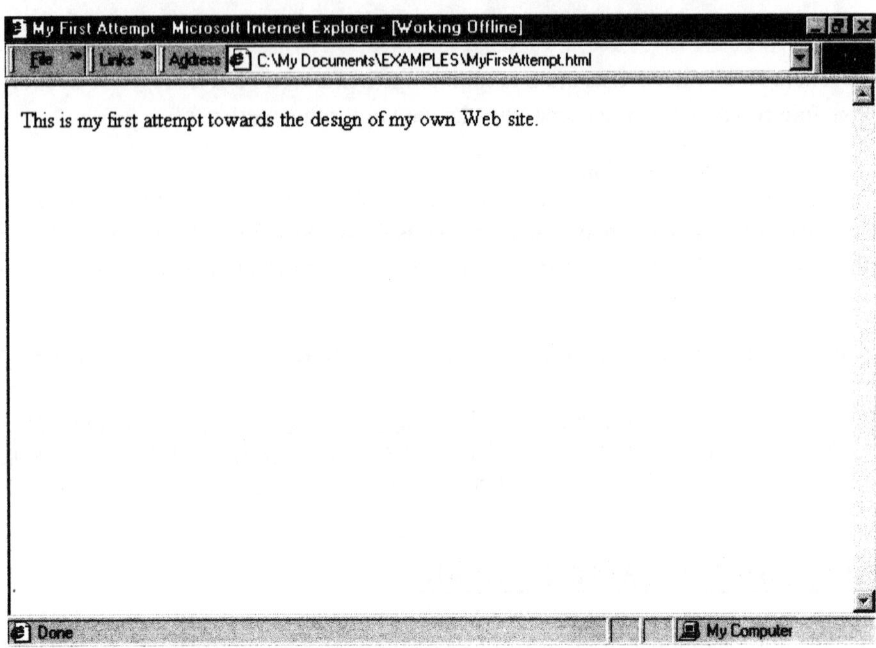

Diagram 2

• Will it work as XHTML document?

In Diagram 2, one can see that the Web browser has accepted the HTML code shown in Diagram 1, and displayed the document in the required format. In fact, this document contains a syntax error, as <Title>, and </title> do not match. When you submit the document to a browser, it parses the document. In other words, it breaks the document into its constituent components. The Internet Explorer(IE) has been tolerant, and thus did not display any error message, instead it has matched the opening and closing tags <Title> and </title) itself.

XHTML uses the vocabulary of HTML, and makes use of the syntax of XML. Therefore, If you try to validate this document, that is to check it for XHTML conformation by the W3C Validation Service as XHTML 1.0 Transitional type document, you will get an error message as shown below in the shaded area . The XHTML Validator (software) cannot validate any document if it fails to meet XML requirements. XHTML combines the best aspects of both HTML and XML, and therefore, the syntax of XHTML document must be structured accordingly.

- Line 5, column 6:
```
<Title>My First Attempt
      ^
```
Error: element "Title" not defined in this HTML version (explanation...)
- Line 6, column 7:
```
</title>
       ^
```
Error: end tag for element "title" which is not open; try removing the end tag or check for improper nesting of elements (explanation...)
- Line 7, column 6:
```
</head>
      ^
```
Error: end tag for "Title" omitted; end tags are required in XML for non-empty elements; empty elements require an end tag or the start tag must end with "/>"
- Line 5, column 0:
```
<Title>My First Attempt
^
```
Error: start tag was here (explanation...)
- Line 7, column 6:
```
</head>
      ^
```
Error: missing a required sub-element of "head" (explanation...)

Sorry, this document does not validate as XHTML 1.0 Transitional.

• Example 2

The aim of this example is to demonstrate further some of the differences between HTML and XHTML regarding the use of tags, and formatting the text for presentation as required.

• Explanation

On examination of HTML document in Diagram 3, you will find that I have extended the application of elements/tags. Thus, this document uses the essential 4 tags <html>, <head>, <title>, and <body>, which all documents should have. In addition, I have implemented the use of :-

• <h2> level 2 heading , and <h3> level 3 heading. Both these headings result displaying the text in bigger font sizes than the normal size. <h2> generates bigger text than <h3>.

- <u> tag is used to underline the markup text, and
- <p> tag creates a new paragraph.
- Now, examine the screen capture of the document previewed in the IE locally. You can see that the document is displayed, with some text underlined, some text printed bigger than the other text, and the document contains four paragraphs. Therefore, this document is structured (font size, underline, text broken down into paragraphs).

The Internet Explorer has passed this document as an HTML document, because the document is displayed in exactly the same way as I intended. Thus, it has met all requirements. In fact, this document contains a number of syntax errors, which will not be accepted by the XHTML Validator. Furthermore, this document contains <u> which has been deprecated (not used any more) in XHTML Strict. This is a text styling or text formatting element. In XHTML Strict, Cascading Style Sheets include this function. The explanation is continued below Diagram 3.

The HTML code for Example 2 – humanBrain.html

```
<Html>
<head>
<title> Example 2 </title></head>
<body>
<h2><u>
    The Human Brain</u>
<P> <h3>
The human brain is as big as a coconut, the shape of a walnut. It has two hemispheres, which are
covered in a thin skin of deeply wrinkled grey tissue called the cerebral cortex.

<P> Each infold on this surface is known as sulcus, and each bulge is known as gyrus. The surface
landscape of each individual's brain is slightly different, but the main wrinkles - like nose - mouth
grooves and crow's feet on an ageing face - are common to all and are used as landmarks.</p>
For further Information: <u> TheBrainSurgeon @home.com
</h3>
</Body>
```

Diagram 3

• Can this document be validated as XHTML document?

The answer is no for the following reasons given by the W3C Validation Service when I submitted this document for validation, as XHTML 1.0 Transitional type document. Certainly, I also tried to validate it as XHTML 1.0 Strict type document, which resulted in more errors pointed out by this service.

•Why?

Because, <u> element does not work at all in Strict XHTML. It is deprecated in Strict. In Strict type XHTML, you have to apply a Cascading Style Sheets (CSS) rule for underlining any text. Of course, you will learn all about it later on as the book progresses.

- However, the following errors are sufficient enough to demonstrate that XHTML may look like HTML, and use HTML vocabulary, but it is a new language in its own right. You must appreciate by now that any book which is on XHTML, and checks XHTML documents with browsers designed for HTML is misleading you in to believing that you are working with XHTML. This is not true as demonstrated in this chapter.

A preview of Example 2 in IE – humanBrain.html

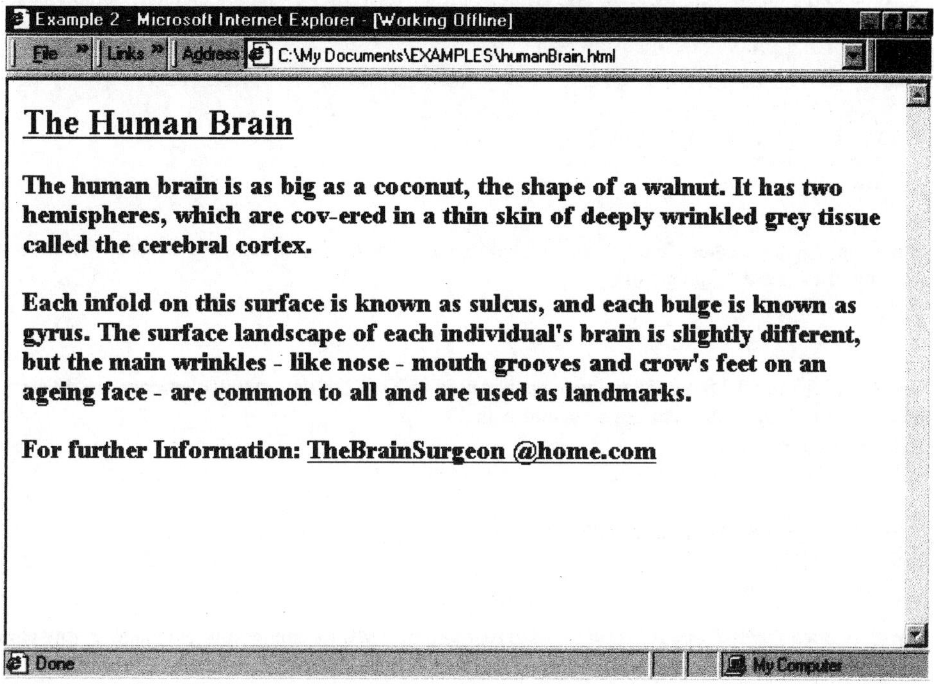

Diagram 4

Error List

Below are the results of checking this document for XML well-formedness and validity.

- Line 2, column 5:
```
  <Html>
      ^
```
Error: element "Html" not defined in this HTML version (explanation...)
- Line 9, column 2:
```
  <P> <h3>
    ^
```
Error: element "P" not defined in this HTML version (explanation...)
- Line 11, column 2:
```
  <p> Each infold on this surface is known as sulcus, and each bulge
is ...
    ^
```
Error: element "p" not allowed here; possible cause is an inline element containing a block-level element (explanation...)
- Line 13, column 4:
```
  </h3>
      ^
```
Error: end tag for "u" omitted; end tags are required in XML for non-empty elements; empty elements require an end tag or the start tag must end with "/>"
- Line 12, column 25:
```
  For further Information: <u> TheBrainSurgeon @home.com
                           ^
```
Error: start tag was here (explanation...)
- Line 14, column 6:
```
  </Body>
        ^
```
Error: end tag for element "Body" which is not open; try removing the end tag or check for improper nesting of elements (explanation...)
- Line 14, column 8:
```
  </Body>
         ^
```
Error: end tag for "P" omitted; end tags are required in XML for non-empty elements; empty elements require an end tag or the start tag must end with "/>"
- Line 9, column 0:
```
  <P> <h3>
  ^
```
Error: start tag was here (explanation...)
- Line 14, column 8:
```
  </Body>
         ^
```
Error: end tag for "h2" omitted; end tags are required in XML for non-empty elements; empty elements require an end tag or the start tag must end with "/>"
- Line 7, column 0:
```
  <h2><u>
  ^
```
Error: start tag was here (explanation...)
- Line 14, column 8:
```
  </Body>
         ^
```
Error: end tag for "body" omitted; end tags are required in XML for non-empty elements; empty elements require an end tag or the start tag must end with "/>"

- Line 6, column 0:
  ```
  <body>
  ^
  ```
  Error: start tag was here (explanation...)
- Line 14, column 8:
  ```
  </Body>
          ^
  ```
  Error: end tag for "Html" omitted; end tags are required in XML for non-empty elements; empty elements require an end tag or the start tag must end with "/>"
- Line 2, column 0:
  ```
  <Html>
  ^
  ```
  Error: start tag was here (explanation...)
- Line 14, column 8:
  ```
  </Body>
          ^
  ```
  Error: no document element

Sorry, this document does not validate as XHTML 1.0 Transitional.

• Differences between XHTML and HTML

XHTML	HTML
The first element in the <head> must be <title>, if not, your document will not be validated as XHTML document.	The <tile> tag is mandatory but Web browsers do not care much if it is missing. In fact, on the Net you can find Web pages on the Internet.
All elements must be properly nested, XML parsers which can read XHTML cannot tolerate any misuse of nested of elements.	In accordance with HTML rules , all elements must be nested but the parser which is built-in in HTML browser allows this illegality.
All tags must have corresponding closing tags for instance: <p> and </p> Empty tags must also be closed. For instance: < br />	You can get away without having corresponding closing tags. <p> will work is accepted
All attributes must be written within double quotation marks	All attributes must be surrounded by double quotes. Your segment of the code without it can work.

• Differences between XHTML and HTML (from Page 31)

XHTML	HTML
For instance: < td colspan =3 width =" 2" > but will be rejected. 3 must be written as "3"	For instance: <TD ALIGN=center >, here it should be " centre", the document was displayed when this rule was violated.
All attributes must be written only in lowercase letters, because XHTML is case-sensitive	Attributes can be written in either lower case or upper case, because HTML is a not case-sensitive language. You can also mix lower and upper cases, again the browser will ignore it.
Minimisation of attributes is illegal. It means that no attribute can be meaningful without its given value. For instance: <hr align = "left" /> - the value of the attribute align must be given in double quotation marks.	Minimisation can occur without any adverse effects. For instance : < hr noshade> -this will display horizontal rule without any shade. No value of the attribute noshade is given, and it is not surrounded with double quotes, but it will still work – this is not workable in XHTML.
Characters "<" and "&" are not allowed	
The top of the document must include XHTML conformation in the form of a DTD.	
Some new elements and attributes have been introduced.	
Style Sheets are used for document formatting and presentation in XHTML 1.0 Strict.	

You will learn more about these differences as the book progresses.

• Summary

You have seen in this chapter that Microsoft Internet Explorer can display XHTML documents. In fact, some other browsers can do the same, but they cannot validate XHTML documents.

Chapter 3
Some Fundamental Ideas of XML

If you are anxious to move on to XHTML, you can read this chapter at a later stage of your learning plane. I would still recommend you to read this chapter, so that you can appreciate more fully the common features, differences and similarities between XHTML and XML.

The prime aim of this chapter is:-

- to enable you to acquire some fundamental understanding of XML

By reading and practising techniques that are demonstrated in this chapter, you should be able:-

- to explain some fundamental ideas of XML and their application
- to explain the basic document structure
- to create a simple XML document and test it locally

. Why is it so necessary?

XHTML is a reformulation of HTML as an XML application. It can be said that XHTML is written in XML. Thus, XML grammar and rules also apply to XHTML. XHTML applies HTML vocabulary and implements the syntax of XML. Therefore, it is desirable to learn what follows here.

In Chapter 2, you were introduced to HTML, where you learnt some basic concepts and Web page development techniques. Through this chapter, you can learn some of the essential ideas of XML, and compare these with the skills and knowledge of HTML you have already acquired.

. Markup tags

The markup takes the form of opening and closing tags, empty –element tags and some other forms.

Like HTML, XML also makes use of markup tags. You already know that a tag (command) is a piece of markup code. The major difference between HTML and XML is that XML is not a fixed markup language. What it means is that unlike HTML, it does not have a set of its own tags as its dictionary. The good news is that the XML developer can make use of HTML tags as well as creating his/her own tags. However, the method for the construction of HTML and XML tags is pretty much the same. The reason for this similarity is the fact that both markup languages inherit tagging method from their mother-language SGML.

For instance, the following XML code has two tags. These are opening and closing tags as identified below:-

- All opening tags in a document must have corresponding closing tags.
- If you do not construct any of these tags correctly, an error will be generated by the XML processor/browser. This is not always the case in HTML.

In HTML, there are occasions when you can ignore the closing tag and your document can still be validated by the browser. Thus, XML is stricter than HTML. No such violation of XML rules is permissible.

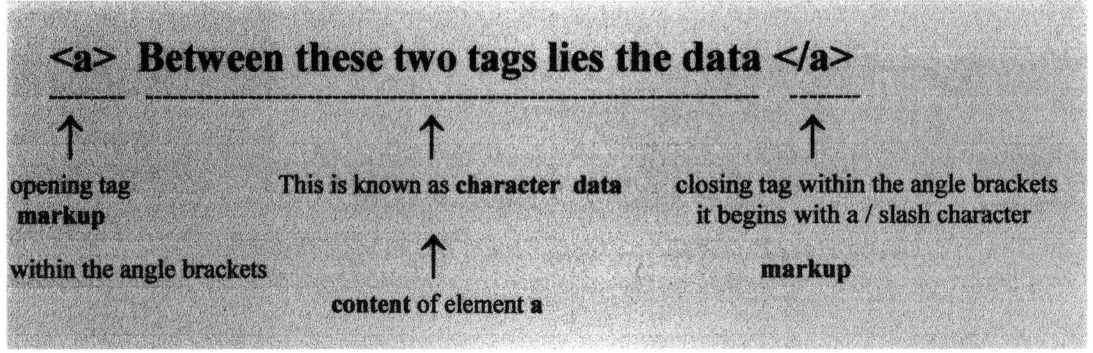

• Is XML case sensitive?

Yes. It simply means that < **name**> and <**NAME**> are two different things in XML. Similarly,

<**SURNAME**> and <**surname**> are also two different names.

This is a very important difference between HTML and XML, as it has a direct implication on XHTML. It will be discussed further in the next chapter. Both opening and closing tags must be either in lower or uppercase. You must remember that unlike HTML, XML does not tolerate the violation of its syntax rules.

• What is an element?

It is often said that the building block of XML is the element. An element has a **name** and **content**. In the above example "**a** " is an element which is enclosed within the angle brackets. So, the name of the element is **a**. The opening and closing tags have the same element and they mean the same. The **content** of the element is within the opening and closing tags. In fact, it is the character data as illustrated above. Of course, the naming of elements is controlled by some rules. These are discussed later on.

• Attributes

• Can elements have values?

Yes. The values attached to elements are known as **attributes**. Elements can have one or several attributes. In fact, an attribute is additional information which concerns the element. This information can be attached to an opening tag in order to modify it. It should also be understood that attributes are not related to the content of the element as its components or parts. These are really values or data which are required by the application. Like elements, attributes have names. Attributes also have values as demonstrated below:-

- The value of the attribute should be written within quotes. These quotes may be double or single.

Illustration 1

< Important notice = “for heads only”>

The content of this document is not for your staff. You should read it for the next meeting.
</Important>

Illustration 2

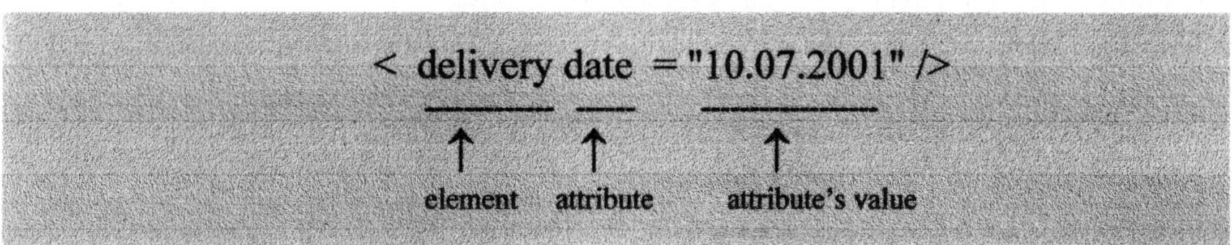

This happens to be an **empty element**, which is discussed in the next section.

Illustration 3

```
< customer regular = "yes" order-over-1000 = "yes">
                                        process the order now.
</customer>
```

It illustrates that elements can have more than one attribute and corresponding value.

• Are there any restrictions in giving values to attributes?

Yes, between the quotation marks there cannot be any of these characters : < , & , ‘ or ” . See also naming the element and attributes below.

• Is it possible to have an element without any content?

Yes, you can have an **empty element**. An empty element does not have any content. Often, an empty element is used for including values of their attributes as illustrated below:-

```
< delivery date = "10.06.2001" />
  -------- ----   ------------ ---
     ↑       ↑         ↑        ↑
  element attribute attribute's character slash essential
                      value     before the closing delimiter
```

- This tag is called an **empty element tag**. Why is it so ? You can easily distinguish this tag from the opening and closing tags, as it has only one pair of angle brackets in which the element 'delivery', its attribute 'date' and its value '10.06.2001' are all put together, and a slash is added to these items before ending the tag with the closing angle bracket '>'.

I list two more examples of empty elements so that you appreciate the use of empty elements in a document:-

• Illustration 4

< sales account = "A10022" /> In this empty element tag, you can identify its parts as shown below:-

- element called ---------------- sales
- attribute called ----------------- account
- value ------------------ A10022

This is an empty element tag as it conforms to XML grammar.

• Illustration 5

< class first = " wagon 5 seat 20R" /> This is another empty element tag. You can identify its parts as shown below:-

- element called ---------------- class
- attribute called ----------------- first
- value ------------------ wagon 5 seat20R

• Are there any rules for naming the element?

The following rules must be applied in accordance with XML grammar:-

- a name can start with a letter as well as with the underscore character '-',
- once started as stated above, it can have letters, digits, hyphens, underscores, colons or full stops
- You cannot begin a name with the string "XML" or "xml", because these characters are reserved for XML itself
- you cannot have any spaces in names

Some examples of valid and invalid names in XML are shown below:-

Valid names	Invalid names
• <surname>	• <capital letters> - because it has white spaces
• <PRICE_IN_Pound>	• <XML-DOCUMENT> - XML is reserved - not allowed

Valid names	Invalid names
. <firstname>	. <20> - you cannot have just digits only
. <-type>	. <26BUSNUMBER> - you cannot start a name with a digit
. <number70>	. <COST*VAT> - * is not allowed
. <umbrella_for_rain_and_hot_sun>	. <cost price > - illegal as it has a white space

. Is there any convention for using upper or lowercase letters for names?

The following two convention are most popular. You can use any of these conventions.

- If a name consists of more than one word, use a hyphen to separate two words. Examples are:-

  - **<national-insurance-number>** and • **<home-phone>**

- Instead of placing a hyphen between two words, you can join two words together, providing each word begins with a capital letter as shown below:-

  - <NationalInsuranceNumber> and • **<LunchHour>**

. How can you name attributes?

Whenever you have to use attributes in your document, you have to name attributes in accordance with the same set of rules which are applied when naming elements. For instance:

< discount maximum percentage allowed = " 0. 35"/> is illegal due to white spaces. It should be:

<discount maximum_ percentage_allowed = ".35"/> is legal.

For now, it is enough to know about elements and attributes. You will meet these topics again.

. Can elements be nested?

The XML document is constructed by means of the **root element and its children**. Yes, indeed, an XML document has just one root element. From this root element you can create as many children as you wish. The XML recommendation does not include a list of defined elements as a ready-made standard name to use. You can give an element any suitable **name** which fits your purpose.

An element does not only contain text. It can also contain other elements as **children** of the element. These children of the element can themselves contain text or have their own children and so on. The XML document can be depicted as a tree of elements. The depth of tree of element can be pretty deep. In fact, there is no limit to the depth of the tree. A very large document will have a much deeper tree than a small document. You will meet this topic again in this chapter for further discussion and tree illustration. Be patient!

. Comments

You can include some comments in your XML document. These are allowed for the benefit of developers so that the document can be identified in the future. They are not part of the document's character data, and thus the XML processor does not process comments. Even so, the following syntax rules must be observed when writing comments:

- they should not appear in the markup. You can place comments before or after the markup.
- they can be written within the document type declaration.
- the structure of a comment begins with " **<!- -** " and ends with " **<!- -** ". Between these the text is enclosed. No space between two hyphens is permissible. For instance:

<!--first XML try by John 02.11.200 -->

- a comment cannot end as " **- - ->"** as it has more than two hyphens. For instance, the following is not permitted:

<!- - Staff record as at 30th November 2000 - - ->

- " --" two hyphens are allowed within any comments without any white space between them.

. Classes of XML documents

There are two classes of documents in XML These are:-

- well-formed and
- valid documents.

Their characteristics are listed in Table 1 below.

Characteristics of XML Documents

well-formed document	valid document
. meets XML syntax requirements	. it has all characteristics of a well-formed document. In addition, it has a DTD, which describes its specific structure.
	. since it has a DTD, the XML processor or browser checks the document to make sure that its structure is drawn in accordance with the structure outlined in the DTD.
. all opening and closing tags must match e.g. <a> … </a> the element **a** in the opening tag <a> matches with the element **a** in the closing tag </a>	
. it has only one root element which contains other elements, if any, in the document	
. all elements must be nested correctly e.g. <World> <Europe> …..</Europe> <Asia> ……..</Asia> <Africa>… …</Africa> <America> ….</America> </World>	
. empty elements of a special form are allowed	
. XML processor/browser checks that the document has met XML syntax rules in all relevant aspects	

Table 1

You can see that the difference between these two classes of documents is due to only one requirement, namely DTD. It raises an important question:

- **Why is there a need for a well-formed document as the valid document includes its characteristics?**

The answer to this question is not straightforward, but requires an appreciation of the following points:-

- The DTD specifies the elements that are allowed in the document.
- The DTD also specifies where in the document allowed elements should be implemented
- Some documents may require a DTD , but not every document needs it.
- A DTD is useful at the time of document creation. **Why?** Because it enforces a specific structure. Thus, it is a good idea to include a DTD.
- A DTD is of least value when the document is being distributed. **Why?** The document is about the structure of a document. If, for instance, there are some XML syntax errors, the document has to be amended by its developers not by the viewer. Therefore, the DTD serves no purpose in such cases.

• Unicode world wide character standard

The information contained in the document has to be transformed into a recognised form for its transmission on line. The process of transformation is known as encoding. Of course, at the destination, the encoded information has to be decoded. Yes, you are right in thinking that the converse of encoding is called decoding. Both coding and encoding can be carried out either by hardware or software.

The Unicode world wide character standard is a character encoding system developed to support the interchange, processing, and display of written text of diverse world languages, mathematical and other symbols. Unicode is a trademark of the **Unicode Consortium (www. unicode. org)**. The same organisation maintain Unicode standard.

The Unicode is an extension to the international 8-bit codes that are themselves extensions of **ASCII**, acronym for American Standard Code for Information Interchange, 7-bit codes.

The 8-bits per character code for English characters is recognised by the XML processor as UTF-8. It is not big enough to include diverse languages of the world. Thus, the Unicode has been developed as 16-bits per character code, which is twice as big as 8-bits character codes, and can accommodate the world's diverse languages, mathematical and other symbols. The 16-bits are recognised in XML processor as as **UTF-16**.

ISO (International Organization for Stadardization) is the body responsible for all international data processing standards. ISO has published Unicode in **ISO 8859** standard series. For instance:-

- **ISO-8859-1** is for Western Europe, and Latin American languages – **Latin –1**, and
- **ISO-8859-2** is for Central and Eastern Europe – **Latin – 2**.

These are recognised by most XML processors. Of course, there are some more Unicode character sets for Japanese, Arabic and many other languages. For further information, try the above listed Web site. XML lets you specify which character encoding schemes must be applied to the document. This way, you can define the language in which your XML document is written. Since UTF-8 is default for XML and your documents are written in English, these can be displayed without any problems. Hurrah!

• XML document design

• Example 1

The above discussion introduces the most essential ideas towards the development of XML documents. It is now time to put XML techniques into practice by means of designing a simple XML document for presenting the following book information:

```
Book Information
Title: Java Simplified
Author: Adam Shaw
Publishers: ADR
ISBN: 1901197 88 3
Publication Year: 1999
Price Pound-Sterling: £15.99
Readership: For students and beginners.
```

The XML document for this book information is shown in Diagram 1. It is simple, but it does demonstrate how to code an XML documents.

```
====================== BookInfor.xml========================
<?xml version ="1.0"?>
<!—document 1-->
<BOOK>
<book> Book Information </book>
<TITLE> Title: Java Simplified</TITLE>
<AUTHOR>Author: Adam Shaw</AUTHOR>
<PUBLISHERS>Publishers: ADR</PUBLISHERS>
<ISBN>ISBN: 1901197 88 3</ISBN>
<DATE> Publication Year: 1999</DATE>
<PRICE Pound-Sterling = ": £15.99" />
<READERSHIP> Readership: For students and beginners.</READERSHIP>
</BOOK>
```

Diagram 1

In order to create and save XML document, I used Microsoft WordPad as discussed in Chapter 1. It was saved on my PC' hard drive as **bookInfor.xml**. It is plain text.

• Explanation

The XML document begins with an **XML declaration** written within **< declaration> angle brackets**. The declaration with which the structure of this code begins is analysed below:-

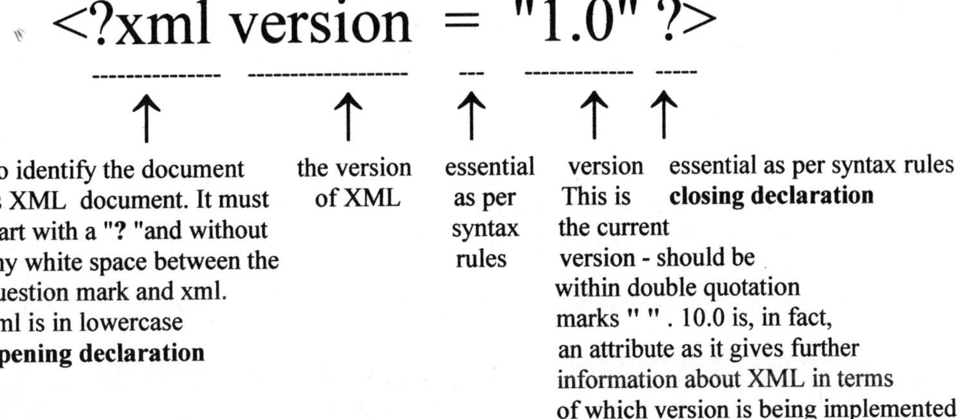
<?xml version = "1.0" ?>
to identify the document as XML document. It must start with a "? "and without any white space between the question mark and xml. xml is in lowercase
opening declaration
the version of XML
essential as per syntax rules
version This is the current version - should be within double quotation marks " " . 10.0 is, in fact, an attribute as it gives further information about XML in terms of which version is being implemented
essential as per syntax rules
closing declaration

- Declaration is on the first line of your XML code and it is written in lowercase.

- Incorrect version will be rejected by the XML processor.

- Another name for this declaration is **prolog**. See prolog.

This piece of code is XML prolog. Its purpose is to inform the receiving application (browser , parser or any other tool) that it is getting an XML document, version 1.0 of XML specification.

- On next line is <!-- **document 1** -->. This a comment. It will be ignored by the processor. Its purpose is no more than to serve as a note about the document for future references. However, if you make any syntax error in writing it, the Internet Explorer 5 will not validate the document as well-formed. Instead, it will generate a message showing error(s). For instance, a white space between **--** will generate the following message.

The XML page cannot be displayed

Cannot view XML input using style sheet. Please correct the error and then click the Refresh button, or try again later.

A comment was not closed. Line 2, Position 5
<!—document 1 - ->
----^

It points out where the violation of XML rule has occurred in the markedup document.

• The root element is called **BOOK.** It has eight children or elements. Each of these elements has its own name and content. These elements within the body of the document must be nested. What it means is that these eight elements must be contained within the root element BOOK. For this reason alone, the document structure can be visualised as follows:-

• Check the document for well-formedness

Having created the file, I saved it as **book . xml** in my folder called **xhtml** on my PC's hard drive. In order to check XML documents for well-formedness, I use Internet Explorer 5. This tool is easy to use.

In order to check XML document for well-formedness, you must open the XML file in the IE5. In this case, my file is **book .xml**. It is the same procedure as you have learnt in Chapter 2 for HTML. In Diagram 2, you can see the document together with the markup code. It is the best way to check your code for well-formedness. There are no mistakes, and therefore, the IE has displayed the document together with markup codes. When the document does not include styling, the IE5 displays it with markup.

The Internet Explorer has parsed the document and displayed it together with markup

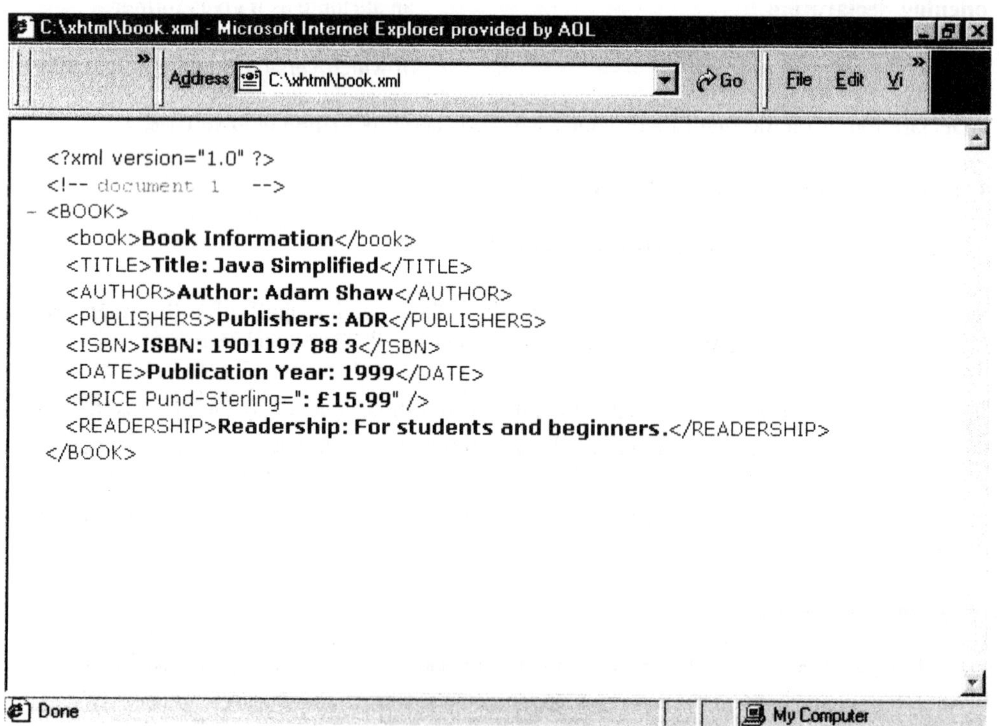

Diagram 2

Now, you can see in Diagram 2 how XML document appears in a Web browser. It is not pretty, but at least the document has been checked for well-formedness.

• What else can be listed in the XML declaration?

In fact, the declaration is itself a **processing instruction (PI)**. It gives vital basic information to the **parser,** which interprets the document. In addition to this version of XML which is being used for the current document, it can also include:-

- **Version information** - which version of XML was used to write the current document? See above example.
- **Encoding information** - this is concerning internationalisation. XML lets you specify which character encoding schemes must be applied to the document. This way, you can define the language in which your XML document is written. The following example declares that the document is written in XML version 1.0 and in the ISO's Latin 1 character set encoding.

<?xml version ="1.0" encoding = "ISO-8859-1"?>

optional attribute can be used to specify the language in which your document is written (i.e. English)

language encoding - character set Latin -1

another example:-

<?xml version ="1.0" encoding "UTF-8" ?>

this language encoding is **default** for XML browsers/parsers should support it. It is also Windows default character set

- The root element <Book > is an opening tag it is then followed by

<book> Book Information </book>

This is the first element within the root element. You can see that it has its own opening and closing tag, and between these tags its own content, " Book Information", as sketched in Illustration 6 below. In the same way, other elements are coded. Of course, the content of these elements is data or the text.

Finally, the root element is closed by its own closing tag </BOOK>. **Why?**

The opening tag for the root element must also have its own corresponding closing tag, so that all other elements within the root element are nested.

Nested of children with the root element

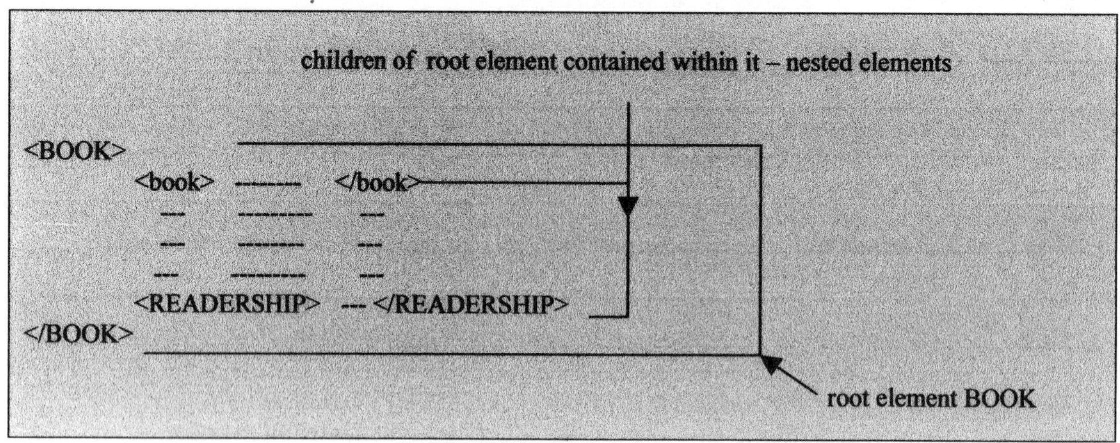

Illustration 6

- **Standalone document declaration -** When a document does not contain any references to any external documents which can affect its processing than it is a ***standalone*** document. In this case, there is only one XML document, which has all requirements in its document type definition (acronym DTD). The standalone attribute accepts any of the two values, namely, 'yes ' or 'no' in order to establish whether the document is standalone or not. If you do not include standalone in your document, then the processing application assumes the value is **'no'** in order to validate the document against the DTD.

In fact, the default value is 'no'. It may be that a document refers to some external entities which affect its processing, in that case, the standalone attribute takes the value of **'yes'**.

Example:

```
<?xml version= "1.0" encoding ="UTF-8" standalone="no"?>
```

Since the default value is **no**, there is no need to declare it. Anyway, to declare it causes no harm. Here, you can appreciate that XML declaration can have :

- the opening tag <?
- version identification
- encoding information
- standalone attribute value declaration
- closing tag ?>

• If the closing tag or any other tags are missing, what will happen?

If you miss out any closing or opening tags, your document will not be validated by the IE5 for well-formedness. It will display an error message. For instance, for the sake of demonstrating this error message, I re-entered this document by missing out "/ " in the following empty element:

<PRICE Pound-Sterling = ": £15.99" >

↑

Error –omitted /

and attempted to check it for well-formedness. The IE5 generated an error message which is displayed in Diagram 3.

You can see that XML is strict and accepts no violation of its syntax rules. In HTML, usually, your document is workable without some matching tags.

Error Message generated as the document is not well-formed

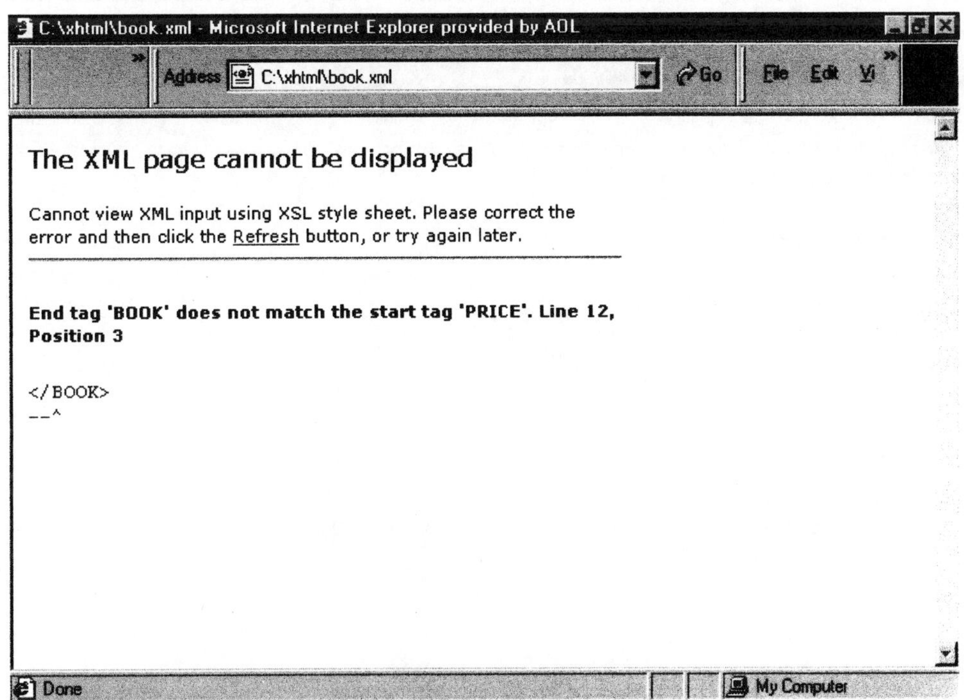

Diagram 3

• Is XML declaration essential?

Its inclusion in every XML document is suggested in the XML recommendation. It does not mean that you must include it in your document. Furthermore, you do not have to include all parts as shown above within the opening and closing tags. At present, XML has only version 1.0. Therefore, if you do not list it in your declaration, the document will still be interpreted as version 1.0.

• Tree-like document structure

You know by now that there can only be one root element or the parent. An element in the document is considered as a **node**. The first node is the root element, which is also the **document node**. Since a document can have many derived elements or **children**, each of these children is also a node. Furthermore, the children can have their own children until all required elements are created. A derived element or child which has its own children, is a also a parent in its own right, and thus it is a **parent node**, and each descending child is a node, where data is stored. The process of deriving a series of nodes from the root element is illustrated below in Diagram 4. It is a tree-like structure, which illustrates the relationship between the document node and derived nodes for each descending child.

Imaginary tree depicting the relationship between the root and derived elements

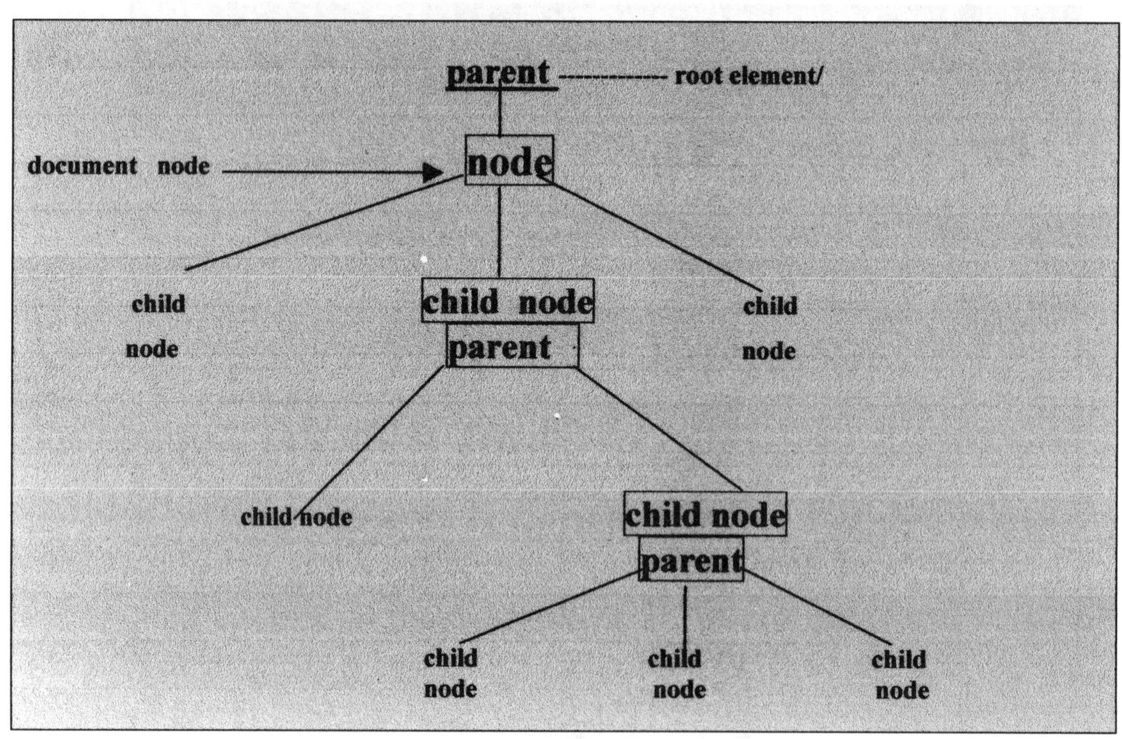

Illustration 7

You can ascend from the bottom of this tree to the top of the tree, and discover that each node has a direct connection with its parent node and through its parent node is connected to the document node. This way, all parts of the document are connected in the hierarchy within the structure of the document.

• Example 2

The purpose of this example is to develop a document which records the following Sales information.

```
                              Sales

Home
      England
                  South        London and Home Counties
                  Midlands     Middle England
                  North        North England
      Scotland
                  Scottish regions
      Wales
                  Welsh regions
Export
      EU          Member countries
      USA         United States of America
      Canada      Canadian regions
```

The document has to be stored and checked for well-formedness.

• Explanation

I have drawn a tree of Sales in order to see the relationship between the root element and derived elements for this document. A tree of Sales is shown in Illustration 8. In this tree, you can see that each discrete object in the document is a node, and every node is related to another node. It illustrates that a node can be either text or an element. If a node is a text node than it does not have any children. You can identify each node in this tree as either text node or an element as listed below:-

Element node	**Text node**
Sales (document node)	Scotland Wales EU USA
Home (parent node)	Canada
Export (parent node)	South
England (parent node)	Midlands
	North

A tree depicting sales

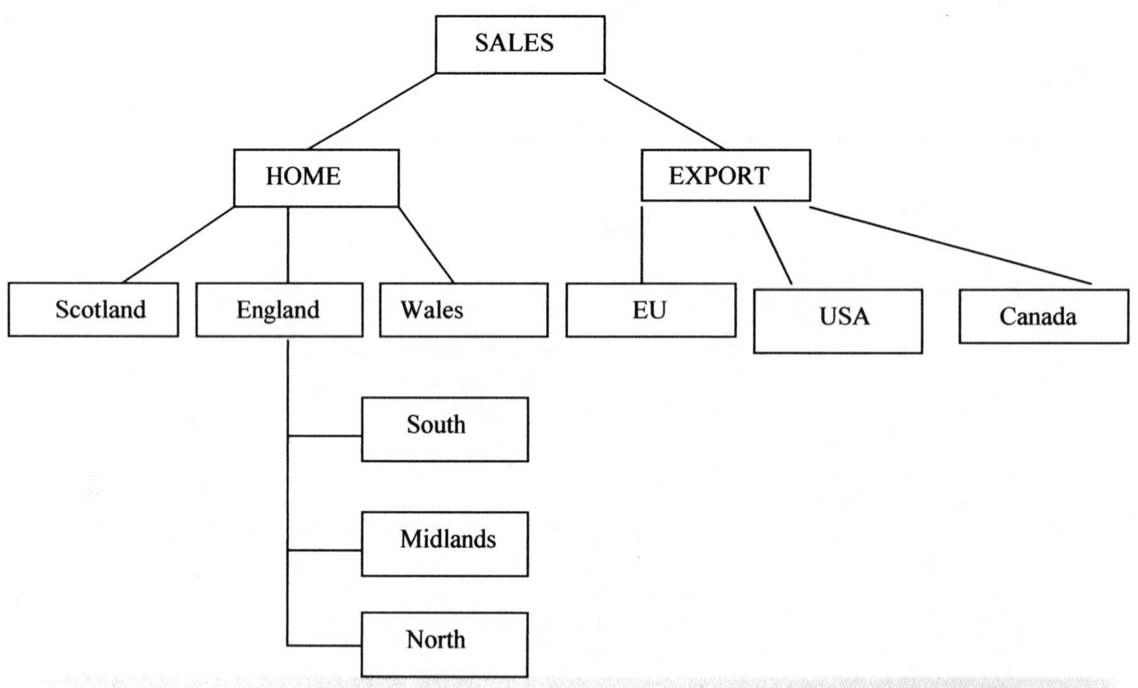

Illustration 8

Text nodes are the smallest items in the tree-like hierarchy. From this tree of the sales, I have created a document and saved it as **sales.xml** as shown in Diagram 4.

In Illustration 8, you can see that the single root element **Sales** contains all other elements. This single element covers the whole body of the document including other elements (children) derived from it. The root element **Sales** is both at the beginning of the document body as well as at the end of its body. This enables the parser to know the start and finish of the document. It also shows that text nodes contain the data or the information which is document's content. Thus, all elements in the body are nested. This way, nesting prevents overlapping, which is illegal in XML. See overlapping below.

The XML document listed in Diagram 4 was tested for well-formedness in the IE5. There were no violations of XML syntax rules and thus the test was successful.

The document is not a table. It contains simple text without any formatting and styling. A document without any styling is parsed and displayed by the Internet Explorer together with markup.

The XML code for example 2

```
============================== sales.xml ==================================
<?xml version ="1.0"?>
<Sales>
    <Home>
      <England>
         <South>London and Home Counties</South>
         <Midlands> Middle England</Midlands>
         <North> North West and North East</North>
      </England>
      <Scotland> Scottish regions </Scotland>
      <Wales> Welsh regions</Wales>
   </Home>
   <Export>
      <EU> EU Members countries</EU>
      <USA> United States of America</USA>
      <Canada> Canadian regions</Canada>
   </Export></Sales>
```

Diagram 4

The IE has parsed the document and displayed it together with markup

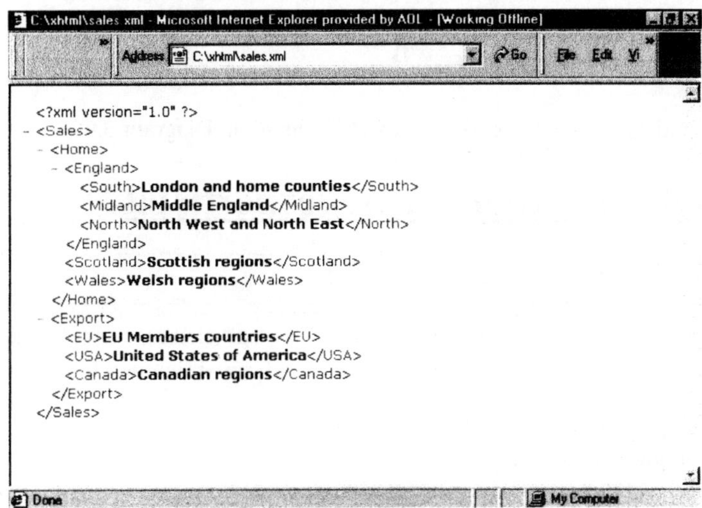

Diagram 5

• overlapping elements

Consider the segment of a markup code listed below:-

< cash> Cash received today <cheque>total = £350 </cash> total = £25000</cheque>

On careful observation, you can see that opening and closing tags do not match. Such a construction leads to overlapping of elements. This is illegal. This sort of markup code can create all kinds of problems, when dealing with real life documents which are usually large and can be complicated. This is demonstrated further through example 3.

• Example 3 & explanation

In example 2, Export Sales has three territories namely EU, USA, and Canada. In order to demonstrate the effects of overlapping, I have added to it **Japan** as a fourth export area. The data for Japan is all regions. Now the parent element has four children as shown in the tree of export sales in Illustration 9.

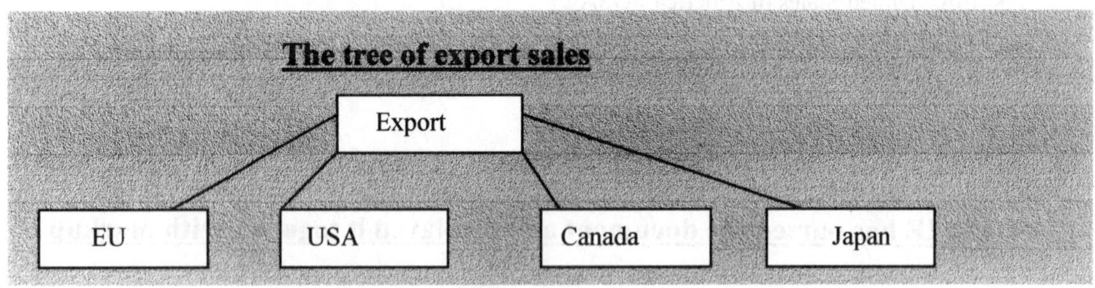

Illustration 9

For export data, I created and saved **export.xml** file, which is shown in Diagram 6.

The XML code for export sales – export.xml

```
========================== export.xml ================================
<?xml version =”1.0”?>
<Export>
        <EU> EU Members countries</EU>
        <USA> United States of America</USA>
        <Canada> Canadian regions</Canada>
       <Japan< All regions</Japan>
</Export>
```

Diagram 6

Document export.xml parsed and displayed together with markup

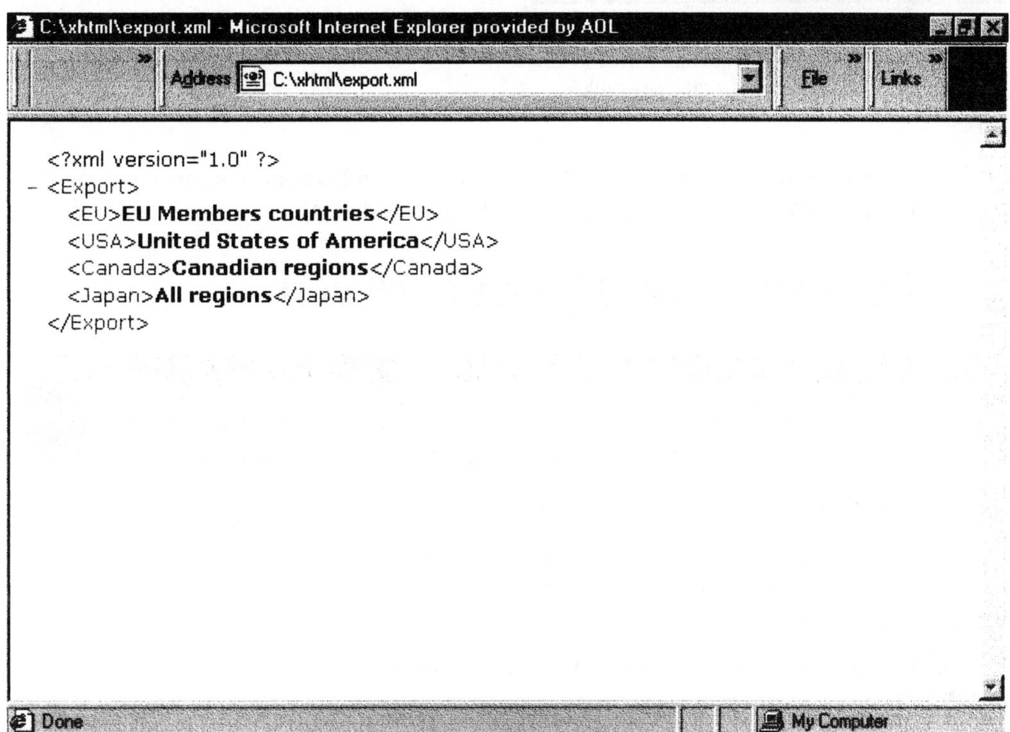

Diagram 6A

- Since all elements are contained within the root element, and thus nested, there is no overlapping. As it contains no violations of XML syntax rules, the IE5 printed no error message. Thus, it was accepted as well-formed document. See Diagram 6A above.

Th XML code for the document re-written as rxportO.salex

```
========================exportO.sales ==============================
<? xml version="1.0"?>
<Export>
        <EU> EU Members countries</EU>
        <USA> United States of America</USA>
        <Canada> Canadian regions</Canada>
       <Japan< All regions</Export>
</Japan>
```

Diagram 6B

• Re-written as 'exportO.sales'

- In order to demonstrate the effect of overlapping elements, I have re-written this code, and saved it as exporto.sales as shown below in Diagram 6B.

- When I tried to check it for well-formedness, the Internet Explorer 5 generated an error message, which is shown in Diagram 6c. Thus, overlapping of elements is illegal.

Document exportO.xml viewed in IE

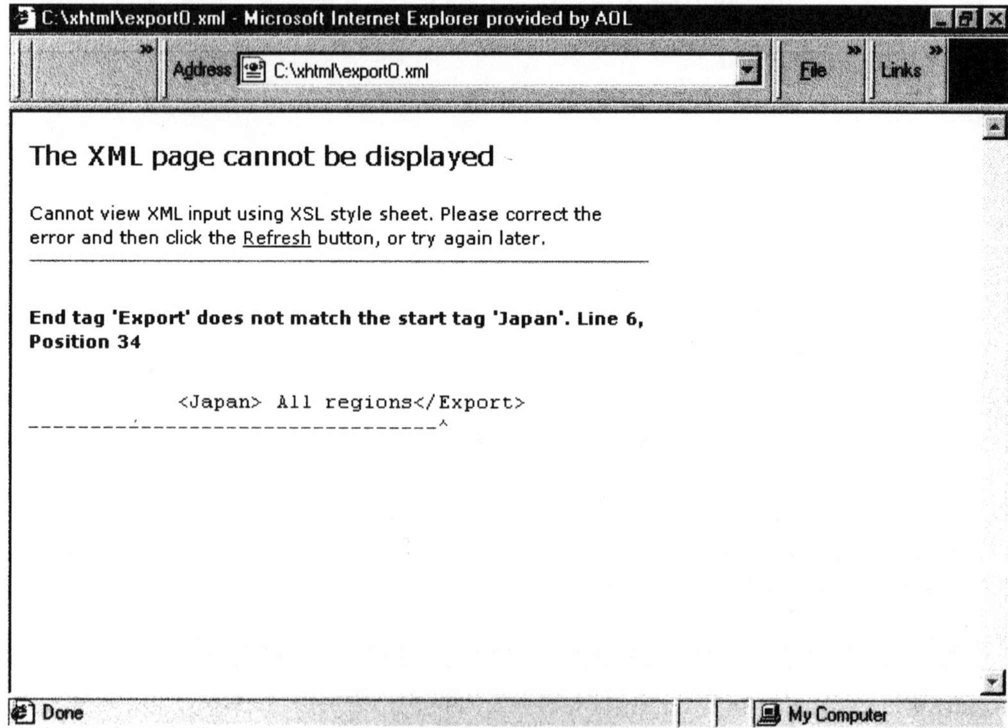

Diagram 6C

• Styling XML documents

Until now, you have created some simple documents without any styling or formatting. This is the reason why in Diagrams 2, 5 and 6A, the text appeared together with markup code.

This is fine for checking the well-formedness of an XML document. Indeed, XML concentrates on the structure of a document, not its appearance (HTML allows it). Anyway, the presentation without any styling or formatting is least desirable for a Web page. As such, it is not good enough for communicating information on the Internet.

Thus, in order to display a document in the browser or any other tool such as the dedicated XML editor, the document has to be formatted or styled. You do so by means of creating some styling information which is related to the structure of the document, and how the document will be displayed.

• How is the link created between the style sheets information and XML document?

A set of styling information is kept separately in style sheets document or file. This style sheets document is associated with the current XML document, so that both the current XML document and styling instructions can be linked together to display the XML document in the desired format. To achieve this aim, the following two steps are necessary:-

• Step 1

In the XML document add the following linking information on the next line below the prolog.

<?xml-stylesheet href = " stylesheet.css " type = " text/css " ?>

↑ ↑

href parameter
this parameter refers to
your file which
contains your own
style sheet instructions/information
for the current document which has to be
associated with this set of styling instructions
This is the file which you must create and saved on the same hard disk

style sheet type parameter
This refers to the type of the style sheet
IE5 or other tools which support css
recognise it

• Step 2

Create a file with **.css** extension and store in it specific styling instruction which will be applied to the XML document. These instructions specify how each element in the document should be formatted, and displayed.

There are scores of CSS properties for adding styles to elements. Among these, font and text properties are widely used. You have to decide which properties are to be included in this file for each element. CSS properties inform the browser which font size, type, style, colour, margin and other values to use to format the text.

There are scores of CSS properties for adding styles to elements. Among these font and text properties are widely used. You have to decide which properties are to be included in your file for each element. These properties inform the browser which font size , type, style colour, margin and other values to use in order to format the content of a document.

• Some CSS properties

Some CSS properties are outlined and demonstrated below:-

• **font-family** - it is for selecting the name of the font. It may be that a particular font may not be available to the browser or any other tool being used for viewing the Web page, it is therefore, suggested to select more than one font type.

• **font- size** - this will let you select the required size of characters. You can select it by naming such as, small, medium, or large. Or you can also describe it in points such as 12pt.

For instance, the following font property will set the font type. It lists two font names. Hopefully, one of them will be available to the browser in which the document will be viewed. You can list several font names as long as there is a comma between each pair and the list ends with a semicolon as shown below:-

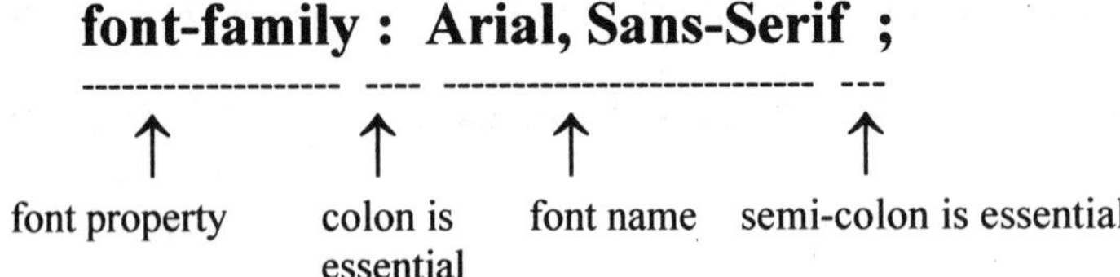

example: font-size: 10pt; This will set the size to 10 point for the selected font type or name.

• **font style** - it is to declare that the font is *italic*. **example:-** font-style: italic;

• **font weight** - this property is used to indicate that the font is bold.
example:- font-style: bold;

• **color** – this property lets you set the text colour of your choice: **example:-** color: blue;
You can also select the colour by means of RGB value. **For instance:-** #0000FF is for blue.
Thus for blue the code is:- color: #0000FF;

• **background color** – if you wish to change the background colour to another colour, you can do so. **For instance:-** background-color: red;

• **text align** – it is used to align the text to left, right, centre or justify. **For example:-**
text-align: centre; - this code will place the text in the centre of a screen.

•**display** – it is used to indicate whether the element is set to rendered or not. It can take none, block, inline values. **For instance:-** display: non; the element will not be rendered.

- **none display** – if you do not want to display the element, you can use this display property value. In this case, the element will be invisible.

- **block display** – it identifies the element as a separate block (a piece of writing treated as a large unit). Each block is considered as a unit and is displayed separately on a new line. The block ends with a break at the end of the element. It is useful for displaying paragraphs, headings and root elements.

- **inline display** - it displays the element, as if it were a part of the current block, on the same line. It is useful for displaying parts of a paragraph or even of a sentence. **For example:- display: inline;** the element will be displayed on the next line, indentation left.

- **text-decoration** – it is very useful if you want to underline, overline or draw a line-through. **for instance:-** text-decoration: line-through; This code will draw a line through.

- **margin** – it is also very useful for setting the size of a margin. You can select any of the following values:- margin-bottom, margin-left, margin-right, and margin-top. **For instance:- margin-bottom: 20 px;** (measurement in *x*- units of pixels)

- **padding** – when the content of an element is within a box/border, you can use the padding property for setting the following margins:

  . padding-top . padding-right . padding-bottom . padding-left

It will set the margin between the text and the border/box drawn around it. You can write just padding only for all four sides in a single setting. **For instance:-** padding: 0. 5in;

Besides these border options, there are some other interested options. Some more properties of CSS will be discussed and implemented as this book progresses. This example illustrates the application of both border and padding properties.

<u>A segment of markup code illustrating how to set both padding for all sides of a border</u>

```
padding:0.5in;
border-top:solid;
border-right:double;
border-bottom:groove;
border-left:double;
```

When this code was implemented it created a border with 5 inches padding all around between the content and border of an element.

The general format of a style sheet file

```
element1
        {
          display: block;
          font-family: Serif, Arial, Helvetica;
          font-size: 12 pt;
          text-margin: left;
        }
element2
         {
           display: inline;
           font-family: Serif, Arial, Helvetica;
font-size: 20 pt;
           color: red;
           text-decoration: underline;
           margin-bottom: 15 px;
        }
   .
   .
   elementn
         {
           display: none;
           font-family: "times New Roman";
           font-size: 14 pt;
           background-color: gray;
           text-align: centre;
           }
```

Illustration 10

The above CSS document is a general example of creating a style sheet for adding individual styles to elements and display them as required.

Indeed, XML concentrates on the structure of a document, not its appearance (HTML allows it). Anyway, the presentation without any styling or formatting is least desirable for a Web page. As such, it is not good enough for communicating information on the Internet.

Thus, in order to display a document in the browser or any other tool such as the dedicated XML editor, the document has to be formatted or styled. You do so by means of creating some styling information which is related to the structure of the document, and how the document will be displayed.

• Example 4

• Part 1

To create a simple XML document in order to display the text shown below in the shaded area. Also save it as testingstyles.xml.

A styled document is displayed in the IE5 without markup.

You can build a style sheet for any Web page by applying some rules/properties of Cascading Style Sheets. For short CSS or css. Try!
You can do so easily once you have built a few style sheets.

This is just a test!

• Part 2

To create a file for styling instructions of your own choice (style sheet) which will be applied to the XML document for this example. You must name it as testingstyles.css, so that it has the same name as XML file, except **.css** file extension.

• Part 3

Display the document testingstyles.xml in the IE5 or any other browser.

• Explanation

• The required XML document is created and saved. It is shown in Diagram 7.

• The following link code is placed between XML declaration (prolog) and the opening tag <test>. This code creates a link between this document and its associated CSS file. This code shows that the style sheet link is in the XML file.

```
<?xml-stylesheet href = " stylesheet.css " type = " text/css " ?>
```

• What is the status of <test> in this example?

It is the parent element. From it, four other elements (children) are derived namely: <para1>,<para2>, <para3> and <para4>.

• In Diagram 7, you can see that these derived elements are contained within the parent element <test>. Each of these elements has some data in the form text or character data, which has to be formatted and displayed as required.

• The next step is to create testingstyles.css file. You can create it by using WordPad text editor and save it as text document. If you wish to use another text editor, well, you can do so. The code, for you to key in and save it, is listed in Diagrams 8 and 8A.

The XHTML code for example 3 – testingstyles.xml

```
========================== testingstyles.xml ============================

<?xml version="1.0"?>

<?xml:stylesheet href ="testingstyles.css" type="text/css"?>
<test>
<para1>
        A styled document is displayed in the IE5 without markup.
</para1>
<para2>
          You can build a style sheet for any Web page by applying some rules/properties
        of Cascading Style Sheets. For short CSS or css. Try!
</para2>
<para3>
           You can do so easily once you have built a few style sheets.
</para3>

<para4>
           This is just a test!</para4>
 </test>
```

Diagram 7

• So, what should be in this style sheet document?

• This file has no prolog . It has the same name as for XML file, except saved with **.css** extension.

• This simple document has four elements namely **<para1>**, **<para2>**, **<para3>** and **<para4>**, it is now necessary to add a style for each of these elements in accordance with some rules of CSS. Thus, the text/data, which is the content of each element will be displayed for each of these elements in the required format as per selected rules or properties of CSS Level 2.

- I want to display element **<para1>** as a box. Furthermore, I wish to specify the style for this element according to which the <para1> should be displayed. The value given to each CSS property is for <para1>, which is my own choice. All properties and their values are listed in Illustration 11 for your ease of learning, so that you can follow CSS in Diagram 8.
- The markup code for the other three elements does not involve placing the text in a box. Therefore, it is comparatively easier to construct. See CSS for more information.
- Of course, you can implement some different CSS properties and give them different values, depending how you want to format and display the document. However, it should be remembered that a style sheet is based on the structure of the document.
- The XML file **testingstyles.xml** was tested in the IE5 successfully. Its screen capture is in Diagram 9 for you to see how this formatted document has appeared in it.

CSS rules for creating the text in a box for paragraph 1

CSS property	Meaning
display: block;	. → data for element para 1 to be displayed as a block
font-size: 14pt;	. → font size 14 point – no font family specified
font-style: bold;	. → font 14 point bold typeface
color:blue;	. → text to be displayed in blue colour
text-decoration:underline;	. → text to be under-lined
text-align: center;	. → text alignment centre
padding:0.2in;	. → margin = 2 inches – all sides of this box equals
border-top:solid;	. → set top border of a box
border-right:double;	. → set right border of a box
border-bottom:groove;	. → set bottom/lower border of a box
border-left:double;	. → set let border of a box.
margin-bottom:20px;	. → it creates white space = 20 pixels between para1 and para2

Illustration 11

• Is styling essential?

It has already been stated that the prime objective of XML is to concentrate on the structure of a document as opposed to its presentation. You have also seen that without any styling or formatting XML document is displayed together with its markup code. This is least desirable for the public viewing of a document on the Web. Once the XML document is linked to a style sheet designed for it, it can be viewed without the markup code, and is thus suitable for displaying on the Internet.

CSS document - testingstyles.css file (cont. in Diagram 8A)

```
=========================testingstyles.css ======================
/* An example of implementing CSS */
para1
    {
    display: block;
    font-size: 14pt;
    font-style: bold;
    color:blue;
    text-decoration:underline;
    text-align: center;
    padding:0.2in;
    border-top:solid;
    border-right:double;
    border-bottom:groove;
    border-left:double;
    margin-bottom:20px;
    }
 para2
   {
    display:inline;
    font-size: 16pt;
    font-style: italic;
    color:black;
    background-color:yellow;
    text-align: left;
   }

  para3
   {
   display: block;
    font-size: 14pt;
    color: red;
```

Diagram 8

CSS document - testingstyles.css file (cont. from Diagram 8)

```
    font-style:bold;
    text-align: left;
    margin-bottom: 30px;
  }
para4
        {
          display: inline;
          font-size: 24pt;
          font-style: italic;
          color: white;
          text-decoration: underline;
          background-color: black;
        }
```

Diagram 8A

The screen capture of document for example 3 - testingstyles.xml file

Colours can only be appreciated on your screen

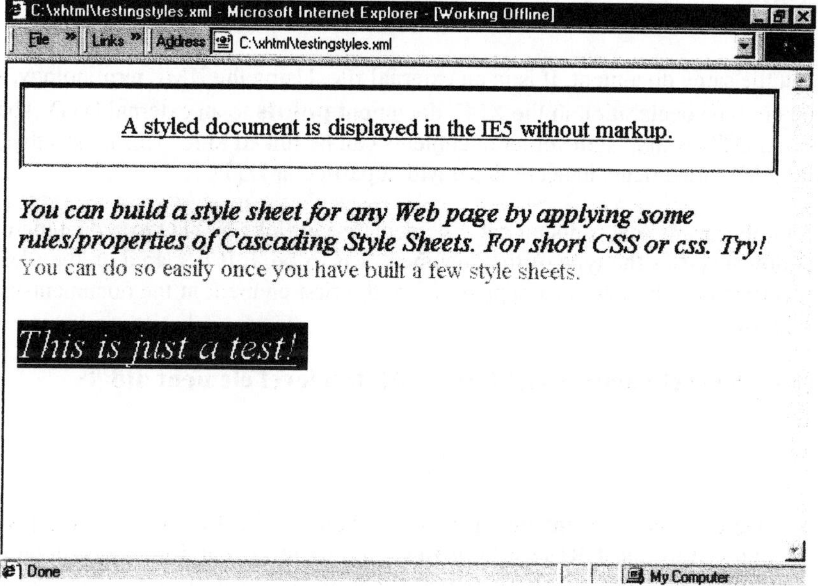

Diagram 9

• Some other related XML concepts

• Can I create my style sheet with the Extensible Stylesheet Language (XSL)?

XSL is more ambitious and powerful than CSS. Indeed, CSS is simpler to use and it is more suited for simple Web pages. XSL has been developed for styling things like tables and complex documents. You can use XSL, but it is better to apply the rules of CSS for less advanced work.

• Document type declaration & DTD

In accordance with the XML 1.0 (Second Edition) Specification, the XML document type declaration contains or points to markup declarations that provide a grammar for a class of documents. This grammar is known as a document type definition or DTD. You have already met document type definition. Before this chapter closes, it is necessary to discuss the relationship between the DTD and document type declaration. It is a pity that in this context the XML terminology is rather confusing here. You have to remember that **DTD** is short only for the document type definition. The document type declaration can point to:-

• an internal DTD

It is written within the same XML document as part of the document type declaration. Or to

• an external DTD

It is **not** written within the same document. It is in an external file. Using the XML terminology, in such cases, the document type declaration in the XML document **points** to an external DTD. The big advantage of an external DTD is that some other documents can be linked to it. This means that you can write a number of XML documents in accordance with a particular DTD.

In practical terms, it simply means that a document type declaration links a DTD to a document. The document type declaration specifies the type of the document it is to be. It is declared on the next line, just below the XML declaration. Thus, it must appear before the first element in the document Its general form is as shown below:-

<!DOCTYPE top level element SYSTEM "URI/ top level element.dtd">

• SYSTEM

SYSTEM is a keyword. Here, it acts as **identifier**. It is used when the DTD is locally developed. The SYSTEM identifier is followed by the **URI** (Uniform Resource Identifier) and the declaration of the DTD. Both of these are within a pair of quotation marks. From all practical purposes, the URI is just the same as the Uniform Resource Locator (URL). This type of declaration points to a Web site, where the DTD can be found. In simple terms, it tells the browser that the DTD is at the Web site whose location is given. This declaration makes it available to other applications.

• PUBLIC

There is another identifier called **PUBLIC**. This points to a DTD, which is for a much larger number of users, and recorded with ISO, as a public standard and part of library of standards. Such DTDs are for larger applications. We are concerned here with the document type declaration for smaller Web sites, where a DTD can be found. It is illustrated below. Furthermore, I have analysed it so that it becomes clearer.

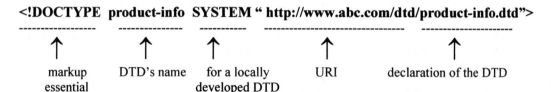

<!DOCTYPE product-info SYSTEM " http://www.abc.com/dtd/product-info.dtd">

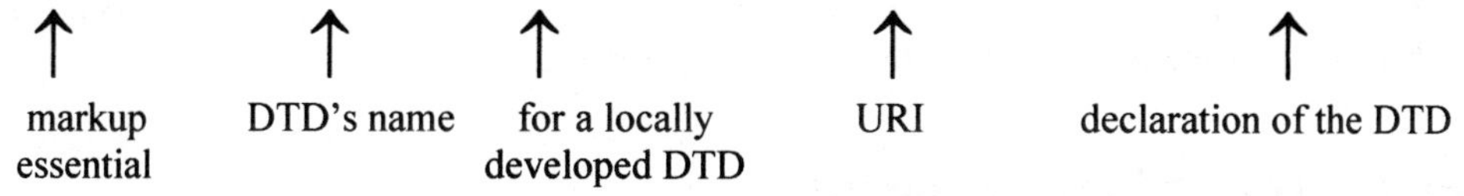

As you can see it is written within the angle brackets. If you examine it carefully, you can appreciate that the purpose of the document type declaration is to link a DTD to the XML document.

• Is DTD absolutely necessary?

If you wish to enforce a specific document structure then it is definitely required. In fact, even so, it is only needed to perform its role at some steps during the process. The reader of your document is not permitted to amend or correct errors in your document's structure. Therefore, the distribution of a DTD as a part of the document is questionable.

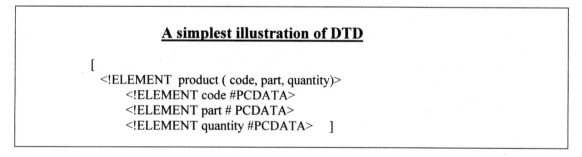

A simplest illustration of DTD

```
[
  <!ELEMENT  product ( code, part, quantity)>
       <!ELEMENT code #PCDATA>
       <!ELEMENT part # PCDATA>
       <!ELEMENT quantity #PCDATA>     ]
```

Illustration 12

The **#PCDATA** code is implemented in Illustration 12. It is helpful to analyse this code below:-

→ It is essential here in order to prevent PCDATA from being interpreted as the name of the element.

P → stands for parsed

CDATA → character data. This code means that the element can have character data which is text.

The above illustration is not a complete DTD. When the DTD is in internal, which means in the same document, then the declaration has to be extended in order to give details of elements and attributes, enclosed within [ ] as shown in Illustration 12 above.

• Prolog

I stated earlier that another name for the XML declaration is prolog. The prolog includes both the XML declaration and document type declarations. As you know by now, the document type declarations include DTDs. Thus, through the prolog, the parser knows what kind of XML document it is going to be. This way, the parser learns how to interpret the document.

• Components of XML document

Until now, you have seen some simple XML documents and some examples of ideas introduced. At this juncture, the XML document and its constitutional parts can be visualised as illustrated below. You can see that diagram 11 represents an XML document which has two major components namely, prolog and elements. Each component has its own two components.

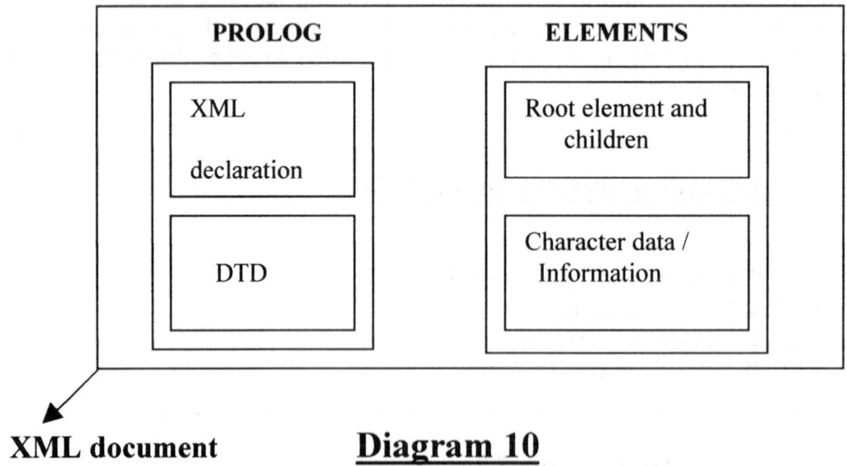

Diagram 10

For advancing your knowledge and skills in XML, you should obtain a copy of XML. Good luck!

Chapter 4

Block-level Elements

The prime aim of this chapter is as follows:-

- to enable you to understand XHTML category of elements called block-level elements, which are used to create the main structure of the document.

By reading this chapter, you should acquire both the knowledge and the skill of including in your XHTML documents the following features:-

- organising the text into manageable paragraphs
- heading a document and its different paragraphs with appropriate headings of different sizes
- highlighting quotes
- making use of 'preformatted text' element in order to include special text such as Java script, Perl script or any other programming code in its original format
- generating line breaks to make text both presentable and meaningful
- including contact address of the Webmaster in a Web page
- understanding the meaning of semantics or built-in semantics
- aligning text

. Introduction

The XHTML document design is for the electronic publication for whatever purpose it may be designed. The document designer has to shape the document in such a way that a document has some headings in order to distinguish one component of the document from some other components, each part of the document is organised in sections or paragraphs, and that text within each paragraph is legible.

It is also desirable that a reader does not experience unnecessary eye strain when he/she reads the document on a monitor screen or on printed paper. Furthermore, the individual or the organisation who generates the Web page also has the aim to monitor the format (shape) of the document in order to maintain a laid down standard. A simple laid down standard may include:-

- **text format** - it simply means defining the structure of text to be written in a Web page. It includes such things as headings, paragraphs, line breaks, underline text, margin settings.
- **specify colour** - selecting background colours, presenting text in different colours
- **define text position** - positioning text in the document in the desired place.

However, the main structure of a document has to be created by means of elements known as block-level elements. At this stage of learning, you must know the answer to the question:

• What does semantics mean in XHTML context?

Before going any further, you should have an idea of the practical meaning of 'semantics' here. Browsers designed for HTML have built-in capabilities of displaying elements in the same way. For instance, most browsers have a built-in capability of understanding the <p> element, which is used for creating a blank line of text or white space before and after the paragraph.

In commercial browsers, the application of <p> element generates the same action, and thus the semantics (language) of the <p> element is the same across almost all commercial HTML browsers.

Since XHTML is comparatively new, there are not yet so many browsers or other user agents specifically designed for this new technology. Nevertheless, similar semantics are recommended in XHTML Recommendation. In Table 1, I have listed some XHTML block-level elements together with their semantics or scope. These elements are often used in Web page design. In Table 2, you can find the most used element called heading. The word "heading", seems to have a variety of meanings. For all practical purposes, it means heading in the sense of a heading of a page, or a paragraph.

• Creating headlines

The element which is used for making a headline is called headline element , as well as heading tag. There are six levels of headline tags. These are useful tags in making headings at different levels, such as main heading, sub heading and other levels of heading if you like. Browsers do not see the visual layout of the text as human eyes can see it. It is for this reason that you have to use basic tags in your document.

• Example 1

This example demonstrates how to create headlines of different sizes in your document by implementing **headline tags.** The text for each headline is shown below in the shaded area.

Text to be used as the content of all six headlines

h1 displays the largest size headline. This is level 1.
h2 displays a larger size headline. This is level 2.
h3 displays a large size headline. This is level 3.
h4 displays a small size headline. This is level 4.
h5 displays a smaller size headline. This is level 5.
h6 displays smallest size headline. This is level 6.

Each headline element is a container of its text. The task is to design a simple XHTML document by using 6 different headline elements, one for each line of text shown above.

• Explanation

The XHTML code shown in diagram 1 is designed to create six different headlines. I analyse each line of this code now:-

- The code starts with a set of meta –data as required. Once again, it is to remind you that the XHTML Recommendation strongly encourages you to use XML declaration:

```
<?xml version= "1.0" encoding = "UTF-8"?>
```

- It is also required that an XHTML document must validate against one of the three DTD's already discussed. Here, the Transitional DTD is implemented. It is also required that a **DOCTYPE** declaration should be with the Formal Public Identifier (FPI). In order to meet this requirement, the following segment of the code is essential:

```
<!DOCTYPE html
                PUBLIC "- //w3C//DTD XHTML 1.0 Transitional//EN"
"http://www.w3.org/TR/xhtml1/DTD/xhtml1-transitional.dtd">
```

- It is also required that the root element must designate the XHTML namespace by means of **xmlns attribute**. For this reason, the following segment of the meta-data must be part of the markup code.

```
<html xmlns= "http://www.w3.org/1999/xhtml" xml:lang= "en" lang= "en">
```

- Having declared the essential meta-data in the head section of the document, the next thing is to set the title of the document, so that it can appear in the title bar of a browser. It is an essential requirement It is set in within the <head> element as shown below.

```
<head>
<title>Largest to smallest headlines</title>
</head>
```

- The head tag is needed as it enables the browser to correctly interpret the document. Within the head section, the title tag <title> is enclosed. The title tag is immediately followed by the title given to this document. It is Largest to smallest headlines.

- At the end of text for this title, there is a closing title tag </title>as required by rules.

- The next requirement is to declare the body of a Web page. This is done by declaring <body> element. In the last chapter, it is stated that the body contains much of the information that forms your Web page. In this example, the body contains all six heading tags: The following segment of the code is for displaying the content of the <h1> element:

```
<h1>
   h1 displays the largest size headline. This is level 1.
</h1>
```

This will be the first line of information in this Web page called Largest to smallest headlines. Once again, notice that the text for this heading is enclosed within the opening and closing tags of level 1 headline. Now, examine the rest of this code to discover that the pattern is repeated for each type of heading.

- The body of X HTML code has to be closed. This is achieved by < /body> as shown in this diagram.

- This is to remind you that <html> is the root element and thus the closing tag </html> is essential in order to mark the end of the XHTML file.

- Prior to previewing the document in the IE, it was submitted to the W3C HTML Validation Service for checking it for XML well-formedness and validity. The W3C result stated. "No errors found!". For information on "Submitting your documents to W3C Validator", see Appendix C.

• Previewing document: headings.html

The code shown in Diagram 1 was saved as headings.html file. I have viewed it in IE locally. Of course, this can also be viewed on-line as a part of a Web page or itself as a Web page.

Diagram 1- The XHTML markup code for example 1 - headings.html

```
<?xml version= "1.0" encoding = "UTF-8"?>
<!DOCTYPE html
                    PUBLIC "- //w3C//DTD XHTML 1.0 Transitional//EN"
 "http://www.w3.org/TR/xhtml1/DTD/xhtml1-transitional.dtd">
<html xmlns= "http://www.w3.org/1999/xhtml" xml:lang= "en" lang= "en">
<head>
<title>Largest to smallest headlines</title>
</head>
<body>
<h1>  h1 displays the largest size headline. This is level 1.</h1>
<h2>  h2 displays a larger size headline. This is level 2.</h2>
<h3> h3 displays a large size headline. This is level 3.</h3>
 <h4> h4 displays a small size headline. This is level 4.</h4>
<h5> h5 displays a smaller size headline. This is level 5.</h5>
<h6>h6 displays smallest size headline. This is level 6.</h6>
</body></html>
```

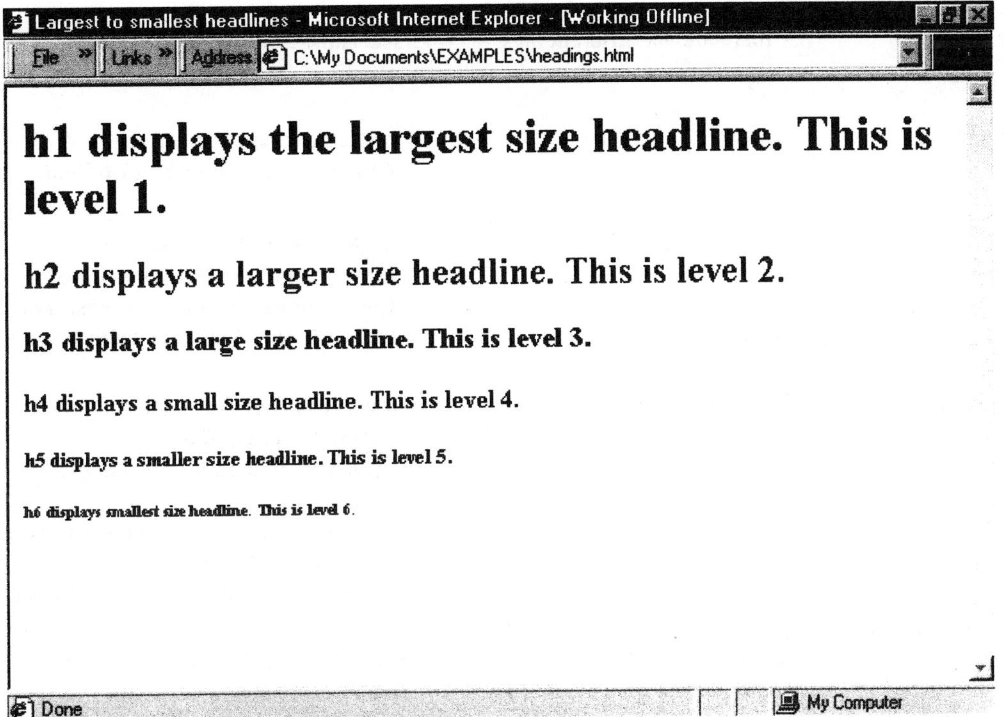

Diagram 2 - Preview of document for example 1 in IE locally

The preview is shown in Diagram 2. It can be seen that an XHTML code is excluded from this display. It shows only the required information in the desired format. You can see that each heading is on a separate line.

• What is the reason for this occurrence?

Simply because a headline creates **an automatic line break**. There are some other ways of creating line breaks, which you will learn soon.

You might have already noticed that headlines text created by heading tags <3> to <<6> is smaller than regular text size. For this reason, their use is rather limited.

Some Block-level elements

Element name	Tags	Scope
• Headline	there are six different tags.	see Table 2 for largest to smallest heading elements.
• Paragraph	<p></p>	it is used to create paragraphs. A paragraph is a single block of text.
• Preformatted text Or preserve	<pre></pre>	its purpose is to maintain the formatting of the text with white spaces in the document. It preserves the white space in the document.
• Blockquote	<blockquote></blockquote>	it was primarily intended for displaying quotations. it can also be used as a block level element. it can also act as styling element, when you are not using style sheet. It can indent text – both left and right margin.
• Address	<address></address>	it is used to provide contact information at the base line of a Web page.

Table 1

Headline Tags

Level	Tag	Size	Scope
1	<h1></ h1>	largest headline	often in use for top level heading
2	< h2></ h2>	large headline	often in use for secondary level heading
3	< h3></ h3>	small headline	often in use for third level heading
4	<h4></ h4>	smaller headline	seldom in use due to size too small
5	< h5 </ h5>	smallest headline	seldom in use due to very small size
6	<h6></h6>	tiniest headline	seldom in use due to tiniest size

Table 2

. Paragraph Formatting

Text for example 2

'Like tends to cause confusion. It is a preposition meaning 'resembling, similar to', as in 'houses like castles', gardens like jungles', 'actors like Olivier'.

To be grammatically correct like should not be used as a conjunction. Thus 'The house looks like it has been deserted' is incorrect. It should read 'The house looks as though/if it has been deserted'.

'Like his mother said, he has had to go to hospital' should read 'As his mother said, he has had to go to hospital.'

. Example 2

Here, the idea is to learn how to organise text into paragraphs so that your text can be shown by a variety of browsers on a variety of computers with varying graphics capabilities correctly in the desired format. The paragraph element <p> is powerful enough to let you achieve your objectives of paragraph formatting as desired. This example illustrates the rule of making paragraphs with the aid of paragraph tags <p></p>.

Write XHTML code for a document called paragraphs, whose content is shown above in the shaded area. Save your XHTML markup code as **paragraphs.html**. Check it for XML well-formedness and validity as XHTML 1.0 Transitional document. View this document locally in the IE5 or any other user agent.

The XHTML markup code for example 2

```
<?xml version= "1.0" encoding = "UTF-8"?>
<!DOCTYPE html
            PUBLIC "- //w3C//DTD XHTML 1.0 Transitional//EN"
 "http://www.w3.org/TR/xhtml1/DTD/xhtml1-transitional.dtd">
<html xmlns= "http://www.w3.org/1999/xhtml" xml:lang= "en" lang= "en">
```

```
<head>
<title>Paragraphs</title>
</head>
<body>
<p>
   Like tends to cause confusion. It is a preposition meaning 'resembling, similar to', as in 'houses like
castles', gardens like jungles', 'actors like Olivier'.</p>
<p>
    To be grammatically correct like should not be used as a conjunction. Thus 'The house looks like
    it has been deserted' is incorrect. It should read 'The house looks as though/if it has been deserted'.
 </p>
<p>
    'Like his mother said, he has had to go to hospital' should read 'As his mother said, he has had to
go to hospital.'</p>
</body>
</html>
```

Diagram 3

. Explanation

- Upon examining the markup code in Diagram 3 you can see that the application of <p>element is simple enough. In order to delineate a paragraph, you must place the closing tag</p> at the end of a paragraph. In HTML, there is no need for </p>, but XHTML is much stricter, and you must observe its syntax rules. The spacing between any two paragraphs is the same as for any other two paragraphs. The document was checked by W3C HTML Validation Service for XMK well-formedness and validity as XHTML 1.0 Transitional document. It meets all requirements. See it as screen capture in Diagram 4.

• Can one align paragraphs?

Certainly, you can control the alignment of paragraphs in your document. This is achieved by applying the **align attribute**. It is discussed under attributes in this chapter. In fact, this is the only attribute, that is implemented with the <p> element. See example 7.

Paragraphing.html viewed in I

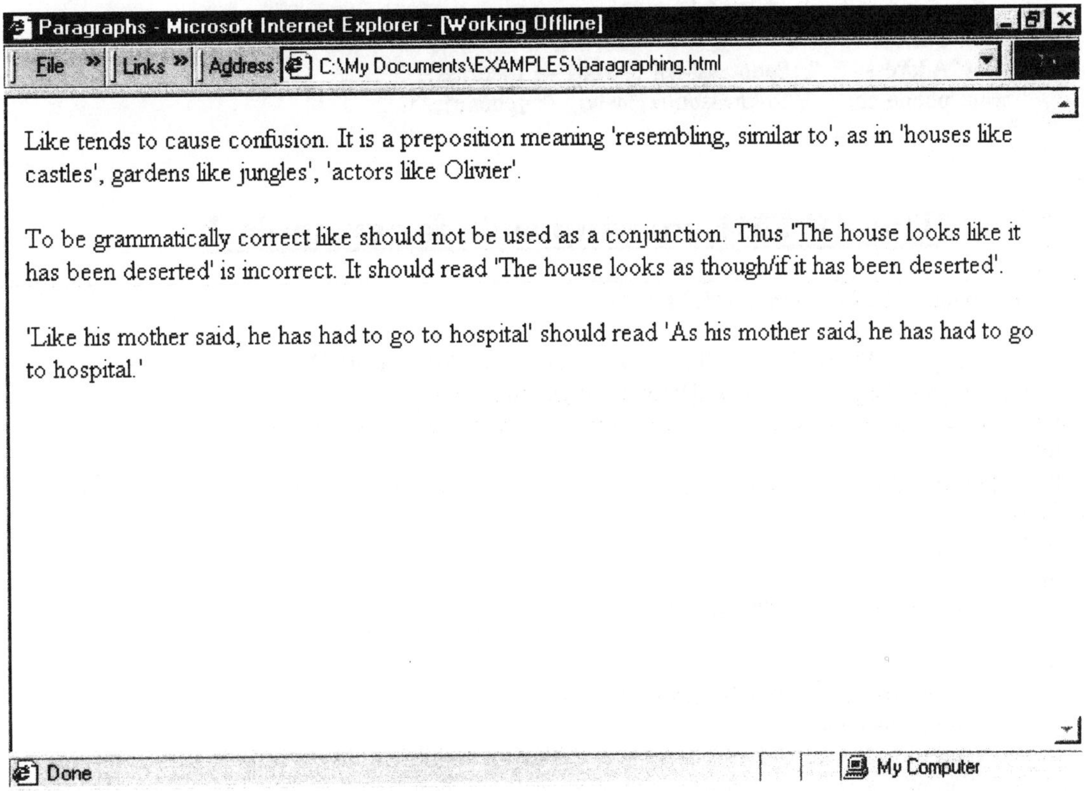

Paragraphs - Microsoft Internet Explorer - [Working Offline]

File » Links » Address C:\My Documents\EXAMPLES\paragraphing.html

Like tends to cause confusion. It is a preposition meaning 'resembling, similar to', as in 'houses like castles', gardens like jungles', 'actors like Olivier'.

To be grammatically correct like should not be used as a conjunction. Thus 'The house looks like it has been deserted' is incorrect. It should read 'The house looks as though/if it has been deserted'.

'Like his mother said, he has had to go to hospital' should read 'As his mother said, he has had to go to hospital.'

Done My Computer

Diagram 4

• Preformatted text

see next page ⇒

• Example 3

A segment of some scripting code is listed in the shaded area below. The idea is to reproduce it together with all white spaces and line breaks (multiple spaces), so that it is preformatted. To write an XHTML code which can generate this required presentation, save your file under any other suitable name, check it for XML Well-formedness and Validity as XHTML 1.0 Transitional document. You must display it to confirm that it is in the required format.

Text for example 3

A segment of some scripting code

```
if ( exists $addressbook {$who} {
   print "$who\n";
   print "Address:      ", $addressbook{$who} -> {address}, "\";
   print "phone no:     ", $addressbook{$who} -> {phone}, "\"
   }
```

The XHTML markup code for example 3

```
<?xml version= "1.0" encoding = "UTF-8"?>
<!DOCTYPE html
                    PUBLIC "- //w3C//DTD XHTML 1.0 Transitional//EN"
 "http://www.w3.org/TR/xhtml1/DTD/xhtml1-transitional.dtd">
<html xmlns= "http://www.w3.org/1999/xhtml" xml:lang= "en" lang= "en">
<head>
<title>Preserve</title>
</head>
<body>
<h2>
      A segment of some scripting code
</h2>
<pre>
           if ( exists $addressbook {$who} {
            print "$who\n";
            print "Address:      ", $addressbook{$who} -> {address}, "\";
            print "phone no:     ", $addressbook{$who} -> {phone}, "\"
           }
</pre>
 </body></html>
```

Diagram 5

• Explanation

The required code is shown in Diagram 5. It was saved as **preserve.html** and then tested locally. In Diagram 6, its screen capture is shown. As you can observe, the headline is not part of the preformatted text.

A segment of some scripting code

It is generated as Level 2 heading in order to label this document. The scripting code is displayed as required, with all white spaces and line breaks preserved. The browser has aligned the text by using fixed-width font. Fixed–width is also known as mono-space font. For instance, 'Courier New' is mono-spaced font type.

Preview of Preserve in IE5

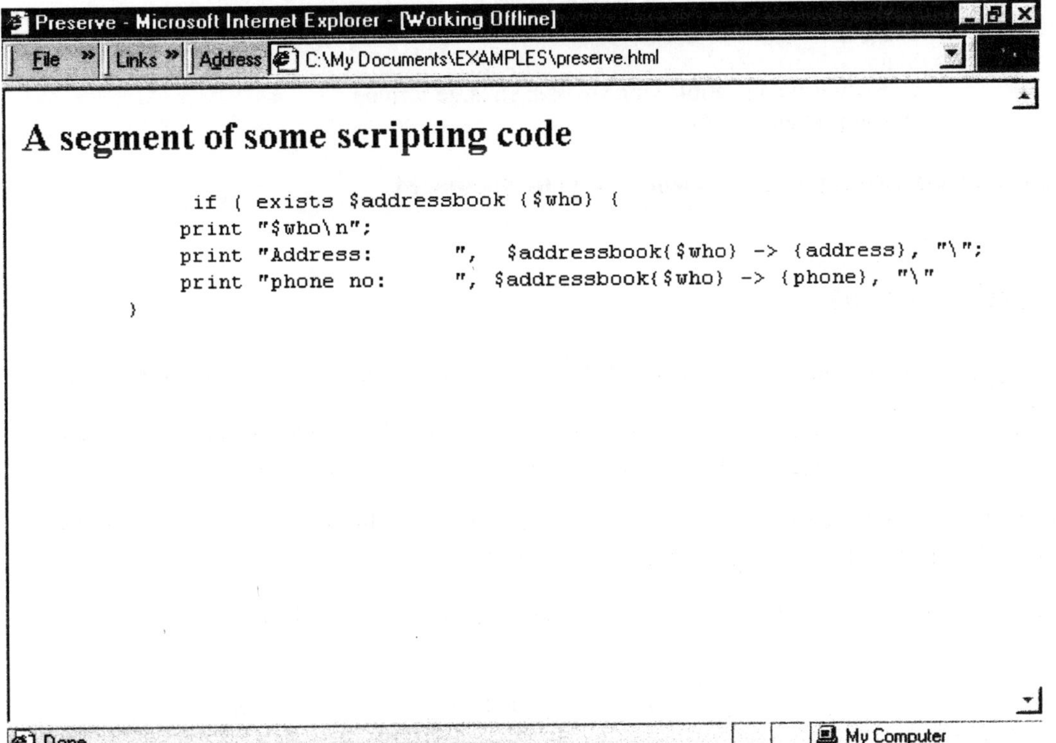

Diagram 6

• Including quotes in your document

see next page ⇒

You know well that sometimes it is necessary to quote the words of someone else for whatever reason. Indeed, one can include quotations with the **<blockquote>** element as demonstrated below.

• Example 4

Create an XHTML document for displaying the following two quotations and the accompanied text in the given format. Save your document as **quoteIt . html**, and display it in the IE5 or any other user agent. You must also carry out XML and XHTML check for both well-formedness and validity.

Quotations!

> **What difference does it make to the dead, the orphans and homeless, whether the mad destruction is wrought under the name of totalitarianism or the holy name of liberty or democracy?**
> **Mahatma Gandhi 1942**
>
> **Honesty is incompatible with amassing a large fortune.**
> **Mahatma Gandhi 1948**

You can include quotations anywhere in your document.

• Explanation

The required XHTML code for this example is shown in Diagram 7. It was saved as **quoteIt . html**.

- You can examine in Diagram 7, how the quoted text is placed with the <blockqoute></blockquote> tags. It follows the same pattern as you have already seen in previous examples.
- In Diagram 8, display starts with level 2 headline, "Quotations!". This is obviously outside the scope of the <blockquote> element, and thus the text is automatically left aligned.
- The <blockquote> element generates a block of everything which is placed within the container tags <blockquote> -------- </blockquote>.
- In order to print the source of each quotation on a separate line, I have placed <br /> element at the end of the cited text. As in XHTML, it is vital to have an end tag. For this reason, a slash mark "/ " is added to the <br> element.

  As opposed to the container element, <br / > element is **an empty element.** This is the reason for < **br** /> tag appearing at the end of each quoted text, before the source of each quotation. It should be noted that there is a space between "**br"** and "/ ".
 meets a strict XHTML requirement that each opening tag must have its corresponding closing tag.

- Now, you know that **
 element** is used here as a line break. In XHTML, it starts a new line. It is for this reason that the source of each quote has appeared on a new line just below each block of quoted text, without any white space (empty line) between the quoted text and its source.
- It provides styling without the application of any styling sheets. Thus, it is a very useful element.
- If you examine the document displayed in Diagram 8, you can see that the text, within the element <blockquote>, is intended. So, it has styled the text in accordance with the traditional way of writing the citing text with some indentation. This is an extra advantage of <blockqute> element.

• Can one use <blockquote> element for just indentation purposes instead of citing some text?

Yes indeed, it is a very useful element when no style sheets are used and you want to indent some text. It is suggested that you make use of it whenever there is a need to indent some text passages. The text does not have to be any citation.

• Does the <blockquote> element take any attribute?

Yes, it does take the **cite attribute**. If you want to include the URL of the quotation's source, you can include it in the <blockqoute> element as demonstrated below:-

```
<blockquote  cite = "http://www.Gandhi.org/quotes">

Honesty is incompatible with amassing a large fortune. <br />

                Mahatma Gandhi 1948 </blockquote>
```

This segment of the XHTML code will display the URL (the Internet address) of the quotation source in the status bar of a browser, providing the browser can accept the URL generated by the **cite** attribute.

• Isn't it worthless to use cite attribute as the chances are that some browsers do not interpret it as required?

To include it in your source code will not do any harm at all. If the URL is not displayed by the browser or any other user agent, the URL is still in the source code. If a reader wants it, he/she can view the source code.

Diagram 7: The XHTML markup code for example 4 – quotIt.html

```
<?xml version= "1.0" encoding = "UTF-8"?>
<!DOCTYPE html
                    PUBLIC "- //w3C//DTD XHTML 1.0 Transitional//EN"
 "http://www.w3.org/TR/xhtml1/DTD/xhtml1-transitional.dtd">
<html xmlns= "http://www.w3.org/1999/xhtml" xml:lang= "en" lang= "en">
<head>
<title>Quotations</title>
</head>
<body>
<h2> Quotations! </h2>
<blockquote>
          What difference does it make to the dead, the orphans and homeless, whether the mad
          destruction is wrought under the name of totalitarianism or the holy name of liberty or
          democracy? <br />   Mahatma Gandhi 1942   </blockquote>
 <blockquote>
 Honesty is incompatible with amassing a large fortune. <br /> Mahatma Gandhi 1948 </blockquote>
<h3>You can include quotations anywhere in your document.</h3>
</body></html>
```

The document entitled **Quotations** was previewed in the IE5. You can see its display in Diagram 8.

Diagram 8: Preview of document quoteIt.html in IE

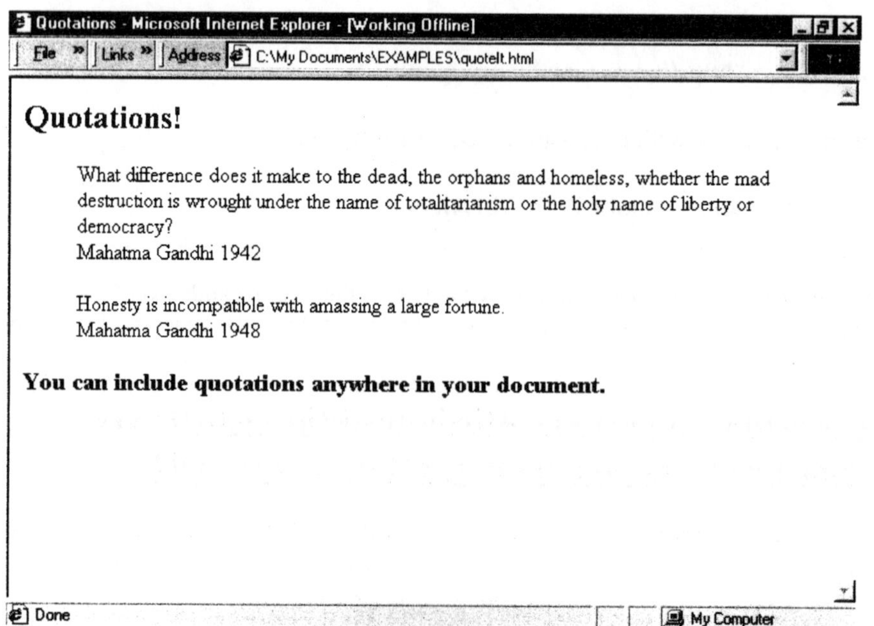

• Horizontal line across the page

You have already learnt that the application of an empty element <br /> produces a line break or an empty line of text between two paragraphs. This is an invaluable method, where it is vitally important to display a line break. Similarly, you can implement **<hr / >**element to generate a horizontal line across the page. Note a space between **hr** and **/. Why is this space desirable?**

Just like <br /> element, the element <hr /> is a not a container. It is an empty element. In HTML, you do not have to place an end tag. On the other hand, in XHTML, an opening tag must have its corre-sponding tag. Therefore, if you leave a space between hr and the slash, browsers can display this ele-ment.

• Example 5

Internet is not a single entity

The Internet does not exist as an entity in its own right. Therefore, it is not owned by any one organisation or a group of companies, or any government.

There is no single centre or organisation to manage the Internet world wide. It is managed and owned by thousands of individual organisations who own and manage these individual networks throughout the world, which constitute the Internet.

Extract from: Web Site Development Simplified, ISBN 1901197 808

- Write a Web page in order to display the above text. The text should be centre aligned. You must save your document, check it for XML well-formedness and validity as XHTML 1.0 Transitional document. Preview it to test that it meets your requirements.

• Explanation

The XHTML code for this example is listed in Diagram 9. Its structure is similar to the structure of documents designed in this chapter. In Transitional DTD the <hr /> element can take **align**, **noshade**, **size** and **width** attributes. Here, I have made use of size attribute. The <hr /> element is written as follows:-

```
<hr size  =  "5" />
-------  ----------   -------
  ⇑         ⇑           ⇑
an empty  attribute   attribute's value in pixels
element   thickness   height of line in pixel – bigger number results
          of line     in thicker line
```

- Since the text has to be centred, I have surrounded , “The Internet ---- which constitutes the Internet." by <blockquote></blockquote> tags. This way, it is centred aligned. If you wish, you can achieve the same aim by means of <centre> ...</centre> tags.
- I wanted to create white space twice as wide as single line break between two paragraphs. For this reason,

 tags are placed at the end first paragraph. See Diagram 10.
- Like other documents, I checked this document for XML well-formedness and validity as XHTML 1.0 Transitional document. The W3C HTML Validation Service found no errors in it. It reported:

  “Congratulations, this document validates as XHTML 1.0 Transitional !”. See Illustration 1.

The XHTML markup code for example 5 – horizontal.html

```
<?xml version= "1.0" encoding = "UTF-8"?>
<!DOCTYPE html
                    PUBLIC "- //w3C//DTD XHTML 1.0 Transitional//EN"
 "http://www.w3.org/TR/xhtml1/DTD/xhtml1-transitional.dtd">
<html xmlns= "http://www.w3.org/1999/xhtml" xml:lang= "en" lang= "en">
<head>
<title> Horizontal Line </title>
</head>
<body>
<center><h2>

          Internet is not a single entity</h2></center>

 <hr size = "5" />

<blockquote>

   The Internet does not exist as an entity in its own right. Therefore, it is not owned by any one
    organisation or a group of companies, or any government. <br /><br />

    There is no single centre or organisation to manage the Internet world wide.
    It is managed and owned by thousands of individual organisations who own and manage these
    individual networks throughout the world, which constitute the Internet.
</blockquote>

<hr size = "5" />
<cite> Extract from: Web Site Development  Simplified, ISBN 1901197 808</cite>
</body></html>
```

Diagram 9

Preview of horizontal.html in IE5

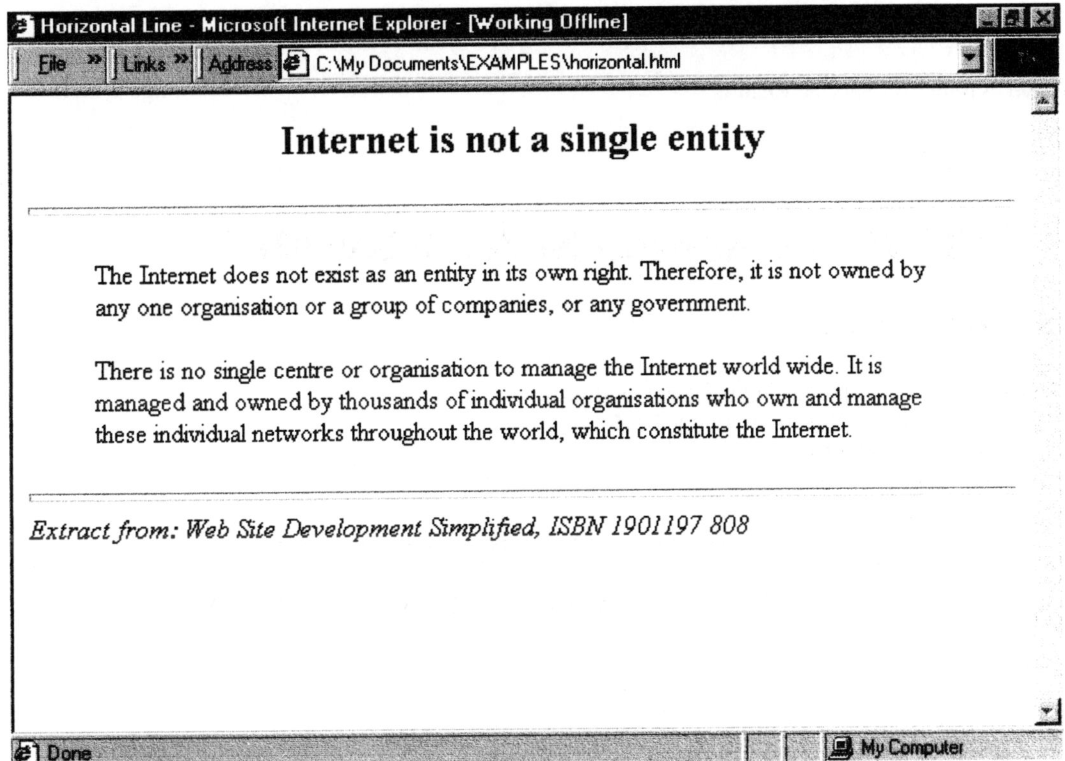

Diagram 10

. XHTML Strict DTD

- It is to remind you that XHTML has three DTDs, namely Strict, Transitional and Frame. Both Transitional and Frame DTDs have all tags and attributes which are in Strict XHTML DTD. In addition, Transitional and Frame DTSs have some additional tags and attributes of their own. For instance, the element <centre> is not included in XHTML Strict DTD, but you can still use it in XHTML Transitional 1.0

- The code listed in Diagram 9 included the implementation of the element<centre>. When it was checked by W3C's HTML Validation Service as XHTML Transitional 1.0 document. At that time, this document was validated as "XHTML 1.0 Transitional". This is shown below in Illustration 1 .

Document: horizontal.html checked and validated by W3C as XHTML 1. 0 document under Transitional DTD

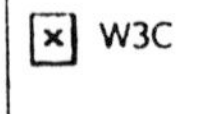

HTML Validation Service Results

Document Checked

- URI: http://www.adrlondon.ltd.uk/horizontal.html
- Last modified: Wed May 16 21:06:19 2001
- Server: Microsoft-IIS/4.0
- Content length: 1014
- Character encoding: utf-8
- Document type: XHTML 1.0 Transitional with namespace http://www.w3.org/1999/xhtml

Below are the results of checking this document for XML well-formedness and validity.

```
No errors found! *
```

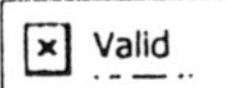

Congratulations, this document validates as XHTML 1.0 Transitional!

To show your readers that you have taken the care to create an interoperable Web page, you may display this icon on any page that validates. Here is the HTML you could use to add this icon to your Web page:

Illustration 1

- The same document was re-submitted to W3C HTML Validation Service, but this time, as XHTML **Strict** document. It was not validated, and the end result stated:

"Sorry, this document does not validate as XHTML 1.0 Strict."

Now, examine Illustration 2, to see how many errors it has listed, due to the inclusion of just one element, namely, <centre> from XHTML Transitional 1.0 used in XHTML 1.0 Strict type document.

Document: horizontal.html checked and invalidated by W3C as XHTML 1. 0 document under Transitional DTD

HTML Validation Service Results

Document Checked

- URI: http://www.adrlondon.ltd.uk/horizontal.html
- Last modified: Wed May 16 21:06:19 2001
- Server: Microsoft-IIS/4.0
- Content length: 1014
- Character encoding: utf-8
- Document type: XHTML 1.0 Strict with namespace http://www.w3.org/1999/xhtml

Below are the results of checking this document for XML well-formedness and validity.

- Line 11, column 7:

```
<center><h2>
      ^
```

Error: element "center" not defined in this HTML version (explanation...)

- Line 13, column 11:

```
<hr size = "5" />
          ^
```

Error: there is no attribute "size" for this element (in this HTML version) (explanation...)

- Line 16, column 0:

```
The Internet does not exist as an entity in its own right. Therefore.   ...
```

Error: text is not allowed here; try wrapping the text in a more descriptive container

- Line 17, column 62:

```
organisation or a group of companies, or any government. <br /><br />
                                                               ^
```

Error: element "br" not allowed here; possible cause is an inline element containing a block-level element (explanation...)

- Line 17, column 68:

```
organisation or a group of companies, or any government. <br /><br />
                                                                     ^
```

Error: element "br" not allowed here; possible cause is an inline element containing a block-level element (explanation...)

- Line 27, column 5:

```
<cite> Extract from: Web Site Development
     ^
```

Error: element "cite" not allowed here; possible cause is an inline element containing a block-level element (explanation...)

Sorry, this document does not validate as XHTML 1.0 Strict.

If you use CSS in your document, you should also check it for validity using the W3C CSS Validation Service.

Gerald Oskoboiny
Last modified: Date: 2001/03/08 01:57:52

Valid

Illustration 2

- It is highly likely that all elements and attributes of XHTML 1.0 Transitional and Frame DTDs will eventually be deprecated (phased out) as XHTML 1.0 develops further.

• The address of the Webmaster

The Webmaster/ Web designer/Web creator can include his/her Internet address at the bottom of the page. This way, the Webmaster can provide an address for correspondence. The element used for this purpose is **<address>.**

• Example 6

Human Brain!

> The brain has 100 trillion connections joining billions of
> neurons and each junction has the potential to be part of a memory.
> So the memory capacity of a human brain is effectively infinite.

BrainStudy@BrainForm.co.uk

Design a Web page for displaying the above text. Save it as addressing .html file. Run it on your system in order to display the document entitled Addressing by means of IE5 or any other user agent.

• Explanation

The required XHTML markup code is listed in Diagram 11. Its structure is similar to the structures of the last four examples in this chapter. However, it gives you another opportunity to examine the application of some other elements which we have already discussed, besides how to code the <address> element. The following segment of the code results in displaying the address the contact address of the Webmaster.

```
<address> Brain Study, <a href = "mailto:
                         BrainStudy@BrainForam.co.uk">BrainStudy@BrainForam.co.uk
 </a> </address>
```

You should carefully examine the structure of the <address> element, which contains the **<a> element**. Within the **<a> element** is the URL of the Webmaster. Also note that </a></address> should be placed in this sequence, which is the order in which the opening tags are used here.

- The <a> element is called the anchor element. It is certainly a special kind of element. For more in formation, see anchors.

The XHTML markup code for example 6 – addressing.html

```
<?xml version= "1.0" encoding = "UTF-8"?>
<!DOCTYPE html
                    PUBLIC "- //w3C//DTD XHTML 1.0 Transitional//EN"
 "http://www.w3.org/TR/xhtml1/DTD/xhtml1-transitional.dtd">
<html xmlns= "http://www.w3.org/1999/xhtml" xml:lang= "en" lang= "en">
<head>
<title>Addressing</title>
</head>
<body>
<h2>
     Human Brain! </h2>

<blockquote>
      The brain has 100 trillion connections joining billions of
      neurons and each junction has the potential to be part of a memory.
      So the memory capacity of a human brain is effectively infinite.
</blockquote>

<address> Brain Study, <a href = "mailto:
                    Brain Study@BrainForam.co.uk">BrainStudy@BrainForam.co.uk
 </a> </address>
</body>
</html>
```

Diagram 11

It was tested for XML well-formedness, and validated as XHTML 1.0 Transitional document. See its screen capture in Diagram 12. It is displayed as required.

. Text Alignment

There is often a need to align both text and images on your Web page. An alignment is a method of Web page lay out. It simply means positioning the text or images on your Web page. Here, the alignment of text is discussed.

Some attributes are supported by Transitional DTD, but the same attributes do not work in the Strict DTD. For instance, **attribute align** is not supported by the Strict DTD. In Table 1, You can find elements which take align attribute, and perform well in the Transitional DTD. If you include an alignment attribute in the Strict DTD, your document will not be validated by W3C as XHTML Strict document.

This is discussed next in example 7.

Preview of Addressing in IE 5

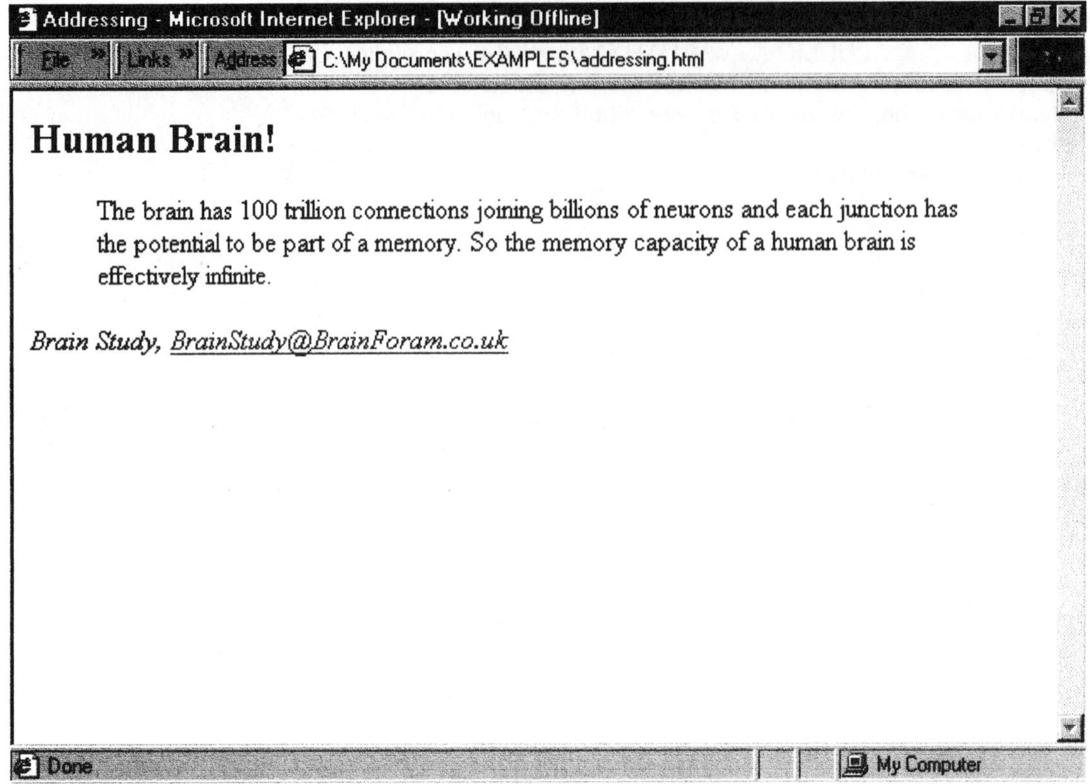

Diagram 12

• Example 7

- Write an XHTML code for displaying the text shown below in the shaded box. Your design of Web page should include the following page layout requirements:-

- heading in the centre of the page, size of heading /headline must be Level 2
- first paragraph to be left aligned
- middle paragraph to be right aligned

- last paragraph to be centre aligned

Save your document, and check it twice for XML well-formedness and validity. First check should be under XHTML 1.0 Transitional DTD, and the second under XHTML Strict DTD. Comment on results of checks carried on by W3C HTML Validation Service.

Stress

"Stress can make your heart beat harder and faster. In fact, I believe that stress is a major cause of elevated blood pressure. Under stress we may feel that as though everything is going wrong.

With chronic stress, the blood vessels constrict, they tighten up and narrow. When that happens, it is harder for the blood to flow through, which means blood pressure goes up.

With chronic stress, the chemistry of blood changes, making it more likely to clot.... a clot will form and trigger a heart attack by getting stuck in a partially narrowed artery in the heart, or prompt a stroke by getting stuck in a narrowed artery in the brain."

• Explanation

The XHTML code is listed in Diagram 13. The align attribute can be used for aligning block elements. The following segment of the code shows how the align attribute is coded.

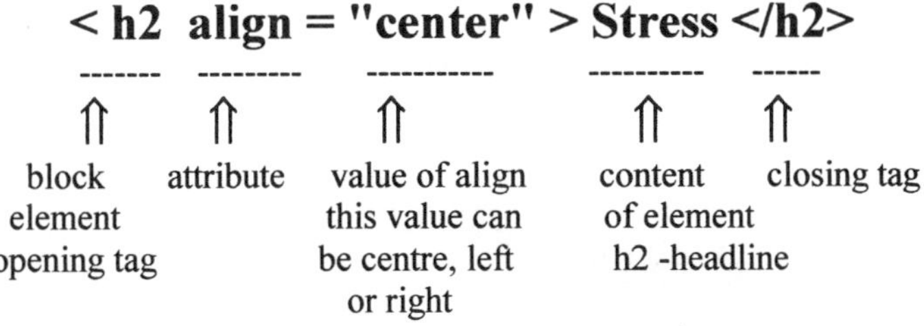

- The XHTML 1.0 Transitional DTD does not allow justify alignment. This code generates headline, in the centre of the page, and aligns it horizontally across the page.
- Since the default alignment of the block element is **left**, then why is there a need for setting left alignment? You will soon learn about style sheets. Just for a moment imagine that your document included style sheet coding, and for some reason, you decided to change it. In that case, left alignment would be useful.
- This code was checked for XML well-formedness and validity as XHTML 1.0 Transitional document. It was validated alright. See Illustration 3, which is self-explanatory.

The screen capture of the document align was previewed in IE successfully. See Diagram 14.

The XHTML code for example 7

```
<?xml version= "1.0" encoding = "UTF-8"?>
<!DOCTYPE html
                    PUBLIC "- //w3C//DTD XHTML 1.0 Transitional//EN"
 "http://www.w3.org/TR/xhtml1/DTD/xhtml1-transitional.dtd">
<html xmlns= "http://www.w3.org/1999/xhtml" xml:lang= "en" lang= "en">
<head>
<title> Text Alignment </title>
</head>
<body>
<h2 align = "center"> Stress</h2>

<p align = "left"> "Stress can make your heart beat harder and faster.
        In fact, I believe that stress is a major cause of elevated
        blood pressure. Under stress we may feel that as though
        everything is going wrong.</p>
<p align = "right">
        With chronic stress, the blood vessels constrict, they
        tighten up and narrow. When that happens, it is harder for the
        blood to flow through, which means blood pressure goes up.</p>
 <p align = "center">
        With chronic stress, the chemistry of blood changes, making
        it more likely to clot...... a clot will form and trigger a heart
        attack by getting stuck in a partially narrowed artery in the
        heart, or prompt a stroke by getting stuck in a narrowed
        artery in the brain."</p>
</body></html>
```

Diagram 13

- In order to check it under **XHTML Strict DTD**, I made the following adjustment to the code listed in Diagram 13.

In Diagram 13 under Transitional DTD

```
<!DOCTYPE html
                    PUBLIC "- //w3C//DTD XHTML 1.0 Transitional//EN"
 "http://www.w3.org/TR/xhtml1/DTD/xhtml1-transitional.dtd">
```

Diagram 13 amended to read as shown below under Strict DTD

```
<!DOCTYPE html
                    PUBLIC "- //w3C//DTD XHTML 1.0 Strict//EN"
 "http://www.w3.org/TR/xhtml1/DTD/xhtml1-Strict.dtd">
```

• This amended document was invalidated. See Illustration 4. The align attribute is not one of the attributes of XHTML Strct DTD. Certainly, it does perform well under Transitional DTD.

Document align previewed in IE

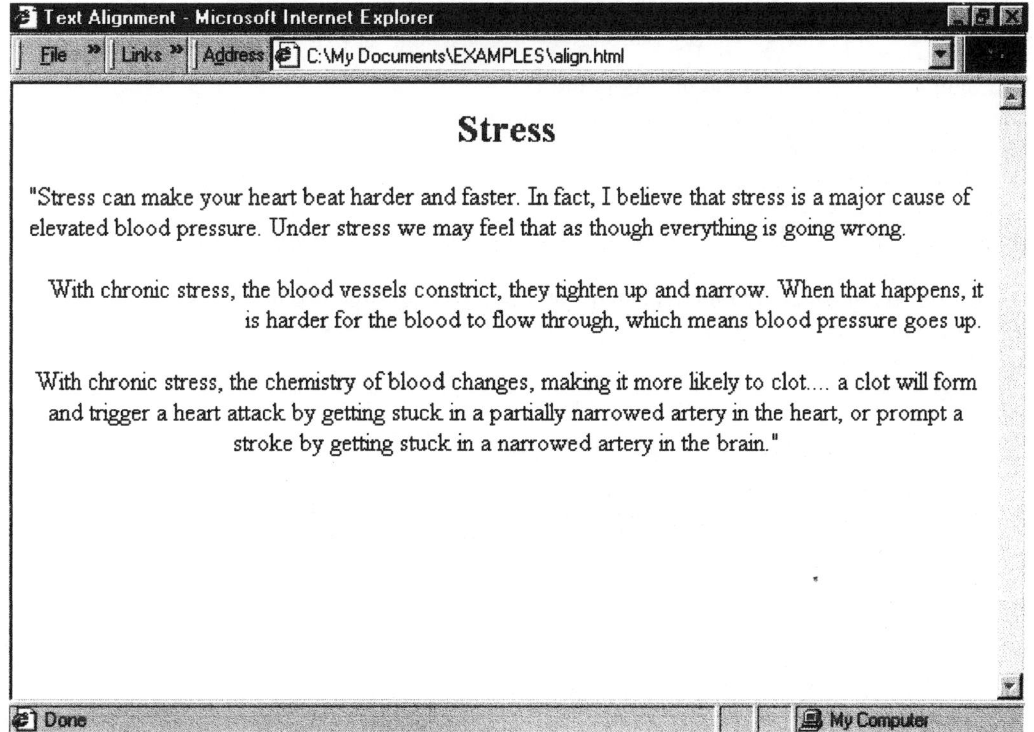

Diagram 14

This chapter has demonstrated the application of block-level elements. These elements generate blocks of text, such as paragraphs. They start on a new line, and thus have a line break above and below the block of text. You will meet more block-level elements as the book progresses. In XHTML, there is another category of elements known as **inline**. Inline elements are discussed in the next chapter.

Document: align.html checked and validated by W3C as XHTML 1. 0 document under Transitional DTD

W3C HTML Validation Service Results

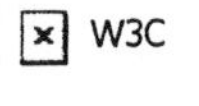

HTML Validation Service Results

Document Checked

- URI: http://www.adrlondon.ltd.uk/align.html
- Last modified: Fri May 18 16:54:47 2001
- Server: Microsoft-IIS/4.0
- Content length: 1264
- Character encoding: utf-8
- Document type: XHTML 1.0 Transitional with namespace http://www.w3.org/1999/xhtml

Below are the results of checking this document for XML well-formedness and validity.

```
No errors found! *
```

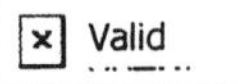

Congratulations, this document validates as XHTML 1.0 Transitional!

To show your readers that you have taken the care to create an interoperable Web page, you may display this icon on any page that validates. Here is the HTML you could use to add this icon to your Web page:

```
<p>
  <a href="http://validator.w3.org/check/referer"><img
      src="http://www.w3.org/Icons/valid-xhtml10"
      alt="Valid XHTML 1.0!" height="31" width="88" /></a>
</p>
```

If you like, you can download a copy of this image (in PNG or GIF format) to keep in your local web directory, and change the HTML fragment above to reference your local image rather than the one on this server.

Illustration 3

Document: align.html checked and invalidated by W3C as XHTML 1. 0 document under Strict DTD

W3C HTML Validation Service Results

W3C

Results

Document Checked

- URI: http://www.adrlondon.ltd.uk/align.html
- Last modified: Fri May 18 21:26:36 2001
- Server: Microsoft-IIS/4.0
- Content length: 1258
- Character encoding: utf-8
- Document type: XHTML 1.0 Strict with namespace http://www.w3.org/1999/xhtml

Below are the results of checking this document for XML well-formedness and validity.

- Line 11, column 12:

```
<h2 align = "center"> Stress</h2>
            ^
```

Error: there is no attribute "align" for this element (in this HTML version) (explanation...)

- Line 13, column 10:

```
<p align= "left"> "Stress can make your heart beat harder and faster.
          ^
```

Error: there is no attribute "align" for this element (in this HTML version) (explanation...)

Sorry, this document does not validate as XHTML 1.0 Strict.

If you use CSS in your document, you should also check it for validity using the W3C CSS Validation Service.

Gerald Oskoboiny
Last modified: Date: 2001/03/08 01:57:52

Valid

Illustration 4

Chapter 5

Inline Elements

The aims of this chapter are:-

- to enable you to understand XHTML category of elements called inline elements;
- to make a distinction between different types of elements within two broad categories of elements namely, block and inline;
- to provide you with an opportunity, through examples, to use some inline elements in order to affect the overall structure of the document in some way;

By reading this chapter, you will acquire both the knowledge and the skill of coding XHTML documents and including in your documents the following text presentation features:-

- different font sizes
- bold style text
- *italic style text*
- monospaced font
- underlined text
- text strikethrough
- text subscripted
- text superscripted
- text emphasised
- word or phrase abbreviated
- word or phrased displayed as an acronym
- text/phrases defined
- text cited – citation
- text quoted - quotation
- coding/programming text
- variables, or mathematical text presented

• A classification of XHTML elements

The XHTML classification of elements depicted in Diagram 1 is self-explanatory. It is suggested that you read this diagram first, so that the following text becomes clearer.

Block-level elements are the subject of the last chapter. Here, it can be added that a block-level element may contain another element. They can also contain inline elements and character data. On the other hand, **inline elements** can only contain other inline elements or character data. When an inline element is implemented, it affects text within the block of some text. In accordance with Diagram 1, inline elements fall within the following three categories. It is worth knowing that inline elements are also known as physical elements.

• Styling inline elements

These are used for such things as highlighting some text in **bold**, or generating some quotations in *italics*, or rendering some part of the document underlined, or displaying some text as larger text than the base text, and adding such other styling details which can enhance the overall structure of the document. Like in HTML, there are some tags in XHTML, which have **built-in styling semantics**. See Table 1. It can be added that a styling element explicitly specifies the style of an element. I have demonstrated the application of these inline elements through solved examples.

• What does built-in styling semantic or semantic markup mean?

You and I can deduct from **<bold>** tag that its purpose is to display a piece of text in bold type face style. A computer can only do so, if we build in a program, such as a browser software, the meaning of a markup tag, in this case, the **bold** tag, and instruct it that when you come across this tag, the text should be displayed in **bold style**. A markup language is designed to be understood by browsers. Therefore, HTML browsers and XHTML browsers have built-in knowledge of some styling tags, and display the text in a standard style. Without a browser's ability to have built-in semantic, a Web page designing task would be tedious, as one would have to write a separate set of instructions for instructing the computer how to interpret each tag.

• Descriptive inline elements

This category of inline elements includes those elements whose names indicate the style in which the text is rendered when any of these elements is implemented. They are based on meaning or structure as opposed to style as in the case of styling elements in Table 1. In Table 2, you can see some descriptive inline elements. Sometimes, these elements are also known as phrasal or logical elements. Here, some solved examples demonstrate the use of these inline elements.

Classification of XHTML Elements

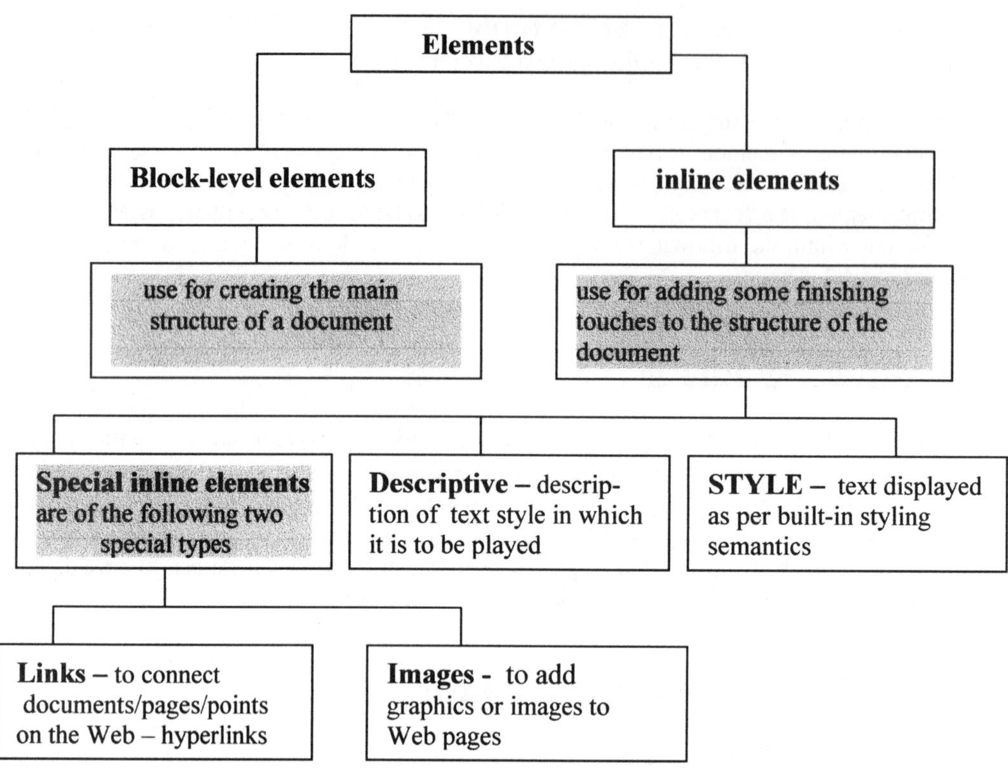

Diagram 1

• Special elements

As shown in Diagram 1, these are categorised as links and images elements. <Link> elements are very important types of inline elements. They are used to create hyperlinks in your XHTML document in the same way as in HTML documents. Without links in Web documents, documents would be just another means of display and no Internet communication would take place. Link elements give location of the resource on the Net. **<a>** and **<link>** are two examples of link elements. The <link> element takes at least two attributes. These are **rel** and **href**. Links elements are discussed and their application is demonstrated in the chapter on **Links in Documents**. The other type of special inline element is the **<img>** element**.** It is used to include an image, such as a company logo in an XHTML document. It is an empty inline element. It takes two attributes, namely, **src** and **alt**. It is implemented whenever, an image, or graphics have to be included in an XHTML document. You will meet these attributes again.

When you include a built-in semantic markup in your XHTML document, the browser already knows what to do with it, and acts accordingly. For instance, the following code will display text larger than the base text.

<big> text will be displayed larger than the base text </big>

Some styling inline elements are listed in Table 1 together with an outcome of each when applied. I have demonstrated the application of these inline built-in styling semantics through solved examples 1 to 5.

Some styling inline elements – built- in semantics

Element	Tags	Outcome
Big	<big>……</big>	Generates text bigger than the base text
Bold	<b>……..</b>	Generates text in **bold** form
Cite	<cite>…..</cite>	Generates text in **italic** style. It can be considered as descriptive because it indicates what it does.
Italic	<i>………</i>	Generates in *italic* form
Keyboard	<kbd>…….</kbd>	Generates text similar to text produced by a typewriter. It is also known as mono-spaced type text.
Small	<small> ------</small>	Renders text smaller in size than the base text
Strikethrough	<strike>…….</strikethrough>	Renders text as crossed off
Subscript	_{…….}	Renders text as subscript
Superscript	^{…….}	Renders text as superscript
True type	<tt>……</tt>	Generates mono-spaced type text similar to that produced by old typewriters
underline	<u>------</u>	Text displayed as underlined

Table 1

Some Descriptive Inline Elements

Element	Tags	Outcome
Abbreviation	<abbr>……</abbr>	it is used for abbreviating some text – very convenient tag when it is needed
Acronyms	<acronym>……</acronym>	An acronym is not an abbreviation , but it is a word formed from or based on the initial letters or syllables of other words, such as radar. (Chambers Dictionary)
Code	<code>……</code>	It allows you to include code in your documents. The code will be rendered in monospaced font
Definition	<defn>……</defn>	You can include definition in your documents by means of element. The default display for this element is *italic* text
Emphasis	<em>……</em>	It is used for emphasising some text. The text appears in *italic*
Quotation	<q>……</q>	It is used for including quotations in your document. It does not render text in any other style than the style of the text that surrounds it
strong	<strong>….</strong>	It is like <em>. It is useful to emphasise text instead of characters. It renders text in bold
Variable	<var>…..</var>	Its purpose is to let you handle mathematical type variables. It renders variables in *italic*

Table 2

• Example 1

Read the following text.

Yoga

The Hindu school, associated with the school of Samkhya as the practical method for achieving the understanding of the self.

Design an XHTML document in order to meet the following requirements:-

- Yoga – display this word on a separate line as a heading and underline it
- The Hindu school - display this phrase as larger text than the base text
- Samkhya – display this word in italic style
- self – display it as underlined and in **bold characters**
- Save the document, check it for XML well-formedness and validity, and view it in any user agent.

• Explanation

The required XHTML code is listed in Diagram 1. The document is saved as **Presentation.html**.

- For the heading, I implemented heading element <h1>, and to underline 'Yoga', I applied inline style element <u>.
- In order to place some emphasis on the phrase "The Hindu school", I have made use of inline style element <big> . The effect of this element is the increase size of the text to which it is applied.
- To display "Samkhya" in *italic style*, I used inline style element < i>.
- To display "self" in bold font and all characters underlined, I applied two inline elements namely, <b> and <u>.
- Like other documents, the document was checked for XML well-formedness and validity by W3C HTML Validation Service. After that, I viewed it in the IE successfully. You can see it in Diagram 3.

XHTML Strict document - <u> will not be recognised. For underlining, you have to develop a style sheet rule - 'text-decoration'. See CSS. W3C will invalidate this document under Strict DTD.

The XHTML markup code for example 1 – Presentation1.html

```
<?xml version= "1.0" encoding = "UTF-8"?>
<!DOCTYPE html
                    PUBLIC "- //w3C//DTD XHTML 1.0 Transitional//EN"
 "http://www.w3.org/TR/xhtml1/DTD/xhtml1-transitional.dtd">
<html xmlns= "http://www.w3.org/1999/xhtml" xml:lang= "en" lang= "en">
<head>
<title>Text presentation</title>
</head>
<body>
<h1><u>
     Yoga</u></h1>
<big> The  Hindu school</big>, associated with the school of <i>Samkhya</i> as the practical method
        for achieving the understanding of the <b><u> self. </u></b>
</body></html>
```

Diagram 2

Presentation 1.html viewed in IE 5

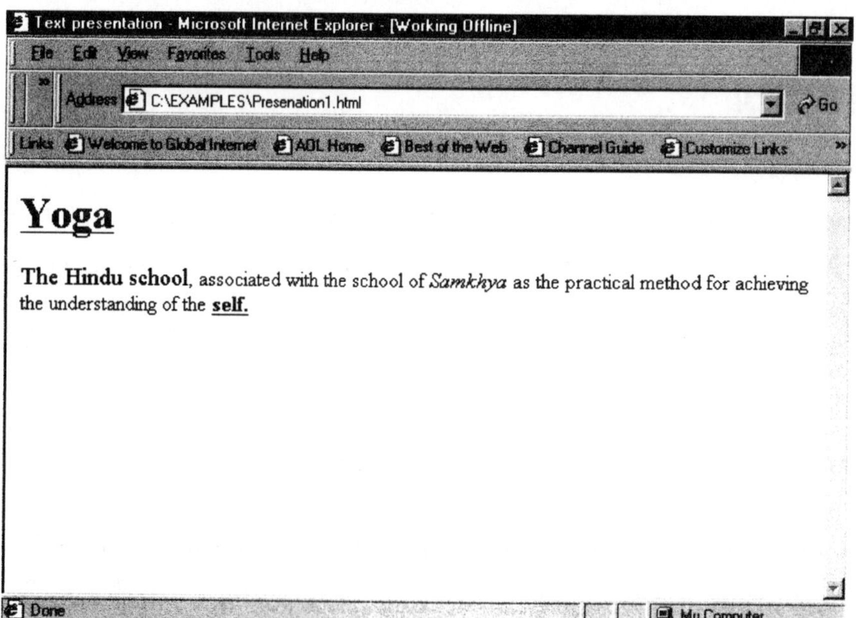

Diagram 3

. Example 2

Your task is to design a Web page for displaying the text shown below in the shaded area. You should apply superscript, subscript, and monospace inline style elements, where you think these are needed. Your document should have its heading, and it must consist of four paragraphs as shown here. You can highlight (place emphasis) any part or word or number, if you wish. Save your document. Check it for XML well-formedness and validity. Also view it in IE or any other user agent.

Board Meeting on 20th September 2001

This is an example of the use of inline style superscript element. A superscript is written above something, such as 'th' on a number in a date.

A subscript is a character written or printed beneath the normal line of script or type, especially in chemistry, mathematics, etc. For example: H2O. Here, the number 2 is a subscript.

Typewriters create text on a piece of paper with uniform spacing between letters. This fixed-width font is called monospaced font.

This is an example of monospaced font.

. Explanation

- The XHTML code for example 2 is listed in Diagram 4.
- For a heading, I have used Level 1 heading. If you wish, you can choose another level of heading.
- Note carefully the places where in the date the […] are placed - **20th**.
- **<b>H₂O</b>** - here also tags should surround the correct text in order to yield the required result. I wanted the subscripted text emphasised. This is why **<b>** tag comes before **H**, and </b> after **O**. Note again where these tags are placed.
- I wanted to display the 'monospaced text' larger in size than the base text, and as **bold** text. For this reason, **<big><b>** tags come before the monospaced tag **<tt>**.
- Like other documents, the document was checked for XML well-formedness and validity by W3C HTML Validation Service. After that, I viewed it in the IE successfully. You can see it in Diagram 5.

W3C will validate this document under Strict DTD. Why? Because these elements are in XHTML 1.0 Strict Version. Experiment!

Diagram 4: The XHTML markup code for example 2

```
<?xml version= "1.0" encoding = "UTF-8"?>
<!DOCTYPE html
                    PUBLIC "- //w3C//DTD XHTML 1.0 Transitional//EN"
 "http://www.w3.org/TR/xhtml1/DTD/xhtml1-transitional.dtd">
<html xmlns= "http://www.w3.org/1999/xhtml" xml:lang= "en" lang= "en">
<head>
<title> Text Presentation </title>
</head>
<body>
<h1> Board Meeting on 20<sup>th</sup> September 2001</h1>
 <p> This is an example of the use of inline style superscript element.
     A superscript is written above something, such as 'th' on a number in a date.</p>
<p>
    A subscript is a character written or printed beneath the normal line
    of script or type, especially in chemistry, mathematics, etc. For example:
    <b>H<sub>2</sub>O</b>. Here, the number 2 is a subscript.</p>
<p>Typewriters create text on a piece of paper with uniform spacing
    between letters. This fixed-width font is called monospaced font.</p>
 <p> <big><b><tt> This is an example of monospaced font.</tt></b></big></p>
  </body></html>
```

Diagram 5: Text Presentation.html viewed in IE 5

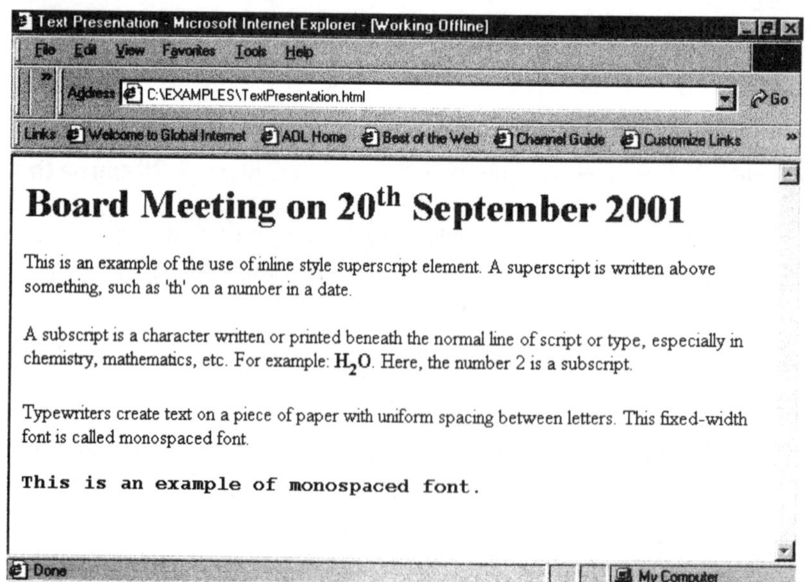

• Example 3

The Internet

World Wide Web **WWW**

It is a distributed information service. It was developed in the early 1990's at the **European Centre for Practical Physics, Geneva** GERN.

World Wide Web **Web**

It is another term for WWW. Web is the most exciting and popular part of the Internet.

Compiler - it translates the source file into a self-contained program called object program that can be run.

- Design a document in order to display the text shown above. It should have the same number of headlines, and paragraphs. In addition to tags which you think are necessary, you should use:
- element abbreviation <abr>…<./abr> for text: **World Wide Web**, which appears twice in this text
- element acronym <acronym>…</acronym> for phrase: European Centre for Practical Physics, Geneva
- element definition <dfn>…</dfn> to define compiler.
- save your document, check it for XML well-formedness and validity. Also view it in IE or any other user agent.

• Explanation

- The XHTML markup code is listed in Diagram 6. It was validated as XHTML 1.0 Transitional document by W3C HTML Validation Service. It means that it has met XML well-formedness and validity requirements.
- You should carefully study the code in order to learn how acronym, abbreviation and definition elements are implemented. It should be noted that acronym and abbreviation elements take a **single attribute** with its value.

For instance:

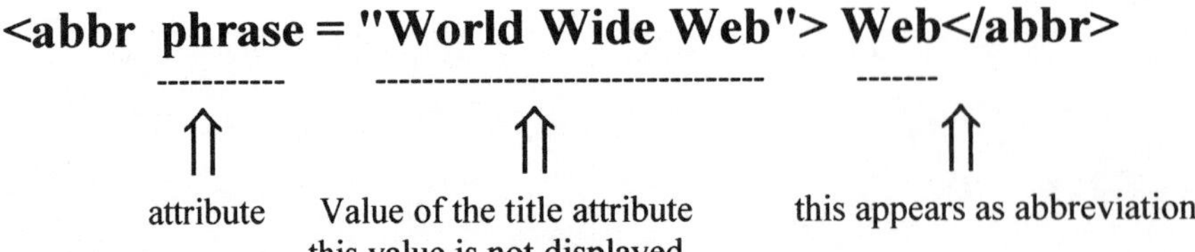

You can call your attribute by another suitable name. In the same way, the code for acronym is constructed. See Diagram 6.

- In Diagram 7A, you can see what happens when the cursor is held over GERN. The acronym element displays, "European Centre for Practical Physics, Geneva ". It is, in fact, the value of the **attribute name.** It is a full presentation of acronym, GERN. In general, when the cursor is placed on an acronym, the value of the attribute is displayed. Now key in the code and experiment with it.

- **<dfn>** element is easy to use, as shown in Diagram 6. It displays text in the *italic style*. This is a useful tag, as it can let you point out the definition of any technical terms or whatever.

The XHTML markup code for example 3 –Descriptive1.html

```
<?xml version= "1.0" encoding = "UTF-8"?>
<!DOCTYPE html
                  PUBLIC "- //w3C//DTD XHTML 1.0 Transitional//EN"
 "http://www.w3.org/TR/xhtml1/DTD/xhtml1-transitional.dtd">
<html xmlns= "http://www.w3.org/1999/xhtml" xml:lang= "en" lang= "en">
<head>
<title>Text presentation 3</title>
</head>
<body>
<h1><u>
     The Internet</u></h1>
 <h3> <abbr phrase = "World Wide Web"> WWW</abbr></h3>It is distributed information service.
       It was developed in the early 1990's at

 <acronym name = "European Centre for Practical Physics, Geneva">GERN</acronym>.
 <h2>  <abbr  phrase = "World Wide Web"> Web</abbr></h2> It is another term for WWW. Web is
        the most exciting and popular part of the Internet.

<p> <dfn> Compiler  - it translates the source file into a self-contained program called object program
           that can be run</dfn>. </p>
</body></html>
```

Diagram 6

Diagram 7: Descriptive1.html previewed in IE successfuly

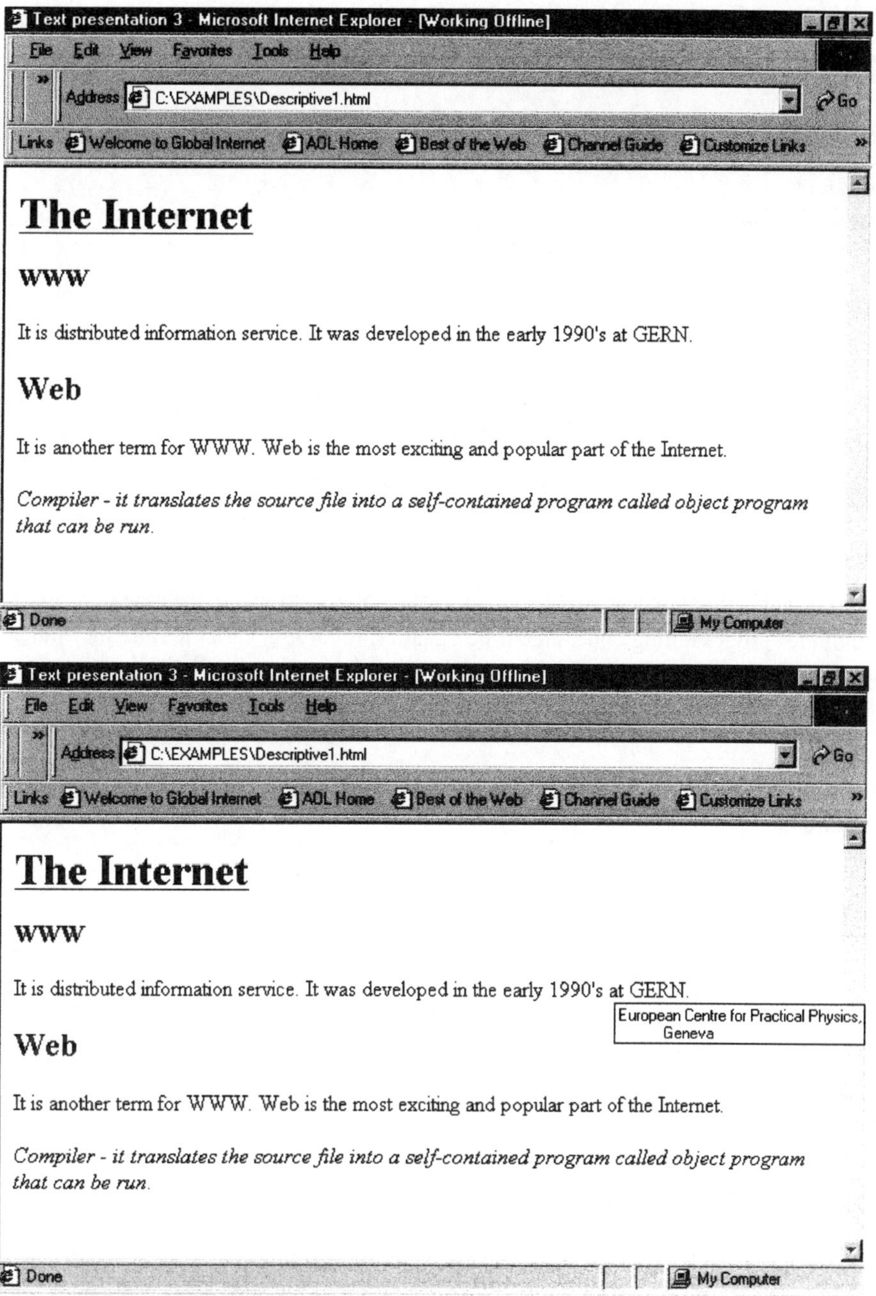

Diagram 7A: When the cursor is held on GERN the full name of the centre appears in a box

• Example 4

To test the account number against the condition laid down.

```
{ int account;
cout<<"Enter account number: ";
cin>>account;
if (account>=1000)
count <<"Wrong number. Try again!"<< endl;
}
```

To workout sales price.

Here, the following variables stand for:
s for sale price, m for material, o for overheads and mr for markup/profit.
S =(m+o+mr)

Extract from:C++ Simplified, ISBN 1901197 999

- Your task is to design a document in order to display the above text in any user agent. Since the above text includes programming code, algebraic equation involving variables and the source of this text, you must apply descriptive inline elements namely **code**, **variable** and **citation**, where each type is required. In your document design, you must include headings, line breaks and paragraphs where you think these are required to create the document in the above text format.

  Save your document, check it for XML well-formedness and validity. Finally, view it to see if it meets all requirements.

• Explanation

- You can examine the code for this example in Diagram 8. It was saved as Descriptive2.html, and then checked by HTML Validation Service for XML well-formedness as XHTML 1.0 Transitional type document. See Diagram 9 for this document display in IE. It has met all requirements.
- In Diagram 9, you can find that the application of <code> element has generated the programming code in **monospaced** font.
- In the above text, the programming code consists of six lines. The idea is to display it in exactly the same way. For this reason, the end of line < /br> tag is added where it is necessary. Without this tag, the entire code would have been displayed as a single continuous line. The reason is that the <code> element does not generate any line breaks. In fact, it compresses multiple spaces or line breaks within the code text. It is a serious drawback as without line breaks or multiple spaces this code would be difficult to read and comprehend. The point is further discussed with an example below Diagram 9.

- The next section of this text contains **S =(m+o+mr)**. It is a mathematical expression, and differs from the ordinary text. It has some variables, which have to be manipulated to produce the required answer. In XHTML, variables are displayed in ***italic*** by applying the descriptive inline element , **<var>**. It is easy to use. See Diagram 9.

- The last requirement is to display the source of this text in the following format:

Extract from: C++ Simplified, ISBN 1901197 999

The descriptive inline element, **<cite>** allows you to cite or refer to the source of the text. The <cite> element displays reference or source of text in **italic**. It is easy to use. Now, examine the entire XHTML code listed in Diagram 8.

The XHTML markup code for example 4 – Descriptive2.html

```
<?xml version= "1.0" encoding = "UTF-8"?>
<!DOCTYPE html
                    PUBLIC "- //w3C//DTD XHTML 1.0 Transitional//EN"
 "http://www.w3.org/TR/xhtml1/DTD/xhtml1-transitional.dtd">
<html xmlns= "http://www.w3.org/1999/xhtml" xml:lang= "en" lang= "en">
<head>
<title> Text Presentation </title>
</head>
<body>
<h3>
   To test the account number against the condition laid down.</h3>
<h4>
<code>
     {
      int account;<br />
      cout<<"Enter account number:  ";<br />
      cin>>account;<br />
      if (account>=1000)<br />
      count <<"Wrong number. Try again!"<< endl;<br />
     }<br /> </code>
         To workout sales price.</h4>
 <p> Here, the following variables stand for:<br />
   s for sale price, m for material, o for overheads and  mr for markup/profit.<br />
 <var>
    S =(m+o+mr)</var> </p>
<p><cite> Extract from: C++ Simplified, ISBN 1901197 999</cite></p>
</body></html>
```

Diagram 8

Descriptive2.html viewed in IE5.5

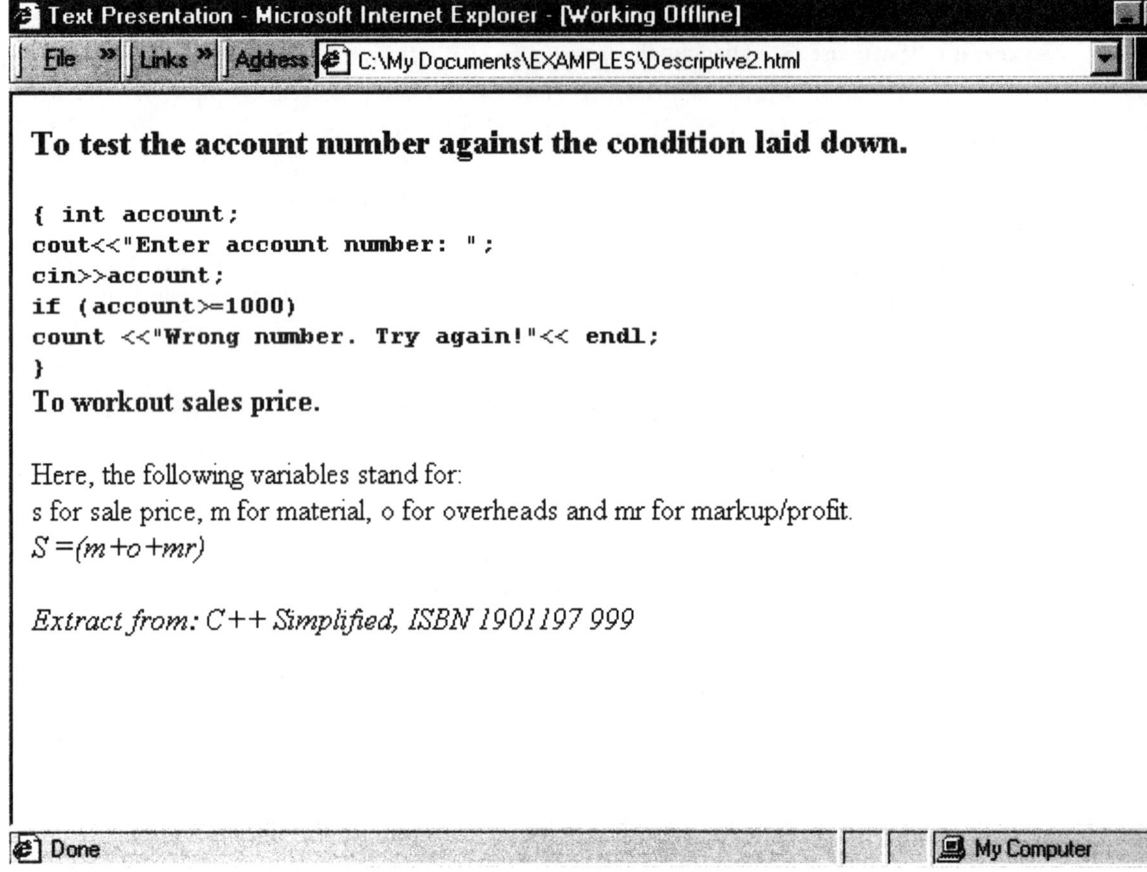
Text Presentation - Microsoft Internet Explorer - [Working Offline]
File
Links
Address
C:\My Documents\EXAMPLES\Descriptive2.html
To test the account number against the condition laid down.
{ int account;
cout<<"Enter account number: ";
cin>>account;
if (account>=1000)
count <<"Wrong number. Try again!"<< endl;
}
To workout sales price.
Here, the following variables stand for:
s for sale price, m for material, o for overheads and mr for markup/profit.
S =(m+o+mr)
Extract from: C++ Simplified, ISBN 1901197 999
Done
My Computer

Diagram 9

- **What can be done to display coding methods in the required format without using <br /> tag?**

Indeed, it is somewhat boring and time consuming to place <br /> at the end of each line of any coding methods, such as in this example. You can overcome this problem by containing the preformatted code within :-

<pre> ...</pre> - **preformatted text element for positioning text blocks.**

This is demonstrated by example 5.

• Example 5

The purpose of this example is to demonstrate the application of <pre> element for preformatted text. The preformatted text to be displayed is shown in a box below. It is a segment of a Java applet program. Design a document, save it and check it for XML well-formedness and validity as XHTML 1.0 Strict type document. Preview it locally in order to test that it meets all requirements. Your document must contain this code in exactly the same way as it is shown below, without using <br /> element.

A segment of a Java program

```
public class GroupCheckBox extends JApplet
{

JCheckBox  payment      = new JCheckBox (" Payment Method " );
JCheckBox  cash         = new JCheckBox (" Cash " );
JCheckBox  creditCard   = new JCheckBox (" Credit Card ");
JCheckBox  debitCard    = new JCheckBox (" Debit Card ", true );
```

Extract from: Java Simplified, ISBN 1901197 883

W3C Validation result – Descriptive.html

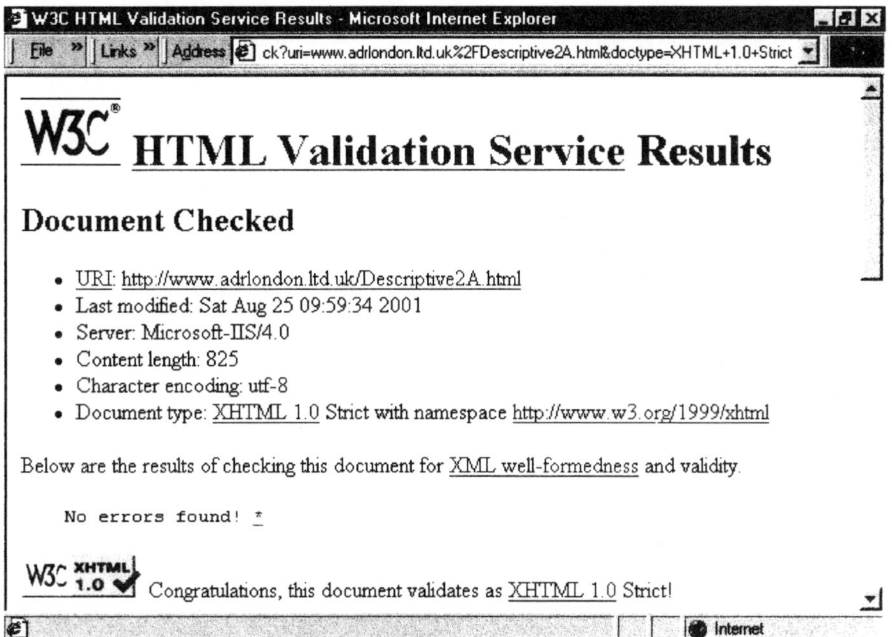

Diagram 10

• Explanation

The XHTML code for the required document is listed in Diagram 10A. It is similar to the code you already have met in the previous example. It makes use of <pre> element, which eliminates the effect of <code>, <br /> elements. It displays all spaces as in the original Java applet program. Whenever, the code is to be displayed with all spaces and line breaks to maintain, in such a case, it is recommended to apply <pre> element.

- Prior to previewing it locally, it was submitted to W3C Validation Service, as shown in Diagram 10. It was tested successfully in IE. See Diagram 11.

XHTML code for example 5 – Descriptive2A.html

```
<?xml version= "1.0" encoding = "UTF-8"?>
<!DOCTYPE html
                PUBLIC "- //w3C//DTD XHTML 1.0 Strict 1.0//EN"
 "http://www.w3.org/TR/xhtml1/DTD/xhtml1-strict.dtd">
<html xmlns= "http://www.w3.org/1999/xhtml" xml:lang= "en" lang= "en">
<head>
<title> Text Presentation </title>
</head>
<body>
<h3>
        Preformatted text element for positioning text blocks</h3>
<pre>
public class GroupCheckBox extends JApplet
{
     JCheckBox  payment      = new JCheckBox (" Payment Method " );
     JCheckBox  cash         = new JCheckBox (" Cash " );
     JCheckBox  creditCard   = new JCheckBox (" Credit Card ");
     JCheckBox  debitCard    = new JCheckBox (" Debit Card ", true );
</pre>
 <p>
<cite>Extract from: Java Simplified, ISBN 1901197 883</cite></p>
</body>
</html>
```

Diagram 10A

• What will happen if you nest <pre> within <h4>.... <h6)?

W3C HTML Validation service will report an error as listed below.

Below are the results of checking this document for XML well-formedness and validity.

- Line 14, column 4:

  <pre>
  ^

  Error: element "pre" not allowed here; possible cause is an inline element containing a block-level element (explanation...)

Sorry, this document does not validate as XHTML 1.0 Strict.

Descriptive2A.html viewed in IE5.5

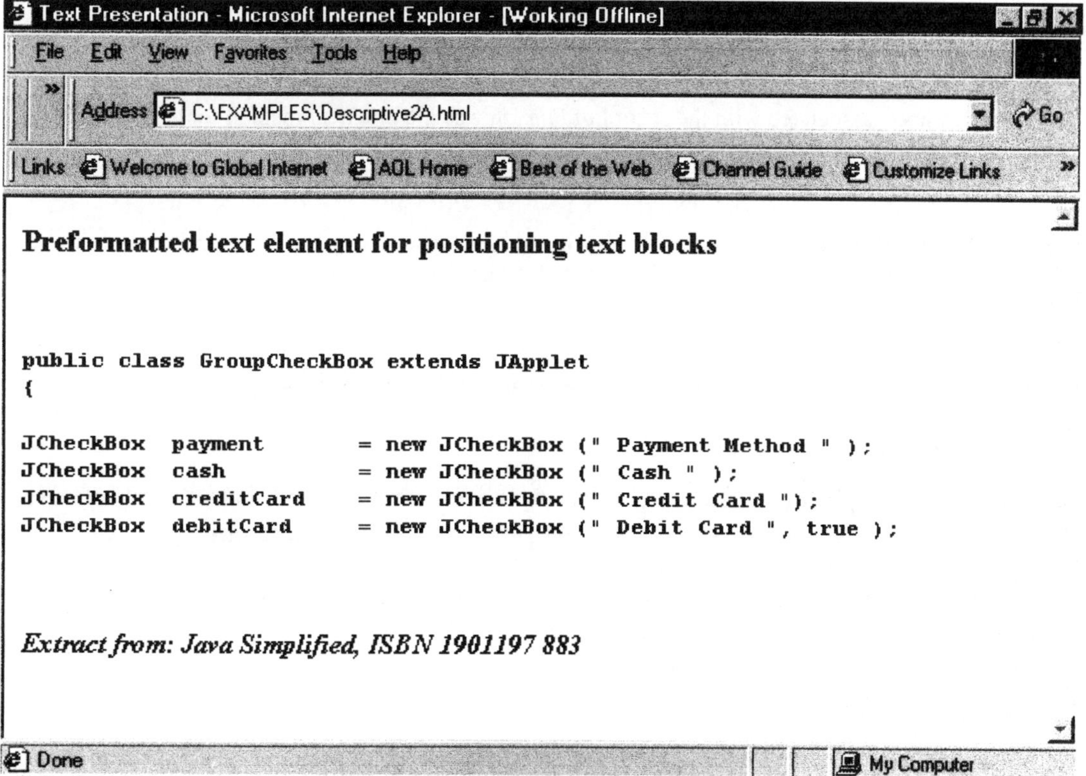

Diagram 11

• Example 6

- Text enclosed within a box below is the same text used for example 1. It is extended by the text shown below the box in the shaded area. You are asked to complete the following tasks:-

- design an XHTML document for the entire text in order to display the whole text in any IE or any other browser/user agent
- all headings should be underlined
- words which are emphasised in different ways and differ from the style of the base text should be displayed in the same way
- save your document under an appropriate name, and test it to make sure it meets all requirements.

Yoga

The Hindu school, associated with the school of *Samkhya* as the practical method for achieving the understanding of the **self.**

Yoga is the discipline or YOKE necessary for the pure subject to recognise itself, and separate itself from the empirical reality with which it is confused. ~~Yoga is just massage.~~

Yoga

Yoga includes moral restraints, spiritual imperatives and exercises - ***Asanas***.

Exercises

Asanas designed to withdraw consciousness from the senses, focus the mind, and ultimately achieve meditation in which the self is completely and transparently understood - ***Samadhi***.

Reading Philosophy.

• Explanation

- The required code for example 6 is listed in Diagram 12.
- Since this text includes the whole text of example 1, I started writing the code for this example by reproducing the code shown in Diagram 2.
- The phrase, ***Yoga is the discipline***, since it begins a new line, it has to start with <p>, the paragraph tag. The phrase is in italic and bold style. In order to achieve this distinctive style, I made use of two inline style elements namely, **<em> and <b>**. As you know, **<em>** is a descriptive element, which renders text as *italic text.* The **<b>** element is an inline style element that renders as **bold text**. The combination and implementation of these two tags resulted in the required style for this phrase.

- YOKE – this word has to be displayed in larger text than the base text. In order to accomplish this requisite, I applied descriptive element <q>, which is for quotation. This element has no structural semantics, and thus has no style. This word is not an abbreviation of any other word, but from Sanskrit language. Therefore, I treated it as quotation.
- The next requirement is to strikethrough, "~~Yoga is just massage.~~ Inline style element <strike> carries out this task easily. It strikes through text.
- The heading **Yoga** has to commence on a new line. You do not need <p> here, because <h2> Level 2 heading element automatically starts a new line. I used <h2>, as it is renders heading large enough, and still smaller in size than the heading generated by <h1>.
- ***Asanas*** – to display this word, three inline style elements are applied. These are <i><b><u>.

The XHTML markup code for example 6 - Presentation2.html

```
<!DOCTYPE html PUBLIC "-//W3C//DTD XHTML 1.0 Transitional//EN"
                "http://www.w3.org/TR/xhtml1/DTD/xhtml1-transitional.dtd">
 <?xml version= "1.0" encoding = "UTF-8"?>
 <!-- <!DOCTYPE html
            PUBLIC "- //w3C//DTD XHTML 1.0 Transitional//EN"
  "http://www.w3.org/TR/xhtml1/DTD/xhtml1-transitional.dtd"> -->
<html xmlns= "http://www.w3.org/1999/xhtml" xml:lang= "en"lang= "en">
<head>
<title>Text presentation 1</title>
</head>
 <body>
 <h1><u> Yoga</u></h1>
 <big> The  Hindu school</big>, associated with the school of
  <i>Samkhya</i> as the practical method for achieving the understanding of the <b><u> self.
  </u></b>
 <p><em><b> Yoga is the discipline </b></em> or <q>YOKE</q> necessary for the pure
  subject to recognise itself, and separate itself from the empirical reality with which it is confused.
  <strike> Yoga is just massage.</strike></p>
  <h2><u> Yoga </u></h2> Yoga includes moral restraints, spiritual imperatives
  and exercises - <i><b><u> Asanas </u></b></i>.
 <h2><u> Exercises </u></h2> <b><u> Asanas</u></b> designed to withdraw  consciousness from
the senses, focus the mind, and ultimately achieve meditation in which the self is completely and trans-
parently understood - <em><b><u>Samadhi </u></b></em>.
 <p><cite> Reading Philosophy. </cite></p>
  </body>  </html>
```

Diagram 12

- The rest of the code follows the same pattern. It is saved as **Presentation2.html**. I viewed the document in the IE. See Diagrams 13 &13A. Since one screen capture could not hold the whole text. I have made two screen captures, so that it can be proved that it was tested successfully.

Diagram 13: Presentation2.html previewed in IE 5.5 (upper part)

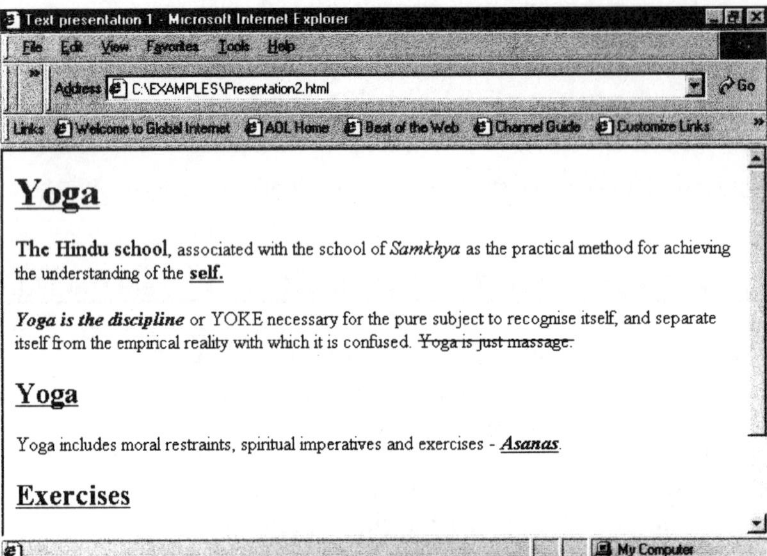

Diagram 13A: Presentation2.html previewed in IE 5.5 (lower part)

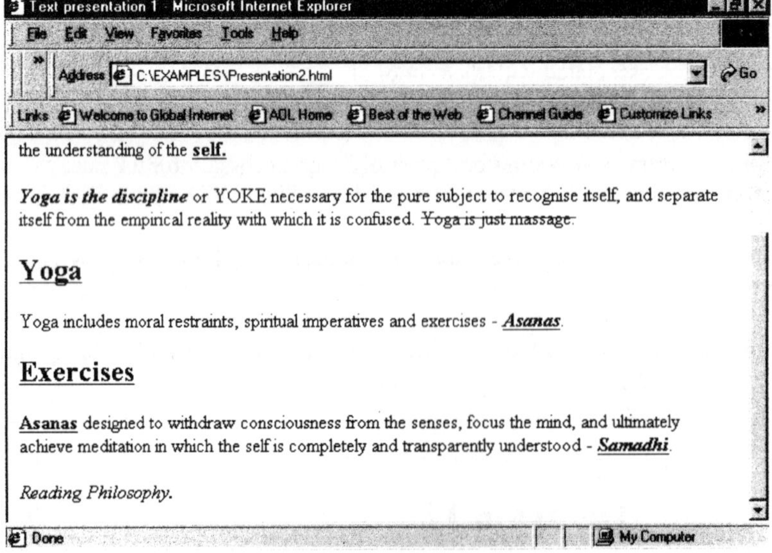

• Example 7

Brain Study

Certain brain areas take many years to mature. The frontal lobes do not become fully myelinated, until full adulthood. This is one reason, perhaps, why younger adults are more emotional and impulsive than those who are older.
Brain Study.

It does not matter who we are, who our parents are, where we came from, or where we are now. ***We are all the same.*** We were all given life and potential by **the Creator.**

The Creator has filled me to the brim with enthusiasm. I gladly and generously pour my unlimited enthusiasm over my every day thought and action. ***I find excitement and adventure in every day.***

~~**The source of happiness is money.**~~ **No. It is good health and confidence in one's own abilities. So, be positive. *Ideas for good living!!!***

- Your task is to design a Web page for displaying the above text in the same format and style. It must have as many paragraphs as shown above. Note that "*Brain Study.*", is a reference or source of heading of the paragraph just above it.

  Having designed the document, you must save it, check it for XML well-formedness and validity, as XHTML 1.0 Transitional document. Also, preview it in order to test that it meets your requirements.

• Explanation

The XHTML code for this example requires the application of both descriptive and style inline elements. It is suggested that you write the required XHTML code yourself, carry on all the necessary steps before displaying it. Compare your code with the code shown in Diagram 12. Your own display should match the display of document **Descriptive2.html**. This is shown in Diagram 13.

The XHTML markup code for example 7 (BePositive.html)

```
<?xml version= "1.0" encoding = "UTF-8"?>
<!DOCTYPE html
            PUBLIC "- //w3C//DTD XHTML 1.0 Transitional//EN"
 "http://www.w3.org/TR/xhtml1/DTD/xhtml1-transitional.dtd">
<html xmlns= "http://www.w3.org/1999/xhtml" xml:lang= "en" lang= "en">
```

Diagram 14

The XHTML markup code for example 7 (BePositive.html)(cont.)

```
<head>
<title> Text Presentation </title>
</head>
<body>
<h3><u>
            Brain Study</u></h3>
<p>
<q>
  Certain<big> brain areas</big> take many years to mature.
  The frontal lobes do not become fully myelinated, until full adulthood.
  This is one reason, perhaps, why younger adults are more emotional and
  impulsive than those who are older.</q><br/>

 <cite> Brain Study.</cite></p>

<p> It does not matter who we are, who our parents are, where we came from,
   or where we are now.<b><u><i> We are all the same.</i></u></b>
  We were all given life and potential by <big><b><u>
   the Creator.</u></b></big></p>

<p><strong> The Creator</strong> has filled me to the brim with enthusiasm.
        I gladly and generously pour my unlimited enthusiasm over my every day thought
        and action.<b/>
  <em> I find excitement and adventure in every day.</em></p>
<p><strike> The source of happiness is money.</strike><b>
  No. It is good health and confidence in ones own abilities.
  So, be positive.</b>
<cite> Ideas for good living!!!</cite></p>
</body>
</html>
```

Diagram 14A

- **What changes to the XHTML code shown in Diagrams 14 and 14 A can be made to run this document under Strict DTD ?**

I have made the following amendments:-

. Diagram 14 – replaced 'Transitional' by 'Strict' and 'transitional' by 'strict'
. Diagram 14A - removed from the code <u> and </u> as this underline element is not defined in XHTML 1.0 Strict
. Diagram 14A - removed from the code <strike> and </strike> as this strike-through element is not defined in XHTML 1.0 Strict

. save the entire document as BePositiveSt.html

- The amended document was validated by the W3C Validation Service under XHTML Strict DTD. See Diagrams 16 and 16A. These are self-explanatory.

BePositive.html viewed in IE 5.5

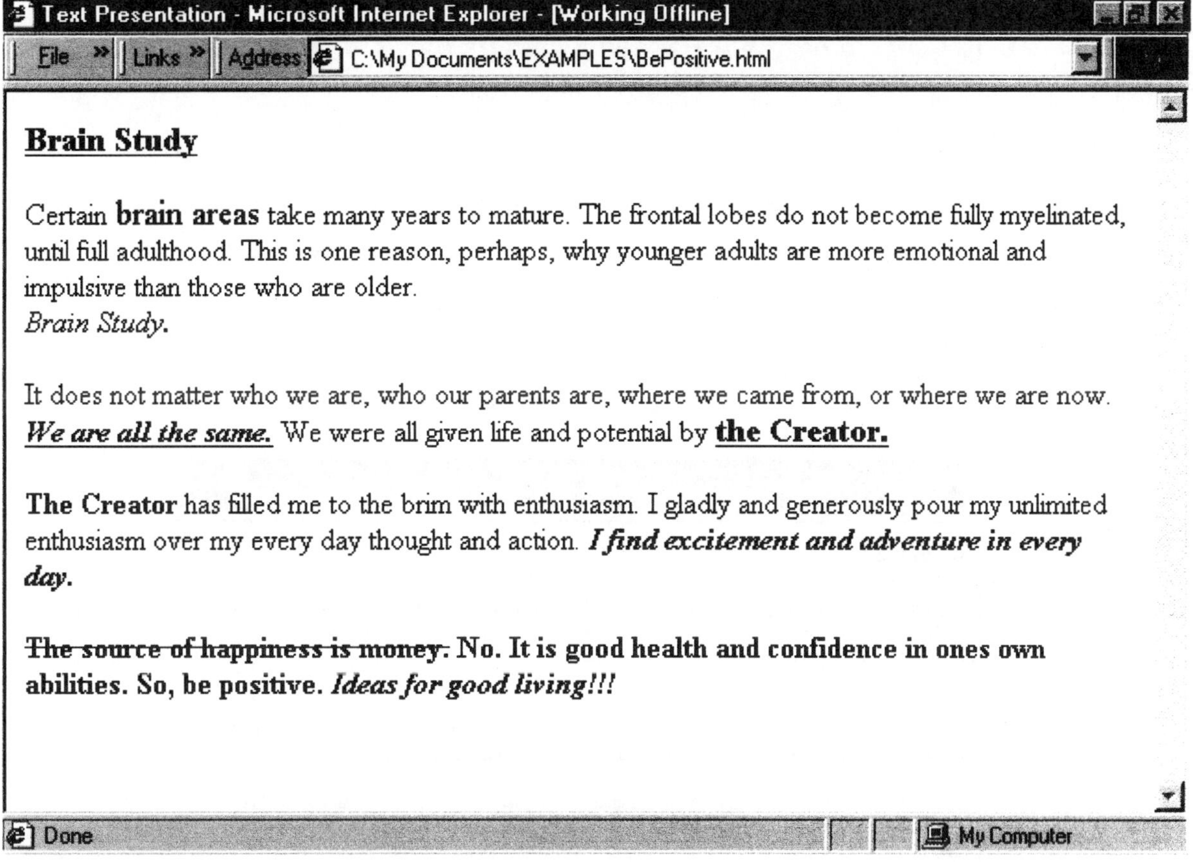

Diagram 15

. A word of warning

Any document written under XHTML 1.0 Strict definition, which has inline built-in style semantics, as well as structural or descriptive inline elements is invalidated by the W3C HTML Validation Service. The XHTML Strict definition requires the application of Cascading Style Sheets (CSS), which have been developed for Strict XHTML documents. See CSS.

Diagram 16: W3C Validation result – document BePositiveSt.html

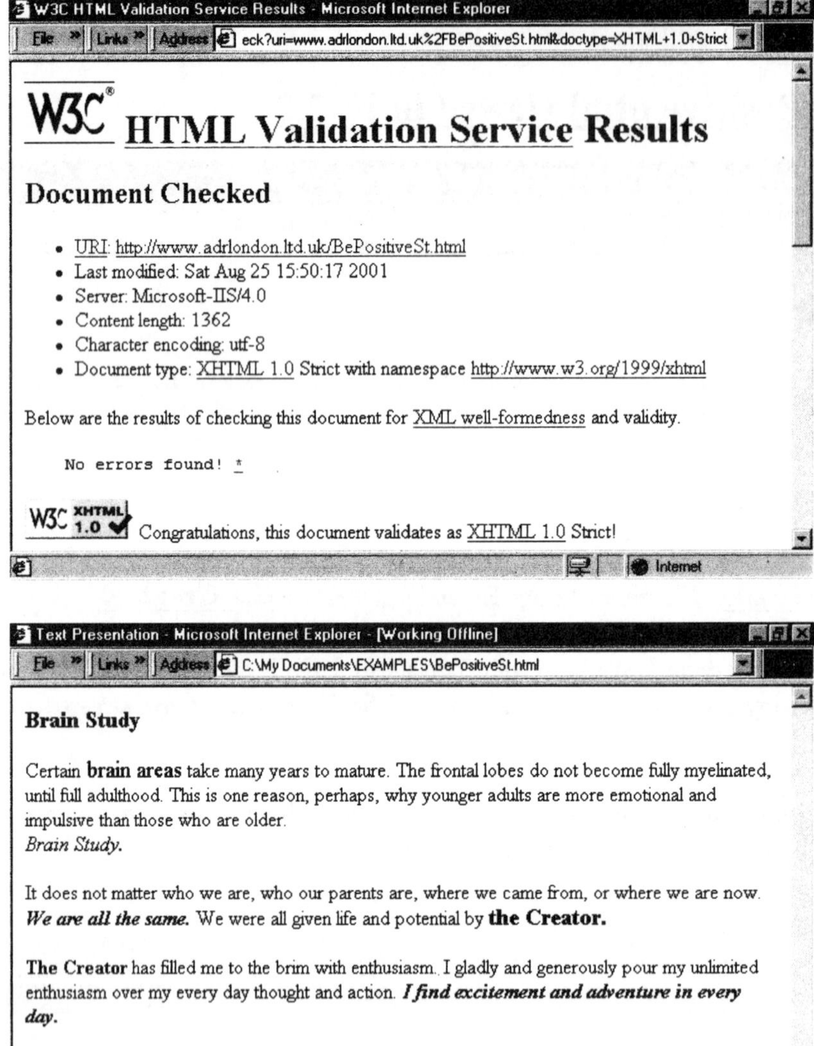

Diagram 16A: Preview of document BePositiveSt.html

Style sheets are introduced in Chapter 7.

Chapter 6

Including Lists in Your Web Pages

The prime aim of this chapter is as follows:-

- to equip you with both the knowledge and the skills necessary to include lists type of text in your Web pages whenever necessary.

By reading and practising lists techniques that are demonstrated in this chapter, you should be able:-

- create ordered lists
- create unordered lists
- create nested ordered lists
- create nested unordered lists
- create definition/glossary lists

• A definition of a list

A list is a series of names, items, figures, etc written or printed. Indeed, lists are very useful means of presenting information in a suitable format whenever there is a need to document data, such as some stock items in a shop or list chapters and their contents, and the like. Thus, a list is a series of some items organised in accordance with some aims of presenting information, so that it is easily understood. In XHTML, you can construct three different types of lists. See illustration 1 for summary information on these lists. In HTML as well as in XHTML, you can also create nested lists.

• A nested list

A nested list is a list within a list. A nested list can help to analyse, organise and present complex data in an easy to read and visualise format. One can apply the nesting technique in order to analyse a set of complicated data or information into its components. Each components can be further analysed until the required level of analysis is reached. You can create nested ordered list, nested unordered list.

Furthermore, you can also combine both ordered and unordered list features to create a nested list.

The following illustration presents summary information on three main types of lists. The nested list is derived from ordered and unordered lists.

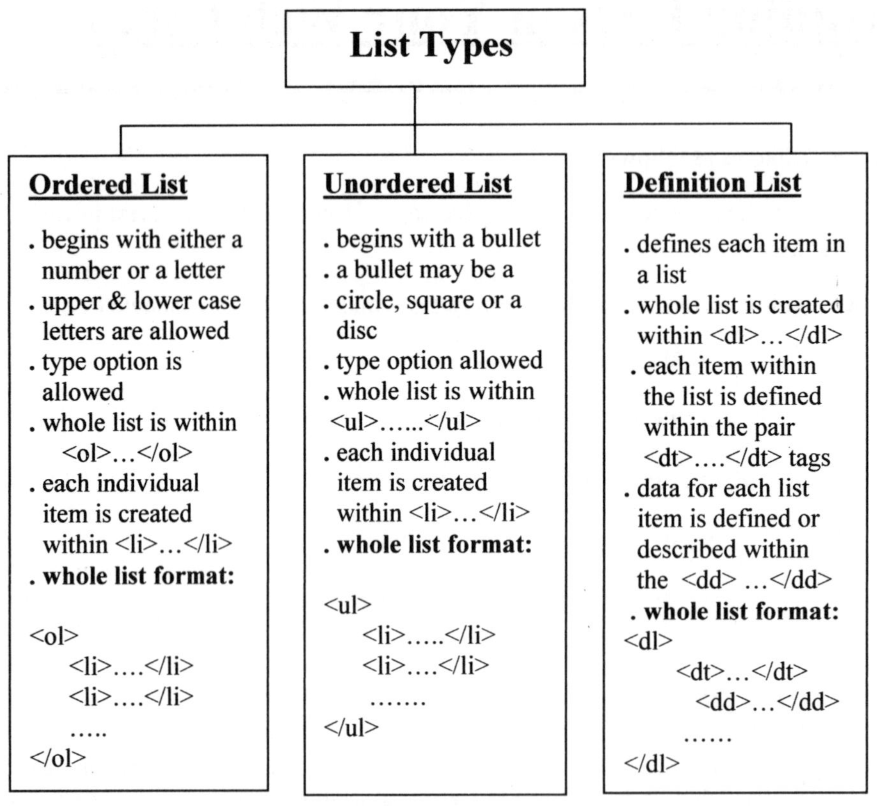

Illustration 1

• Example 1
Ordered Lists

In order to structure an ordered list, one has to decide on the relative position of each item that constitutes it. There are no hard and fast rules concerning the relative positions, except that it depends on the purpose of the list and the level of preference one attaches to a member of the list in the hierarchical list structure.

<u>Methods of Payment</u>

A. By Cash
B. By Cheque
C. By Credit Card
D. By Debit Card

- It is required to construct an ordered list entitled Methods of payment, which should list its four items in the order given above in the shaded area. The first item should be marked by an uppercase letter '**A**'.

  Save your file, check it for XML well-formedness and validity as XHTML 1.0 Transitional document. Also display it in any browser to see that it meets all requirements.

• Explanation

It is likely that you are wondering why I have chosen the order of placing these four items in this sequence.

The order of placing list items apparently is not easy to infer from an ordered list. It is, therefore, suggested that one should include a key or a simple note for the preference of listing items in the order given. Here, I placed '**By Cash**' at top of the list, because it is the preferred method of payment for, say, a retailer. I also started the list with the uppercase letter 'A'. I could have started with a numerical value, say '1' or any other number, or any other letter in uppercase or lowercase.

- In Diagram 1, you can see that the whole list is contained within the **element <ol>. ol** stands for the ordered list. You can think of ol as an overall list element.

- As the list must commence with an uppercase letter **A**, you must assign an attribute called A to this overall ordered list element **ol**. This is achieved by the following segment of the code:-

<ol type ="A" >

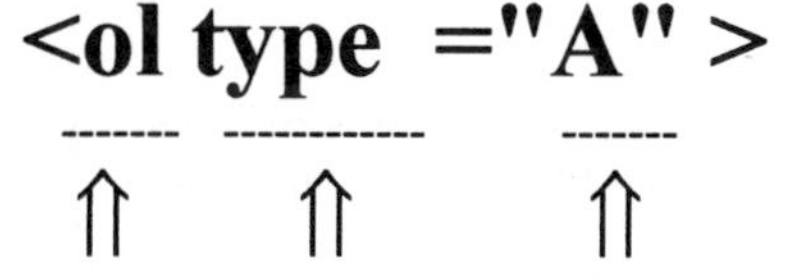

element for ordered list | attribute | attribute's value – it starts the list and allocates uppercase letters to list members You can start a list at any number or letter

- The list item element is **<li>**. It contains the list item. Each item must be contained within <li> and </li>, as shown below:-

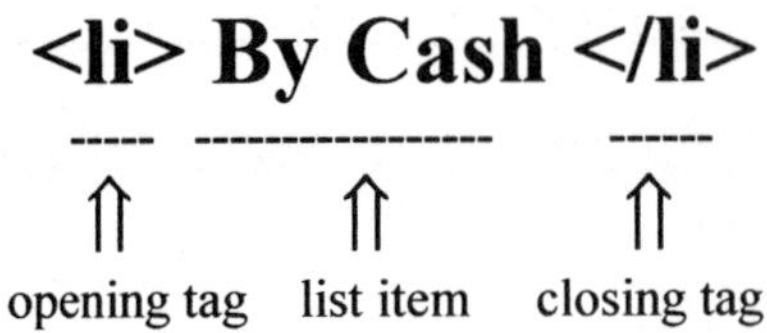

- The whole XML code is listed in Diagram 1. It was checked as required and displayed in the IE5. It meets all requirements. See Diagram 2.

The XHTML code for example 1 – ordered.html

```
<?xml version= "1.0" encoding = "UTF-8"?>
<!DOCTYPE html
                    PUBLIC "- //w3C//DTD XHTML 1.0 Transitional//EN"
 "http://www.w3.org/TR/xhtml1/DTD/xhtml1-transitional.dtd">
<html xmlns= "http://www.w3.org/1999/xhtml" xml:lang= "en" lang= "en">
<head>
<title> Ordered List </title>
</head>
<body>
<h2><u> Methods of Payments</u></h2>
<ol type ="A" >
<li> By Cash </li>
<li>By Cheque </li>
<li>By Credit Card</li>
<li>By Debit Card</li>
</ol>
</body>
</html>
```

Diagram 1

In fact, the **type** attribute in XHTML **strict** is not allowed. It is deprecated. It works in XHTML Transitional 1.0. The cascading style sheet technology (CSS) has replaced it. The problem is that still not all browsers can interpret CSS rules. It is for this important reason alone, you should make use of the **type** attribute, as long as you are working with XHTML Transitional 1.0. Eventually, you have to make use of CSS. The **type** attribute can take values shown in Illustration 2 below Diagram 2.

ordered.html previewed in IE 5.5

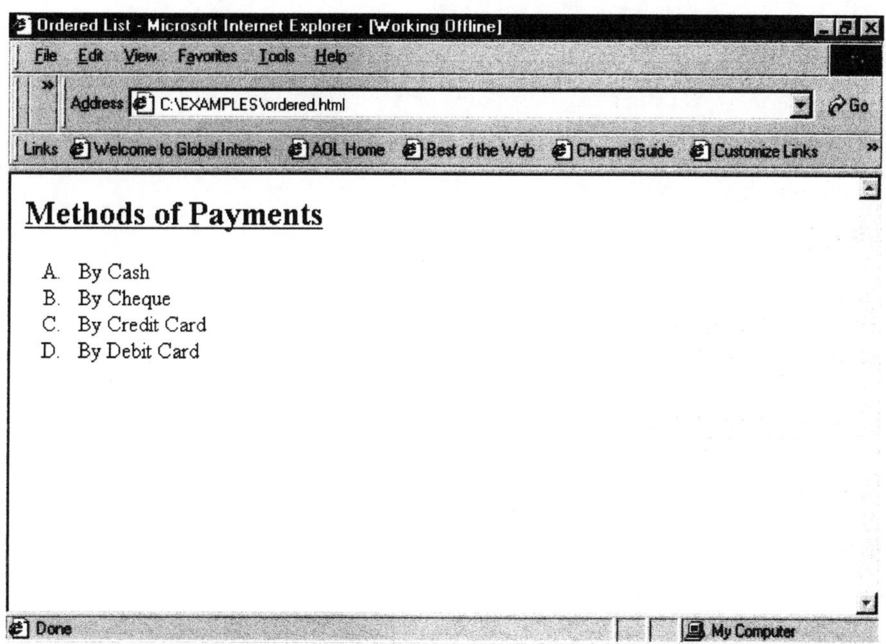

Diagram 2

Type attribute Values & definitions for ordered lists

Attribute Value	Definition
1 (number one)	sets decimal numbers – 1,2,3,… default - no need to set it .
A	generates uppercase letters - A, B, C….
a	generates lowercase letters – a,b,c,…….
I	starts uppercase Roman numbers – I,II,III,..
i	begins lowercase Roman numbers - i,ii,iii,..

Illustration 2

• Example 2 – Ordered list letters & Numerals

Uppercase alphabetic

A. By Cash
B. By Cheque
C. By Credit Card

Decimal numbers

1. If statement
2. Compound Conditions
3. Non-numeric Values

Lowercase Roman numerals

i. Appendix A
ii. Appendix B
iii. Appendix C

• Design an ordered list in order to display the information in the format shown above in the shaded area. Save your file, check it for XML well-formedness and validity as XHTML 1.0 Transitional document. Also display it in any browser to see that it meets all requirements.

• Explanation

• If you study carefully the XHTML code listed in Diagram 3, you can find out that the main list consists of three individual components. Each component is structured as an ordered list in its own right. Each list begins with a different value attached to **type attribute** as explained below:-

• The **<ol type ="A" >** commences an ordered list with an uppercase letter 'A' for the first component

• The **<ol type ="1" >** starts decimal numbering at 1 for the middle component/ordered list

• The **<ol type ="i" >** begins the last component/ ordered list with 'i' the Roman number

The file was saved as **orderedMixed.html** and checked as required. The screen capture is shown in Diagram 4. It illustrates that the XHTML code has created the document in the required format.

The XHTML code for example 2 – orderMixed.html

```
<?xml version= "1.0" encoding = "UTF-8"?>
<!DOCTYPE html
                    PUBLIC "- //w3C//DTD XHTML 1.0 Transitional//EN"
 "http://www.w3.org/TR/xhtml1/DTD/xhtml1-transitional.dtd">
<html xmlns= "http://www.w3.org/1999/xhtml" xml:lang= "en" lang= "en">
<head>
<title> Ordered list types </title>
</head>
<body>

<b><u> Uppercase alphabetic</u></b>
<ol type ="A" >
<li> By Cash </li>
<li>By Cheque </li>
<li> By Credit Card </li>
</ol>

<b><u> Decimal numbers</u></b>
<ol type = "1">
<li> If statement</li>
<li> Compound Conditions </li>
<li> Non-numeric Values</li>
</ol>

<b><u> Lowercase Roman numerals</u></b>
<ol type = "i">
<li> Appendix A </li>
<li> Appendix B</li>
<li> Appendix C</li>
</ol>
</body>
</html>
```

Diagram 3

W3C Validation Service

This document will be invalidated under Strict DTD, as attribute type and <u> element are not recognised in XHTML 1.0 Strict.

orderMixed.html previewed in IE5.5

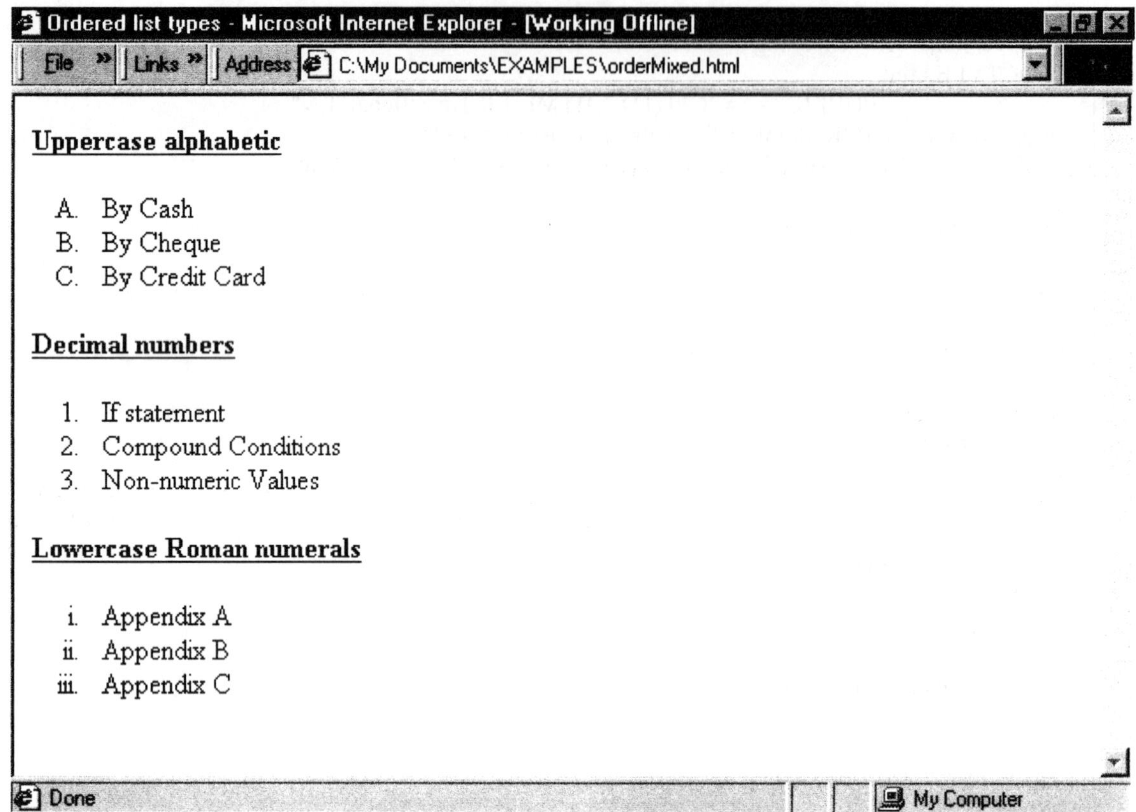

Diagram 4

• Example 3
unordered or bulleted list

Unlike the ordered list, an unordered list is just a collection of data or information. There is no hierarchical structure. Thus, list items are not positioned within the list in accordance with any ranking or priority associated with any specific order, such as age. For instance, if you make a list of 10 persons you meet in the street, you will create an unordered list. It is so, as you have only a collection of people without placing them in the list by determining each person's relative position in the list. You can consider it as a non-sequential list, as it makes no difference which item is listed in what order in the list. The following example demonstrates how one can create such a list.

An example of unordered list

- Software Engineering
- Web Technologies
- Programming Languages
- Hardware
- Databases

- Your task is to create an unordered list in order to display the information listed above in the shaded area.The list should be displayed in the given format. Save your XHTML file, check it for XML well-formedness and validity as XHTML Transitional 1.0 document.

• Explanation

The structure of the required code for this example is shown in Diagram 5. You can see that it is very similar to the structure of code you have met so far in this chapter. However, the crucial difference lies in the overall list elements. For the unordered list, you must implement <ul> element. Within this element, like the ordered list, list items are contained. Each list item is created with <li> element. See Diagram 5.

- It was saved as **unordered.html**, and checked accordingly. The document was previewed in IE 5.5, as shown in Diagram 6. You can see that each list item began with a solid bullet point or disc, as well as being indented. If you do not specify the attribute and its value, an unordered list is rendered as a bulleted list. The default delimiter for the unordered list is disc or solid circle. This is the reason for calling an unordered list as **a bulleted list**.

Type attribute Values & definitions for unordered lists

Attribute Value	Definition
Square	it is a small filled square
Circle	it is an unfilled circle
Disc	it is a filled circle
Default	automatic. XHTML complaint browser generates a filled circle. It is the same as disc.

Illustration 3

The XHTM code for example 3 – unordered.html

```
<?xml version= "1.0" encoding = "UTF-8"?>
<!DOCTYPE html
                    PUBLIC "- //w3C//DTD XHTML 1.0 Transitional//EN"
 "http://www.w3.org/TR/xhtml1/DTD/xhtml1-transitional.dtd">
<html xmlns= "http://www.w3.org/1999/xhtml" xml:lang= "en" lang= "en">
<head>
<title> Unordered List of titles</title>
</head>
<body>
<h1><u>An example of unordered list</u></h1>
<ul>
   <li> Software Engineering</li>
   <li> Web Technologies    </li>
   <li> Programming Languages </li>
   <li> Hardware </li>
   <li> Databases</li>
</ul>
</body></html>
```

Diagram 5

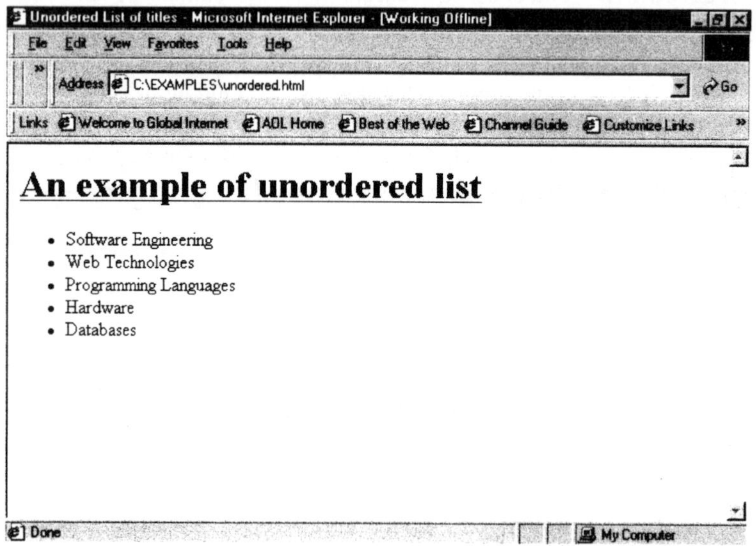

Diagam 6: unordered.html previewed in IE 5.5

• Is it possible to render an unordered list with some other delimiters?

Yes, you can change the type of bullet by means of the **type attribute**. This can be achieved if you are working with XHTML Transitional or Frameset types documents. The type attribute values and definitions for the unordered lists are shown in Illustration 3 above, and example 4 demonstrates their application.

• Example 4
unordered Lists squares & numbers delimiters

An example of unordered list using square

- Chapter 1 - Introduction
- Chapter 2 - Program Structure
- Chapter 3 - Conditions testing

An example of unordered list using circle

- Chapter 4 - Tables
- Chapter 5 - Fonts & Colours
- Chapter 6 - UGI

- Write two unordered lists in order to display in any browser the information listed in the above shaded area. Your Web page display should resemble both lists as shown here. You must save it, and check it as XHTML Transitional 1.0 document in accordance with XML well-formedness.

• Explanation

The required code is listed in Diagram 7. It was checked for XML well-formedness and validity as XHTML Transitional 1.0 document. The list is displayed in Diagram 8. You can see that it resembles the original information given in the shaded area. The following segments of the code have created different
delimiters.

- <ul type ="square"> - The rendering of first unordered list uses squares.
- <ul type =" circle"> - The rendering of second unordered list uses circles.

Diagram 7: The XHTM code for example 4 – unorderMixed.html

```
<?xml version= "1.0" encoding = "UTF-8"?>
<!DOCTYPE html
                    PUBLIC "- //w3C//DTD XHTML 1.0 Transitional//EN"
 "http://www.w3.org/TR/xhtml1/DTD/xhtml1-transitional.dtd">
<html xmlns= "http://www.w3.org/1999/xhtml" xml:lang= "en" lang= "en">
<head>
<title> Unordered Lists</title>
</head>
<body>
<h3><u>An example of unordered list using square</u></h3>
<ul  type ="square">
   <li> Chapter 1 - Introduction </li>
   <li> Chapter 2 - Program Structure  </li>
   <li> Chapter 3 - Conditions testing </li>
 </ul>
<h3><u>An example of unordered list using circle</u></h3>
 <ul type =" circle">
   <li> Chapter 4 - Tables </li>
   <li> Chapter 5 - Fonts & Colours  </li>
   <li> Chapter 6 - UGI </li>
 </ul></body></html>
```

unorderedMixed.html previewed in IE 5.5

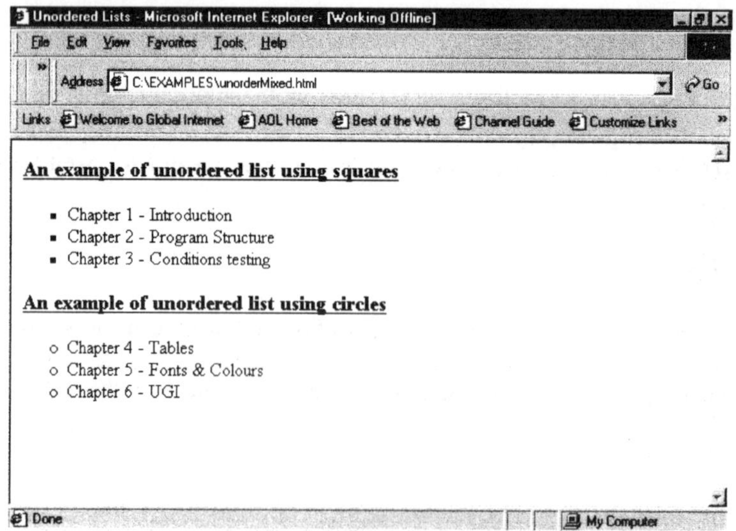

Diagram 8

The rendering of two unordered lists – first uses squares and second list uses unfilled circles.

• Nested ordered and unordered lists

By nesting, it means that one element is contained within the other element, without any overlapping. So, you can nest a list within another list. The list which has to be nested within another list, must be contained within a list item <li> element of the list in which it is nested. This rule is visualised in Illustration 4. In this illustration, the generalised nested unordered list is shown in the white area. Examples 5 and 6 are aimed to demonstrate the construction of nested ordered and nested unordered lists.

Generalised nested unordered lists

```
<ul>
    <li> This is the first item of the list in which another list is nested</li>
      <ul>
         <li> First item of  nested list</li>
         <li> Second item of  nested list </li>
         <li> Third item of nested list</li>
      </ul>

    <li> Second item of the list in which another list is nested</li>
    <li> Third item of the list in which another list is nested><li>
</ul>
```

Illustration 4

• Example 5
nested ordered list

An example of nested ordered list starting with letter a

A. Retail Sales

   1. Cash payments
   2. Credit cards payments
   3. Debit cards payments

B. Regular Customers average annual sales £10,000+
C. Regular Customers average annual sales under £10,000

- The aim of this example is to construct an ordered nested list in order to display the above information in the same format on the Internet. Your task is to write an XHTML code, save it and check it for XML well-formedness and validity as XHTML 1.0 Transitional document. Also preview it in in IE5.5 or any other browser/user agent.

• Explanation

The XHTML code for this example is shown in Diagrams 9 and 9A. It is self-explanatory. It is so, as its structure is based on Illustration 3 and other examples discussed so far in this chapter.

- However, once again, it is worth mentioning that the segment of the code:

```
<ol type ="a">
```

is essential. The **type attribute** together with its **value "a"** sets the starting point to render the outer ordered list.

- Diagram 10 shows the screen capture of the Web page previewed in IE5 5. Here, you can find that the rendering of the nested ordered list began at number 1. The browser generated decimal numbers as it is the default mode for the **type attribute**. For this reason, I have not included a type attribute together with its value to generate these numbers.

The XHTML code for example 5 – nestorder.html (cont.in Diagram 9A)

```
<?xml version= "1.0" encoding = "UTF-8"?>
<!DOCTYPE html
                PUBLIC "- //w3C//DTD XHTML 1.0 Transitional//EN"
 "http://www.w3.org/TR/xhtml1/DTD/xhtml1-transitional.dtd">
<html xmlns= "http://www.w3.org/1999/xhtml" xml:lang= "en" lang= "en">
<head>
<title> Nested ordered list </title>
</head>
<body>
<h3><u>An example of nested ordered list starting with letter a</u></h3>
<ol type ="a">
```

Diagram 9

The XHTML code for example 5 – nestorder.html (cont. from Diagram 9)

```
<li>Retail Sales
<ol>
   <li>Cash payments</li>
   <li>Credit cards payments</li>
   <li>Debit cards payments </li>
</ol>
</li>
     <li> Regular Customers average annual sales £10,000+ </li>
      <li> Regular Customers average annual sales under £10,000</li>
</ol>
</body>
</html>
```

Diagram 9A

nestorder.html previewed in IE 5.5

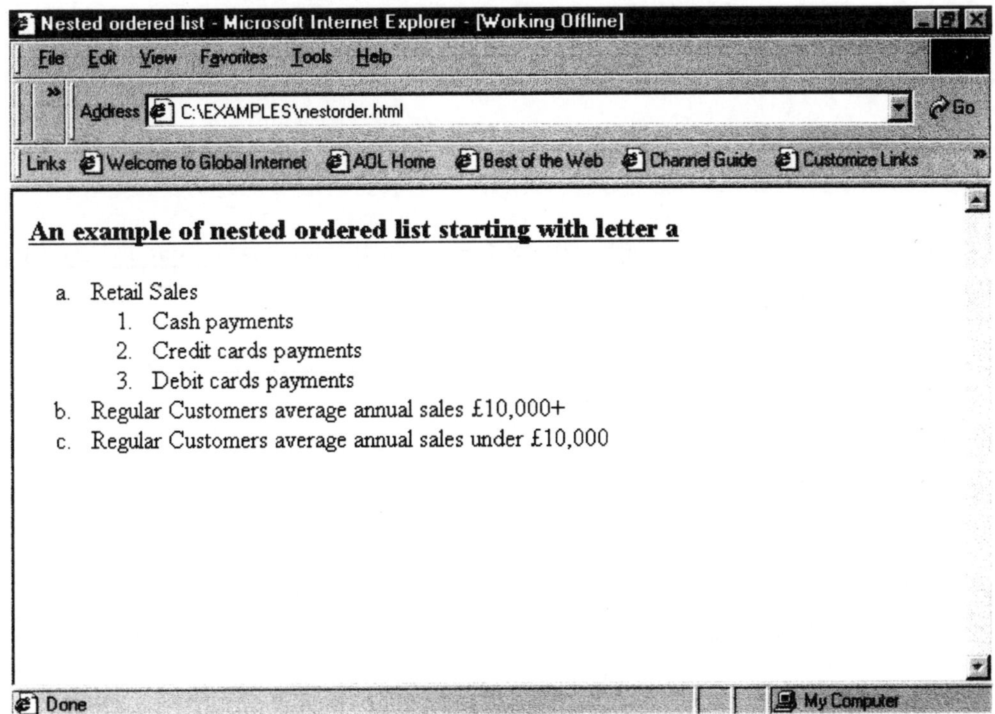

Diagram 10

The above screen capture demonstrates that the Web page was designed and displayed as required. You can see that lists are also indented one in the other as required.

• Example 6 nested unordered list

An example of nested unordered list with circles used as bullets

- Chapter 1 - What is XML?
  - ° Program structure
  - ° Your first XML program
  - ° Preview a document locally
- Chapter 3 - Using Colours
- Chapter 4 - Style Sheets

- The aim of this example is to demonstrate the design of nested unordered list. You are asked to use the text shown above in the shaded area for designing a nested unordered list. Your XHTML code should be written to produce the document whose format and style match the text shown above. You must also save it, check it for XML well-formedness and validity as XHTML Transitional 1.0 document.

• Explanation

The XHTML code for example 6 –nestunorder.html (cont. in Diagram 11A)

```
<?xml version= "1.0" encoding = "UTF-8"?>
<!DOCTYPE html
                        PUBLIC "- //w3C//DTD XHTML 1.0 Transitional//EN"
 "http://www.w3.org/TR/xhtml1/DTD/xhtml1-transitional.dtd">
<html xmlns= "http://www.w3.org/1999/xhtml" xml:lang= "en" lang= "en">
<head>
<title> Nested unordered list </title>
</head>
<body>
<h3><u>An example of nested unordered list with circles used as bullets</u></h3>
<ul>
   <li> Chapter 1 - What is XML?
```

Diagram 11

The XHTML code for example 6 –nestunorder.html (cont. from Diagram 11)

```
  <ul type ="circle" >
          <li> Program structure  </li>
          <li> Your first XML program  </li>
          <li> Preview a document locally  </li>
    </ul>
  </li>
  <li>Chapter 3 - Using Colours  </li>
  <li>Chapter 4 - Style Sheets </li>
</ul>
</body>
</html>
```

Diagram 11A

nestunorder.html previewed in IE 5.5

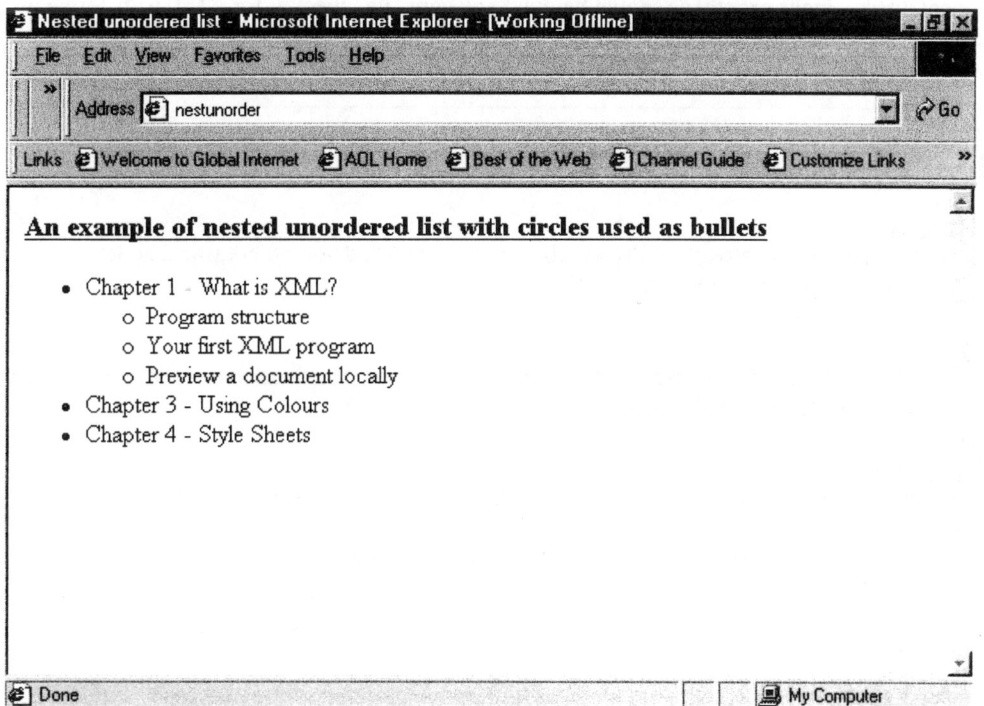

Diagram 12

Upon reading the code listed in Diagrams 11 and 11A above, you can see that its structure is similar to the code for the last example. Also note that lists are indented one in another, and thus it matches the original format and presentation style. See the screen capture of the document previewed in IE 5.5.

• Definition lists

A definition list is a special kind of list. Its prime objective is to display some terms or phrases or pinpoint some terms or phrases in your Web page, and define these or explain them as necessary. In fact, the word definition is somewhat misleading. It creates a list, which is more of a descriptive nature. Anyway, it is a very useful means of describing some words and phrases. The general format of a definition list is shown in Illustration 1. A definition list does not start with any bullets or numbers.

• Example 7
def.html

You are asked to convert the text shown below in the shaded area into a definition type list. Your document should be designed to take into account presentation style and text format, so that the document display looks exactly as shown below. Save your file, check it for XML well-formedness and validity as XHTML Transitional 1.0 document. Preview your document in the IE 5.5 or another browser.

An example of definition list

The Internet
The Internet is a network of thousands of inter-connected computers world wide.
The most popular part of it is the Web.

The Web
The Web or the World Wide Web is a collection of text, graphics, sounds, video clips, pictures
and other information arranged in pages with hyper links.

A Hyper Link
The purpose of a hyper link is to enable the user to link the current document to another
required
document on the Web. The hyper link is in the Web page.

• Explanation

The XHTML code for this example is shown in Diagram 7. If you examine it carefully, you will find out that there is hardly any similarity between the definition list and other types of lists discussed in this chapter.

1. The definition list is handled by the element **<dl>**. You must place it at the beginning of the segment of the code, for creating the definition list.

2. The first descriptive phrase or word is '**The Internet**'. This descriptive phrase is coded as:-

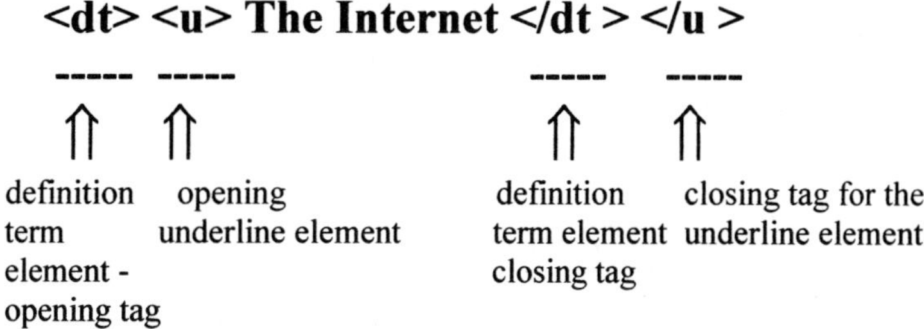

<u>If you do not wish to underline the phrase/word, there is no need to include <u></u> in this code.</u>

3. Now, the next requirement is to set the code for defining /describing the phrase or word.

   The code for it:-

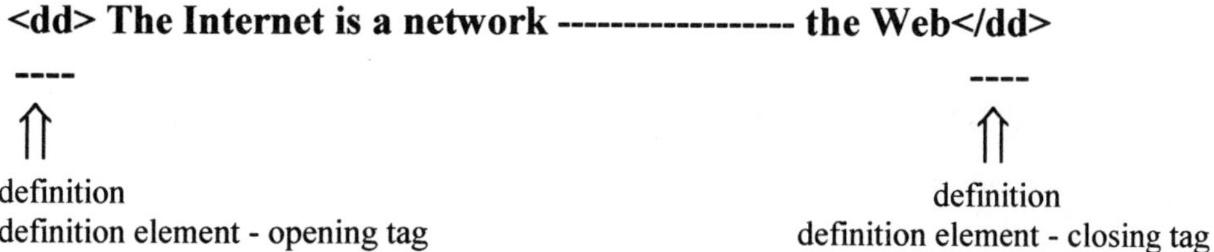

4. This first descriptive phrase 'The Internet' has only one definition/ description, and thus the next step is to code the next descriptive phrase and its description or definition. To do so, you have to repeat steps 2 and 3 as above. This process is repeated until all descriptive phrases and their respective definitions or descriptions have been coded.

5. Having coded the last definition/description, you must place the closing tag **</dl>**. This tags ends the process of coding the definition list. By now, you must be familiar with the rest of the code shown in Diagram 13. The file was saved as **def.html**, checked as required. It was previewed in IE 5.5 You can see that it matches all requirements. See its screen capture in Diagram 14.

> You have to decide yourself which of the lists is most suited for your needs for a particular Web page and a specific purpose. Indeed, a list can be very useful for some kind of information to display on the Internet. Make use of this technique!

Diagram 13: The XHTML code for example 7 – def.html

```
<?xml version= "1.0" encoding = "UTF-8"?>
<!DOCTYPE html
                         PUBLIC "- //w3C//DTD XHTML 1.0 Transitional//EN"
 "http://www.w3.org/TR/xhtml1/DTD/xhtml1-transitional.dtd">
<html xmlns= "http://www.w3.org/1999/xhtml" xml:lang= "en" lang= "en">
<head>
<title> A definition list </title>
</head>
<body>
<h3><u>An example of definition list</u></h3>
<dl>
   <dt><u>The Internet</u></dt>
   <dd> The Internet is a network of thousands of inter-connected computers
       world wide. The most popular part of it is the Web</dd>
<dt><u> The Web</u></dt>
   <dd> The Web or the World Wide Web is a collection of text, graphics,
       sounds, video clips, pictures and other information arranged in pages
       with hyper links.</dd>
<dt><u> A Hyper Link</u></dt>
   <dd>The purpose of a hyper link is to enable the user to link the current
      document to another required document on the Web. The hyper link is
      in the Web page.</dd>
</dl>
</body></html>
```

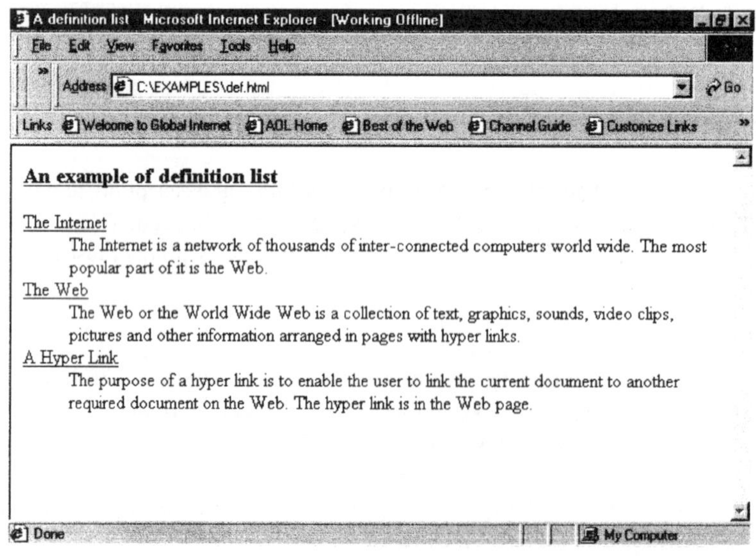

Diagram 14 - def.html previewed in IE5

Chapter 7

Colours & Style Sheets

The prime aims of this chapter are as follows:-

- to enable you to understand the application of different colours on your Web pages.
- to introduce you to cascading style sheets (CSS) and some CSS techniques.

By reading and practising techniques that are demonstrated in this chapter, you should be able :-

- to make a distinction between different methods of specifying colour
- to set the colour of the text
- to set the background colour
- to apply different colours on the same Web page in order to improve its design and highlight some words, phrases, sentences or any other aspect of a Web page
- to explain the advantages of applying CSS rules and techniques
- to create an internal style sheet
- to create and link a document to an external style sheet
- to explain the reasons of an external style sheet preference over the internal style sheet
- to design both internal and external style sheets for applying colours on your Web pages

• Setting colours

You can create attractive Web pages by applying different colours and their combinations to both the text itself and the background. In fact, you should not use colour for just making a Web page colourful. You should use colour on your Web page to improve the design of your Web page, so that it is not only attractive, but it also enables the visitor to your Web site to find some required piece of information easily.

• The RGB colour model

The colour display unit of your computer system has a great number of pixels. A pixel is a single tiny dot on a display unit (screen). All screen images are made up of a collection of pixels. These pixels are so tiny and so close to each other that a human eye cannot distinguish one from the other. Each pixel is either **off (dark)** or **on (illuminated in colour if it is a colour screen).**

The RGB colour model defines colour in terms of **red**, **green** and **blue** components. Thus, the primary colours or lights are red, green and blue. These colours can be combined in order to generate a combined colour. When RGB components are mixed in equal amount of light intensity they produce white. When RGB components are combined in other proportions they generate a mixed colour representing the proportional amount of intensity of light of RGB components. This is how you can create virtually countless mixed colours.

• Standard & Hexadecimal colours

In order to represent the intensity of red, green and blue lights/colours in the mixed colour, the mixed colour is specified by a number or value. This number itself consists of three different sets of numbers, each representing the intensity of red, green and blue in the mixed colour. The system used to describe this mixed colour is called **hexadecimal** (base 16). The hexadecimal numbering system is commonly used in the computing field. The reason for preferring this numbering system is that it can represent any number between 0 - 255 with just **two hex digits** in accordance with the hexadecimal system. For instance:

- **000000** - it represents **black colour** as it has no RGB components, just no colour
- FF0000 - it means **red colour** as it has 100% red light, and the other two are not present
- FFFFFF - this represents **white colour** - no other colours in it

Table 1 contains the hexadecimal equivalent of 16 standard colours. The hexadecimal numbers are known as hexadecimal, the **triplets** or hexadecimal pairs or **hex pairs**. In passing, there is no harm in mentioning that the base 16 is easier to use in the computing field than base 10. For example, it is easier to convert a hex number into binary and vice versa. Binary numbers are the backbone of computer systems. In table 1, you can see that hex pairs begin with the symbol # in order to distinguish them from other numbering systems. The hex pairs are written without quotation marks.

The **16 standard (or simple) colours**, to choose from for your Web page, are shown in table 1. By applying hexadecimal values, in theory you can specify colours from a palette of 24 million colours. In fact, it is highly likely that your system is capable of no more than 256-colour default display. It is a wide range of colours. Wide enough for most needs!

• Standard colours

Standard colours are Windows colours, which are defined in HTML 3.2 and 4.0. These colours correspond to the basic VG monitor on most PCs. For ease of use, you can declare colour by its name for displays on a 16-colour monitor. These colours are pretty bright, but the fact of the matter is that on most PCs they can render displays. For complex colour schemes, you have to apply the hex pair values.

The biggest drawback is that different manufacturers have different standards. For instance, Netscape has countless colours. Scores of browsers do not even have the same colour names. However, there is one important aspect which must not be overlooked which is the fact that most manufacturers base their colour systems on 256 different colours. These are almost the same throughout the industry. Thus, it is a good idea to design Web pages using these colours.

It is worth knowing that there are many different browsers and often several different versions of the same browser in use across the Internet. You may have the latest version of a particular browser running on your computer system, and thus your Web page on your system appears brilliant. On the other hand, the same document, on someone else's system with a rather older version of the same browser or a different browser, may look dull, or may not even display clearly the image(s) in your document.

Standard colours & their equivalent Hex pair values

Colour Name	Hex Pair Triplet	Colour Name	Hex Pair Triplet
Black	#000000	Gray	#808080
White	#FFFFFF	Lime	#00FF00
Red	#FF0000	Olive	#808000
Green	#008000	Yellow	#FFFF00
Blue	#0000FF	Maroon	#800000
Navy	#000080	Purple	#800080
Silver	#C0C0C0	Fuchsia	#FF00FF
Teal	#008080	Aqua	#00FFFF

Table 1

In addition to these standard and hexadecimal specifying colour methods, there is another method of specifying colour, which is known as **decimal colour value**. It is based on 0 to 255 values. By this method, each colour component red, green and blue is specified as three sets of numbers, ranging from 0 to 255. Despite the fact that this method does not have any letters, as in the case of the hexadecimal system. It is least used by Webmasters.

. Which is the colour scheme for you ?

Your design of Web page must get your message across on the Net. For simple displays, it is, therefore, recommended to design Web pages with a standard colour scheme. This way, it is likely that your colourful visual presentation will be rendered across the Internet in the same way and as you want. Remember, the whole idea is to communicate with viewers, with the main aim to do business with them. You should always bear in mind that you are investing both time and money in your Web page design for your business, and thus its complex colourful visual presentation must not hinder your principal goal.

. Cascading style sheets

Until now, you have learnt how to give instructions to the browser thorough the XHTML code for your document style, text format and display. The formatting and styling of text imply defining the structure of text for your Web page. It includes font size, styles and faces, headings, line breaks, underline text, margin settings, and positioning the text on a Web page. In order to insert these presentational features in Web documents, some relevant elements and attributes were used. The XHTML 1.0 Strict version has excluded these presentational features by adopting cascading style sheets technologies.

Style sheets can enable you to control the appearance of Web pages. By means of style sheets, you can format your text, font sizes and types, spacing between lines, word and letters, control margin, background colours, thickness of the border of a table, and other visual features of tables. In fact, style sheets can be applied to all aspects of XHTML. The most popular style sheet language is Cascading Style Sheet (CSS). The W3C recommended CSS Level 1 in 1996. The CSS Level 2 was introduced in 1998. The CSS Level 2 includes CSS Level 1.

The reason for its popularity is that the leading browsers' manufacturers have implemented it. The Internet Explorer and Netscape Navigator have adopted it, but the manner of adoption differs, and thus both browsers interpret style sheets in their own way. One can only hope that by the time you read this book these differences are minimal. The older browsers cannot handle style sheets at all. It means that older browsers and those do not support CSS will set aside your style sheet markup code.

Until now, you have made use of some elements and attributes that have been deprecated by the World Wide Web Consortium (W3C). With these elements and attributes, W3C HTML Validation Service successfully validated the code as XHTML 1.0 Transitional 1.0 document, and stated:

"Valid – Congratulations, this document validates as Transitional!"

When it was tried to validate the same document under XHTML Strict version, W3C HTML Validation Service did not validate the code as XHTML 1.0 Strict document, and reported:

"Sorry, this document does not validate as Strict."

When any feature is deprecated, W3C replace it by another feature, which is functionally equivalent. The continuous deprecation of HTML and XHTML elements and attributes will, most certainly, lead to a wider adoption of CSS. Therefore, it is advisable to apply CSS now and save time and efforts in altering Web pages in the not too distant future.

• How can you write your own style sheet rules?

In XHTML emphases are on content-oriented or functional aspects of the document as opposed to presentational features in the case of HTML. Indeed, style sheets are concerned with the presentational features of a document. These presentational features are the styles. If you organise these features as a set of rules, you will, indeed, develop a style sheet. The general format of the syntax for setting a style sheet rules is as follows:-

selector {declaration }

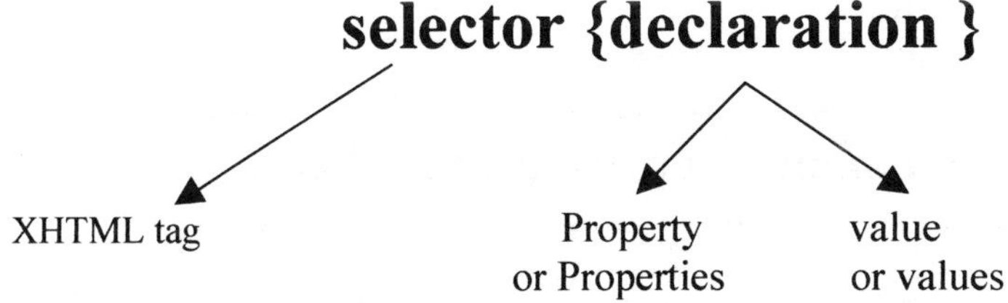

In the following code, you can identify each component in the syntax of style sheet rule:

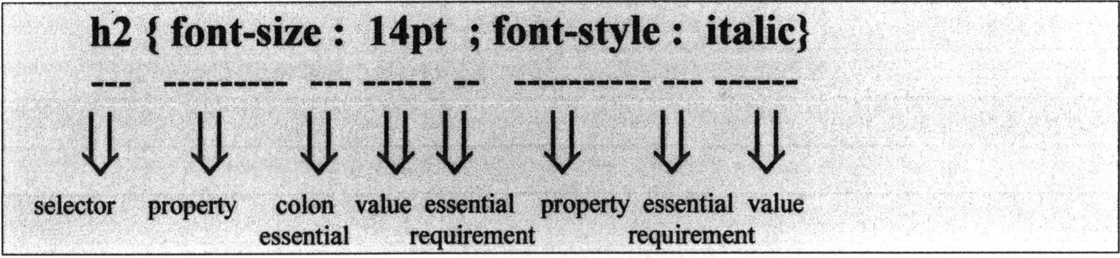

- The property can be single or plural – as in this example, size and style are two properties.

- The semicolon is used to separate a property and its value (pair) from the other property and its value (pair).

- Property and value are used as a pair.

- Within the pair is a colon to separate its components.
- The property list must be within curly brackets.
- **selector** - it sets the scope of the style. For instance, **<h2> element** can be used as a selector, whose scope is to create a headline of level 2. Thus, the selector is the name of the tag (element). You will soon learn that selectors are not always based on element names. There is another type of selectors called classes. See class selector.
- **declaration** - it is within the **curly brackets {...}**, which consists of some X HTML features concerning the required typographic style. For instance, **{ font-size: 14; font-style:normal }**

In fact, the purpose of the declaration is to set the typographical effect of the selector. For example:

h3 { font-size:20pt; font-style:*italic* }

This XHTML code will result in setting the headline in level 3 **(scope),** but in font size 20 using *italic* style typeface **(typographical effect)**. Of course, your style sheet can have one or more style definitions.

Methods of creating style sheets

Internal style sheet - it is within the document. It is created with the **style** element and placed inside the **head** element.

External style sheet - it is a separate file which is saved with the **.css** file extension. It is linked to the document by means of the **link** element inside the **head** element. It is also known as **linked** style sheet.

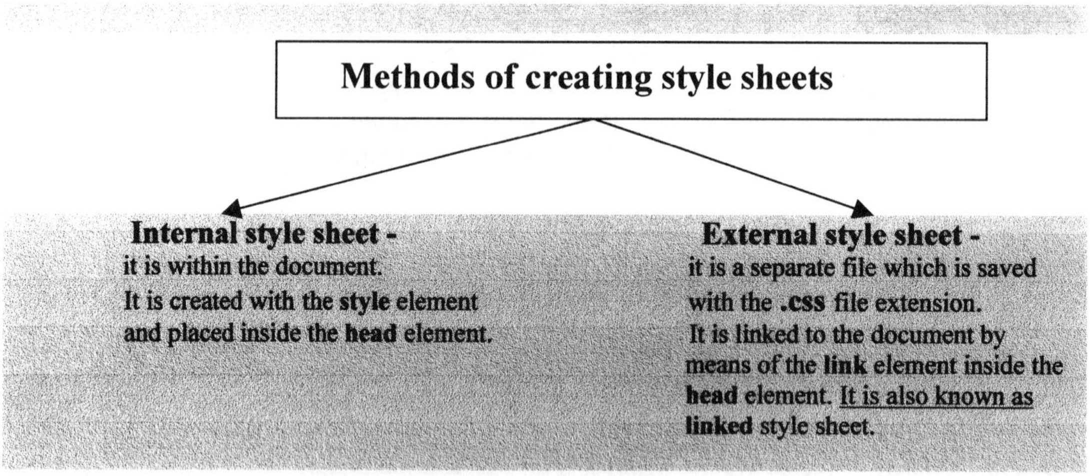

How can you place an internal style sheet definition on your Web page?

The style definition or style information or style blocks or stylistic rules all these phrases refers to style sheet features. A complete and workable style sheet can have one or more style definitions/rules. These rules are contained within the **<style> element**. The general format is as follows:-

The <style> element is inserted in the **Head** part of the Web page. Within it, the style sheet definition is placed. It forms a block of style sheet definition(s). This information affects the style preferences in the **whole XHTML** document. Its simplest form is as shown on the next page.

```
<head>
        < style type = "text/css ">
                                selector {declaration}
        </style>
</head>
```

Often, you need to expand this simple form. The **type ="text/css"** - it is an essential attribute. It is required to specify that you are using css (Cascading Style Sheets) language.

• Example 1
creating an internal style sheet

The task is to design a Web page for displaying the following text in the same format. Your design should include the following stylistic rules:-

- heading - font style italic, its colour green, and choose any size for it
- main text – "The earliest---linguistics." – font style normal and its colour blue, and select any font size
- last line of text – it is a reference. display it as citation, and use any font size, but it must be in red.

You must save it, and check it for XML well-formedness and validity as XHTML 1.0 Strict document. In order to check that it meets all requirements, display it in any browser.

> ***Mathematics in Asia***
>
> The earliest known evidence of mathematics in Asia comes from the Harappan civilization of the Indus Valley (now Pakistan) around 3000 BC. The earliest documents, though difficult to decipher, seem to deal with trading accounts, and weights and measures, with special reference to an advanced brick-making technology.
>
> If Greek mathematics can be said to have arisen out of philosophy, then Indian mathematics has its roots in linguistics.
>
> *History of mathematics*

. Explanation

The required code XHTML code is listed in Diagram 1. This document is written under XHTML **Strict DTD**. This DTD differs from the DTD you have met so far. For this reason , in Diagram 1, the segment of the code that refers to XHTML 1.0 Strict is written on a shaded background. Examine it.

The segment of the code that creates an internal style sheet and sets different colours for the text is shown in the shaded area in this diagram. It is contained in the head section of the document. Now, it is suggested that you read the entire code, and run it on your machine in order to check it and display it on your monitor.

The XHTML code for example 1 – style1. html

```
<?xml version= "1.0" encoding = "UTF-8"?>
<!DOCTYPE html
PUBLIC "- //w3C//DTD XHTML 1.0 Strict//EN"
 "http://www.w3.org/TR/xhtml1/DTD/xhtml1- Strict.dtd">

<html xmlns= "http://www.w3.org/1999/xhtml" xml:lang= "en" lang= "en">
<head>
<title> My first style sheet </title>
<style type ="text/css">
h1{font-size:22pt;  font-style:italic; color: green}
h2{font-size: 14pt;font-style:normal; color: blue}
h3{font-size:16pt; color: red}
</style>
</head>
<body>
    <h1> Mathematics in Asia </h1>
  <h2>
    The earliest known evidence of mathematics in Asia comes from the
    Harappan  civilization of the Indus Valley (now Pakistan) around 3000 BC.
    The earliest documents, though difficult to decipher, seem to deal with trading accounts,
    and weights and measures, with special reference to an advanced brick-making technology.
    If Greek mathematics can be said to have arisen out of philosophy, then Indian mathematics
    has its roots in linguistics.</h2>
<h3><cite> History of mathematics</cite></h3>
</body>
</html>
```

Diagram 1

- Here, you can see how stylistic rules are written within each pair of curly brackets. This is the required and complete internal style sheet. It is contained within the <style> element. If you examine the entire code, you will learn that in accordance with the above explanation, the <style> element is itself within the document head.

- File style.html was checked by W3C HTML Validation Service. The result stated,“ No error found!” The screen capture of its display in IE 5.5 is shown in Diagram 2. It meets all requirements. Of course, you cannot appreciate different colour effects in black and white if you run this code on your PC, you should be able to see its display in colour.

<u>style1.html previewed in IE 5.5</u>

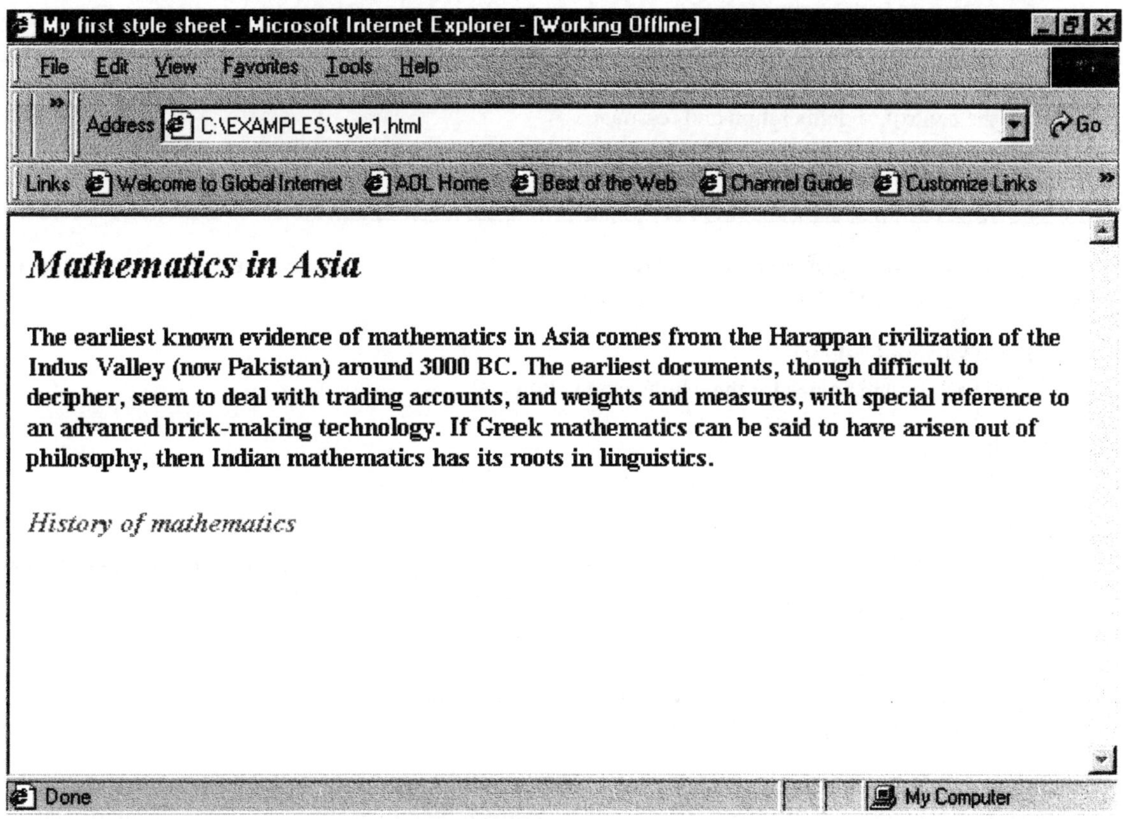

<u>Diagram 2</u>

<u>If you display it on your screen, you should be able to see all colours, providing you have a colour monitor of VGA type.</u>

So far so good, you have seen in action an internal style sheet. You can also create an external style sheet and link it your XHTML document. In fact, the external style sheet is given preference over the internal style sheet. Why? It is quicker to maintain external style sheets. To create an external style sheet is easy enough. Like an internal style sheet, an external style sheet can contain only a single rule.

• Example 2
a link or an external style sheet

> ***Philosophical Ideas***
>
> **Innate ideas** that are inborn and not the product of experience. There is a great controversy over their existence.
>
> ***Instinct*** - the term implies innately determined behaviour, inflexible to change in circumstance and outside the control of deliberation and reason.
>
> ***Integrity*** - most simply a synonym for honesty.

Design an XHTML document for displaying the text shown in the shaded area above. It should be displayed in accordance with the following requirements:-

- **The background colour:**
  Set the background colour for the whole page yellow.

- **Text heading:**
  Level 1 heading, *italic* font of any size, but colour should be red.

- **Paragraph 1:**
  Begins with phrase, "Innate Ideas" – this phrase should be displayed in bold style. For the remaining text in this paragraph, use any font of any size, normal style, and colour should be grey.

- **Paragraph 2:**
  First word "Instinct" should be displayed in *italic* style by applying <i> element. The whole paragraph should be in font style normal of any size, and colour green.

- **Paragraph 3:**
  First word "Integrity" – this word should be ***highlighted/emphasised*** by using <em> element. The rest of the paragraph should also be in normal style. Use a font of any size, and colour red.

Check your code for XML well-formedness and validity as XHTML 1.0 Strict document. At the same time, use the W3C HTML Validation Service to validate your **css file** prior to previewing your document in IE 5.5 or any other browser.

The XHTM code for example 2 – style2.html

```
<?xml version= "1.0" encoding = "UTF-8"?>
<!DOCTYPE html
                    PUBLIC "- //w3C//DTD XHTML 1.0 Strict//EN"
 "http://www.w3.org/TR/xhtml1/DTD/xhtml1-Strict.dtd">
<html xmlns= "http://www.w3.org/1999/xhtml" xml:lang= "en" lang= "en">
<head>
<title> My first link style sheet </title>
<link rel ="stylesheet" href="styles2.css" />
</head>
<body>
    <h1>Philosophical Ideas </h1>
  <p>
    <b>Innate ideas</b> that are inborn and not the product of
       experience. There is a great controversy over their existence.
 </p>
 <h2><i> Instinct</i> - the term implies innately determined behaviour,
      inflexible to change in circumstance and outside the control
      of deliberation and reason.</h2>
<h3><em>Integrity</em> - most simply a synonym for honesty.</h3>
</body>
</html>
```

Diagram 3

External style sheet saved as style2.css for example 2

```
/* This style sheet is to be linked to style1*/
body{background-color: yellow}
h1{font-size:22pt; font-style:italic;color:#808000}
h2{font-size:20pt; font-style:normal; color:#ffff00}
h3{font-size:120%;color:red}
p{font-size:150%; color:gray; font-style:normal}
```

Diagram 4

. Explanation

- The XHTML code for this example is listed below in Diagram 3. It is self-explanatory.

- An external style sheet is written in a text editor. So, I just opened NotePad and keyed in the style sheet rules, which are listed in Diagram 4. It is saved as **firstlink.css**. Note that the file extension is **.css**. You can see the effects of colours if you display the file on your machine. The screen captures prove that both files worked well and that the display meets all requirements set for this example.

• In what ways does the structure of this code differ from the structure of the code for example 1?

There are two major differences between the XHTML code that has an internal style sheet and the code without an internal style sheet. These differences are discussed below:-

- The XHTML code listed in Diagram 3 has no <style> element in the <head> element.

- Instead in Diagram 3, within the <head> element, you can find the following segment of the code:-

```
<link rel ="stylesheet" href="first-link.css" />
```

The <link> element is written in the <head> element. This is the link statement, whose purpose is to link the external file style-link.css, which contains style sheet rules to the XHTML file **style2.html**. This link is vital. Why is it so?

The function of this link statement is to let the browser or any other user agent know that the document has to be styled in accordance with the style rules/definitions contained in the file, which is the **value** of the **href attribute**.

- **In Diagram 4A is a portion of screen capture, which proves that the code shown in Diagram 4A was validated by W3C CSS Validator Service**

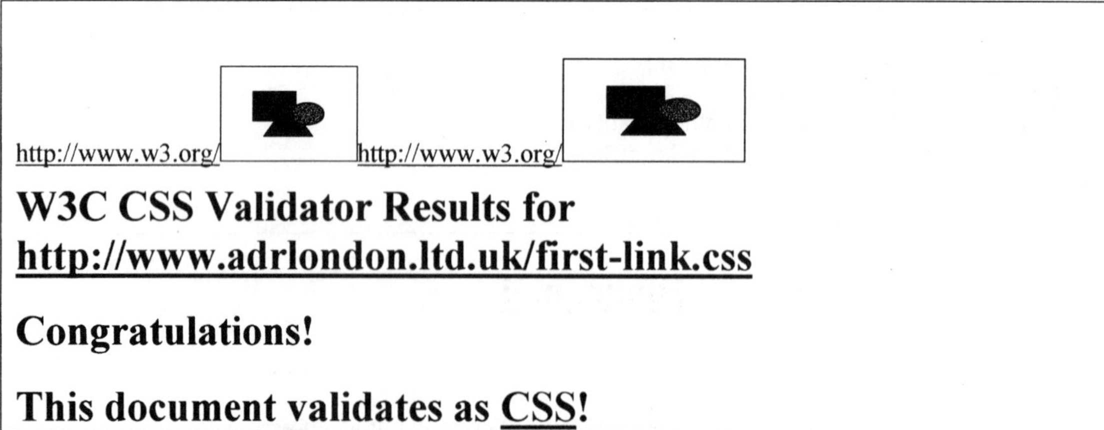

http://www.w3.org/ http://www.w3.org/

W3C CSS Validator Results for http://www.adrlondon.ltd.uk/first-link.css

Congratulations!

This document validates as CSS!

Diagram 4A

style2.html previewed in IE 5.5

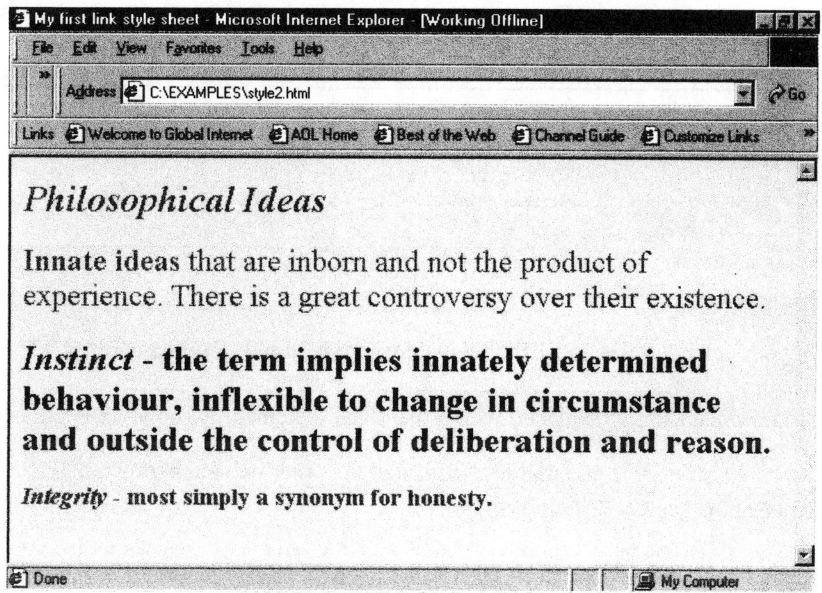

Diagram 5

• What are the advantages of creating an external style sheet?

It is already stated that it is easy to maintain an external file. For instance, a commercial organisation may have standard rules as styles for the production of documents. In such a case, it is feasible to keep all standard rules in an external style sheet file. Whenever, someone within the organisation generates an XHTML document for business communication, and has to include in the document organisation's standard styles, he/she can include, just one line of <link> code in this XHTML file. This way, it is much quicker. With an external style sheet file, it is also easier for the Webmaster to maintain the file on a regular basis.

Furthermore, there is no need to have both CSS and XHTML files in the same folder, or on the same computer or even in the same place or the same country. In order to link the style sheet to the XHTML document, the most important requirement is the correct path to the file given in the link statement as the value of the attribute **href**.

There is no limit on the length of the path to the file. It must be the correct path to the external CSS file. Finally, if the external CSS file is on another computer of the same organisation, but in another country, you have to add in the link statement the **URL** of the location, where the CSS file is stored. The URL is then becomes the part of the link statement. For instance:

<link rel = "stylesheet" href = "http://www. unserdeutschland. de/unserstyles.css" />

- Suppose you want to amend the XHTML code listed in Diagram 4 as you would rather have an internal style sheet for whatever personal reasons, such as your Web page has only a few style rules.

- **<u>How can you incorporate the same external CSS file into your XHTML file?</u>**

The process of amending the file is simple as shown below:-

- Code in Diagram 4 - first step is to replace link statement by **<style type = "text/css">**
- External CSS file in Diagram 3 – second step is to paste this file below the <style> element into the code in Diagram 4
- third step is to save your amended file under the same name: style2.html or under another name

The segment of the code which should be placed within the <head> element is shown in Diagram 5A.

- This CSS file has two font properties given in font sizes and the other two are expressed as a percentage. For explanation, see CSS2 font properties.

The segment of the code which should be placed within the <head> element is shown in Diagram 5A.

```
<style type= "text/css">
<!--
/* This style sheet is to be linked to style1*/
body{background-color: yellow}
h1{font-size:22pt; font-style:italic;color:#80800}
h2{font-size:20pt; font-style:normal; color:#ffff00}
h3{font-size:120%;color:#808000}
p{font-size:150%; color:#808080; font-style:normal}
-->
</style>
```

<u>Diagram 5A</u>

. <u>Comments</u>

In Diagram 5A, the CSS is within comments. Many browsers cannot interpret CSS code. Therefore, if you place the CSS as shown below, you will hide it from such browsers.

```
<! --
 CSS
-- >
```

If you do not code it in this way, the older browser will get confused and attempt to render it incorrectly.

Chapter 8

Working with Cascading Style Sheets

The prime aim of this chapter is to:-

- enable you to gain further knowledge and experience of working with cascading style sheets (CSS).

By reading and practising techniques that are demonstrated in this chapter, you should be able :-

- to understand some CSS properties which are applied to control fonts, text alignment, text indentation, text colour and background colour.
- to explain how CSS properties are passed on to another element as style inheritance
- to create named styles
- to design a document with an internal style sheet, as well as with an external style sheet

• CSS2 font properties

In CSS2, there are some font properties, whose correct application is highly desirable. If any of these properties is incorrectly coded, W3C CSS Validator will not validate your document as CSS. It is a really big topic, and beyond the scope of this book. If you wish to acquire a comprehensive knowledge and skills of using fonts for developing style sheets, it is suggested that you visit W3C site at:

http://www.w3/org/TR/REC-CSS2/fonts.html

At this site, you will be able to print out some comprehensive information, which you may need for some specific requirements. The following account of font properties is aimed at giving you sufficient information on this important topic. CSS2 specifies fonts according to these characteristics:

• Font family

A font family is a group of fonts, which are similar in design. The purpose of fonts is to render the text. Some of their characteristics are outlined below:-

- You can use any of the generic fonts. These are serif, sans-serif, cursive, fantasy, monospace. Generic font family names are keywords, and therefore must not be quoted.
- There are a large number of font family names including, **Helvetica**, **New Century Schoolbook**, and **Kyokasho ICA L**. Other font names such as **Courier**, **Times**, **Times New Roman**, and many other fonts are available on PCs and can be specified by their names.
- If a chosen font is not installed on the system on which the Web page is viewed, in that case, the default font of the viewing browser will be used.

•Example: h1{ font-family: Arial, Times, serif }

This example has named three fonts. The idea is that any of these may be installed on the machine, where the Web page is being viewed. If these fonts are not available, then the default font of the viewing browser will be applied automatically.

- You can also name just one font, as illustrated below:-

body{ font-family: Helvetica}

- Font family names containing 'whitespace' should be quoted. If quoting is omitted, any 'whitespace' characters before and after the font name are ignored and any sequence of 'whitespace' characters inside the font name is converted to a single space. An example of font name with 'whitespaces' is as follows:-

BODY { font-family: "new century schoolbook", serif }

- In fact, you can name any of the fonts running on your machine. For instance:

body{ font-family: " Century Gothic"}

In CSS2, you have a large choice for naming the particular font you want.

• Font weight

- The font weight refers to the boldness or lightness of the font. It can enable you to specify how light or bold the text should be rendered.
- There are two modes of specifying the font weight. You can indicate the weight either by applying the relevant keywords for font weight:-

normal, lighter, bold, and bolder.

- Or use instead their **corresponding numbers**, which are:- **400, 100, 700 and 900** respectively (in the same order in which keywords are listed above).

- The following examples demonstrate their application:-
- p { font-weight: normal } ⇐ this will render text as normal (normal brightness)
- h1 { font-weight: 700 } ⇐ this will set the text as **bold**
- body { font-weight: 400 } ⇐ this will render text as normal (normal brightness)
- h2 { font-weight: lighter } ⇐ this will render text as normal (normal brightness)
- You can also set other weights between 100 –900. If these are available on the viewing computer, the text will be rendered as required. For instance:

STRONG { font-weight: 300 }

- Child elements inherit the computed value of the weight.

• Font style

The font style specifies whether the text is to be rendered using a normal, italic, or oblique face. Italic and oblique are similar.

- The following example demonstrates how you can specify a font style:-
  - p {font-style: italic } ⇐ renders the paragraph in italic
  - em { font-style: oblique } ⇐ renders text/words with emphasis, but in oblique

• Font size

The font size is controlled by means of font–size property. Some font-size characteristics are listed blow:-

- Size is set as absolute, relative, percentage, or length.
- default is medium. • it applies to all elements. • It is inherited.
- Preferred method is the percentage . Reason for this preference is that different browsers render text in different sizes. For instance, 10 point Courier on another PC may look different in size.
  - **Example 1: h1{ font-size: 50%}** ⇐ will render text as half the base size/ parent element.

- **Example 2:** Suppose the base size for a paragraph is 10pt (10 point) *italic*, and you want to express it as:

h2{ font-size: 160%} ⇐ This will render text 16 point **italic** on your screen, as well as of the same size on any other screen.

- size expressed as percentage is relative to the base size/parent element.

- You can specify size as x point as shown below:-

- **Example 3: p{ font-size: 14pt}** ⇐ the viewing browser may not render it as required.

Different browsers may render absolute numbers in their own way, and they may not be of the same size as you wish.

• Properties of inheritance

The idea of inheritance is an important aspect of cascading style sheets. In accordance with the inheritance concept the children elements of a parent element inherit all properties of the parent element. There is an exception to this rule, as some properties are not inherited. Furthermore, in some cases, some properties are not inherited. For instance, if a specific declaration is made in a child element. These aspects of the inheritance concept are explained and demonstrated by the following two solved examples:-

• Example 1

> **Think!**
>
> A thought is what you make of it. Each negative thought represents stress. Rather, each is a stressor, **a cause of stress.**
>
> Stress itself is the response of the body to demands made upon it. Stress is the reaction of the body to the stressors.
>
> **Your mind believes what you tell it to believe.**

- The text shown above in the shaded area has to previewed locally as a Web document. Design the following two separate files:-

File 1 – CSS document to contain the following presentational and styles information:-

- Web page must be displayed on **yellow** background and the font style has to be **normal**.
- For the heading of this text apply Level 1 element, and display it in the centre of a top line, but the text colour should be green.
- Paragraph - a thought .... stress. Apply <p> element in order to make it a paragraph. The font size should be increased from its base size to 120%. The phrase, **a cause of stress,** in this paragraph should be highlighted by making its size even bigger than the size of the font by increasing it from 120% to 160%.
- Paragraph – Stress....stressors. Apply Level 2 headline element. Increase its font base size to 120%. The text should be displayed in the colour blue.
- Paragraph – Your ... believe. Use Level 3 element for this paragraph, font size 150%, and colour green.

File 2 – XHTML document – to contain the document

- This file should be created under XHTML 1.0 strict DTD. Thus, you must use XHTML strict only.
- Save your both documents under appropriate file names. Check your XHTML file for XML well-formedness as XHTML 1.0 Strict document. Also check your CSS document for validity. Both documents can be checked by W3C Validation Service on-line service.

• Explanation

- The XHTML document is listed in Diagram 1. This is saved as inherint.html. Examine it carefully.
- The CSS document is shown in Diagram 2. This is saved as inherint.css.
- The code **<link rel="stylesheet" href="inherint.css" />** in XHTML document links the CSS document to it.
- If you examine CSS file, you can see that <body> element is declared here as a parent element. It means that all other elements in the XHTML document are its children. It is for this reason that the document is displayed on a yellow background. Furthermore, the font-style is the same throughout the document. Why? Because in the <body> element, it is set to normal.
- The text contained within the <big> element is displayed much larger than the text in a paragraph, in which it is displayed. There are two reasons for such a large size of the phrase: **a cause of stress.**

  . Firstly, the <big> element is a child of parent element <p>.
  Thus, it inherits the properties of its parent element <p>, which has font-size 120%

- Secondly, the child element <big> itself has font-size 160%. For these reasons, the phrase is displayed so big.

- Both documents were validated by W3C Validation Service. The document was previewed in the IE 5.5. It meets all requirements. See Diagram 3. You cannot appreciate colours until you run it on your system.

The XHTML document for example 3 – inherent.html

```
<?xml version= "1.0" encoding = "UTF-8"?>
<!DOCTYPE html
                    PUBLIC "- //w3C//DTD XHTML 1.0 Strict//EN"
 "http://www.w3.org/TR/xhtml1/DTD/xhtml1-Strict.dtd">
<html xmlns= "http://www.w3.org/1999/xhtml" xml:lang= "en" lang= "en">
<head>
<title>Inheritance </title>
<link rel="stylesheet" href="inherint.css" />
</head>
<body>
    <h1> Think! </h1>
  <p> A thought is what you make of it. Each negative thought represents
      stress. Rather, each is a stressor, <big> a cause of stress</big>.</p>
 <h2> Stress itself is the response of the body to demands made upon it.
      Stress is the reaction of the body to the stressors. </h2>
<h3>Your mind believes what you tell it to believe. </h3>
</body></html>
```

Diagram 1

The CSS code for example 3 – inherent.css

```
/* style sheet link to inherint.html*/

body { font-style:normal; background-color:yellow;}
h1{color:green; text-align:center;}
h2{font-size:120%; color:blue;}
h3{ font-size:150%; color:green;}
p{font-size:120%;}
big{ font-size:160%;}
```

Diagram 2

Previewed of inherent document in IE 5.5 – example 1

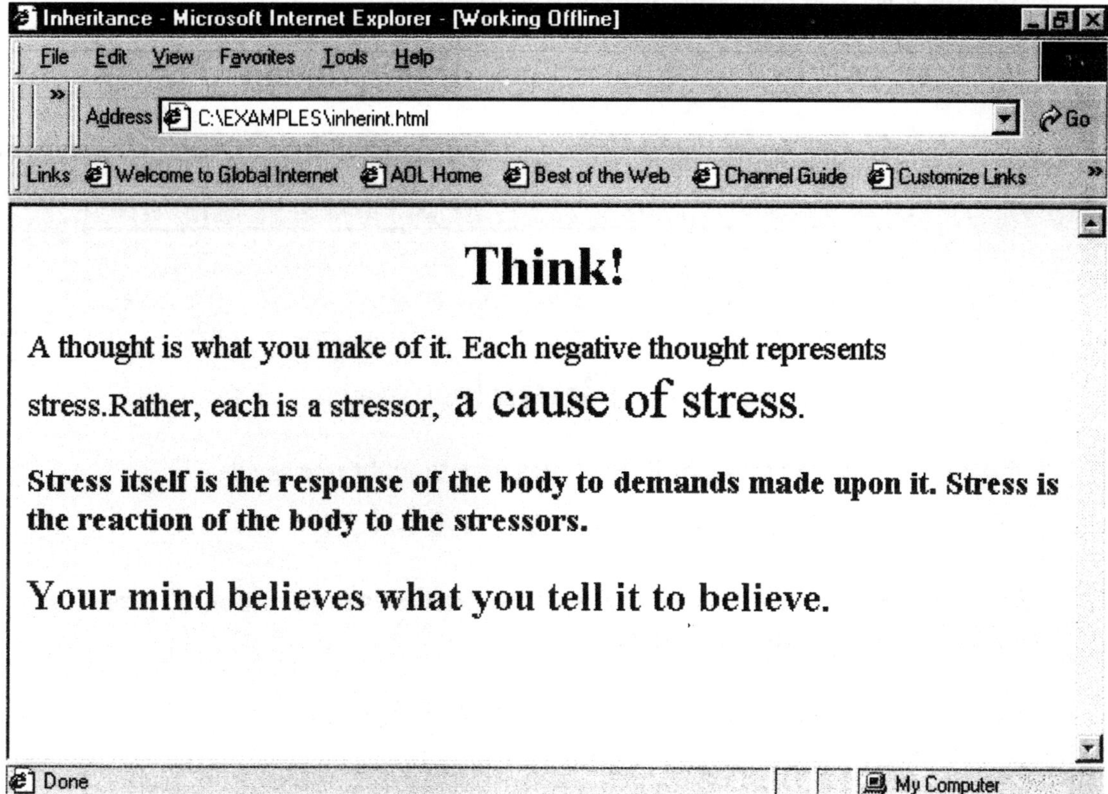

Diagram 3

- **Some child elements are not affected by the inheritance.**

To prove this exception, I amended the XHTML code shown in Diagram 2. The amended segment of the code is shown below.

```
<h3>Your mind believes what you tell it to believe.<br />
 <em>Stress Study</em> </h3>
```

- With this amendment, I saved the document as **inheritanceA.html**. This way, it became a different document.

- The amended document was previewed in the IE 5.5, as shown in Diagram 3A. You can see that the text contained within the child element <em> is not affected by the inheritance rule. In fact, it is shown in italic style, which is the characteristic of the <em> element. Thus, a specific property of a child element is not overridden by the property of the parent element.

The screen capture of the preview of the amended document

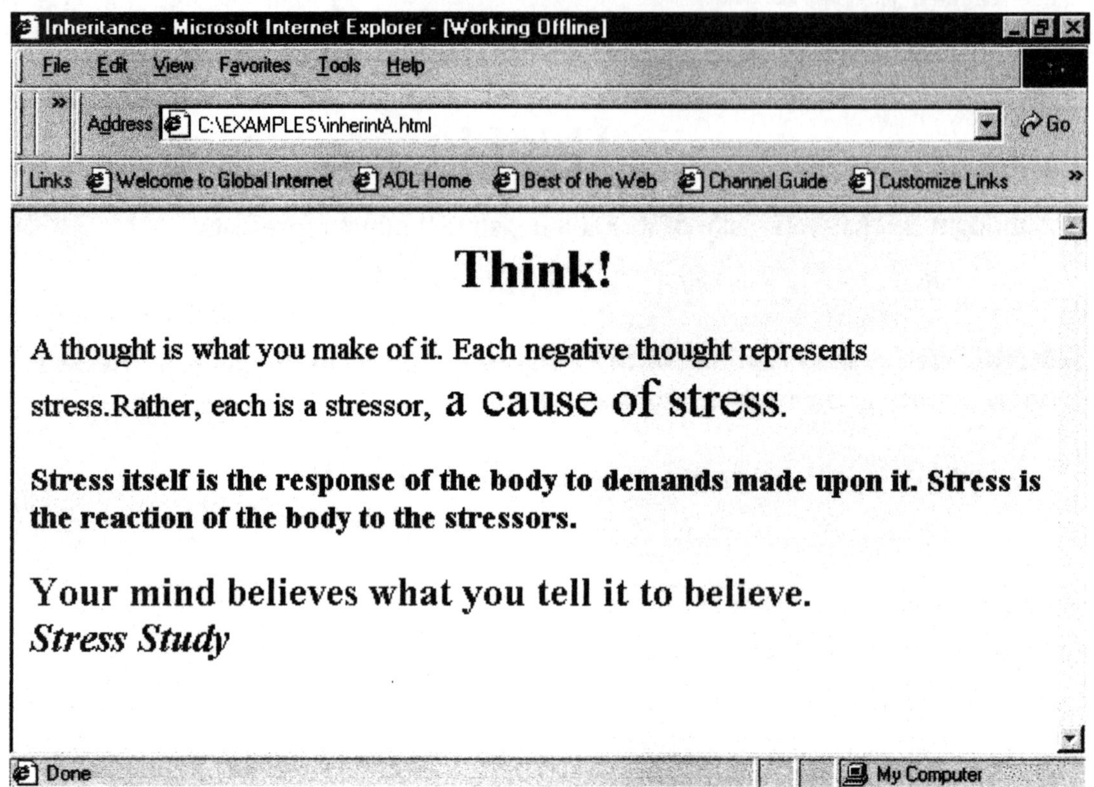

Diagram 3A

• Example 2

The purpose of this example is to demonstrate that the child element inherits the properties of its immediate parent. In order to demonstrate this concept, I have re-modelled example 7 in Chapter 6, by amending the XHTML document, so that it is re-written under XHTML 1.0 Strict DTD, and applies the CSS inheritance rule. Before proceeding any further, you should now find this example in this book.

• Your task involves the following amendments:-

- display this definition list on a yellow background. Set the font-size for the entire body of the document to 120% of the base size, font-style **bold**, and the text should be printed in the colour red.
- Set the new list heading, “Style inheritance & list presentation” as headline Level 2, by increasing the font size to 150%.
- dd – definition element <dd> – make its font-style normal, text colour white, and display it on a black background.
- For the above requirements, you have to write an internal style sheet, and insert it in the XHTML code shown in Diagram 7 in Chapter 6.
- Also replace ‘Transitional’ by ‘Strict’, ant ‘transitional’ by ‘strict’ in the original XHTML document, so that it can be validated W3C Validation Service as XHTML 1.0 Strict document. Prior to previewing it locally, you should validate your document for XML well-formedness and validity as XHTML 1.0 Strict document.

• Explanation

In Diagram 4, you must examine the XHTML document. You can see that it meets all above requirements It was validated by W3C, as shown below in the screen capture.

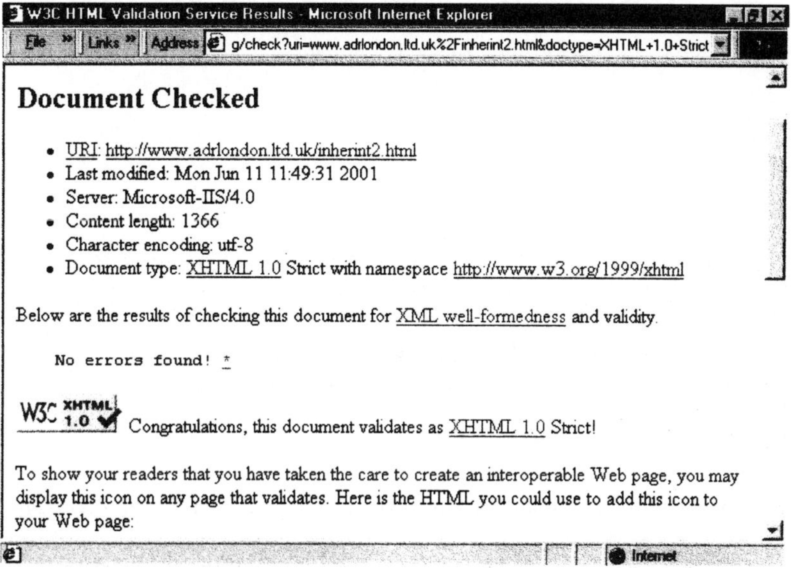

The preview of this document is shown in Diagram 5. In this screen capture, you cannot see the effects of colours, and thus cannot fully appreciate the outcome of amendments. It is therefore necessary to run the example on your PC.

Anyway, if you key in this example, you will be able to see all the colours and appreciate that the <dt> element has taken on the properties of the parent element <body>. All definition terms <dt> are displayed according to the properties of the parent <body> element.

On the other hand, the element<dd> has assigned all properties, which are given in style rule element <style>. Thus, all descriptions/ definitions are displayed in the same presentational style.

It should also be noted that the element <h2> has also taken on the properties of the <body> element, which is also its parent element. Note that the element <h2> has no children. This is why the immediate parent element for the element < dt> is the <body> element. Think!!!

The XHTML code for example 2 – inherint 2.html

```
<?xml version= "1.0" encoding = "UTF-8"?>
<!DOCTYPE html
                    PUBLIC "- //w3C//DTD XHTML 1.0 Strict//EN"
 "http://www.w3.org/TR/xhtml1/DTD/xhtml1-Strict.dtd">
<html xmlns= "http://www.w3.org/1999/xhtml" xml:lang= "en" lang= "en">
<head>
<title> Second example of inheritance </title>
<style type="text/css" >
body{font-size:120%;color:red;font-style:bold; background-color:yellow;}
h2{font-size:150%;}
dd{font-style:normal; color:white; background:black;}
</style>
</head>
<body>
<h2>Style inheritance & list presentation</h2>
<dl>
<dt>The Internet</dt>
        <dd> The Internet is a network of thousands of inter-connected computers
      world wide. The most popular part of it is the Web.</dd>
<dt> The Web</dt>
   <dd> The Web or the World Wide Web is a collection of text, graphics,
      sounds, video clips, pictures and other information arranged in pages
      with hyper links.</dd>
<dt> A Hyper Link</dt>
   <dd>The purpose of a hyper link is to enable the user to link the current
     document to another required document on the Web. The hyper link is in the Web page.</dd>
</dl>
</body></html>
```

Diagram 4

The document for example 2 previewed in IE 5.5

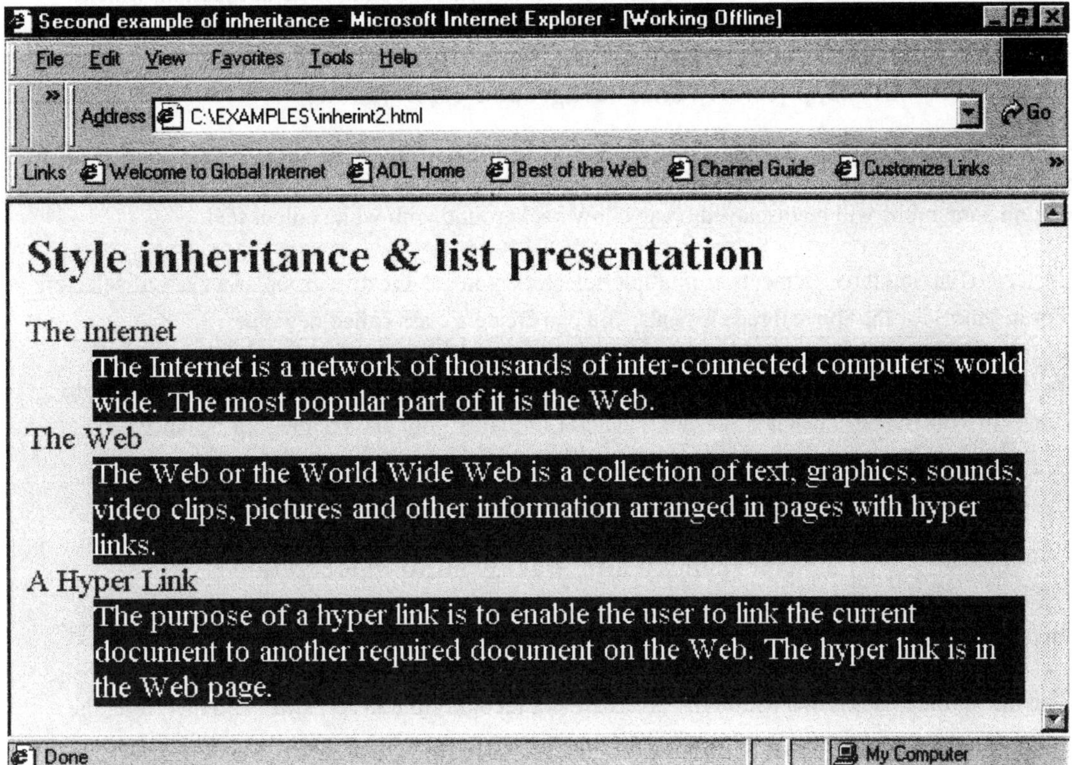

Diagram 5

It demonstrates the usefulness of style inheritance in creating and displaying some information organised in the form of a list.

• Classes

Once again, consider the following general format of the syntax for setting style sheet rules:-

selector{declaration}

It is further analysed as:

selector {property: value}

When it is put into practice, until now, XHTML elements, such as h1, h2 and the like are used as selectors. The declaration consists of property, such as 'color', and its value such as 'red'.

- You can also have multiple selectors. Multiple selectors can share the same declaration, which contains properties and values. For instance:

h1, h2, p {color:white; background-color:yellow}

In this case, each element has the same properties and their respective values. This style sheet rule means that all headings of Levels 1 and 2 will have white colour text on a yellow background. Similarly, all paragraphs will be displayed on a yellow background with white colour text.

- Instead of having three elements as multiple selectors, you can create a group or a class of selectors. For instance, for the above three elements, you can create a class called newtype.

- A class is then used as a class selector (or a class attribute selector), which may appear numerous times in a document. The class selector's general format is:- dot class name. For instance:-

. newtype ⇐ the class attribute selector or class as a selector is denoted in a style rule with a dot.

- For example: **. newtype {color:white; background-color:yellow}**

In fact, as such, it is unworkable in an XHTML document. Why?

- The fact of the mater is that names of classes are not recognisable in XHTML, and therefore, the **.class name** does not invoke class style by itself. So, how do you make it work?

The good new is that this problem is overcome by adding to the class attribute selector, the element to which the class style is required. For instance, the paragraph is marked up as shown below:-

< p class = "newtype"> .... </p>

The advantage of this method is the style will apply to all paragraphs of class **newtype** in the document.

• Example 3

Applying named styles - classes

- Your task is to design a Web page in order to display the text shown below in a box. Your design should make use of class attribute selectors in order to set styles.

- Write an internal style sheet for style sheet rules listed below the text for the document to be created. These styling rules will be applied to the same XHTML document.

Text for the document to be created

Success!

Get started now. Get started with the idea that you are going to succeed. Lack of success is not failure. It is simply some feedback.

Without some feedback we will never reach our goals!

The feedback information can help you to know where you are going wrong. Analyse it and take an appropriate action to put things right.

Go for it!

- Both headlines which are shown on the first and last lines should have the same style. Use any font properties and values.
- Paragraph – "Get …… feedback." and " paragraph – "The ---- right."
  For these two paragraphs, set one named style, so that they have the same look. Text should be of white colour on a black background. You can also apply some other properties and values of fonts.
- For paragraph – "without …..goals!" set another named style, which should apply to this paragraph only.
- The entire text should be displayed on a yellow background.
- Prior to viewing your saved document locally, check your code for XML well-formedness and validity, as XHTML Strict document.
- Use W3C Validation Service for validity, so that you are sure that it meets all requirements of XHTML Strict.

• Explanation

The XHTML code together with an internal style sheet is listed in Diagram 6. You must read it carefully. The document was checked and validated by W3C Validation Service. Its preview is shown in diagram 7. It meets all requirements.

It is suggested that you analyse the content of Diagram 6 in relation to the above discussion about classes, named styles and class attribute selector. Also critically examine Diagram 7, so that you can identify all styles set for this example.

XHTML code with an internal style sheet for example 3

```
<?xml version= "1.0" encoding = "UTF-8"?>
<!DOCTYPE html
                    PUBLIC "- //w3C//DTD XHTML 1.0 Strict//EN"
 "http://www.w3.org/TR/xhtml1/DTD/xhtml1-Strict.dtd">
<html xmlns= "http://www.w3.org/1999/xhtml" xml:lang= "en" lang= "en">
<head>
<title> Classs styles </title>

<style type="text/css" >
body{background-color:yellow}

p. start{
      font-size:120%;
      font-style:bold;
      color: white;
      background:black;
      }

p. feedback{
        font-style:italic;
        font-size:150%
       }

h1. headings{
        font-style:normal;
        font-size:150%;
        }
 </style>
 </head>
<body>
 <h1 class ="headings">Success!</h1>
 <p class ="start">
                      Get started now. Get started with the idea that you are going to succeed.
                      Lack of success is not failure. It is simply some feedback.</p>
<p class ="feedback">
                       Without some feedback we will never reach our goals!</p>
<p class ="start">
                      The feedback information can help you to know where you are going wrong.
                      Analyse it and take an appropriate action to put things right.</p>
<h1 class ="headings">Go for it!</h1>
</body></html>
```

Diagram 6

Document for example 3 previewed in IE 5.5

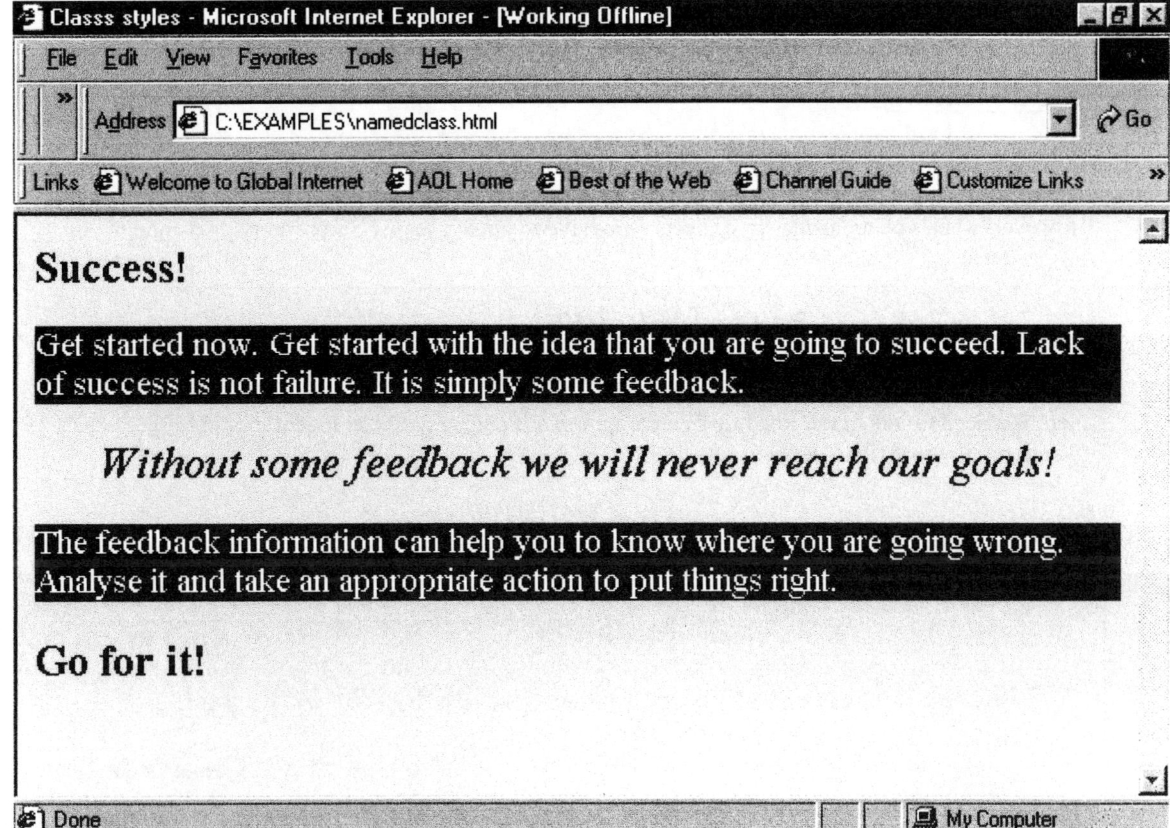

Diagram 7

• Alignment and indentation

• **Text alignment** – you have the following four options to select from:-

- **left margin -** left alignment aligns the text to the left of lines.
- **right alignment** - it aligns the text to the right end of lines.
- **centre alignment** - aligns the text in the centres of lines between the left and right margins.
- **Justify or justified** - aligns both the left and right end of lines.

The CSS property for text alignment is **text-align**. For instance, the following code in a style sheet will align the paragraph to the centre of a page.

```
p{text-align:centre}
```

• Indentation

You have already met the <blockquote> element. Any text contained within this element is intended. The element is still in Strict DD, and thus it can be used for both quoted and unquoted blocks of text. However, when you are using style sheets, you have to make use of CSS property: text-indent.
For instance:

```
h4 { text-indent:5%}
```

Here, 5% is the amount of available space within the block. It is very a useful CSS property, when there is a need to indent the first line of a paragraph. Of course, you can indent the first line of each paragraph, if you wish to do so.

• Example 4

A Quotation

I like the dreams of the future rather than the history of the past.

Who said that? Thomas Jefferson

Success is having vibrant health. Success is being the person you want to be, having the things you want to have, and doing the things you want to do. Being, having, and doing do not necessarily mean accumulating possessions and money. Being, having and doing mean exploring life in hundreds of different ways, living life to its fullest.

There is enough for the needy but not for the greedy – Mahatma Gandhi

- The task is to design a Web page in order to display the text shown in a box above. Your design should be based on the following requirements:-
- Background colour - yellow or any colour of your choice.
- Heading - it must be aligned to the centre of the line, font style *italic*, and text should be in red colour. Make it Level 1 heading, with font size 120% of the base size.

- Paragraph - I like --- past. – a paragraph to be displayed in normal font style, font style 120% of the base size, and text colour grey. Align the text to the left margin.
- Paragraph - Who… Jefferson – align the text to the right, font style normal, size 140% of the base size, and text colour green.
- Paragraph – Success---fullest – make it Level 3 headline, font size 110% of the base size, justified, and text display red.
- Last paragraph – font size 180% of the base size, font style italic, text colour blue, but it must be in dented by 10% of the space available on the line, so that the first line is intended.
- You must write and save an external style sheet, so that it can be linked to the separate XHTML file, which contains the information on a Web page.
- Prior to previewing your document locally in any user agent, use W3C HTML Validation Service in order to check your **.html** file for XML well-formedness and validity. You can also use the same W3Cservice to validate your **.css** file.

• Explanation

For this example, you have to design two files.

File 1: External style sheet saved as style4A .css. This files contains presentational requirements for the XHTML document. See Diagram 8.

- Note the use of semicolons **(;)** between the properties and at the end of the last property in the list as shown below.

h4 { font-size:180%; font-style:italic; color:blue; text-indent:10%;}

It is advisable to place the semicolon at the end of the last property as well.

File 2: The XHTML code saved as style4.html. It contains the XHTML document.

- The file style4A.css is linked to file style4.html, because this file contains the href attribute. This attribute links both files together.
- The CSS file was validated by W3C Validator service. It stated, "To show your readers that you've taken the care to create an interoperable Web page, you may display this icon on any page that validates…."

External style sheet saved as style4A.css for example 4

```
/* This style sheet is to be linked to style4*/
body{
   background-color: #ffff00;
   }
h1{
   font-size:120%;
   font-style:italic;color:#ff0000;
   text-align:center;
  }
h2{
   font-size:140%;
   font-style:normal;
   color:#008000;
   text-align:right;
  }
h3{
   font-size:160%;
   color:#ff0000;
 text-align:justify;
}
p{
  font-size:120%;
  font-style:normal;
  color:#808080;
  text-align:left;
 }
h4 {
   font-size:180%;
   font-style:italic;
   color:#0000ff;
  text-indent:10%;
}
```

Diagram 7

- The code shown in Diagram 14 was also validated by W3C service. The preview of the document is shown in Diagram 15. It meets all requirements. It is suggested that you run these two files on your own PC, so that you can gain first hand experience of creating external style sheets and linking it to the XHTML document.

The XHTML code for example 4 – style4.html

```
<?xml version= "1.0" encoding = "UTF-8"?>
<!DOCTYPE html
            PUBLIC "- //w3C//DTD XHTML 1.0 Strict//EN"
 "http://www.w3.org/TR/xhtml1/DTD/xhtml1-strict.dtd">
<html xmlns= "http://www.w3.org/1999/xhtml" xml:lang= "en" lang= "en">
<head>
<title> CSS Application </title>

<link rel ="stylesheet" href="style4A.css" />

</head>
<body>

  <h1>A Quotation </h1>
  <p>
    I like the dreams of the future rather than the history of the past.</p>

<h2>
    Who said that? ><cite>Thomas Jefferson</cite></h2>

<h3 >  Success is having vibrant health. Success is being the person you want to be, having
       the things you want to have, and doing the things you want to do. Being, having, and
       doing do not necessarily mean accumulating possessions and money. Being, having
       and doing mean exploring life in hundreds of different ways, living life to its fullest.
</h3>
 <h4> There is enough for the needy but not for the greedy - Mahatma Gandhi </h4>
</body>
</html>
```

Diagram 8

Indeed, by now, you can appreciate that styles are defined within rules. A set of such rules is called cascading style sheet (CSS) or just a style sheet. There are two types of style sheets, namely internal and external. An internal style sheet is written within the XHTML document. On the other hand, the external style sheet is a separate document, which is saved as **. css** file. This file has to be linked to the XHTML document. The link element for creating the link, and making it work is in the XHTML document.

The preview of document created for example 4

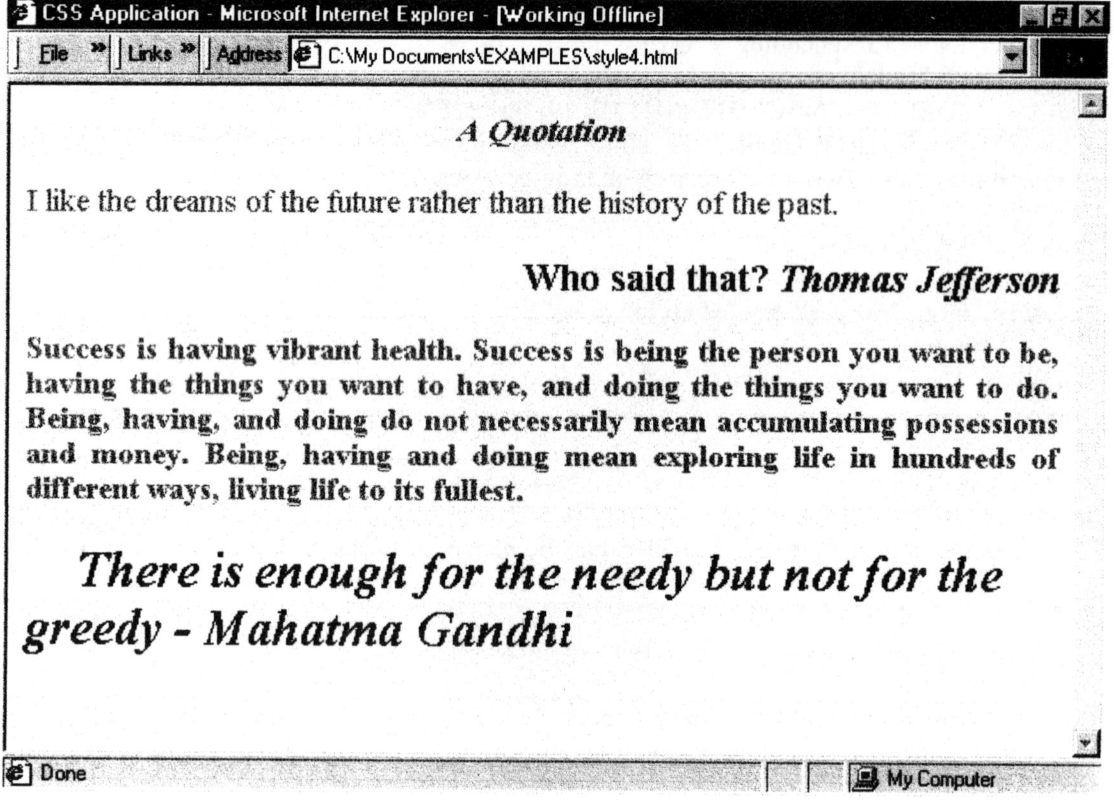

Diagram 8

Often the use of styles concerns the application of fonts, colours and alignment. This chapter has introduced you to some basic ideas and demonstrated by means of solved examples, methods of using these CSS techniques. You will learn more about CSS techniques as the book progresses.

Chapter 9

Handling Tables

The prime aims of this chapter are as follows:-

- to enable you to understand that the structure of a table as a two-dimensional form consists of rows and columns
- to construct some tables in order to present information

By reading and practising techniques that are demonstrated in this chapter, you should be able :-

- to create a simple two-dimensional table for the presentation of information
- to apply techniques for controlling rows and columns in a variety of ways
- to create a complex table involving grouping of columns for the presentation of information
- to create both internal and external Cascading Style Sheets for presentational and styling information

• What is a table?

The practical definition of a table for this book is that a table is a two-dimensional form, in which information can be stored or recorded. A column is the vertical section, and a row is the horizontal section of a table. The intersections of rows and columns in a table are known as cells, where the information is stored/recorded. In fact, a table can also be visualised as a number of lists placed side by side together. For instance, the figure shown in Diagram 1 is a table. It consists of four rows and four columns. Its size is generally expressed as four-by-four (4x4). It means four rows and four columns. In computer programming, a table is usually known as 'a matrix'.

In order to organise the table and store information in it, its structure is divided into recognisable parts. These are known as **header**, **body** and **footer**. In addition, a table usually also has a **title or caption**. Furthermore, you can add a border to a table by means of the **border attribute,** which the <table> element allows.

All of these aspects of a table's structure are identified through solved examples in this chapter.

An empty table consists of four rows and four columns

Diagram 1

XHTML elements for constructing a table

Element	tags	Function
table element	<table>...</table>	It marks the start and end of the entire table.
header row	<th>---</th>	It sets each header row of a table and indicates the end of each header row. Within these tags are the text for each heading of a table.
table row	<tr>....</tr>	It sets each row of a table. It contains <th> and <td> elements. It a is sub-section within a table. </tr> marks the end of each row.
data/information	<td>....</td>	In each cell of a table data is entered from the left to the right. This element marks the beginning of data entry into each cell, and the end of data entry into each cell. This is how columns are created.

Table 1

- In XHTML, all the contents of a table are contained within the **table element, <table>**. All other elements, namely:

  <caption>,<thead> <tbody>,<tfoot> and <tr>

are included within it. The elements listed in Table 1 are required for constructing a basic structure of a table and placing information into each cell of a table.

• Example 1

The task is to convert the following simple table with its title into an XHTML document. Save it as **simple.html file**. Prior to previewing it in IE5.5 or any other user agent, check it for XML well-formedness and validity as XHTML 1.0 Strict document. Use W3C Validation Service to validate it.

A Simple Table

Date	Invoice No.	Amount
01.05.2001	A00101	£750.00
12.05.2001	A00200	£1250.00
30.05.2001	A00324	£1376.89

• Explanation

The XHTML code for this example is in Diagram 3.

- The above table is surrounded by a border. The thickness or width of edges of the border around the table, and between its cells is measured in pixels. If you do not set this width, the browser will automatically set it. Some browsers set it as zero, which is their default value, and it means no border. On the other hand, some other browsers set it as one pixel (default). For this example, I have declared it:

<table border = “2”>

Note that it is a numerical value and written within double quotation marks.

- This table has its title or caption. It must be declared within the <table> element. The code for it is

<caption> A Simple Table</caption>

This segment of the code is essential when you want to attach a title to a table. Thus, it is an optional requirement..

- The next requirement is to create a header (table head). This table has three headings. Therefore, the table header is divided into three headings, which are Date, Invoice No., and Amount. The segment of the code for creating these headings is:-

```
<tr>
    <th>   Date </th>
    <th>   Invoice No.</th>
    <th>   Amount </th></tr>
```

- **<th> element must be contained within the <tr> element as shown above.**

- Each **<th>** is for an individual cell in the table head. The next requirement is to place data under each heading. The data items are entered in the body cells of a table body. The body of the table is below the header row (table head). In this case, it contains only three rows for data entry. The data has to be entered in each individual cell. The element **<td>** performs this task. This element must be contained within the **<tr>** element. The segment of the code for entering data in cells of the first row is as follows:-

```
<tr>
    <td>   01.05.2001</td>
    <td>   A00101</td>
    <td>   £750.00</td></tr>
```

- This process is repeated for entering data in the remaining cells of the table body.

The preview of a document for example 1 - simple.html

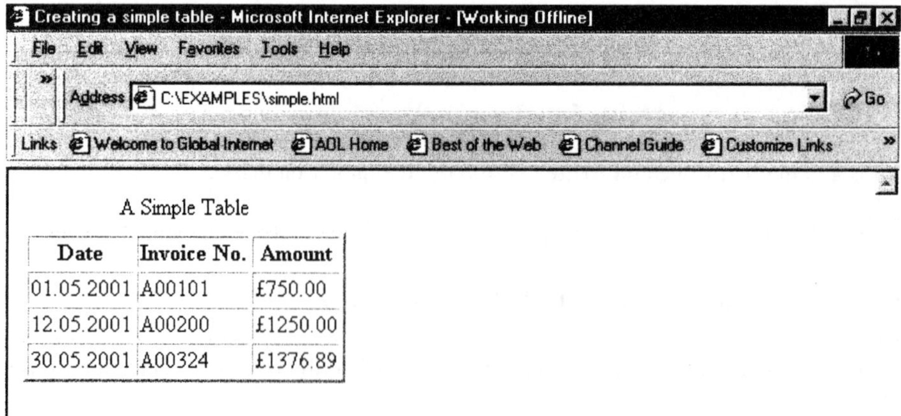

Diagram 2

- Prior to previewing this document in the IE 5.5, the document was validated by W3C Validation Service. See the screen capture in Diagram 2. It has met all requirements.

The XHTML code for example 1 – simple.html

```
<?xml version= "1.0" encoding = "UTF-8"?>
<!DOCTYPE html
        PUBLIC "- //w3C//DTD XHTML 1.0 Strict//EN"
 "http://www.w3.org/TR/xhtml1/DTD/xhtml1- Strict.dtd">
<html xmlns="http://www.w3.org/1999/xhtml" xml:lang="en" lang= "en">
<head>
<title> Creating a table</title>
</head>
<body>
          <table border ="2">
          <caption> A Simple Table</caption>
 <tr>
        <th>   Date </th>
        <th>   Invoice No.</th>
         <th>   Amount </th>
</tr>
 <tr>    <td>   01.05.2001</td>
        <td>   A00101</td>
        <td>   £750.00</td>
</tr>
 <tr>
        <td> 12.05.2001</td>
         <td> A00200</td>
        <td> £1250.00 </td>
</tr>
<tr>
         <td> 30.05.2001</td>
        <td> A00324</td>
        <td> £1376.89</td>
</tr>
</table>
</body>
</html>
```

Diagram 3

• Alignment of text in cells

You can align text in a cell of a row by means of **align attribute** or **valign attribute**. The difference between these two attributes is that valign sets vertical alignment, whilst the align attribute creates the horizontal alignment. These attributes, values and a general syntax format are listed in Table 2.

The Alignment attributes

Attribute	Value allowed	syntax format
. **align**	centre, left, right, and justify	**<tr align = "center">** • Since the alignment of data/text in all cells in a row has the same format this code aligns text in the centre of each cell in a particular row. • As <td> and <th> elements are declared within the <tr> element, this applies to data within these elements.
. **valign**	top, bottom, middle, and baseline	. **<tr valign = " top">** • It also affects all cells in a row like the align.

Table 2

• Example 2

Your task is to design an XHTML document for previewing and displaying the table titled, **Senior Staff Confidential File**, shown below. You should make sure that all headings and data entries are aligned horizontally in the centre of each cell. You must save it, and check it for XML well-formedness and validity as XHTML 1.0 Strict document.

Senior Staff Confidential File

Surname and Initials	Job Title	Sex	NI.No.	Emp.started	Current Salary
Smith, J.M.	Technical Director	Male	MN123456BY	12.12.1998	£55000
Taylor, R.	Sales Director	Male	YY654321BA	23.10.1978	£59000
Blankett, N.Y.	IT Director	Female	VH098765CV	01.01.1988	£44000

The XHTM code for example 2 – tabletwo.html (cont. in Diagram 4A)

```
<?xml version= "1.0" encoding = "UTF-8"?>
<!DOCTYPE html
        PUBLIC "- //w3C//DTD XHTML 1.0 Strict//EN"
 "http://www.w3.org/TR/xhtml1/DTD/xhtml1- Strict.dtd">
<html xmlns="http://www.w3.org/1999/xhtml" xml:lang="en" lang= "en">
<head>
<title>Table and Alignment </title>
</head>
<body>
<table border ="2">
<caption> Senior Staff Confidential File</caption>
<tr align ="center">
                <th> Surname and Initials </th>
                <th>  Job Title</th>
                <th>  Sex </th>
                <th>  NI.No.  </th>
                <th>  Emp.started </th>
                <th> Current Salary  </th>
</tr>
<tr align ="center">
                <td>Smith, J.M.</td>
                <td>Technical Director</td>
                 <td >Male </td>
                <td> MN123456BY</td>
                <td> 12.12.1998</td>
                <td> £55000</td>
</tr>
```

Diagram 4

The XHTM code for example 2 – tabletwo.html (cont. from Diagram 4A)

```
<tr align ="center">
                    <td > Taylor, R. </td>
                    <td > Sales Director</td>
                    <td >  Male</td>
                    <td > YY654321BA</td>
                    <td > 23.10.1978</td>
                    <td > £59000</td>
</tr>
<tr align ="center">
                    <td > Blankett, N.Y. </td>
                    <td > IT Director</td>
                    <td > Female </td>
                    <td > VH098765CV</td>
                    <td >  01.01.1988</td>
                    <td >  £44000</td>
</tr>
</table>
</body>
</html>
```

Diagram 4A

• Explanation

The structure of an XHTML code listed in Diagrams 4 & 4A follows the same pattern as for example 1 .However, you should examine carefully:-

- how in each cell each relevant heading is coded in the table head (row). Since it is required that each heading should be horizontally centred in each cell in the table head, the segment of the code for all six headings is written as <tr align ="center">. Since all <td>...</td> elements with their respective data for all headings are contained within the <tr> ...<.tr> element, this alignment declaration applies to all headings.
- For data entry in each row in the table body for each row, <tr align ="center"> is essential.
- The document was saved, and then presented to W3C Validation Service. W3C Results, Congratulations, this document validates as XHTML 1.0 Strict! See its preview in Diagram 5.

Preview of a document in IE 5.5 for example 2 tabletwo.html

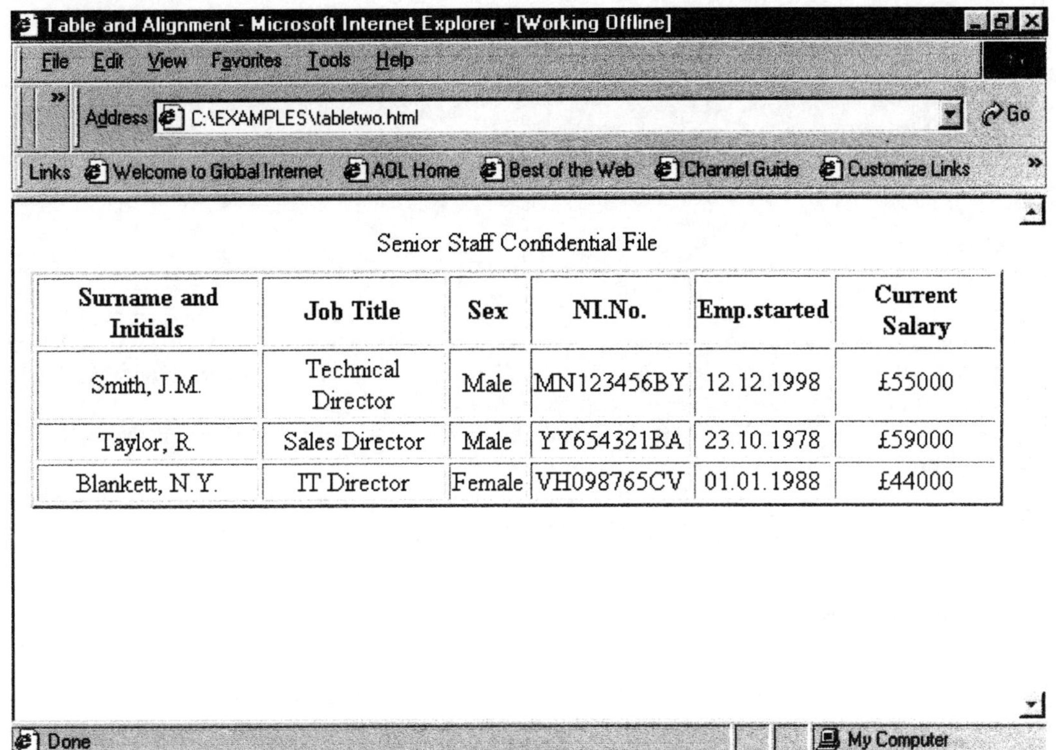

Surname and Initials	Job Title	Sex	NI.No.	Emp.started	Current Salary
Smith, J.M.	Technical Director	Male	MN123456BY	12.12.1998	£55000
Taylor, R.	Sales Director	Male	YY654321BA	23.10.1978	£59000
Blankett, N.Y.	IT Director	Female	VH098765CV	01.01.1988	£44000

Diagram 5

• Table alignment in a document

• Example 3

A table entitled, **"World Atlas Contents"** and some text are shown below in the shaded area. The task is to design an XHTML document in order to place the table in a border, and then the bordered table is to be displayed on the right side of the page (screen). The text should be placed on the left side of the table as a single block of three paragraphs. Save it as **earth.html**.

Prior to previewing it in the IE 5.5 or any other browser, use W3C Validation Service to check it for XML well-formedness as an XHTML 1.0 Transitional document.

World Atlas Contents

Topic	Page No.
Geographical Information	1
The Planet Earth	3
The Solar System	5
The Earth's Structure	7
The Atmosphere	12
Seas and Oceans	17
The Sun	21
The Moon	26
The Stars	30

Earth is the planet which we inhabit, a nearly spherical body. Every twenty-four hours, it rotates from west to east round an imaginary line called its axis. This axis has its extremities, the North and South Poles. In the course of a year it completes one revolution round the sun.
The Earth is nearly 4600 million years old. Life as we know it has evolved over the last 40 to 50 million years.
The Earth's surface layer of rock is known as the crust. It is around 65 Km(40 miles) deep in areas of land mass, and 6 Km (4 miles) deep under the oceans.

• Explanation

The code for Example 3 is listed in Diagrams 6 & 6A. If you do not specify where a table should be displayed, the browser will automatically display it to the left side of the screen. Why? Because it is the default place for displaying a table.

Therefore, in the <table> element, you should use **align attribute** to declare that it must be displayed on the right side of the page. In order to draw a border around the table, you should also include border attribute together with its width in pixels. The segment of the code for these requirements is shown below:-

<table border ="2" align ="right">.

- I have used element <div> which is a generic block level element in order to display the text. If you wish you can implement <p> element instead. The remaining of the code in Diagrams 6 & 6A is straightforward. The document was checked by W3C Validation Service as XHTML Transitional 1.0 document. See the screen capture in Diagram 7. It is displayed as required.

• How can the text be displayed on the left side of the table?

By default the text starts on the left the document.

XHTML code for example 3 – earth.html (cont. in Diagram 6A)

```
<?xml version= "1.0" encoding = "UTF-8"?>
<!DOCTYPE html
        PUBLIC "- //w3C//DTD XHTML 1.0 Transitional//EN"
 "http://www.w3.org/TR/xhtml1/DTD/xhtml1- Transitional.dtd">
<html xmlns="http://www.w3.org/1999/xhtml" xml:lang="en" lang= "en">
<head>
<title>Table alignment relative to a document</title>
</head>
<body>
<table border ="2" align ="right">
<caption> World Atlas Contents  </caption>
  <tr>
        <th> Topic </th>
       <th> Page No.</th> </tr>
 <tr>
      <td>Geographical Information  </td>
      <td> 1 </td>
</tr>
 <tr>
        <td>The Planet Earth </td>
        <td> 3</td>
</tr>
<tr>
     <td>The Solar System </td>
     <td> 5</td>
</tr>
<tr>
    <td> The Earth's Structure</td>
    <td>  7</td>
</tr>
<tr>
    <td> The Atmosphere</td>
    <td>  12</td>
</tr>
<tr>
    <td> Seas and Oceans</td>
    <td> 17</td></tr>
```

Diagram 6

XHTML code for example 3– earth.html (cont. from Diagram 6)

```
<tr>
   <td> The Sun</td>
   <td> 21</td>
</tr>
<tr>
   <td> The Moon</td>
   <td> 26</td>
</tr>
<tr>
   <td> The Stars </td>
   <td> 30 </td>
</tr>
</table>
<div>
   Earth is the planet which we inhabit, a nearly spherical body. Every twenty-four hours, it
   rotates from west to east round an imaginary line called its axis. This axis has its
   extremities, the North and South Poles. In the course of a year it completes one revolution
   round the sun. <br />
  The Earth is nearly 4600 million years old. Life as we know it has evolved over the last 40
   to 50 million  years.<br />
 The Earth's surface layer of rock is known as the crust. It is around 65 Km(40 miles) deep in
  areas of land mass, and 6 Km (4 miles) deep under  the oceans.</div>
 </body>
</html>
```

Diagram 6A

- Note that your document with <table border ="2" align ="right"> as XHTML Strict document will not be validated successfully as XHTML 1.0 Strict document. You will get the following result from W3C:-

```
Below are the results of checking this document for XML well-formedness and validity.
Line 12, column 27:
<table border ="2" align ="right" >
                          ^
Error: there is no attribute "align" for this element (in this HTML version) (explanation...)
Sorry, this document does not validate as XHTML 1.0 Strict.
```

This is really a big difference between XHTML Transitional and Strict versions.

- Apply CSS to align a table in XHTML Strict document - this is explained by means of solved example. See CSS.

Document Earth is previewed in IE5.5 – earth.html

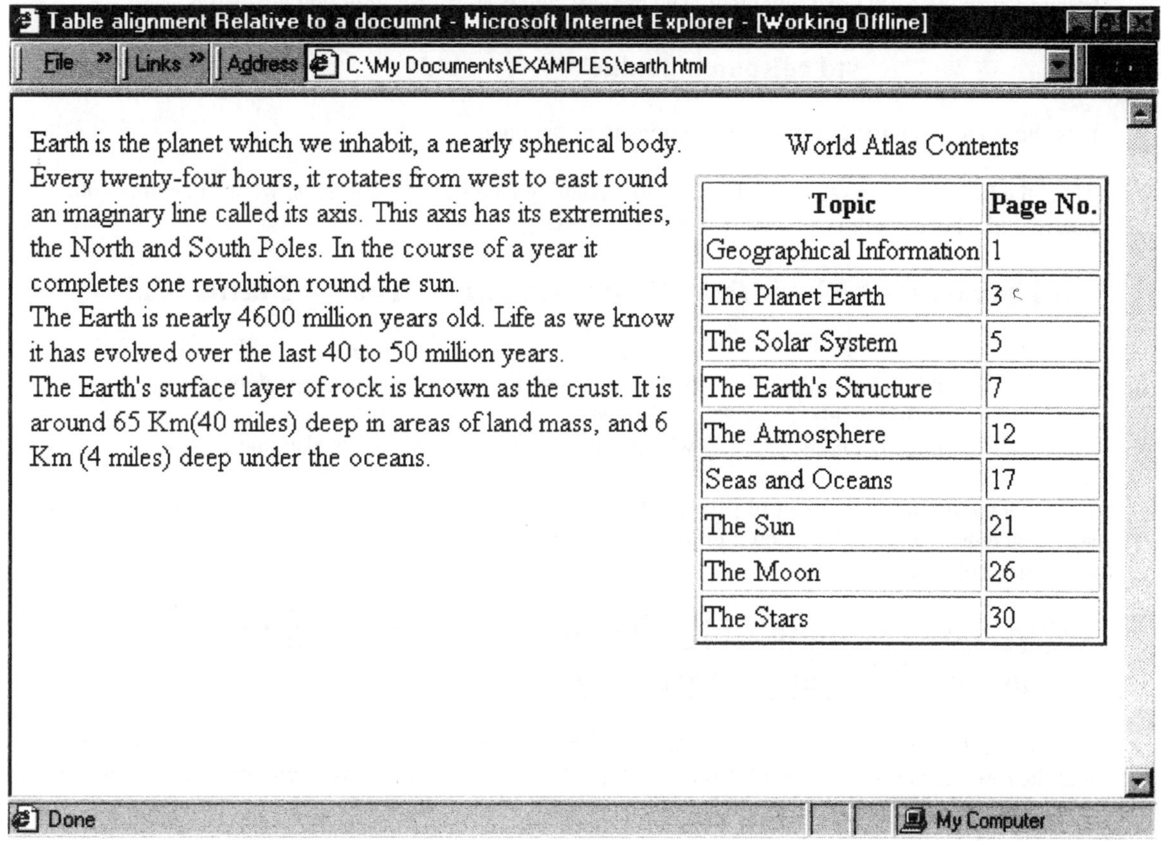

Topic	Page No.
Geographical Information	1
The Planet Earth	3
The Solar System	5
The Earth's Structure	7
The Atmosphere	12
Seas and Oceans	17
The Sun	21
The Moon	26
The Stars	30

Diagram 7

. Controlling rows and columns

You can think of a table as consisting of a number of boxes or compartments, where you can place or store some data. This box or compartment in 'table terminology' is known as a cell. The size of this cell can be manipulated. This is achieved by means of **colspan** and **rowspan** attributes. For instance, you can make a single cell which occupies three columns. In other words, the cell will span over the next three columns. The effect of this column manipulation is that three consecutive columns merge.

So, you decide how many columns a cell should occupy (span). Similarly, you can span more than one row per cell, and thus merge rows.

• Colspan attribute

For example, if you want a cell to occupy three columns of a table, you can achieve it by apply the **colspan** attribute on the <**td** >element. The general syntax form for applying colspan is:-

<td colspan = "value">--------</td>

here the value is a number/integer of columns to be spanned.

Thus, the following is a segment of a code for spanning a cell over 3 columns, whose height is 100 pixels, and whose width is also set to 100 pixels wide.

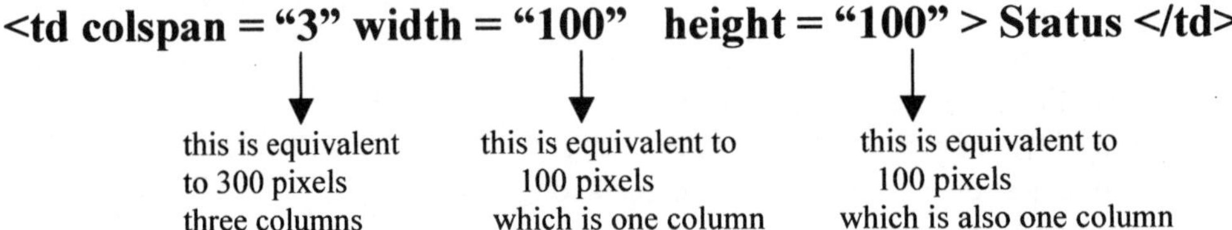

Note that the minimum number of pixels for setting either width or height is 100 pixels. For any large size, you must increase the given number by 100 pixels. For instance "value = 400" is equivalent to 4 columns - 100 times 4.

• Why have I set both width and height as a single column whilst the cell occupies three columns?

The reason for setting the column as a single column despite the fact that it occupies three columns is that the row has not been manipulated by applying the corresponding **rowspan** attribute, which is discussed below:-

• rowspan attribute

The general syntax format for setting the **rowspan** is:-

<td rowspan = "value">.....**</td>**

here the value is an integer/number of rows to be spanned. For instance:-

<td rowspan = "4">....</td> will span the cell over rows.

. Example 4

The aim of this example is to demonstrate the effects of rows and columns attributes in creating a table of rows and columns, where any cell covers more than one row or column.

The XHTML code for example 4 – span.html

```
<?xml version= "1.0" encoding = "UTF-8"?>
<!DOCTYPE html
        PUBLIC "- //w3C//DTD XHTML 1.0 Strict//EN"
 "http://www.w3.org/TR/xhtml1/DTD/xhtml1- strict.dtd">
<html xmlns="http://www.w3.org/1999/xhtml" xml:lang="en" lang= "en">
<head>
<title>Spanning Rows and Columns</title>
</head>
<body>
<table border = "2">
<caption> Experimenting with Rows and Columns formation</caption>
<tr>
      <td colspan ="6" >column span 6 columns </td>
      <td colspan = "4">column span  4 columns</td>
      <td rowspan = "6" colspan ="4">size of this cell= 6x4 </td>
 </tr>
 <tr>
     <td colspan ="3">column span 3 columns  </td>
     <td colspan ="3"> column span 3 columns </td>
     <td colspan ="4"> column span 4 columns </td>
 </tr>
</table>
</body></html>
```

Diagram 8

. Explanation

The idea is to show you how you can devise a table without an equal number of cells in each row, and each column. It is highly unlikely that you will often draw a table like the one shown in a screen capture in Diagram 9, but it does demonstrate the principle of using colspan and rawspan attributes. The XHTML code listed in Diagram 8 is simple enough as both colspan and rowspan have already been discussed above. It was validated as XHTML Strict document by W3C. You should examine it carefully, and match its outcome in Diagram 9.

The screen capture in Diagram 9 illustrates that you can merge either rows or column as you wish. In this display, you can see that all cells except the last cell (far right cell) have spanned over a number of columns written in each cell. Each of these cells occupies a single column. On the other hand, the last cell whose size is stated as 6x4 occupies 6 rows and 4 columns. The segment of the code for creating this cell and the information written in it is as shown below:-

<td rowspan = "6" colspan ="4">size of this cell= 6x4 </td>.

Here, both rowspan and colspan have been implemented.

The document for example 4 previewed in IE5.5 – span.html

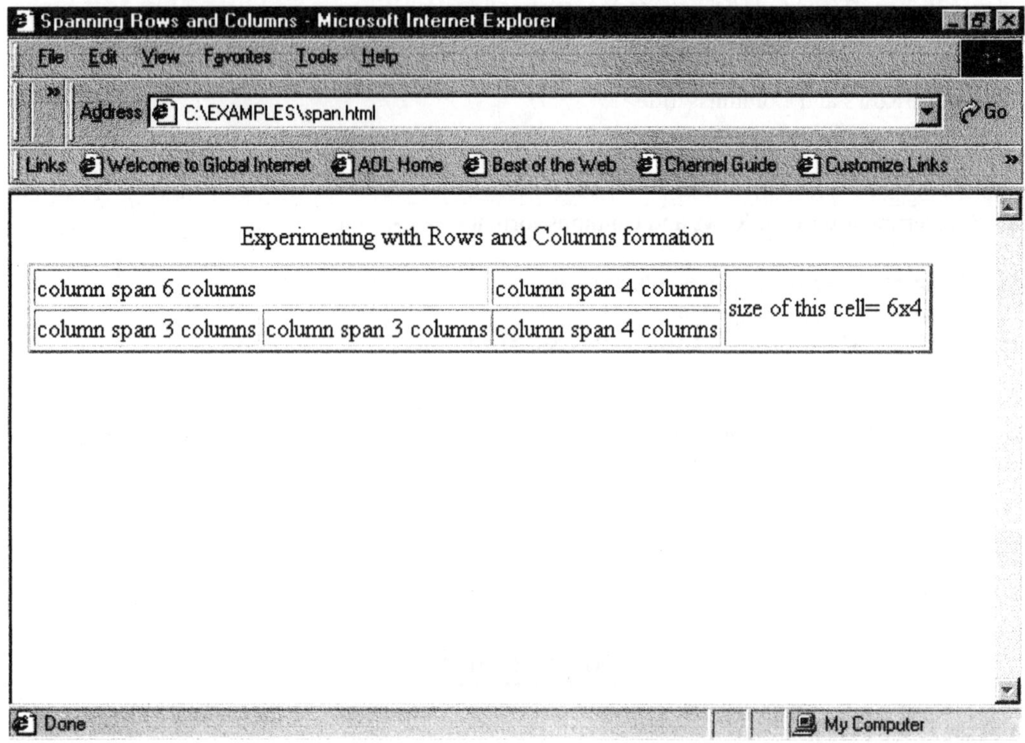

Diagram 9

• How can you style a table by means of CSS rules?

You can apply styles to tables. The current version of CSS is CSS2, which incorporates all CSS1 properties. In addition, CSS2 has also added some properties for tables. The problem is that not many browsers have so far implemented CSS2. However, it is hoped that by the time you read this book, CSS2 is widely handled by almost all major browsers and other user agents. However, some aspects of styling tables are illustrated in this chapter. For tables, you can include an internal style sheet in your XHTML document code or construct a separate external style sheet, which can be linked to the correct XHTML document by means of link the attribute. Both types of style sheets are constructed for tables in this chapter.

• Example 5

The purpose of this solved example is to demonstrate the application of font and colour properties of CSS as applied to a table entitled, " Senior Staff Confidential File" in Example 2. The following rules should be included in the internal style sheet for this example:-

- caption – font style should be italic, and its size 150% of the base font size. Align it in the centre of the line on a black background, but the text should be white.
- all six headings should be displayed on a red background and be aligned in the centre of each cell.
- each entry should be aligned in the centre of each cell and must be displayed on a yellow background.

• Your task is to design an XHTML document in which the above styling rules are included. Save it, and prior to previewing it in IE5.5.5 or any other user agent/browser, use W3C Validation Service to validate your document.

The XHTML code for example 5 – tabletwoA.html (cont. in Diagram 10A)

```
<?xml version= "1.0" encoding = "UTF-8"?>
<!DOCTYPE html
        PUBLIC "- //w3C//DTD XHTML 1.0 Strict//EN"
 "http://www.w3.org/TR/xhtml1/DTD/xhtml1- Strict.dtd">
<html xmlns="http://www.w3.org/1999/xhtml" xml:lang="en" lang= "en">
<head>
<title>Table and Alignment </title>
<style type ="text/css" >
                    td{background:#FFFF00;align ="center" }        /* yellow */
                    th{background:#FF0000;align="center"}          /* red */
                    caption{
                          font-style:italic; font-size:150%;
                          align:"center";
                          color:#FFFFFF;background:#000000}       /*black */
</style>
```

Diagram 10

The XHTML code for example 5 –tabletwoA.html (cont. from Diagram 10)

```
</head>
<body>
<table border ="2">
<caption> Senior Staff Confidential File</caption>
<tr>
        <th> Surname and Initials </th>
        <th>   Job Title</th>
        <th>  Sex </th>
        <th>   NI.No.   </th>
        <th> Emp.started </th>
        <th>Current Salary  </th></tr>
<tr>
        <td>Smith, J.M.</td>
        <td>Technical Director</td>
        <td>Male </td>
        <td> MN123456BY</td>
        <td> 12.12.1998</td>
        <td> £55000</td></tr>
<tr>
        <td> Taylor, R. </td>
        <td> Sales Director</td>
        <td>  Male</td>
        <td> YY654321BA</td>
        <td> 23.10.1978</td>
        <td> £59000</td></tr>
<tr>
        <td> Blankett, N.Y. </td>
        <td> IT Director</td>
        <td> Female </td>
        <td> VH098765CV</td>
        <td>  01.01.1988</td>
        <td>  £44000</td></tr>
</table>
</body></html>
```

Diagram 10A

•Explanation

In order to design an XHTML document for this exercise, I have re-written the code listed in diagrams 4 & 4A in this chapter., The internal style sheet rules are listed in the <head> section. In diagrams 10,I have highlighted the internal style sheet by writing it on a shaded area.

• As per requirement, it was validated by W3C Validation Service. The outcome was:
"Below are the results of checking this document for XML well-formedness and validity. No errors found! Congratulations, this document validates as XHTML 1.0 Strict!" See the display in Diagram 11.

A preview of Table: Senior Staff Confidential File in IE5

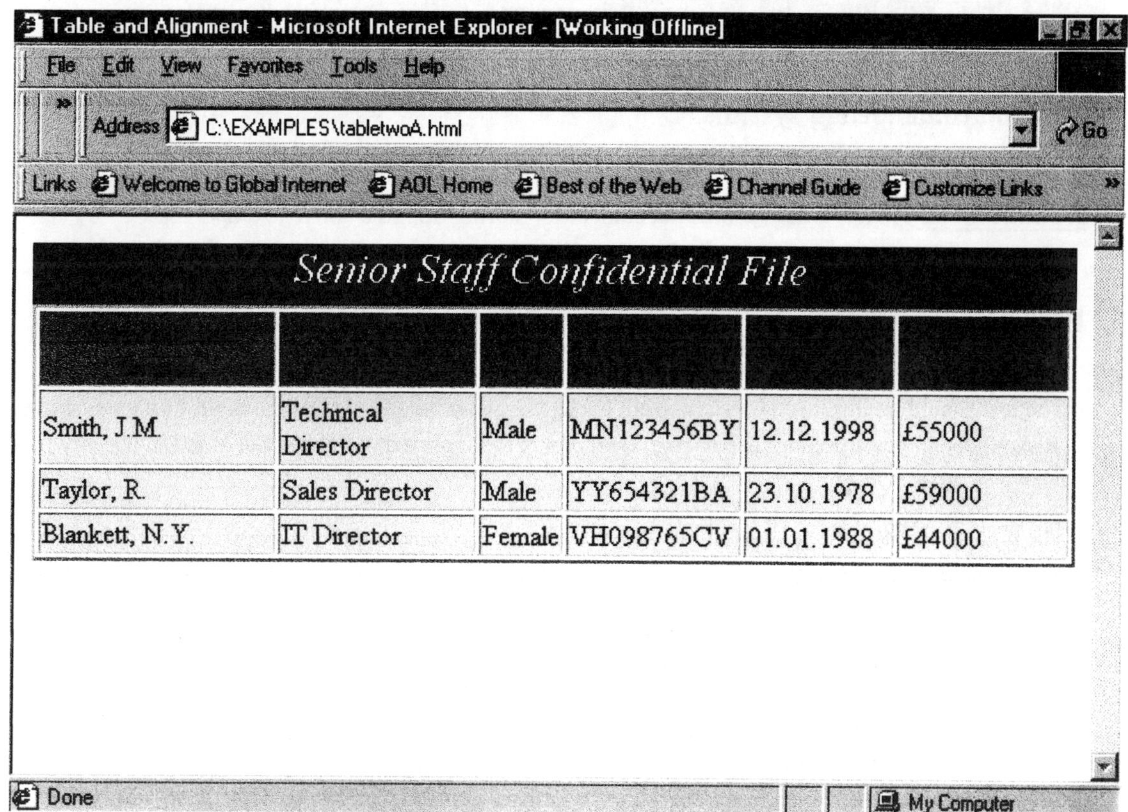

Senior Staff Confidential File

Smith, J.M.	Technical Director	Male	MN123456BY	12.12.1998	£55000
Taylor, R.	Sales Director	Male	YY654321BA	23.10.1978	£59000
Blankett, N.Y.	IT Director	Female	VH098765CV	01.01.1988	£44000

Diagram 11

You can only appreciate the effects of colours, if you experiment by running this example on your system. Examine it carefully to confirm that it meets all requirements set for this exercise.

• Example 6

Your task is to design two separate documents for displaying in the IE 5.5 or any other browser the text and a table shown below in the shaded area.

The text and a table

The hexadecimal numbers are known as hexadecimal pairs or hex pairs. The hex pairs begin with the *symbol* #, so that they can be distinguished from other numbering systems.

Some Standard Colours			
Colour Name	Hex Pair/Triplet	Colour Name	Hex Pair/Triplet
Black	#000000	White	#FFFFFF
Gray	#80808880	Lime	#00FF00
Red	#FF0000	Olive	#808000

Document 1: An XHTML 1.0 Strict document for storing both the above text and the accompanying table. Save this file under any suitable name with **.html** extension.

Document 2: This is the CSS file in which you should save the following styling presentational requirements:-

- The text should be displayed on a colourful background, on the left side of the table, as shown above. It should be in black colour. The phrase ***symbol #*** is to displayed in italic style. You can use any font style and size.
- The table itself should be placed on the right side of the document, that is next to the text. The title of this table should be displayed on a black background, but the text should have a white appearance.
- The text within the table (both table head and its body) can be of any colour of your choice, and of any font style and size.
- The table must have a colourful border, whose width may be thin, or medium, or thick.
- Save both XHTML document and cascading style sheet in two separate files. Use W3C Validation service in order to validate both files accordingly. Finally, preview the document.

• Explanation

- The XHTML code for this document is listed in Diagrams 12 & 12A. It is saved as **hex.html**. An important feature of this document is that it contains information for creating and storing both the text and the table together with its heading. It has the following segment of the code in order to link this file to the CSS file:-

```
<link rel ="stylesheet" href="hex2.css" />
```

- It should be noted that the segment of the code for creating the table is written first, and then the code for the text. It seems odd as above, the text is written first and the table is on its right. Why is it so?
- The reason is that in the CSS document, **hex2.css**, the following rule places the table on the right side of the text.

```
table{
        float:right;
    }
```

The preview of the document saved as hex.html is shown in Diagram 13. It meets all requirements.

The XHTML code for example 6 – hex.html (cont in Diagram 12A)

```
<?xml version= "1.0" encoding = "UTF-8"?>
<!DOCTYPE html
        PUBLIC "- //w3C//DTD XHTML 1.0 Strict//EN"
 "http://www.w3.org/TR/xhtml1/DTD/xhtml1- Strict.dtd">
<html xmlns="http://www.w3.org/1999/xhtml" xml:lang="en" lang= "en">

<head>
<title>Styling a table with CSS</title>
<link rel ="stylesheet" href="hex2.css" />
</head>
<body>
<table>
<caption> Some Standard Colours  </caption>
  <tr>
      <th> Colour Name </th>
      <th> Hex Pair/Triplet</th>
      <th> Colour Name</th>
      <th> Hex Pair/Triplet</th>
  </tr>
<tr>
     <td>Black</td>
     <td>#000000 </td>
     <td>White</td>
     <td>#FFFFFF</td>
 </tr>
```

Diagram 12

The XHTML code for example 6 – hex.html (cont from Diagram 12)

```
<tr>
    <td> Gray </td>
    <td> #80808880 </td>
    <td>Lime</td>
    <td>#00FF00</td>
</tr>
<tr>
    <td>Red </td>
    <td>#FF0000</td>
    <td> Olive</td>
    <td>#808000</td>
</tr>
</table>
<p>
    The hexadecimal numbers are known as hexadecimal pairs or hex pairs.
    The hex pairs begin with the <em> symbol #</em>, so that they can be
    distinguished from other numbering systems.</p>
</body></html>
```

Diagram 12A

External style sheet saved as hex2.css for example 6

```
/* This style sheet is to be linked to hex.html */
caption{
        text-decoration:underline; font-style:italic; font-size:150%;  background:#000000; color:#ffffff;
}
table{
        float:right; border-style:double; border-color:#0000ff; }

th  {
      border-style:solid;border-color:#808080; border-width:thin;}

 td{
      border-style:solid; border-color:#808080; border-width:thin; }
em  {font-size:120%;}

 p{
    font-size:110%; font-style: normal;}
```

Diagram 12A

Table and some standard colours document previewed in IE5.5

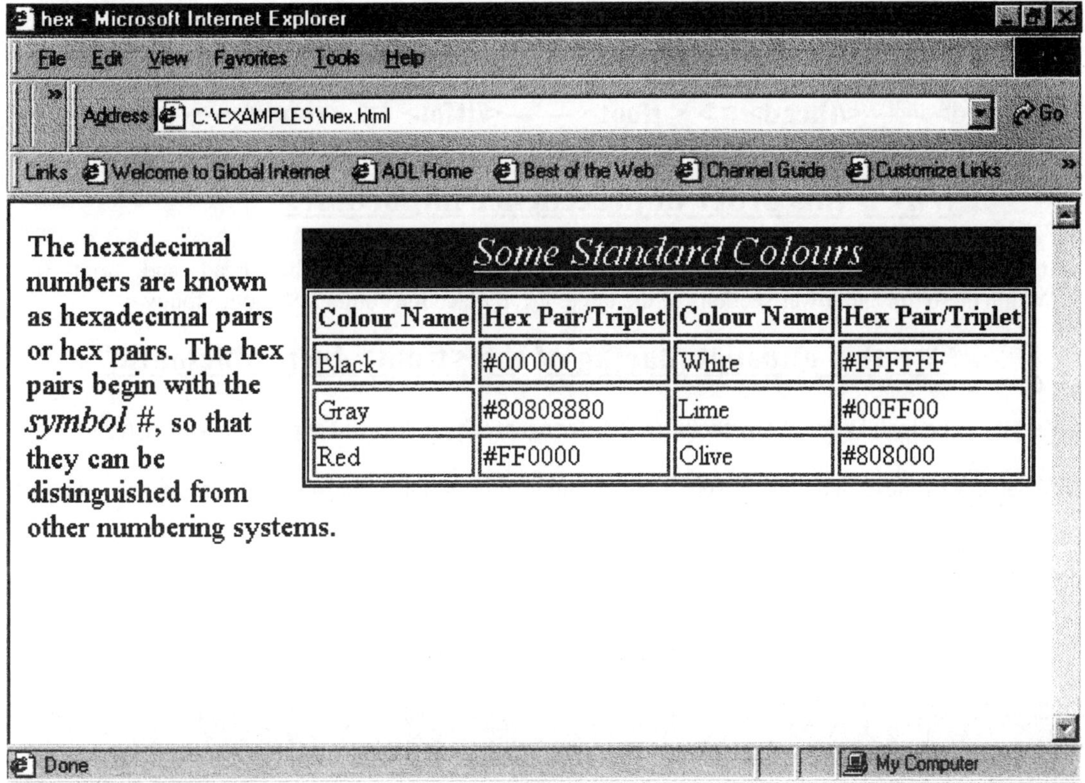

Colour Name	Hex Pair/Triplet	Colour Name	Hex Pair/Triplet
Black	#000000	White	#FFFFFF
Gray	#80808880	Lime	#00FF00
Red	#FF0000	Olive	#808000

Diagram 13

• Table head, body and foot elements

You can organise table rows by means of **<thead>**, **<tfoot>**, and **<tbody>**. These elements can create three distinguishable sections, namely **thead, tfoot** and **tbody** sections of a table. These are optional elements, and thus you do not have to use them in constructing every single table.

• Are there any conditions for including them in your XHTML document ?

Yes indeed, the following requirements are essential:-

- A table can have one <thead> and one <tfoot>, but a number of <tbody> elements

- If either of these elements are used in a document, the **<tr> element** must be nested within any of these elements.

- When all three elements are in the document, the order of precedence is as follows:-

<thead> ------</thead> ⇒ < tfoot> -------</tffot> ⇒ <tbody> -----</body>

- **Why is this order of precedence important?**

It enables the browser or any other user agent to lay out the contents of the <thead> and <tfoot> first. Within these top and lower sections of the table, it can place the content of each <tbody>.

- **Can this unusual placing of the <tfoot> be problematic?**

Yes, it can be rea0d wrongly by the browser/user agent which does not support this element.

- When any of these elements is used, it must contain at least one table row by means of < tr> element.

• Example 7

Sick Staff Report

Name	*Job title*	*Department*	*Status*	*Annual salary*
G.M. Johnson	Accounts Executive	Accounts Dept.	Married	18500
B. V. Blair	Production Asst	Manufacturing Dept	Single	19350
A. C. Clarkson	Buyer	Purchase Dept.	Married	25000
This is strictly confidential information. It is for the use of Personnel Department only.				

- The task is to design two documents one of which is CSS document for style and presentational information. The other is an XHTML document which contains the information to be displayed.

Your designs of these two documents should be for previewing the above table in the IE 5.5 or any other user agent. It should include the following requirements in order to display this table in its given format:-

1. The table should have a border surrounding the whole table. Set border thickness = 10 pixel, style double, and its colour maroon.

2. The caption should be of italic style and displayed on a yellow background.

3. The footer of the table should also be in *italic* style, but the white text is to be displayed on a black background.

4. The header which contains headings of columns should be displayed on a grey background, and in *italic* style, and the text must be white.

5. The remaining part of the table should contain data. If you wish, you can style data cells.

6. Your XHTML document must be written under XHTML 1.0 Strict. In your own interest in order to make sure that documents are correctly designed, get them checked by W3C Validation service.

The XHTML code for example 7 – staff.html (cont. in Diagram 14A)

```
<?xml version= "1.0" encoding = "UTF-8"?>
<!DOCTYPE html
        PUBLIC "- //w3C//DTD XHTML 1.0 Transitional//EN"
 "http://www.w3.org/TR/xhtml1/DTD/xhtml1- Transitional.dtd">
<html xmlns="http://www.w3.org/1999/xhtml" xml:lang="en" lang= "en">
<head>
<title>Header, Footer & CSS </title>
<link rel ="stylesheet" href="staff2.css" />
</head >
<body>
 <table border ="10" >
 <caption> Sick Staff Report </caption>
<thead>
<tr>
        <th> Name </th>
        <th> Job title</th>
        <th> Department</th>
        <th> Status</th>
        <th>Annual salary </th>
</tr>
</thead>
<tfoot>
<tr>
<td colspan ="10"> This is strictly confidential information. It is for the
            use of Personnel Department only.
      </td>
</tr>
</tfoot>
```

Diagram 14

The XHTML code for example 7 – staff.html (cont. from Diagram 14)

```
<tbody>
<tr>
        <td>G.M. Johnson</td>
        <td> Accounts Executive</td>
        <td> Accounts Dept.</td>
        <td> Married</td>
        <td> 18500</td>
</tr>
<tr>
        <td> B. V. Blair</td>
        <td> Production Asst</td>
        <td> Manufacturing Dept</td>
        <td> Single</td>
        <td> 19350</td>
</tr>
<tr>
        <td> A. C. Clarkson </td>
        <td> Buyer</td>
        <td> Purchase Dept.</td>
        <td> Married</td>
        <td> 25000</td>
</tr>
</tbody>
</table>
</body>
</html>
```

Diagram 14A

• Explanation

The XHTML code for this example is in Diagrams 14 & 14A. It was saved as **staff.html**. The other required document is listed in Diagram 15, which was saved as **staff2.css**. This is an external CSS document for which a link is created in staff.html. This link is highlighted in Diagram 14 for your benefit. You must examine these documents carefully.

In Diagram 14 A, you can find **<tbody>** element. It contains within <tr> and <td> elements data items.

• What will happen if you remove <tbody> element from staff.html file ?

Its elimination from **staff.html** will have no adverse effects, as <tbody> element is an optional element.

Note that I have used standard colours. You can use any standard colour for any element. One can specify any colour by its name or RGB- value. Here, I have used hex pair value for colours specified in the external CSS document listed in Diagram 15.

When choosing colours, you have to decide for yourself which colours to apply. Those colours which look attractive on the screen may not even appear when printed on paper.

The external CSS file for example 7 – staff2.css

```
/* This style sheet is to be linked to staff.html */
caption{
      text-decoration:underline;
      font-style:italic;
      font-size:150%;
      background:#ffff00;                    /* yellow */
      color:#000000;                         /* black */
    }
table{

      border-style:double;
      border-color:#800000;                  /* maroon */
    }
thead{
   font-size:120%;
   font-style:italic;
   color: #ffffff;                           /* white */
   background-color:#808080;                /* grey */
  }
 tfoot{
     font-style:italic;
     font-weight:bolder;
     color:#ffffff;              /*white */
     background-color:#000000;   /* black*/
   }
```

Diagram 15

- Having stored these documents, I submitted each document to W3C Validation Service. Both documents were validated by W3C succssfully. The screen capture of the document previewed in the IE 5.5 is shown in Diagram 16. It certainly meets all requirements.

Document for example 7 previewed in IE 5.5

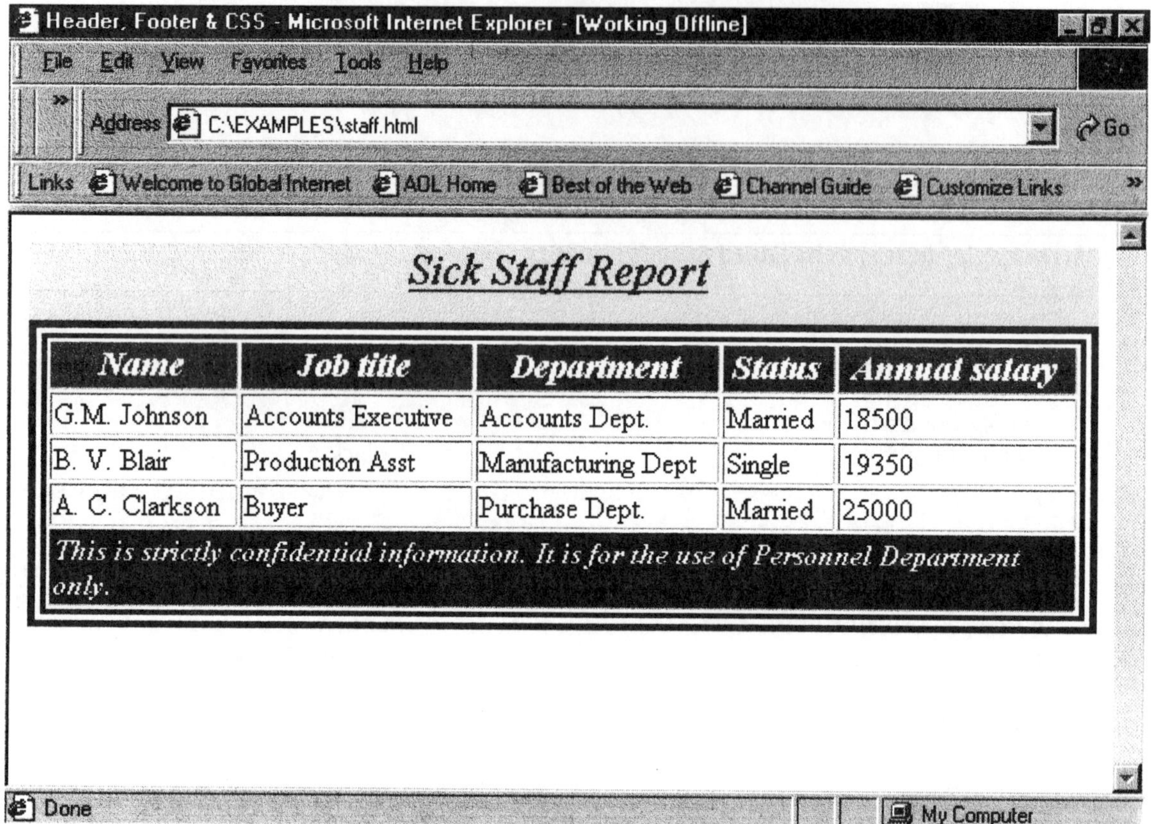

Diagram 16

• Cellspacing and cellpadding attributes

Cell spacing creates a space or distance between individual cells using the optional attribute **cellspacing**. On the other hand, cell padding is used for the space between the cell content and the border of the cell. These spaces are measured in pixels. Once again, it is repeated that different screen resolutions have different fixed pixel widths. It means that a table may not exactly appear on your screen as it does so on my monitor. The general syntax formats for including one or both of these attributes in an XHTML code are:-

<cellspacing = "iteger value" cellpadding = "integer value">

or **<cellspacing =”integer value”>**

or **<cellpadding =” integer value”>**.

The integer value is the number of pixels. It should be a whole number.

• Example 8

In order to demonstrate the application of cellspacing and cellpadding attributes, I have designed the following two documents:-

• **spacing .html** shown in Diagrams 17 and **spacing1.css** shown in Diagram 17A.

spacing.html contains the required data for displaying in the table entitled, “European Marketing Cost”.

The structure of the code follows the pattern of the other XHTML codes in this chapter. The segment of the code shown below lays out the table.

```
<table border = "5" cellspacing = "7"  cellpadding = "10">
```

In accordance with this code, the table will be displayed within a border whose width is 5 pixels wide. The space between individual cells will be equivalent to the width of 7 pixels, and the distance/space between the cell content and border will be 10 pixels wide.

• Another important point to note is the construction of a group column, and its four sub-columns as shown below.

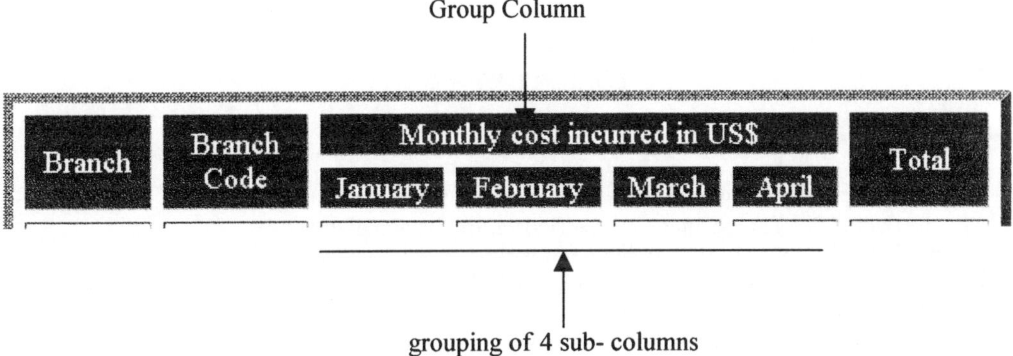

In Diagram 17, the relevant segment of the code is shown on a shaded background.

```
<td colspan = "4" >Monthly cost incurred in US$ </td>
```

In the above shaded area is the segment of the code which spans the column, “Monthly cost incurred in US$” by 4 columns. The numerical value 4 is important here, as under this column, four sub –columns that are highlighted above are created.

The XHTML code for example 8 – spacing.html (cont. in Diagram 17A)

```
<?xml version= "1.0" encoding = "UTF-8"?>
<!DOCTYPE html
        PUBLIC "- //w3C//DTD XHTML 1.0 Strict//EN"
 "http://www.w3.org/TR/xhtml1/DTD/xhtml1- strict.dtd">
<html xmlns="http://www.w3.org/1999/xhtml" xml:lang="en" lang= "en">

<head>
<title>Styling a table with CSS</title>
<link rel ="stylesheet" href="spacing1.css" />
</head>
<body>
<table border = "5" cellspacing = "7"  cellpadding = "10">
<caption> European Marketing Cost </caption>
<thead>
<tr>
     <td rowspan = "2" > Branch </td>
     <td rowspan = "2" > Branch Code</td>
     <td colspan = "4" >Monthly cost incurred in US$ </td>
     <td rowspan = "3" > Total </td>
</tr>
<tr>
     <td> January </td>
     <td>February</td>
     <td>March</td>
     <td>April</td>
</tr>
</thead>
<tfoot>
<tr>
   <td colspan ="10" rowspan ="4">
   To the Group Chief Accountant - these figures are the actual expenses
   paid by each branch. These figures do not include any other expenses
   except marketing expenses - see definition of marketing expenses.</td>
</tr>
</tfoot>
```

Diagram 17

- Furthermore, the spanning of rows for Branch, Branch Code and Total must be spanned at least by the figures shown in the shaded area in Diagram 17. If you do not do so, your four sub-columns will not be created in the same format as shown above.

- If you wish, you can apply column group element, **<colgroup / >** for grouping columns of a table. It is an empty element. This element must appear in the <table> element, just below the <caption> element.

The XHTML code for example 8 – spacing.html (cont. from Diagram 17)

```
<tbody>
<tr>
        <td>London -UK </td>
        <td>250000 </td>
        <td>190000  </td>
        <td>177000 </td>
        <td>210000 </td>
        <td>185000 </td>
        <td>1,012,000 </td>
</tr>
<tr>
          <td> Frankfurt -Germany  </td>
          <td> 180000 </td>
          <td>200000 </td>
          <td>155000 </td>
          <td>190000 </td>
          <td>120000 </td>
          <td>845,000 </td>
</tr>
<tr>
      <td>Paris - France </td>
      <td>350000 </td>
      <td>265000 </td>
      <td>128000 </td>
      <td>250000 </td>
      <td>140000  </td>
      <td>1,133,000 </td>
</tr>
</tbody>
</table>
</body>
</html>
```

Diagram 17A

- The external Cascading Style Sheet rules for this example are listed in Diagram 18. Of course, there is a segment of the code in the XHTML document for linking the XHTML document to the style sheet document.

CSS document for example 8 – spacing1.css

```
/* This style sheet is to be linked to spacing.html */
caption{
        text-decoration:underline;

        font-size:150%;
        font-weight:bold;
        background:#ffff00;                  /* yellow */
        color:#000000;                    /* black */
       }
table{

       border-width:thick;
       border-color:#ccffff;               /* light green */
       }
 thead{
    text-align: center;
    font-size:120%;
    font-weight: normal;
    color: #ffffff;                   /* white */
    background-color:#808080;              /* grey */
   }
 tfoot{
      font-size:110%;
      font-style:normal;
      font-weight:normal;
      color:#ffffff;                 /*white */
      background-color:#000000;           /* black*/
    }
tbody
     {

      text-align:center;
     }
```

Diagram 18

- Prior to previewing the Web page, I used W3C Validation Service to validate these two documents. The XHTML code as XHTML 1.0 Strict and CSS 2 rules were successfully validated. See the screen capture in Diagram 19. You can see that the XHTML code has created the group column, as well as underneath grouped together its 4 sub-columns as required. The styling and presentational aspects are in accordance with the CSS rules listed in the external CSS listed in Diagram 18. The only way, you can further appreciate more the outcome of these two **.html** and **.css** files is to run these on your own machine.

It is suggested that you examine the display of the document in Diagram 19 and relate it to the XHTML code and CSS rules in order to learn how these files have created the document and presented the data in rows and columns, especially the grouping of sub-columns under a group heading.

A preview of a Web page designed for example 8 – spacing.html

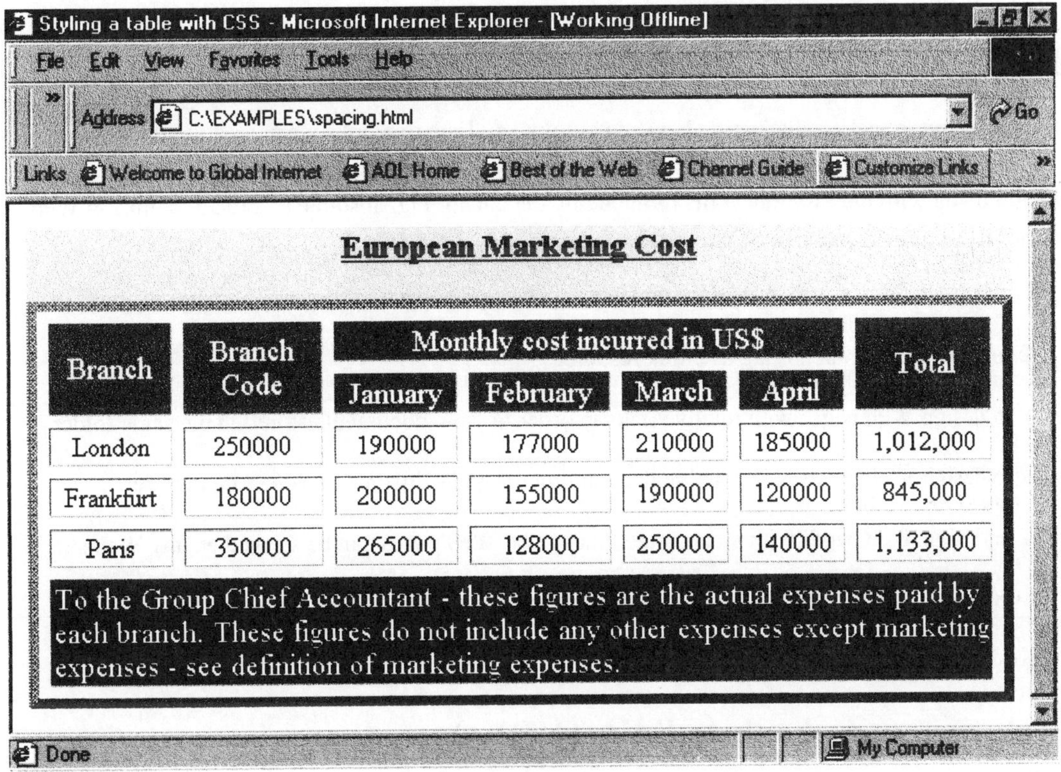

European Marketing Cost

Branch	Branch Code	Monthly cost incurred in US$				Total
		January	February	March	April	
London	250000	190000	177000	210000	185000	1,012,000
Frankfurt	180000	200000	155000	190000	120000	845,000
Paris	350000	265000	128000	250000	140000	1,133,000
To the Group Chief Accountant - these figures are the actual expenses paid by each branch. These figures do not include any other expenses except marketing expenses - see definition of marketing expenses.						

Diagram 19

Sufficient emphases have been placed in differentiating and demonstrating the difference between the structural markup (XHTML) and its style and presentational information (CSS). Of course, there are still some other relevant elements which have not been discussed. In Appendix A, you can find some more elements and their attributes which can also be applied to tables.

Chapter 10

Links in Documents

The prime aims of this chapter are as follows:-

- to assist you to understand the meaning of the anchor tag, absolute and relative links, and protocols
- to enable you to make a distinction between absolute and relative links when creating documents
- to equip you with the essential skills of including the anchor tag, absolute and relative links in Web pages to be previewed locally, and on the Internet

By reading and practising techniques that are demonstrated in this chapter, you should be able :-

- to construct the anchor tag as a link resource
- to design Web pages with relative links in order to view documents stored in the same folder
- to design Web pages with relative links in order to view documents stored on the Web
- to design Web pages with an absolute link so that Web pages can be viewed on any Web site
- to apply mailto:instruction, and explain any likely problems, and recognise its usefulness
- to describe various protocols

• Relative and absolute links (URLs)

In fact, with the <a> element, you can create two kinds of links. These are absolute and relative links. The difference between these two can be simply visualised as:-

- The **absolute link** is equivalent to a full address of someone, which you should write on an envelope in order to make sure that a postman/postwoman can deliver it to the correct address. For instance, if you wish to view a document on the Internet, which is stored on a particular server, you must provide an absolute link or URL, using the HTTP protocol such as: http:// adrlondon.ltd.uk/

- The **relative link** or URL is equivalent to writing on an envelope the address of another member of staff and sending it through an organisation's internal post system. The address of a member of staff in the same organisation is like a ' an internal reference' or 'a relative'. It is not considered as 'a personal relation', but as a reference to a given entity, which is the organisation.

  For instance, on your computer hard disk a number of files are stored. If you refer, say, in file A to another file called file B, then you are creating a relative link between these two files. In your computer system, both files are relative to your computer system (entity). Indeed, it can be said that everything on your hard disk is relative to your computer system. This is the way, how I view my computer system relative to me. Think about it !

  The method of including these links in XHTML documents is demonstrated in this chapter. These links are formed with an important element known as <a> element, which is explored first below:-

. The anchor tag <a>

Some essential feature are outlined below:-

- the **<a>** element creates a link. It is usually called an opening **anchor tag**. Naturally, its closing tag is </a>. It is an inline element, which has a special function of making the World Wide Web work. You cannot nest one <a> within another <a>.
- **'a'** stands for anchor.
- it takes href attribute - **'href'** stands for hypertext reference.
- **href** attribute takes the URL of the document to which the link is to be made. The href attribute can also accept other attributes.
- The general syntax for creating the anchor tag as a **resource link** is given below:-

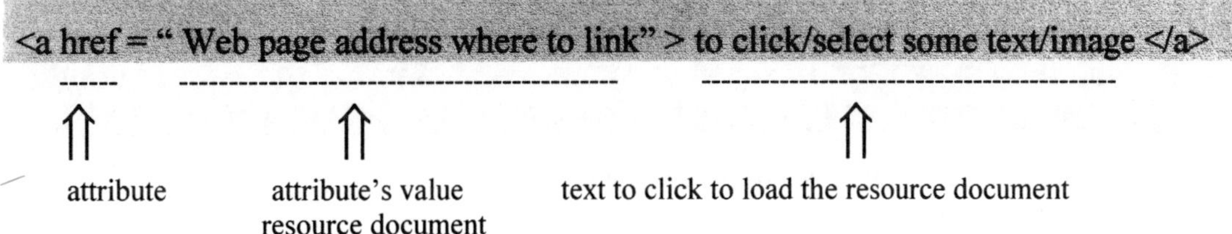

. Example

The following example illustrates the application of the anchor tag when the source document is on the same system:-

Example

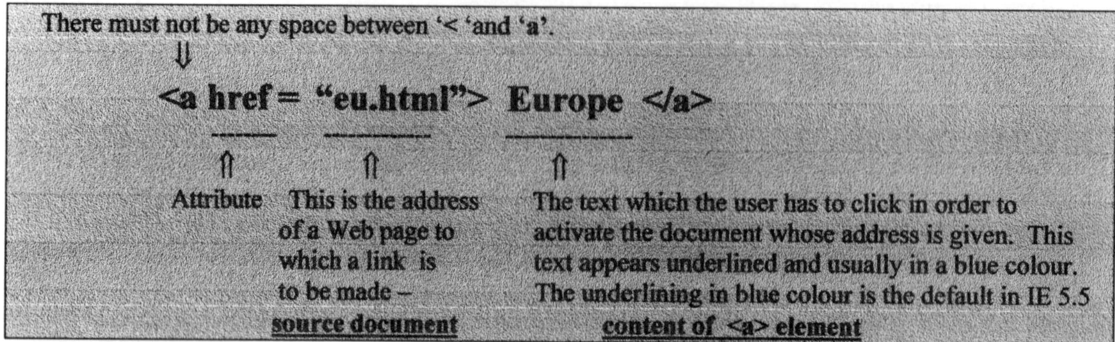

There must not be any space between '< 'and 'a'.
<a href= "eu.html"> Europe </a>
Attribute
This is the address of a Web page to which a link is to be made – source document
The text which the user has to click in order to activate the document whose address is given. This text appears underlined and usually in a blue colour. The underlining in blue colour is the default in IE 5.5
content of <a> element

• What happens when the user clicks this text ?

The clicking action sends a signal to the browser which starts searching/navigating for the address listed in the anchor tag. If the browser finds a document at this address in the opening tag, it invokes the document.

• Legal and illegal content of <a>

The following rules must be observed when constructing the content of element <a>:-

•The content of the <a> can be some text, or an image or an inline type of element. For instance:-

```
<a href = "ger.html"> Germany - please click here</a>
```

content as simple text is legal

```
<a href = "ger.html"> <i> France - please click here </i></a>
```

content as simple text to be displayed in *italic style* is legal - <i> is an inline element

• A document containing an image can be the content of <a>:-

```
<a href = " rach.html"> <img src = "angelika.gif" alt = "Single picture –click here" /></a>
```

here the document containing the image acts as a source link - it is legal construct.

• The anchor element <u>cannot</u> take a block element. For instance the following construction is **illegal**.

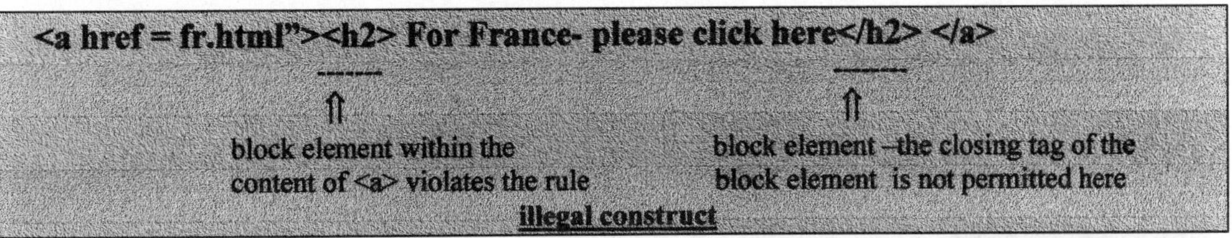

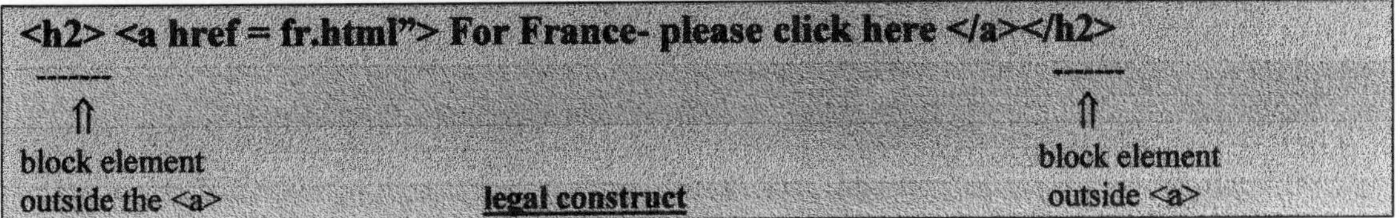

It is **legal** as the block element is outside the content of <a>.Thus a block element cannot be the content of the <a> element.

• Example 1

There are two pieces of text marked as Text 1 and Text 2, shown below. In Text 1, 'email' is an important word whose definition is given in Text 2. Your task is as follows:-

• Design two XHTML documents. Each document must contain a reference to each other in such a way that if a reader wants to find the meaning of the word 'email' in Text 1, the reader just simply clicks on this word. This click action should open the second file which contains Text 2. When a reader wants to return to the file containing Text 1, the reader must click 'email' in this second document in order to return to the first document. A reader should be able to jump from one document to another document, if he/she wants to do so.

• The XHTML files for both documents should be saved and kept in the same folder.

Prior to previewing these documents, as usual, check them for XML well-formedness and validity, as XHTML 1.0 Strict type.

<u>Text 1</u>

There are private networks. These are installed mainly in larger organisations. Now-a-days, these networks are linked to Internet and its associated information on-line systems such as the Web, and email to exchange information within an organisation. You can also link your organisation's information system to another organisation's information system.

Text 2

Email (electronic mail) is another method of communication. By this method, messages are sent from computer to computer.

• Explanation

The XHTML code for Text 1 is listed in Diagram 3. The segment of the code that is essential for creating a link, when the word e-mail is clicked by the user is as follows:-

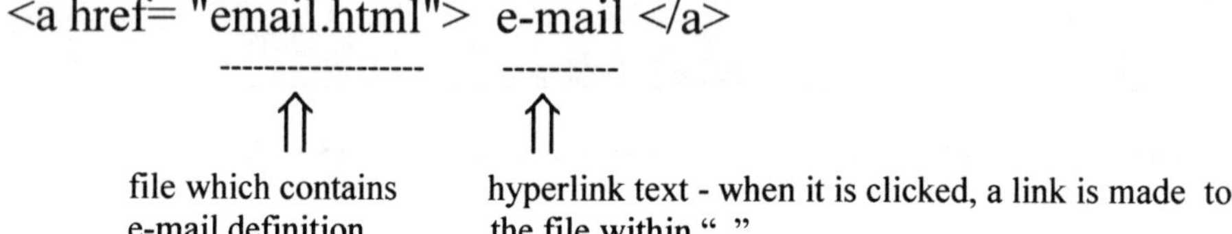

• The markup code for the other required file is shown in Diagram 4. This file is also stored in the same folder called example on my system. It also has a reciprocal anchor tag, so that the user can return to the first document, if necessary.

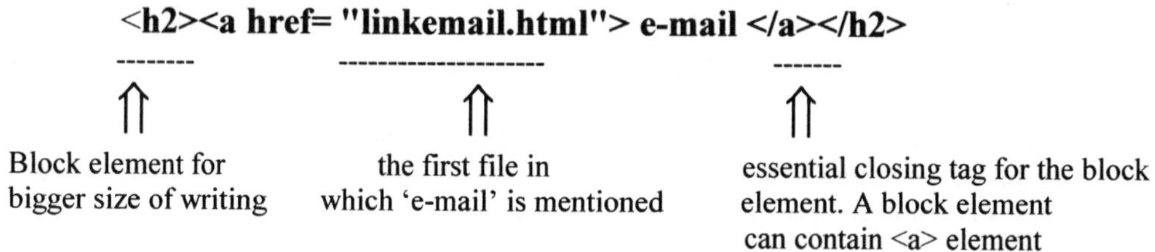

• In both cases, when the user click on the link , 'e-mail' the browser searches for **href**. When it finds it, the browser reads its value, which is, in both cases, .html file. As there is no other information, such as a name of a directory in this value of attribute **href**, the browser assumes that both files are in the same folder. Therefore, it looks for the required file. Having found the file, it loads it for displaying its content. If the browser cannot load the required file, it may be the result of some error, such as :-

< a href = "email.html"> e-mail</a>

The gap between '<' and '**a**' is not allowed. Try it out yourself to find out that it does not work!

The XHTML code for Text 1 – linkemail.html

```
<?xml version= "1.0" encoding = "UTF-8"?>
<!DOCTYPE html
        PUBLIC "- //w3C//DTD XHTML 1.0 Strict//EN"
 "http://www.w3.org/TR/xhtml1/DTD/xhtml1- strict.dtd">
<html xmlns="http://www.w3.org/1999/xhtml" xml:lang="en" lang= "en">
<head>
<title> Hyperlinks </title></head>
<body>
<p>
  There are private networks. These are installed mainly in larger organisations. Now-a-days, these
  networks are linked to Internet and its associated information on-line systems such as the Web, and
  <a href= "email.html">  e-mail </a>, to exchange information within an organisation.</p>
 <p>  You can also link your organisation's information
      system to another organisation's information system. </p>
</body>
</html>
```

Diagram 1

The XHTML code for Text 2 – email.html

```
<?xml version= "1.0" encoding = "UTF-8"?>
<!DOCTYPE html
        PUBLIC "- //w3C//DTD XHTML 1.0 Strict//EN"
 "http://www.w3.org/TR/xhtml1/DTD/xhtml1- strict.dtd">
<html xmlns="http://www.w3.org/1999/xhtml" xml:lang="en" lang= "en">
<head>
<title> hyperlink </title>
</head>
<body>
    <p>  Email ( electronic mail) is another method of communication. By this method, messages are
sent
          from computer to computer. </p>

<h2><a href= "linkemail.html"> e-mail </a></h2>
 </body>
</html>
```

Diagram 2

The preview of Text 1 in IE 5.5 – example 1

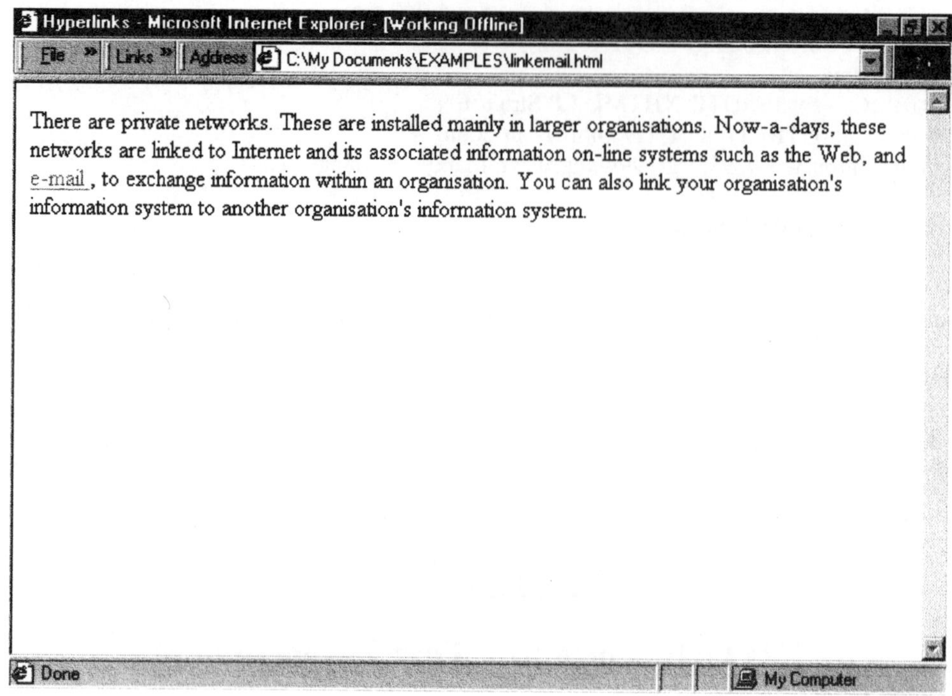

Diagram 3

The preview of Text 2 in IE 5.5 – example 1

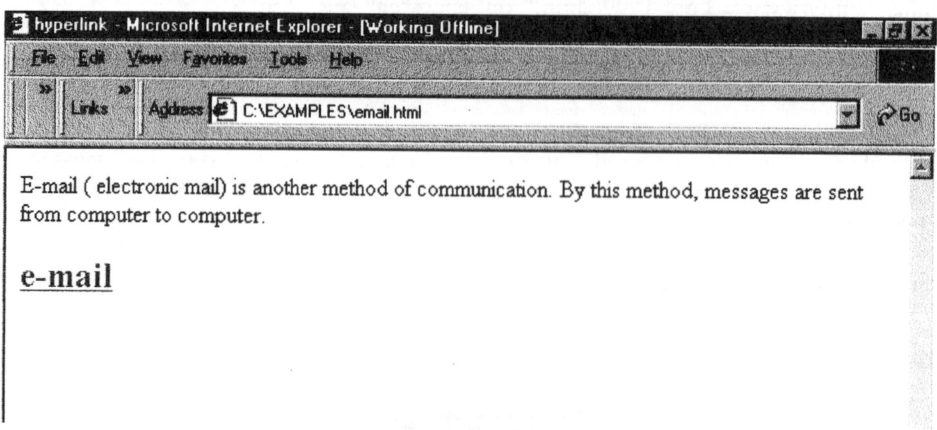

Diagram 4

- By clicking on the underlined text in both Diagrams 3-4, you can navigate between two files.

. Example 2

The aim of this example is to demonstrate how you can create and store several links in one document in such a way that any of the links can be selected in order to retrieve the relevant information kept in another file. Therefore, your task is to design four XHTML documents. The first three XHTML Strict type documents should correspond to the following three chapters listed in a box.

Save each source document as **chap1.html**, **chap2.html**, and **chap3.html**. Keep these in one folder. You must also include in each source document some hypertext, which a user can click, if he/she wishes to return to the document containing links to all three chapters.

The purpose of the fourth XHTML document is to store the required four links with their hypertext. When this document is loaded in the IE 5.5 or any other user agent, the user should be allowed to select any of the three links in order to retrieve information on a screen. Save it as **links.html**, or give it another name, but it must also be in the same folder as the other three source documents.

Each of these four documents should be checked for XML well-formedness and validity, prior to any previewing.

Chapter 1 - Introduction

Introduction 1
What is a network?
What is the Internet?

Chapter 2 - Foundation of Web Page Design

What is XHTML?
Creating your first XHTML document
Validating your XHTML document

Chapter 3 - Shaping your Web page

What are Cascading Style Sheets (CSS)?
Creating headlines
Internal and external CSS

. Explanation

- Th XHTML markup codes for three source documents are listed in Diagram 5, 6 and 7 respectively.

These files are simple enough to follow. However, one element, < **hr** /> is introduced for the first time. As you might have gathered by now, it is an empty element. It is really a useful element, when you want to draw/display a horizontal line. In Diagram 10, a horizontal line can be seen. Here, it separates source information from the hypertext.

- In each source document, the following anchor tag is listed:

<a href = "links.html" Table of Contents – click </a>

Without the segment of this code in each source document, the user will not be able to return to the links document – links.html. When the user clicks on a link in each page, the browser searches for **href** attribute. When it finds it, the browser looks for its value to read it. There is no other information such as a name of a directory or another folder in this segment of the code. Thus, the browser assumes rightly that **links.html** is also in the same folder in which the source file is stored. Thus, it gets it, and loads it for displaying it on your screen.

- In Diagram 8, you can study the XHTML code for the **links document**. The structure of the code of this document is pretty similar to the structure of codes in Diagrams 5-7. The vital difference between this document and the other three documents is that it has three anchor tags, each of which relates to a different document. On the other hand, the other three documents have the same anchor tag, pointing to this page.

The XHTML code for creating Chap1.html

```
<?xml version= "1.0" encoding = "UTF-8"?>
<!DOCTYPE html
        PUBLIC "- //w3C//DTD XHTML 1.0 Strict//EN"
 "http://www.w3.org/TR/xhtml1/DTD/xhtml1- strict.dtd">
<html xmlns="http://www.w3.org/1999/xhtml" xml:lang="en" lang= "en">
<head>
<title> Chapter 1 </title>
</head>
<body>
 <h2> Chapter 1 - Introduction</h2>
 <p>
   Introduction 1 <br />
   What is a network? 3<br />
   What is the Internet? 5 </p>
<hr />
<h2><a href ="links.html"> Table of Contents - click </a></h2>
</body></html>
```

Diagram 5

The XHTML code for creating Chap2.html

```
<?xml version= "1.0" encoding = "UTF-8"?>
<!DOCTYPE html
        PUBLIC "- //w3C//DTD XHTML 1.0 Strict//EN"
 "http://www.w3.org/TR/xhtml1/DTD/xhtml1- strict.dtd">
<html xmlns="http://www.w3.org/1999/xhtml" xml:lang="en" lang= "en">
<head>
<title> Chapter 2</title>
</head>
<body>
 <h2> Chapter 2 - Foundation of Web Page Design </h2>
 <p>
   What is XHTML? 20 <br />
   Creating your first XHTML document 22 <br />
   Validating your XHTML document 24</p>
<hr / >
<h2> <a href="links.html">Table of Contents - click</a> </h2>
</body></html>
```

Diagram 6

The XHTML code for creating Chap3.html

```
<?xml version= "1.0" encoding = "UTF-8"?>
<!DOCTYPE html
        PUBLIC "- //w3C//DTD XHTML 1.0 Strict//EN"
 "http://www.w3.org/TR/xhtml1/DTD/xhtml1- Strict.dtd">
<html xmlns="http://www.w3.org/1999/xhtml" xml:lang="en" lang= "en">
<head>
<title> Chapter 3</title>
</head>
<body>
 <h2> Chapter 3 - Shaping your Web page </h2>
 <p>
   What are Cascading Style Sheets (CSS)? 25 <br  />
   Creating headlines 27 <br  />
   Internal and external CSS 33 </p>
<hr  / >
<h2>
 <a href = "links.html"> Table of Contents - click</a>
</h2></body></html>
```

Diagram 7

The XHTML code for creating links.html

```
<?xml version= "1.0" encoding = "UTF-8"?>
<!DOCTYPE html
        PUBLIC "- //w3C//DTD XHTML 1.0 Strict//EN"
 "http://www.w3.org/TR/xhtml1/DTD/xhtml1- strict.dtd">
<html xmlns="http://www.w3.org/1999/xhtml" xml:lang="en" lang= "en">
<head>
<title> Inter-links</title>
</head>
<body>
 <h1> Table of Contents</h1>
<p>Please click any of the following chapters for further information.</p>
 <hr />
<h2>
   <a href ="chap1.html">Chapter 1 - click</a><br />
   <a href ="chap2.html">Chapter 2 - click</a> br />
  <a href ="chap3.html">Chapter 3 - click</a>
</h2  ></body></html>
```

Diagram 8

A preview of links documents in IE 5.5 - links.html

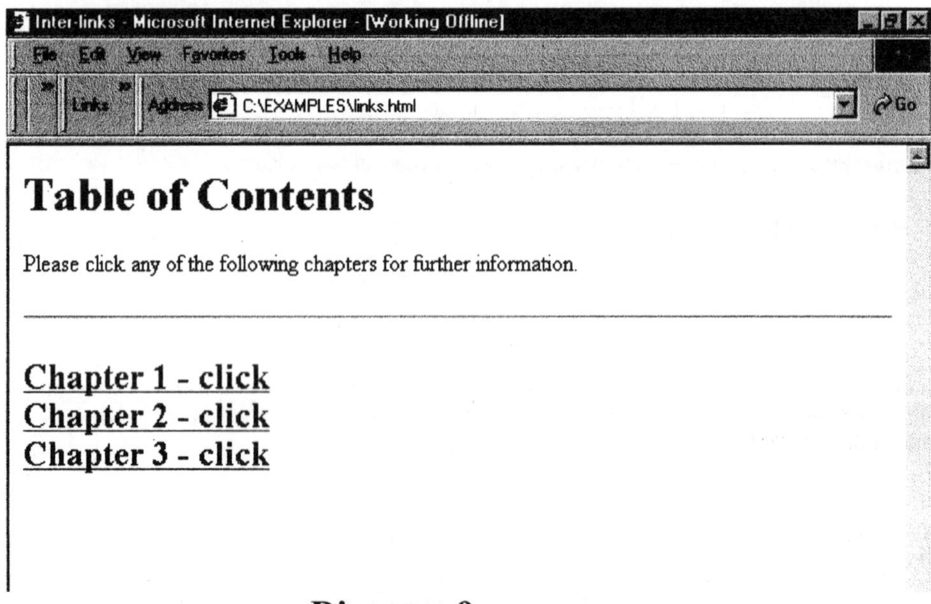

Diagram 9

A preview of Chap.3 in IE 5.5 – chap3.html

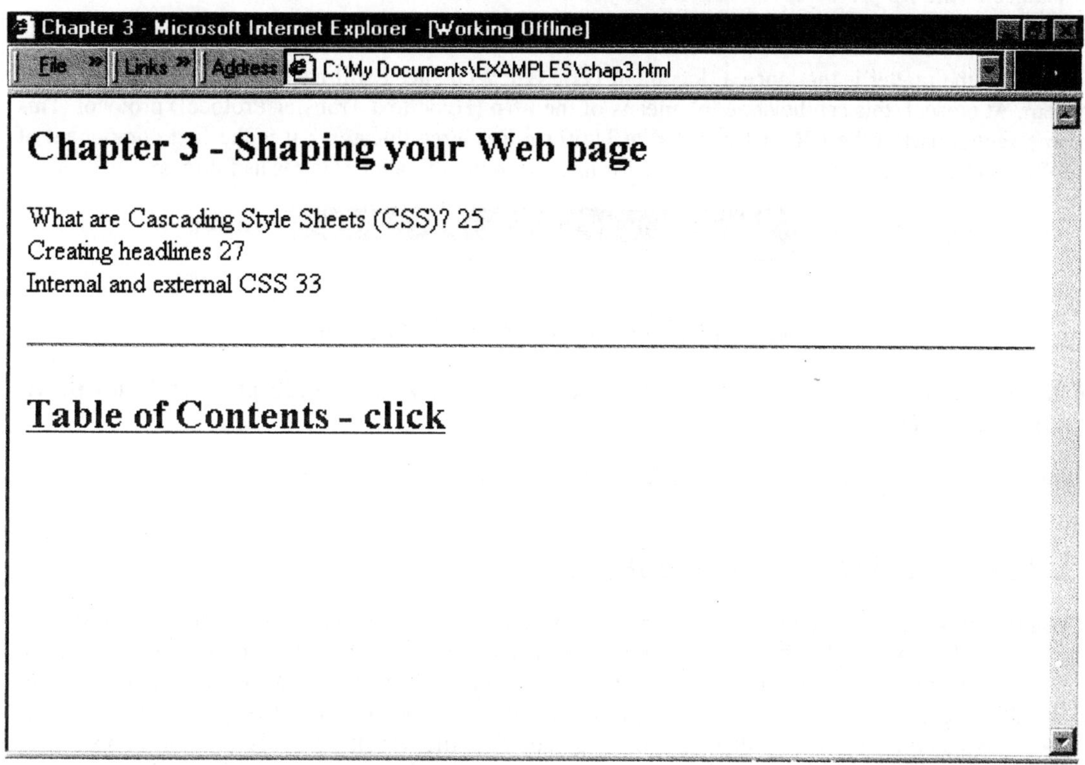

Diagram 10

• Linking across the Web

• How can you create links within your documents so that some resources across the Internet can be accessed?

The idea of URL (Universal or Uniform Resource Locator) is to enable you to link to any other site on the World Wide Web. As you know that the Internet is a giant library of all kinds of resources one can think of, you can get all kinds of information on the Web, and do shopping as well. There are numerous protocols for traversing the Web. For instance, the **ftp protocol** is for transferring files across the Net.

I myself use ftp every day. All practical solved examples containing XHTML codes have to be up-loaded to our Web site by the FTP browser. For this transfer, I use Terrapin FTP Browser, which I found reliable. By this process, all Web pages, which form our Web site are transferred to it.

Once the file, say, shown in Diagram 11, is on our Web site, I can then link this file to W3C Validation Service for XML well-formedness and validity as XHTML 1.0 Strict document. You may require the assistance of the ftp protocol, for instance, if you want to load a browser from the Internet. Thus, it is commonly used.

The fact of the matter is that once a document is on our Web site, I still have to upload it to the W3C system. At present, this can be done by means of the **http** (Hypertext Transfer Protocol) protocol. This is an essential part of the **URL** (Universal or Uniform Resource Locator). It is the first component of the Web address. The general syntax format for using http in your anchor tag is as follows:-

⇑

This is the **URL** (Uniform or Universal Resource Locator)

In the real world, the above general format becomes:- **http:// www.adrlondon.ltd.uk/ index.html** It is the Web address of ADR.

- Some other address types also form part of URLs. See Table 1 for their features.

. What do we mean by uploading?

If you design your own Web site, in the first instance, all your documents which constitute your Web site are stored on your PC's hard disk. These documents have to be copied to the server/computer of your Internet Service Provider (ISP). Once they have been transferred (copied) , they make up your Web site. The process of transferring/copying your Web pages/documents to your ISP's server is known as uploading, and the method is called upload. This file transfer process is wholly opposite to the process known as loading something from the Internet on to your system, or a file from one folder to another folder on a PC.

. What is a resource locator?

A resource locator or resource location is the name of the file on the server. In the above example, index.html is the resource locator. This is the file in which the home page of ADR is kept. This way, Web site operation is simplified in such a way that all documents are stored in one folder. In the home page, you find the links to navigate to the page you want to see.

. Hypertext links

Historically speaking, the term hypertex is not the invention of the 1990s, alongside the explosion of the Web. It is said that its origin goes back as far as the 1940's. For all practical purposes, it can be best stated as a method for linking pages, both off and on-line, by selecting a text, or any symbol which is underlined and highlighted in a colour. This method allows the reader/viewer to move from viewing/reading from one page to another. You can even move from a current place to another place on the same page. The application of anchor tag is not too hard to grasp. One should not be overexcited about its usefulness, and start inserting too many hypertext links in Web pages . The inclusion of too many links in Web pages can be confusing, time consuming and discouraging to your viewers.

Furthermore, the maintenance of a Web site, which has lots of links can also cause problems. Whenever, you have to up-date your site, you have to make sure links still exist in the correct places. Far too many links are likely to break, and thus can create unnecessary maintenance problems.

Of course, you can apply different colour schemes. You have to be careful in choosing colours. For instance, the use of bright colours may make the underlining of a link invisible. A reader expects a link to be underlined. Therefore, you must pay attention to the use of colour for hypertext links. It is suggested that you apply any colour for hypertext link which is different from the colour of the text, not bright, and can be distinguished from the text colour. Also, keep in mind that some of your viewers may be colour-blind, and unable to see the difference between certain colours, especially red and green.

The good practice is to design your Web site first. Once you are happy with your pages, consider objectively the inclusion of a number of essential links in pages. In the light of colours used in each page, both for the background and the text itself, consider objectively the use of colours for hypertext links. If you still wish to use any colour for any links, apply the above suggestions for making your links visible, easy to maintain a Web site, and keep viewers interested in your Web pages. Finally, remember that the whole idea of a Web site is to communicate with a large number of visitors for whatever reasons your Web site is on the Web. It is for this very reason, you should not try to influence the user with your considerable knowledge and skills of creating hyperlinks with pictures, logos and so on all over the page. Many viewers find these links childish, and distracting.

Remember!!!

This chapter is about hypertext links, and linking one Web page to another page. It is worth pointing out that there are other types of things to which you can link your page. For instance, the <link> element can link a page to an external style sheet. See style sheets. You can also link to other items such Java applet .

. The mailto:

You may come across another type of address, which may look like a protocol, but it is not a protocol. It is called mailto. This address form does not use **://** instead, it has '**:**' which is followed by an e-mail address as its URL. Its function is to call up a mail client, so that an e-mail can be sent. It is easy to use this method of sending e-mails, but it may not work on the end user system. **Why?**

The browser has to be set to interpret an email link by this method. If a browser is not set for it, you, the end user, cannot make it interpret incoming emails sent by this method. On the other hand, this method of sending emails has its uses when implemented with <form> element.

• You may see in some other publications the anchor link is overloaded with other parameters, such as

cc=me@me.com&subject=a subject&body = enter data here

An XHTML document with any of these or all of these parameters will not be successfully validated by W3C Validation Service. It does not matter, if you try to validate as XHTML Transitional 1.0 type or Strict type document. It is suggested that if you wish to use '**mailto**:' in your documents, you should not add any additional values to the following general syntax:-

```
<a href = "mailto: e-mail address" > Mail to someone </a>
                                     ----------------------
                                              ⇑
                                     click action apply on it
```

See example 3 for its application.

Address Types

Type	Features
http://	Hypertext Transfer Protocol - it links to a Web Site, and returns a Web page.
https://	As above, but it has security features. It is more protective for financial services, such as money transfers with both debit and credit cards.
ftp://	File transfer Protocol . You can also write it as FTP. It is used for copying files across the WWW. It works fine, if you create links to some files stored on some public sites.
gopher://	An old system, which is still useful, mainly in the academic world. Once, it was the only search tool which existed for users.
file://	It is a file link within your own system. This part of the address has an additional forward slash.
localhost://	Local Web server - for information from your own server.

Table 1

• Example 3

The purpose of this example is to demonstrate how to implement **mailto: action form** by sending email to Anne@adrlondon.ltd.uk

• Explanation

The XHTML code for calling up Microsoft Outlook Express on my system in order to send an e-mail to Ann@ adrlondon.ltd.uk is listed in Diagram 11. It is a simple document which involves the implementation of <a> element, with which you are familiar. However, the process of sending an e-mail by filling in a form requires some explanation. For this reason, I have sketched out all necessary steps as shown in Illustration 1 below.

The process of sending an e-mail by means of mailto: instruction

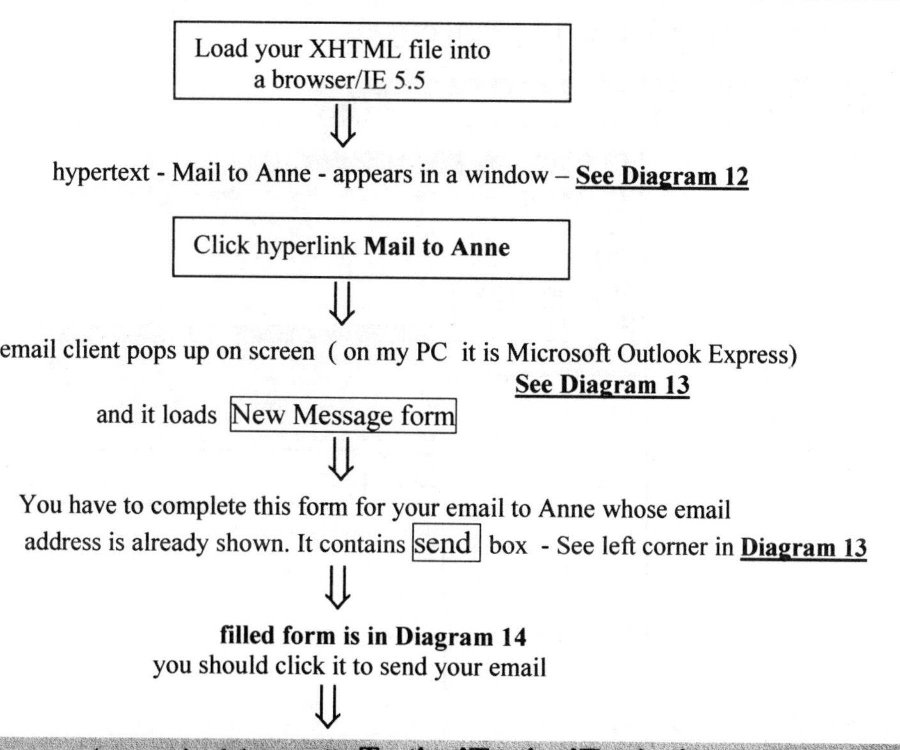

Load your XHTML file into a browser/IE 5.5
hypertext - Mail to Anne - appears in a window – See Diagram 12
Click hyperlink Mail to Anne
email client pops up on screen (on my PC it is Microsoft Outlook Express)
See Diagram 13
and it loads New Message form
You have to complete this form for your email to Anne whose email address is already shown. It contains send box - See left corner in Diagram 13
filled form is in Diagram 14
you should click it to send your email
Ann received the e-mail : Testing!Testing!Testing!

Illustration 1

The XHTML code for malito: form action - mailto.html

```
<?xml version= "1.0" encoding = "UTF-8"?>
<!DOCTYPE html
        PUBLIC "- //w3C//DTD XHTML 1.0 Strict//EN"
 "http://www.w3.org/TR/xhtml1/DTD/xhtml1- strict.dtd">
<html xmlns="http://www.w3.org/1999/xhtml" xml:lang="en" lang= "en">
<head>
<title> Mailto </title>
</head>
<body>
 <h3>
  <a href="mailto:Anne@adrlondon.ltd.uk"> Mail to Anne</a></h3>
</body></html>
```

Diagram 11

Diagrams 12, 13 and 14 respectively

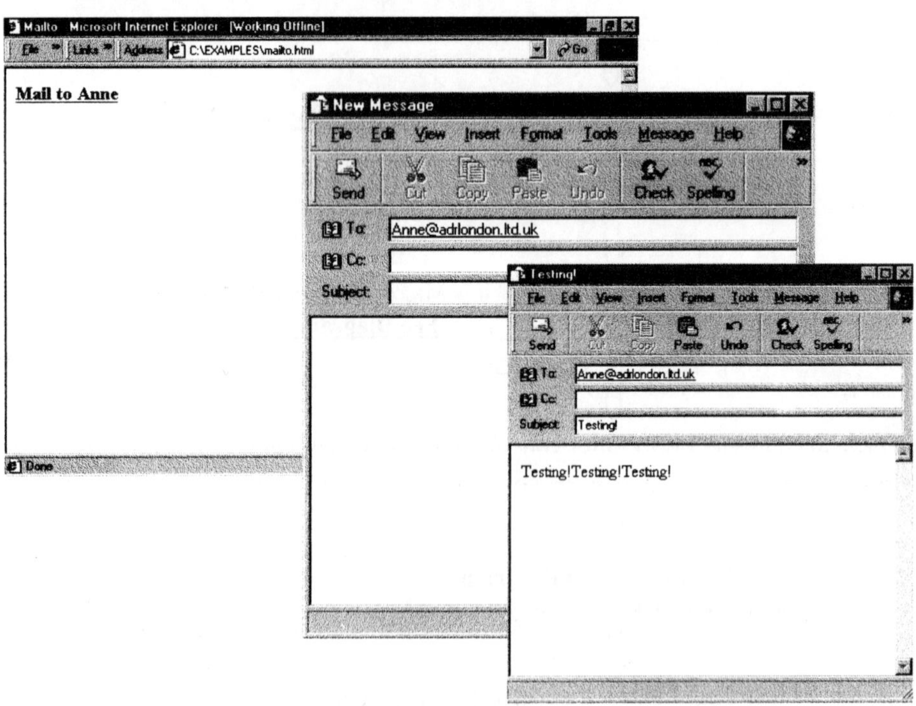

• Example 4

• Links across the Web

Table 2 shows a Web Site Address Book. If this address book is stored as an XHTML document, you should be able to load the file, say, in the IE 5.5, and click the hypertext of the required Web site for visiting it. Your task is to design an XHTML document for storing these addresses in this file.

Save it as **waddress.html**, or under any other suitable name. Check your document for XML well-formedness and validity as XHTML 1.0 Strict document. Finally, preview your document in order to check that it works satisfactorily.

Web Site Address Book

Organisation	Web Address	Hypertext to click
World Wide Web Consortium -	http://validator.w3.org/check/	W3C HTML Validation Service
Yahoo UK and Ireland -	http://www.yahoo.co.uk/	Yahoo
Waterstone's Booksellers -	http://www.waterstones.co.uk/	Watersone's
Microsoft Developer Network –	http://msdn.microsoft.com/developer/	Microsoft
A.D.R.(London)Ltd -	http://www.adrlondon.ltd.uk/	Home Page

Table 2

• Explanation

- This is an example of an absolute link type, when files are stored on different servers/computers. The source file, **waddress.html** is stored on your own computer, in which you must specify the full address of each Web site. The XHTML code for this file is listed in Diagram 11.
- In order to place Web site addresses in the form of a list, I have made use of XHTML list technique by creating an unordered list, **<ul>**. Within this list, the full address of each Web site is given as a list item,**<li>**.You have already learnt the techniques of creating lists in the last chapter. Therefore, it should not be too difficult for you to grasp this method.

The structure of each list item is pretty much the same, except, as one can expect, the full address of each Web site is different in each list item. The following analysis of a list item in this particular case, will help you to appreciate its structure and fully understand its function.

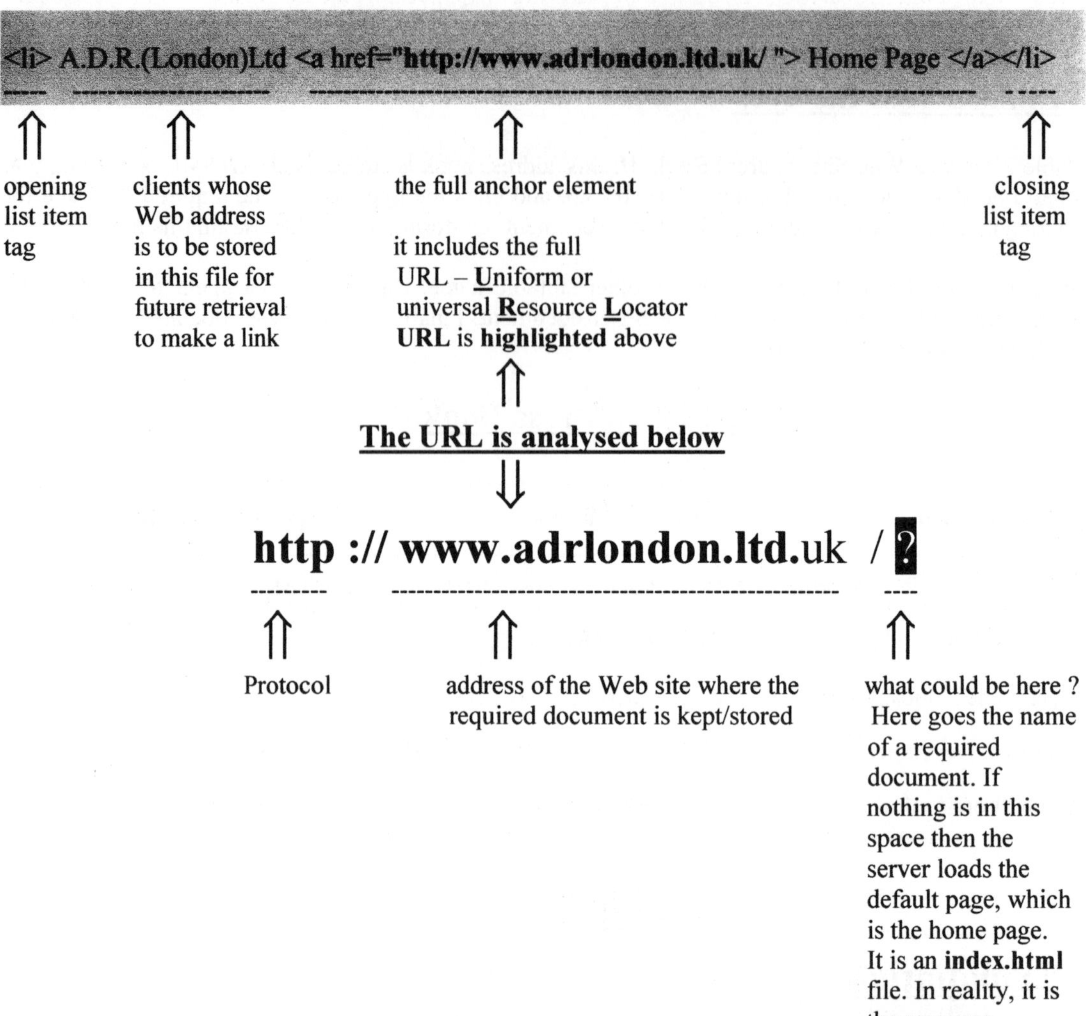
<li> A.D.R.(London)Ltd <a href="http://www.adrlondon.ltd.uk/ "> Home Page </a></li>
opening list item tag
clients whose Web address is to be stored in this file for future retrieval to make a link
the full anchor element
it includes the full URL – Uniform or universal Resource Locator
URL is highlighted above
closing list item tag
The URL is analysed below
http :// www.adrlondon.ltd.uk / ?
Protocol
address of the Web site where the required document is kept/stored
what could be here ? Here goes the name of a required document. If nothing is in this space then the server loads the default page, which is the home page. It is an index.html file. In reality, it is the resource location or the required document.

- Prior to previewing the document, it was validated as XHTML 1.0 Strict type document. The preview is shown in Diagram 12. Here, you can see that it matches with the information in Table 1. If you run this example on your machine, you will see that all hyperlinks are underlined and in a blue colour in IE.

  In fact, it is ready to operate as your 'Web Address Book', on-line. I made use of it by clicking the hypertext -Home Page of the last list item. I was immediately connected to ADR Web site, and their Home Page was displayed on my screen, ready for me to navigate it. See it Diagram 13.

ADR Home Page appeared in response to my clicking action, despite the fact that I did not specify the **waddress.html** in the above ADR URL. Thus, you can achieve the same result without specifying index.html file in a web site's URL. You can also link several documents together.

The XHTML code for waddress.html

```
<?xml version= "1.0" encoding = "UTF-8"?>
<!DOCTYPE html
        PUBLIC "- //w3C//DTD XHTML 1.0 Strict//EN"
 "http://www.w3.org/TR/xhtml1/DTD/xhtml1- strict.dtd">
<html xmlns="http://www.w3.org/1999/xhtml" xml:lang="en" lang= "en">
<head>
<title> Links across the Web </title>
</head>
<body>
<h1>Some Examples of URLs</h1>
<h2>You can click any of the following links to make a connection.</h2>

<ul>
   <li> World Wide Web Consortium
         <a href="http://validator.w3.org/check/">
         W3C HTML Validation Service</a></li>
   <li>Yahoo UK and Ireland
          <a href="http://www.yahoo.co.uk/">Yahoo</a></li>
   <li> Waterstone's Booksellers
           <a href="http://www.waterstones.co.uk/">Waterstone's</a></li>
   <li> Microsoft Developer Network
          <a href ="http://msdn.microsoft.com/developer/">
          Microsoft</a></li>
    <li>A.D.R.(London)Ltd<a href="http://www.adrlondon.ltd.uk/">Home Page </a></li>
</ul>
</body>
</html>
```

Diagram 15

You are given the opportunity of running solved examples on your system, so that you can learn more by doing, and consolidate your acquired knowledge and skills gained. **Practice makes perfect!**

Diagram 16 : A preview of Web Sites Address Book - linksWeb.html

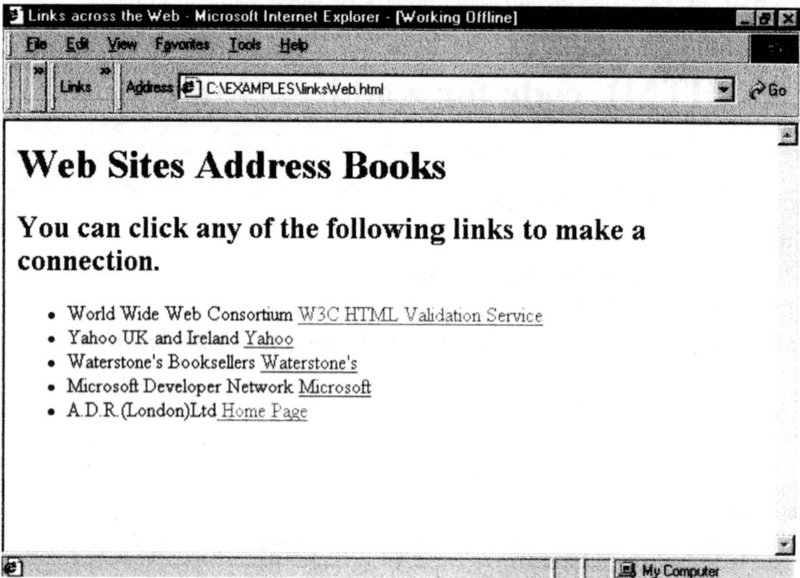

Diagram 17: Home Page loaded in response to a clicking action

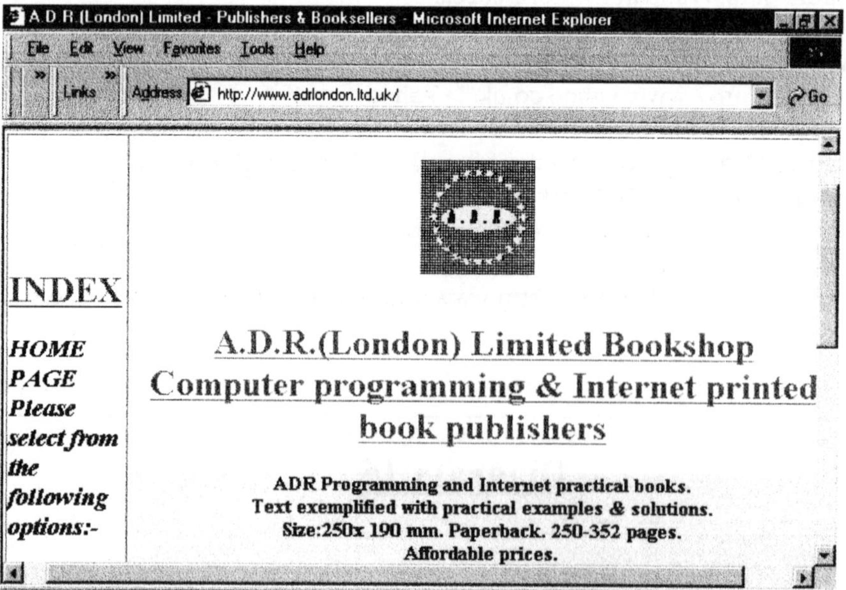

Chapter 11
Forms for Online Application

The prime aims of this chapter are as follows:-

- to assist you to understand the importance of forms in "dot com" commerce
- to enable you to understand that the design of on-line forms involves both a markup code and a programming code
- to equip you with XHTML techniques for form design
- to provide you with some practical information for learning script programming

By reading this chapter and practising techniques that are demonstrated here, you should be able:-

- to appreciate that the form content should be well thought out
- to explain the need for CGI script either embedded within the XHTML document or as an external CGI programming code needed for on-line data processing
- to know sources of CGI scripts on the Internet, and how to set up Perl on your PC
- to design forms by implementing a number of form controls and associated attributes and their values
- to validate document/form in order to prove that it meets XHTML 1.0 Transitional requirement
- to use input controls which are in a particular form in order test locally that these input controls are set correctly and that data can be collected by means of the form being tested

. Introduction

In today's "dot com " world of commerce, you meet all sorts of on-line forms. Any buying and selling or just obtaining some information from the Web, usually involves a form. The handling and processing of forms online has tremendously influenced the way paperwork was dealt with in the world of commerce, just a few years ago. Of course, there are still many commercial organisations which do not operate online commerce, but increasingly it is becoming likely that electronic commerce will be a way of life for the majority of people.

On the Web, the end user is directed to fill in the form online. Having filed in the form, the end user should submit it, there and then, usually to the same server from which the end user received the form. The server processes the information given, an action is taken, and the decision is displayed on the screen, there and then, in the form of another page/form.

Indeed, in business, form design for a good response is the responsibility of someone who specialises in this field. If you have to design online yourself, it is suggested that you should consider the proposed form design objectively, and seek answers, at least, to the following questions:-

- What is the purpose of the proposed form?
- What sort of concise and precise information should be collected?
- For what purpose is each piece of information needed?
- Who is likely to complete the form?
- What sort of precise and concise information will the respondent be able to provide freely?
- Will the respondent be in a position to have the required information?
- How and when will the collected information become meaningful, and useful?
- Will the decision on the information processed be in the form of a form? if so,
- Will the form on which the decision is to be communicated have sufficient information for the form receiver's use?

On a number of occasions, I have bought some goods from well-known companies on the Internet, and paid in advance. When I wanted to return goods, I could not communicate with the department responsible for payment or complaint, as the form which served as acceptance of my order, and demanded payment in advance, had no address, phone, fax, or even e-mail address for further communication. Such a form design does not encourage me to place another order with the same company again!

It will not serve any useful purpose if you just include form filling in your Web pages without the careful planning and consideration of your requirements and the users' perceived responses, and contact information for customer care or for a better relationship. You may consider modifying your current business forms and converting them into your XHTML format, if you think that these forms are still relevant for on-line business. In this chapter, I have demonstrated some essential tools for creating forms for on-line use. No emphases are placed on information content of any form for any commercial purposes.

• Forms for online data processing

The task of creating forms for data processing on-line entails XHTML markup code and CGI script.

1. XHTML markup code

The information needed to create a blank form is coded in XHTML, and some presentation styles incorporated into the form design to create a Web page, which is a form for data collection.

2. Common Gateway Interface (CGI) script

When a user requests information from the Web, the browser finds out which computer has the information and sends a request to it. The computer that has the information receives the request, understands it, and then sends back a response to the browser. This relationship between the browser and the program on the other computer is known as a client –server relationship. The browser is the client, and the other computer, where the program resides, is the server.

It is the client/browser, which is requesting the services from the server. The server is residing on the other computer. In this client/server relationship, the server understands the request from the web browser, and responds to it. This server is known as a **Web Server**. This relationship is visualised as a communication between client/Server and WWW in Illustration 1.

Now imagine that you are sitting by your PC, which has a Web browser, and that you can link to the Net through a Web server which resides at another computer, say at your ISP. If you start viewing Web pages on line, your PC becomes a client, and the other computer at your ISP is your Web server. Further, assume that the Web page has a form, on which you must provide some information to buy something on the Net. So, you must fill in a form on-line, and submit it by clicking on a submit button. The data/information you have provided on this form has to be processed. For this data processing task, a CGI script is required. The CGI script collects the data, and processes it.

The Common Gateway Interface (CGI) is a well-known data processing method used by Web servers in order to process data. This is usually called server-side programming. Thus, it is a programming activity, which involves writing a piece of programming code. CGI programs can be written in several programming languages, such as Perl, JavaScript, C++, C, Python and some other languages.

• Perl

It is the first popular language for CGI programming. It has been in use since 1987, and has been developing ever since.

It originated at Unix. Perl programs work well with Unix servers. At the time of writing, the current stable release is 5.6. Its popularity is due to its simplicity and usefulness as it is a portable language. It means that Perl programs can be run on a large number of computers and operating systems, including Microsoft Windows.

A visualised communication between Client/Server and WWW

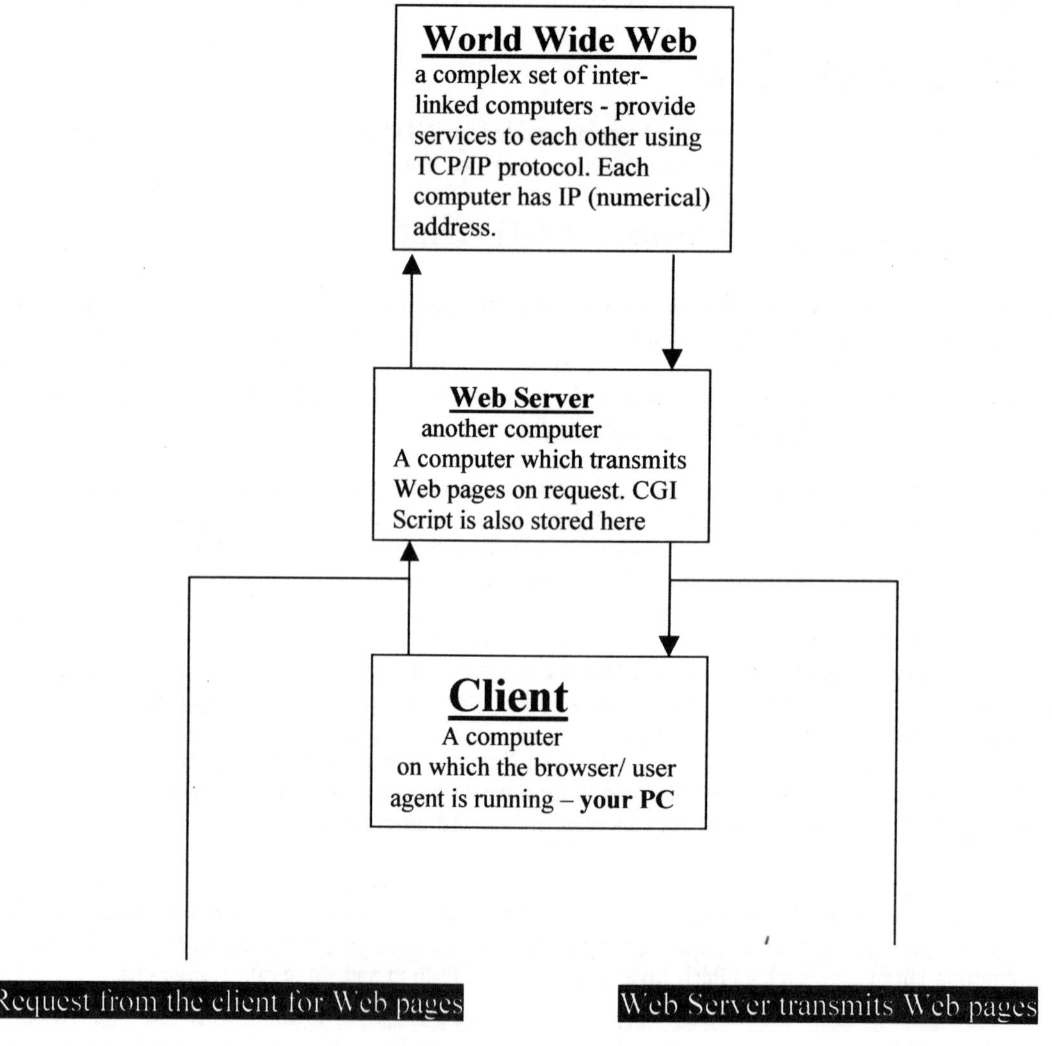

Illustration 1

• JavaScript

It is another popular scripting language. To complicate matters, both Microsoft and Netscape have their own JavaScripts. JavaScript from Java has 'Active Server Pages' (ASP), and Netscape offer 'Server-side JavaScript' (SSJS). One can include ASP or SSJS code in an XHTML document. If you do so, it is the server which executes the script to create the Web page. ASP is a part of Microsoft's Internet Information Server (IIS). In the next section, I have listed some useful Web site addresses on CGI resources.

• What should you do about CGI Script?

This book is about XHTML. Of course, in order to collect form data and process it, you must make use of CGI code either embedded in your XHTML document or written and stored as an external program. In this chapter, you will learn how forms are designed and how they work. However, in order to make a form perform its function, you have to have a relevant CGI script. There are a number of Web sites from where one can download CGI scripts. It is suggested that you consult CGI Resource Index at the following Web site:

http://www.cgi-resources.cm/

You will find more than 3300 CGI resources listed in some 270 categories. So, there must be some scripts in Perl, JavaScript, and so on for your particular data processing requirements. You can obtain Free CGI scripts. You must visit it to find out how many scripts are there, and available free of charge. You can adopt the chosen script for form data processing.

On the other hand, if you are a student or hoping to become a professional Webmaster, then you must acquire practical knowledge and skills of developing workable CGI scripts in Perl, JavaScript, or any other CGI languages. I prefer Perl. So, take the next step of visiting a big technical bookshop or a campus bookshop, which is well equipped with Internet/Web/computer programming books. Your investment in a good Perl book will yield fruitful results in the future. Of course, you need Perl itself.

• The <input> element & input controls

When completing a form, there has to be some sort of standard space or input area on the screen in which the user can enter the data. At one time, there was only one element <input> to enter data in this input area. So, a form could have a number of <input> elements.

For instance, if there were five <input> elements, there were five spaces, or say, five boxes in which the user could enter data. This was the only input control for entering data. At present, there are ten different types of input controls. These are outlined in Tables 1,1A and 1B. Like other elements, these control elements can take some relevant attributes. The attributes which are associated with input controls are listed in Tables 2 and 2A.

Form input controls (cont. in Table 1A)

Control	Nature	Tag used for creating control
. buttons	. A form should have a minimum of one button. This button is known as **submit**. What is its purpose? The submit button sends the data back to you. . There is another useful button called **reset** It is very useful, as it lets the user clear the response so that you can re-enter it - change of mind allowed!	. <input type = "submit" /> . <input type = "reset" />
. radio buttons	. A number of radio buttons can be put together as a group, but you are allowed to select just one of the **predefined choices** at a time. . When you create a group, you can assign it a particular **name** of your choice, but different **values**. Reason for it → . Unselected buttons → called inactive →	. <input type = "radio" name = "radio" value ="3" / > in this tag, you have to include **name** and **value** for a group otherwise, default value is returned . name = value → a pair . to match answers to relevant questions . no value returned and thus ignored
. checkboxes	. Useful for selecting several choices from a list of **predefined choices**. . A checkbox can be **checked** by the the user. This is useful for simple yes/no type responses.	. <input type = "checkbox" name = "cbx" value = "1" /> . name = value as for radio buttons OR . default value →**on** for the checked box
. text boxes	. Use for entering a single line text. . It is the most applied element. . This is the most versatile element and it can take a number of options → . Useful for many user entries.	. Please enter your surname <input type = "text" name="name" size = "no" / > . It can take the following attributes: . name . value . size .maxlength

Table 1

Form input controls (cont. from Table 1)

Control	Description	Example / Notes
. text areas	. Gives the user the choice to enter several lines of text. You can fix its size in terms of rows & columns . Anyway, it is still limited to what a user's browser can display . It is commonly used	. <textarea name ="name" cols ="40" rows = "4"> Please type here </textarea> . the column **width** is one character . the default size = 20 column by 2 rows . Maximum size cannot be specified
. drop-down menus and scrollbarboxes/bars *other names for this control: select box, option group and list box*	. For multiple choices . User must press CTRL+ mouse.	. <select name = "ss " size ="no."> </select> It can let you select a number of options or the user can select the whole list. The option tag is . <option value = "1" > </select>
	. An option can be "selected" first to encourage the user to choose it as his/her answer	. <option selected>**LONDON** is the name already selected , but the user can change it
	. When size is given with multiple choice, no scroll bar appears	. for choosing just a single option from an <option> **Birmingham**, where Birmingham is the option
	. For a single choice, scroll bar is displayed, so that a choice can be made	
. password	. similar to the text **box** . user's input is hidden for security purposes . typed characters are masked as asterisks	. <input type = “password” name = “ss” size = “25” />
. file input	. accepts a file as an input . it creates a browser button so that the user can click it to locate the desired file . displays an input filed in which a file can be placed for upload	. <input type =“ file” name = “ss” />

Table 1A

Form input controls (cont. from Table 1A)

. **hidden**	. this is hidden form control . it contains data which is is invisible to the end use but a Web author wants to include as part of data for some other specific reason	. <input type =" hidden" name = "ss" value = " value" /> . it always requires these three attributes type, name and value
. **image**	. it is a graphical submit control . image is in a separate file	. <input type = "image" src = Anne.gif" alt = picture" /> . **src** attribute is essential

Table 1B

Attributes associated with input element<input>

Attribute	feature
type	. it is used with all controls, as it establishes which input control is going to be created.
name	. it is used with all <input> elements. The submit button does not need it. Use it for naming controls, so that you can receive information from controls.
value	. the value is passed to the server when you click the submit button.
disabled	. if you click the 'disabled' button, the control remains visible but unusable, and thus no input is allowed.
size	. the size of a control is set in numeric value.
maxlength	. it sets the maximum number of characters which can be input
. **checked**	. usually in buttons, radio buttons , checkboxes and drop-down menus, an item is pre-selected.
accept	. it is used with file control in order to specify the media type which can be accepted.

Table 2

Attributes associated with input element<input> (cont. from Table 2)

Attribute	feature
. src	. it is used with image file in order to link the external resource.
. alt	. it specifies the text which should appear if the graphic image cannot be displayed
. align	. it can align the control physically.

Table 2 A

. How do you create a form?

- **The <form> element** is at the heart of creating any form, in the same way as the **<TABLE...> tag** is for designing tables. It takes two mandatory attributes namely, **action** and **method**.
- **A fine distinction** between the mandatory attribute **action** and **method** is illustrated below.

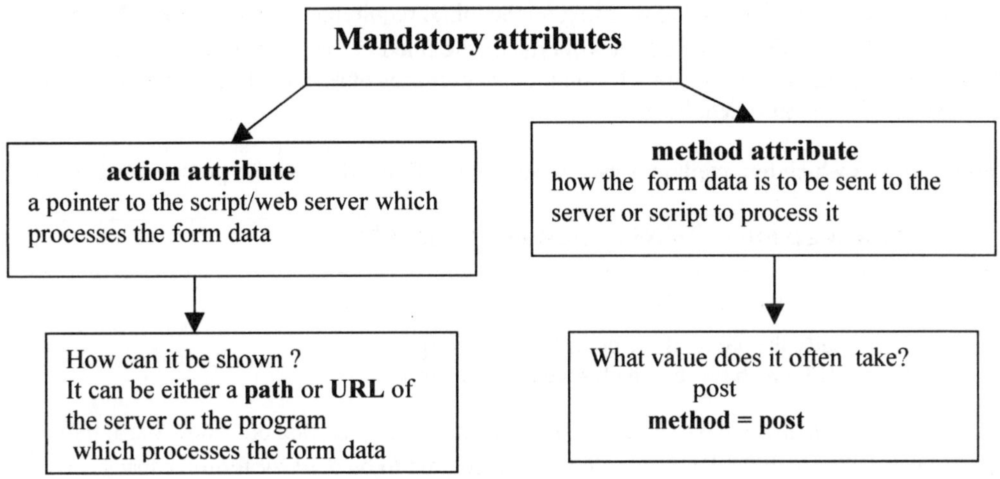

Illustration 2

Now that ten input controls and some attributes which are associated with these controls have been explained, it is time to demonstrate their use by means of some solved examples. These examples create simple forms.

• Example 1

• Creating text boxes & submit button

The purpose is to design a simple form using the text boxes control. The form is to be filled in by the user, by entering his/her name in a one-line box. This is to be followed by his/her address in three simple boxes, each will have only one line of text.

At the end of the address, the user must write free booklet number available from you. Since the form has to be processed using the CGI, the user must be given the opportunity to send it off to the server, by simply clicking the submit button. You can incorporate some style sheet rules, if you so desire.

Prior to previewing it in the IE5.5 or any other user agent, check your XHTMlL 1.0 Transitional document for XML well-formedness and Validity by submitting it to W3C Validation Service.

• Explanation

The XHTML code for this example is listed in diagram 1. It has been validated successfully by W3C Validation Service. In Diagram 1, I have shown style sheet rules on a shaded background.

- The following line contains the code for setting up the initial requirements to get feedback from a form. '**action**' specifies CGI script which will process the filled in form. Here, it is "URL" (see below). Since, this form is not for any commercial purposes other than demonstrating how to create a form, "URL" is sufficient here.

  '**method**' specifies which http method is used to submit the form with data for processing. here, it is **post**.

  <form action = "URL" method = "post">

  It is usually the name of the program (CGI script)
  at your ISP /Web server which processes the form

- It is emphasised that when you have to set up your Web site, you must find out from your Internet Service Provider (ISP) the full URL of the CGI script/program to be used for form feedback purposes. You must also discuss with your ISP firm, if they offer any programs which can make feedback from the form easier and present it in a meaningful format. It may be that you are expecting a large number of forms, and therefore, it is worth sorting out from the start, if there is any likely text tidying up to do, when the form feedback is returned to you, and how to achieve it.

- The segment of the code **<div> Please enter your full name:- </div>** - here the heading of the text box is contained within a generic block level element <div>. 'div' stands for division.

It is ideally suited for use with Cascading Style Sheets. It creates a line break before and after the element. It does not create any vertical white space, except a line break. In Diagram 1, you can see that I have placed all three headings within this element If you examine carefully Diagrams 2 and 3, you can find out that its application has resulted in creating line breaks between each heading and a text box that follows it.

- **<input type = "text" name ="name" size = "40" />
** It creates a text box, 40 characters long. The value of text boxes are data items which the end user enters into them. See the screen capture in Diagram 3 in which all text boxes are filled in with data/information – values of boxes.

- **<input type = submit value = "send it now!">** - this segment of the code creates the submit button.

This caption is printed on the submit button, which the user must click in order to submit data to the server.

• What happened when the submit button "send it now!" was clicked?

<form action = "URL" method = "post"> - this segment of the code does not points to an actual URL of any programming script designed for data processing. Thus, it is not a workable URL. When clicked the submit button, IE 5.5 generated an the following error message. The message does not point to this reason, but now you know why this has occurred.

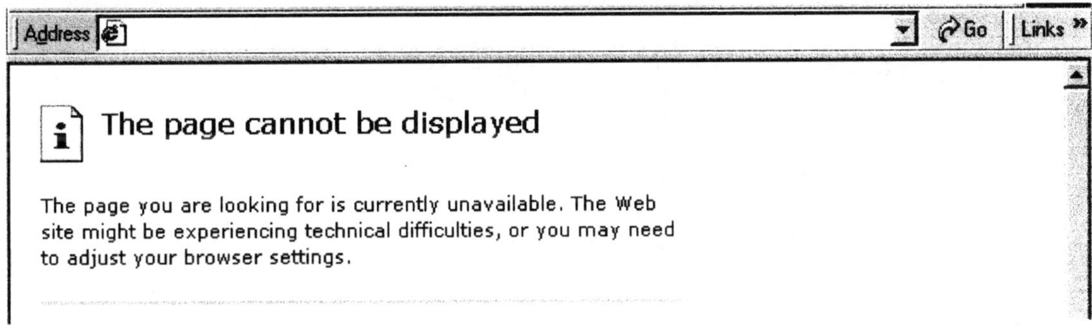

Error Message

The XHTML code for example 1 – form1.html

```
<?xml version= "1.0" encoding = "UTF-8"?>
<!DOCTYPE html
        PUBLIC "- //w3C//DTD XHTML 1.0 Transitional//EN"
 "http://www.w3.org/TR/xhtml1/DTD/xhtml1- transitional.dtd">
<html xmlns="http://www.w3.org/1999/xhtml" xml:lang="en" lang= "en">
<head>
<title> A Simple Form </title>
<style type ="text/css">
body{
        background-color:aqua;   }
h2{
     color = black;
      font-size =110%;
      font-style:normal;}
div {
      color = black;
      font-size =120%;
      font-style:italic; }
</style>
</head>
<body>
<h2>
       Please help us to help you by sending your completed form to us   </h2>
       <form action = "URL" method = "post">
 <div> Please enter your full name:- </div>

<input type = "text" name ="name" size = "40" /><br />

 <div>   Please enter your address below:- </div>

       <input type = "text"   name = "add1"   size = "30" /> <br />
       <input type = "text"   name = "add2"   size = "30" />  <br />
       <input type = "text"   name = "add3"   size = "30" /> <br />

   <div> Please enter free booklet number:- </div>
      <input type = "text"   name ="no."   size ="12" /> <br />
       <input type = "submit"  value = "send it now!" />
</form>
</body>
</html>
```

Diagram 1

Diagram 2: This preview shows blank form ready to be completed by the end user

A Simple Form - Microsoft Internet Explorer

File Links Address C:\EXAMPLES\form1.html Go

Please help us to help you by sending your completed form to us

Please enter your full name:-

Please enter your address below:-

Please enter free booklet number:-

send it now!

A Simple Form - Microsoft Internet Explorer - [Working Offline]

File Links Address C:\EXAMPLES\form1.html Go

Please help us to help you by sending your completed form to us

Please enter your full name:-

Mr John Smith

Please enter your address below:-

1 High Street

Nocity

NO11 2AA

Please enter free booklet number:-

12348901

send it now!

Diagram 3 above: you can examine the whole form together with data entered in all text boxes. It has worked, as it was successfully tested and previewed in the IE 5.5

- **Example 2**

- **Checkboxes, radio buttons and text area**

Credit Assessment Form A

Status - please tick an appropriate box for status:-

Married Single Co-habitation ⇐ **Checkboxes**

Employment - Please tick an appropriate box for employment:-

Employed Unemployed Self-employed Retired ⇐ **Checkboxes**

Annual income - Please tick an appropriate box for annual income in UK Pounds:-

25000 20000 –24999 16000-19999 12000-15999 8000-11999 Under 8000 ⇐ **Check-boxes**

Type of accommodation - Please select type of accommodation:-

Property Owner Council/Housing Trust Accommodation Private Rented Accommodation ⇐ **Radio Buttons**

Full Name and address - Please enter your full name and current address:-

⇐ **Text area**

Send it now! ⇐ **Submit Button/caption on it**

Illustration 3

The task is to design a Credit assessment Form A in order to enable the interviewer to complete it, on the screen, with a client for a personal loan. Your form design should include some pre-defined choices. During the interview with a client, the interviewer clicks the correct answer given by the client, and records the full name and address of the person being interviewed.

In Illustration 3, I have listed seven different sections of this proposed form. Where necessary, I have also indicated which 'form input controls' should be used for these pre-defined choices, recording the full name and address of the client being interviewed. Finally, you should also include a submit button with a caption on it. The form should be on a yellow background, text in black, and each section heading highlighted.

Save your XHTML document as **from2.html**, or under any other suitable name. Prior to previewing it in IE or any other user agent, submit it to W3C Validation Service for validation as XHTML 1.0 Transitional type document.

The XHTML code for example 2 – form2.html (cont. in Diagram 4A)

```
<?xml version= "1.0" encoding = "UTF-8"?>
<!DOCTYPE html
        PUBLIC "- //w3C//DTD XHTML 1.0 Transitional//EN"
 "http://www.w3.org/TR/xhtml1/DTD/xhtml1- transitional.dtd">
<html xmlns="http://www.w3.org/1999/xhtml" xml:lang="en" lang= "en">

<head>
<title> Checkboxes, radio buttons and Text area </title>
<style type ="text/css">
body{ background-color:#ffff00;}          /*yellow*/
h2{  color =#000000;                      /*black*/
     font-size =110%;
     font-style:normal;
     text-decoration:"underline";
     text-align:"center";  }
 div { color =#000000;
      font-size =110%;
      font-style:normal; }
</style></head>
<body>
<h2>Credit Assessment Form A</h2>
   <form action = "URL" method = "post">
<div>Status - please tick an appropriate box for status:-</div>
     <input type = "checkbox" name ="status" value ="married" />Married
     <input type = "checkbox" name ="status" value ="single" />Single
     <input type = "checkbox" name ="status" value ="cohabit" />Co-habitation
<div> Employment - Please tick an appropriate box for employment:-</div>
     <input type = "checkbox" name ="employment" value ="emp" />Employed
     <input type = "checkbox" name ="status" value ="unemp " />Unemployed
     <input type = "checkbox" name ="status" value ="selfemp" />Self-employed
     <input type = "checkbox" name ="status" value ="ret" />Retired
```

Diagram 4

The XHTML code for example 2 – form2.html (cont. from Diagram 4)

```
<div> Annual income - Please tick an appropriate box for annual income in UK Pounds:-</div>
    <input type = "checkbox" name ="income" value ="earnings" />25000 +
    <input type = "checkbox" name ="income" value ="earnings" />20000-24999
    <input type = "checkbox" name ="income" value ="earnings" />16000-19999
    <input type = "checkbox" name ="income" value ="earnings" />12000-15999<br />
    <input type = "checkbox" name ="income" value ="earnings" />8000 -11999
   <input type = "checkbox" name ="income" value ="earnings" />Under 8000

<div> Type of accommodation - Please select type of accommodation:-</div>
    <input type = "radio" name ="accommodation" value ="owner" />Property Owner
    <input type = "radio" name ="accommodation" value ="council" />
    Council/Housing Trust Accommodation<br />
     <input type = "radio" name ="accommodation" value ="private" />
     Private Rented Accommodation

<div>Full Name and address - Please enter your full name and current address:-</div>
    <textarea  name ="address" rows ="5" cols="60" ></textarea><br />
     <input type = "submit"  value = "Send it now!" />
</form>
</body>
</html>
```

Diagram 4A

• Explanation

The structure of the code listed in Diagrams 4 & 4A is pretty much the same as for the previous example. I have shown style sheet rules on a shaded background in Diagram 4 for your ease of learning.

As in Example 1, the segment of the code: **<form action = "URL" method = "post">** is not pointing to any CGI program or a Web site, where such a script is stored. The URL is here to construct the code, so that its application can be demonstrated. Even so, it is the right time to ask:-

. Which values should be passed to CGI script?

- Enter your answers on this form, and click the submit button, it will not transmit anything, and you will get an error, as shown above. There is no action.

A preview of Credit Assessment Form A in IE 5.5

Example 2 - form2.html

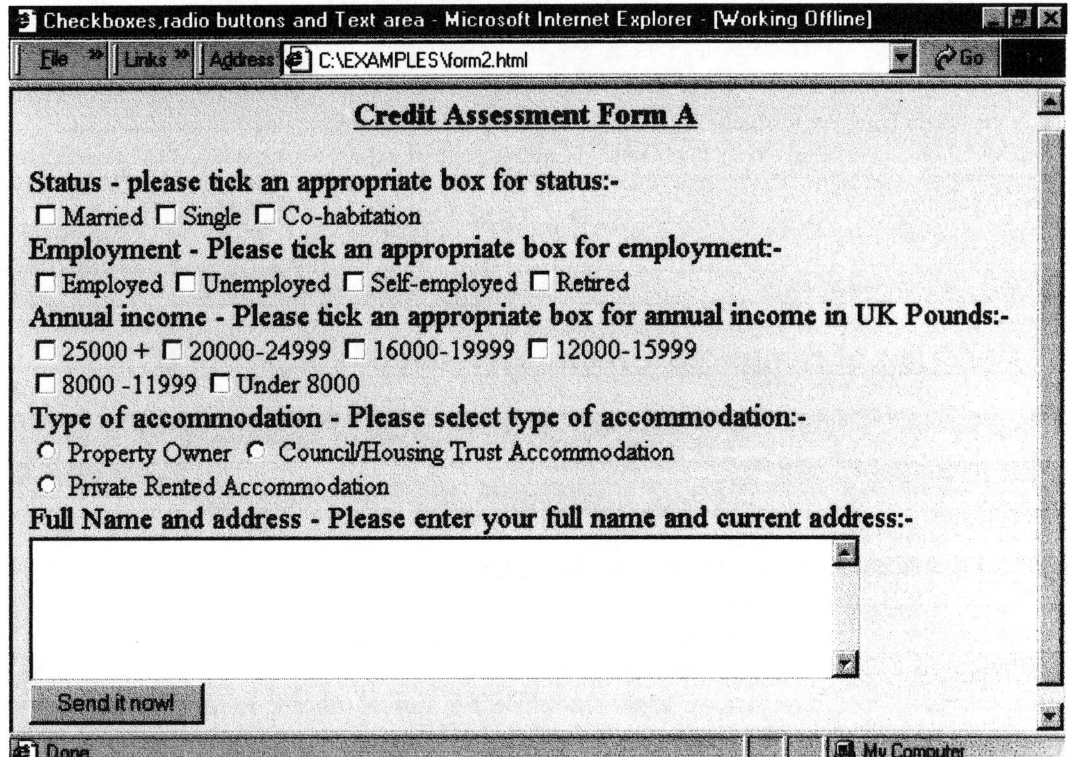
Checkboxes,radio buttons and Text area - Microsoft Internet Explorer - [Working Offline]

File » Links » Address C:\EXAMPLES\form2.html Go

Credit Assessment Form A

Status - please tick an appropriate box for status:-

☐ Married ☐ Single ☐ Co-habitation

Employment - Please tick an appropriate box for employment:-

☐ Employed ☐ Unemployed ☐ Self-employed ☐ Retired

Annual income - Please tick an appropriate box for annual income in UK Pounds:-

☐ 25000 + ☐ 20000-24999 ☐ 16000-19999 ☐ 12000-15999

☐ 8000 -11999 ☐ Under 8000

Type of accommodation - Please select type of accommodation:-

○ Property Owner ○ Council/Housing Trust Accommodation

○ Private Rented Accommodation

Full Name and address - Please enter your full name and current address:-

Send it now!

Done My Computer

Diagram 5

The above form is ready to be completed by the interviewer. The interviewer has completed it on behalf of a client. See Diagram 6.

- **Which values should be passed to CGI script when URL is pointing to a CGI script?**

However, assume that the URL in **<form action = "URL" method = "post">** is pointing to a CGI script. Now, enter answers, and click submit button. In this case, the following value in pairs will be transmitted to the server:-

Single	checked,
Employed	checked
2000 – 24999	checked
Property Owner	checked

- Checkboxes and radio buttons are controls, which can be either checked (true) or unchecked(false). You can see in Diagram 6 which of the checkboxes and radio buttons the interviewer clicked in response to the answers given by the client. The above pairs of values correspond to the answers give.

- The value of text area are the data entered in it. It is also transmitted to the CGI script as

full address	name and the address entered

A preview of completed Credit Assessment Form A in IE 5.5

Checkboxes,radio buttons and Text area - Microsoft Internet Explorer - [Working Offline]

File » Links » Address C:\EXAMPLES\form2.html Go

Credit Assessment Form A

Status - please tick an appropriate box for status:-
☐ Married ☑ Single ☐ Co-habitation

Employment - Please tick an appropriate box for employment:-
☑ Employed ☐ Unemployed ☐ Self-employed ☐ Retired

Annual income - Please tick an appropriate box for annual income in UK Pounds:-
☐ 25000 + ☐ 20000-24999 ☑ 16000-19999 ☐ 12000-15999
☐ 8000 -11999 ☐ Under 8000

Type of accommodation - Please select type of accommodation:-
◉ Property Owner ○ Council/Housing Trust Accommodation
○ Private Rented Accommodation

Full Name and address - Please enter your full name and current address:-

```
Mr Jonh Bull
100 High Road
High City
HG1 2CIT
```

Send it now!

Done My Computer

Diagram 6

• Example 3

• Drop-down menus and scrollboxes

Drop-down menus and scrollboxes offer multiple choices to the respondent. In order to design a form containing these features, besides other required elements, you must implement <select> and <option> elements in the same document. The technique is demonstrated below:-

Test Cricket 2001 England

Please select place(s) to watch test matches. If several selections, press CTRL key and click left mouse simultaneously:-

London
Manchester
Nottingham
Leeds
Birmingham
Cardiff

Please select one travel mode. If several selections, press CTRL key and click left mouse simultaneously:-

By air
By car
By train
By coach

Please write below your telephone number and fax number (if any):-

Send it now!

- Your task is to design a Web page in order to display the above form for on-line completion by the respondent. Use style sheet rules for text formatting, and displaying the form on a yellow background. It is in your own interest to check the document for XML well-formedness and validity as XHTML 1.0 Transitional. Preview it in the IE or any other user agent before public viewing.

• Explanation

The XHTML code for this form design is shown in Diagrams 7 and 7A. Having being validated by

W3C Validation Service, I previewed it in my IE 5.5. The XHTML document has met all the above requirements. See the screen capture in Diagram 8.

- The structure of this document is similar to the structure of the document in the example. The major point to remember is that elements <select> and <option> should be used one after the other in order to allow selection of any items from a given number of choices. Furthermore, to let the respondent select more than one place to visit and more than one mode of travel, you must place the attribute in the <select> element, as shown below:-

```
<select name ="test" multiple ="multiple">
```

do not write a number here as in HTML 4.0

This segment of the code defines the selection process for an unlimited number of options to choose from. The selecting of each option is set by the following segment of the code, say for selecting London for watching the test cricket:-

```
<option value ="Lond"> London</option>
```

For each selection, you must have a separate <option> ....</option> code. When all selections are coded, you must not forget to place the </select> tag. This way, all options are within the selection process defined as multiple selection.

- The function of the following segment of the code is to display the instruction given without allowing the respondent to alter it at all. This way, the option is visible, but unchangeable(disabled).

```
<option disabled ="disabled"> Please write below your telephone number and fax number (if any):-
```

The XHTML code for example 3 form3.html (cont.in Diagram 7A

```
<?xml version= "1.0" encoding = "UTF-8"?>
<!DOCTYPE html
        PUBLIC "- //w3C//DTD XHTML 1.0 Transitional//EN"
 "http://www.w3.org/TR/xhtml1/DTD/xhtml1- transitional.dtd">
<html xmlns="http://www.w3.org/1999/xhtml" xml:lang="en" lang= "en">
<head>
<title> Drop-down menus and scrollboxes </title>
<style type ="text/css">
body{background-color:#ffff00; }              /*yellow*/
```

Diagram 7

The XHTML code for example 3 - form3.html (cont. from Diagram 7)

```
h2{
      color =#000000;                        /*black*/
      font-size =100%;
      font-style:normal;
      text-decoration:"underline";           /* underline */
      text-align:"center"; }
 h3 {
      color =#000000;
      font-size =80%;
      font-style:normal;
      text-align:"center";
      text-decoration:"underline";}
</style></head>
<body>
  <h2> Test Cricket 2001 England </h2>
  <form action = "URL"   method = "post">
<h3>Please select place(s) to watch test matches. If several selections,
      press CTRL key and click left mouse simultaneously:- </h3>
  <h3>
         <select name ="test" multiple ="multiple">
        <option value ="Lond">  London</option>
        <option value ="Man">   Manchester</option>
        <option value ="Nott">Nottingham </option>
        <option value ="Le" >   Leeds</option>
        <option value ="Bir" >  Birmingham</option>
        <option value ="Card" > Cardiff </option>
</select></h3>
 <h3>  Please select one travel mode. If several selections,
        press CTRL key and click left mouse simultaneously:-</h3>
             <select name ="jour" multiple ="multiple">
             <option value ="air">  By air    </option>
             <option value ="car">  By car    </option>
             <option value ="train">By train  </option>
             <option value ="coach"> By coach </option>
</select>
<select>
    <option disabled ="disabled"> Please write below your telephone number and fax number (if any):-
</option>
</select><h3>  <textarea  name = "com" cols = "50"   rows ="2" ></textarea></h3>
                  <input type = "submit" value = "Send it now!" />
</form></body></html>
```

Diagram 7A

A preview of the document in IE 5.5 – form3.html

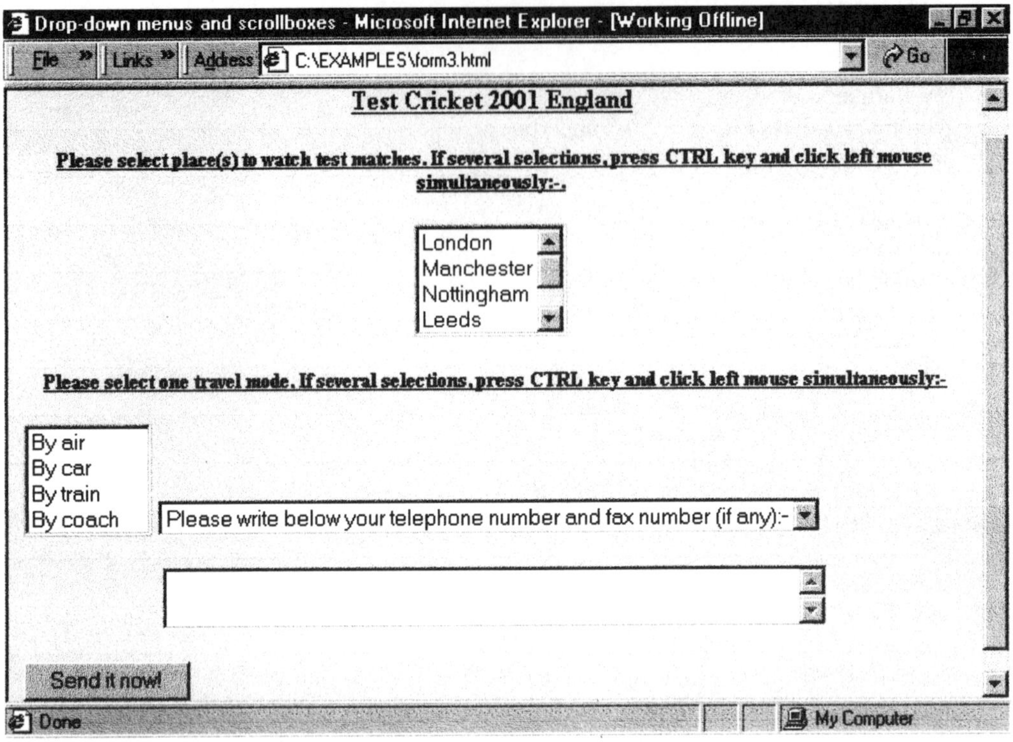

Diagram 8

The form is ready to be filled in by the end user.

• Example 4

• Some input controls & associated attributes

The task is to design a form for collecting and maintaing staff personal records and private addresses. The areas of this proposed form are shown below in the shaded area. You should save your XHTML document. Prior to previewing it locally, it must be checked for XML well-formedness and validity as XHTML 1.0 Transitional document. Your form design should provide the end user with some boxes in which the text can be entered. In addition, the end user should be given the opportunity to make a selection. Use relevant input controls and associated attributes for different areas of the form.

Furthermore, the end user should be able to submit and resubmit the form. The entire form should be displayed on a coloured background. You can also apply some style sheet rules in order to make the form display attractive, but do not over do it.

GlobalWeb PLC			
Staff Personal Record and Private Address			
National Insurance No.		Date of Birth	
Employment commenced		Employment Ended	
Full Name/Mr/Mrs/other status			
Street			
Town		Country	Code:
Telephone:	Fax/e-mail	Job Title	Dept:
Full Time Staff	Part Time Staff	Male	Female
	Note :-	⇐ **this note should be by itself as a box on a separate line**	
	Send button	resubmit button	⇐ **both button should be side-by-side**

• Explanation

The XHTML code is listed in Diagrams 9 and 9A. Its structure is similar to the structure of the documents developed in this chapter. It was submitted to W3C Validation Srvice, and validated successfully as XHTML Transitional 1. 0 document. Its preview is shown in Diagram 10. You should run it on your PC to learn from personal experience.

The XHTM code for example 4 - form 4.html (cont. in Diagram 9A)

```
<?xml version= "1.0" encoding = "UTF-8"?>
<!DOCTYPE html
        PUBLIC "- //w3C//DTD XHTML 1.0 Transitional//EN"
 "http://www.w3.org/TR/xhtml1/DTD/xhtml1- transitional.dtd">
<html xmlns="http://www.w3.org/1999/xhtml" xml:lang="en" lang= "en">
<head>
<title> Staff Record </title>
```

Diagram 9

The XHTM code for Example 4 - form 4.html (cont. from Diagram 9)

```
<style type="text/css">
body{background-color:#00ffff;}                                    /* Aqua colour *?
h3{ font-size =110%; font-style:normal; text-align ="center";  text-decoration:"underline";   }
 p {text-align ="center"; }
</style></head>

<body>
     <form action = "URL"   method = "post">

      <h3> GlobalWeb PLC<br />
               Staff Personal Record and Private Address </h3>
  <fieldset>
           National Insurance No. <input type = "text" name ="NI" size= "20" />
           Date of Birth<input type ="text" name ="dob" size ="10" /> <br /><br />
           Employment commenced. <input type = "text" name ="EmpC" size= "10" />
           Employment Ended: <input type ="text" name ="EmpE" size ="10" /><br />
           Full Name/Mr/Mrs/other status: <input type = "text" name ="FulN"   size = "80" /><br />
           Street:  <input type = "text" name ="st"   size = "80" /> <br />
           Town:<input type ="text" name ="town" size =" 30" />
           Country:<input type ="text" name ="count" size ="20" />
           Code:<input type ="text" name ="code" size ="8" />
           Telephone: <input type = "text" name ="phone" size = "20" />
           Fax/e-mail:<input type = "text" name ="phone" size = "20" />
</fieldset>
<fieldset>
           Job Title: <input type = "text" name = "JB" size = "30" />
           Dept:  <input type = "text"  name = "Qant" size ="20" />
</fieldset>
          <input type = "radio" name = "staff" value = "fts" /> Full Time Staff
          <input type = "radio" name = "staff" value = "pts" /> Part Time Staff
          <input type ="checkbox"  name = "staff" value = "1" /> Male
          <input type ="checkbox"  name = "staff" value = "1" /> female
   <p>   Note:- <textarea  name =" com"   cols = "40"  rows = "1"> </textarea><br />
         <input type = "submit" value = "Send it now!" />
         <input type = "reset" value ="Resubmit" /></p>
</form>
</body>
</html>
```

Diagram 9 A

A preview of document designed as a form for example 4

Staff Record - Microsoft Internet Explorer - [Working Offline]

File » Links » Address C:\My Documents\EXAMPLES\form4.html Go

GlobalWeb PLC
Staff Personal Record and Private Address

National Insurance No. Date of Birth

Employment commenced Employment Ended
Full Name/Mr/Mrs/other status:

Street:

Town: Country: Code:
Telephone: Fax/e-mail:

Job Title: Dept:

Full Time Staff Part Time Staff Male female

Note:-

Send it now! Resubmit

Done My Computer

Diagram 10

. From where can I get Perl?

There are several releases of Perl. Therefore, it is important to understand which release is the most suitable for your requirements. You can get some information on Perl software from:-

http://www.perl.com/print/language/info/software.html

This document tells you about Perl software. For ActivePerl for Windows, you can get product information from:- **http://www.acivestate.com/Products/ActivePerl/**

I have installed on my machine, ActivePerl 5.6 for Windows. If you wish to install this release, it is suggested that first you download **ActiveState's Perl 5.6** installer
Windows from:- **http://www.activestate.com/ActivePerl/download.html**

In addition, if you are running Windows 95 or 98, you will require the latest version from Microsoft of Windows Installer. It is suggested that you get on-line product information first, so that you have up-to date information.

. Installing ActivePerl on your system for Windows

- Download ActivePerl From ActiveState - it is recommended to install it using the default: **C:\Perl** when prompted for the installation component. Just follow the instructions.
- Installing Perl for ISAPI is recommended, so that you can run programs within the Web server. Perl for ISAPI, is an extension that can speed up Web script launching by using the ISAPI interface.
- By default:
- A script ending with **.pl extension** is processed by the standard Perl interpreter
- A script ending with **.plx extension** is processed by Perl for ISAPI – helps to run Perl programs
- You can re-run the Installer, if you want to re-install, modify or even wish to remove Perl from your machine.

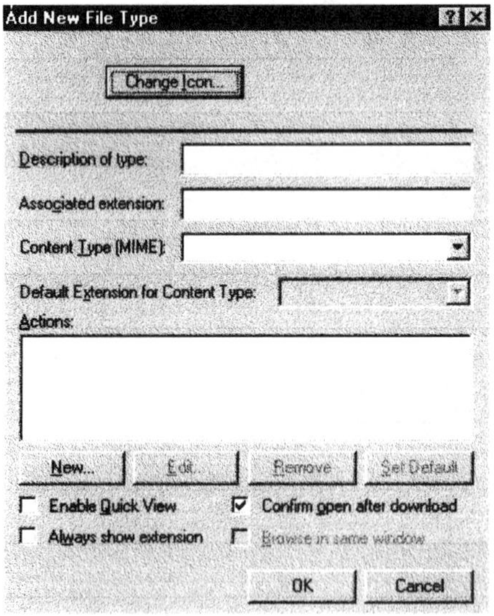

Illustration 4

- You must make sure that Perl is associated with the **.plx extension**. You can check it by following the steps listed below:-

- Open Windows Explorer
- From the View menu - select Folder Options
- In the Folder options dialog box – click File Types and then click New Type
- Now you are in the **Add New File Type** dialog box as shown in Illustration 4
- Enter PLX file in Description of type box
- Enter .plx in Associated extension text box
- Select text/plain in Content Type (MIME)

- Click New button - either of the following two things can happen now. these are:-
  - If Perl already has an association with the**.plx** extension, then you will get a message shown below in Illustration 5.

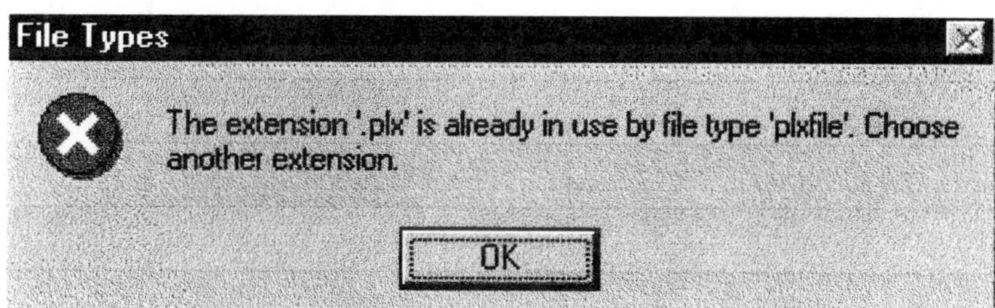

Illustration 5

- If Perl has been unable to associate itself with the .plx extension, then instead of the above message, you will see in Actions box "open" and New Action Dialog box on your screen.

- At this stage, enter in 'Application used to perform action:' box the path to Perl on your computer, that is the location of Perl, where you have installed Perl. On my machine, I must enter:

C:\Perl\bin\Perl. exe

This location is also default. Most people prefer it to over some other locations. Now, click on OK to close the New Action dialog box. On your screen the following Folder Options window will appear. In this dialog box, you can see extension PLX next to the Perl icon, which means that Perl is set up correctly on your machine, and that it has associated itself with **.plx**. See Illustration 6. You can start working with your Perl. Good luck!

The CGI script for your particular need for a particular application has to be linked to your XHML page (form), or CGI code can be embedded in your XHTML document. In this chapter, Perl is recommended for readers who have programming aptitude and students who may be studying to become Webmasters.

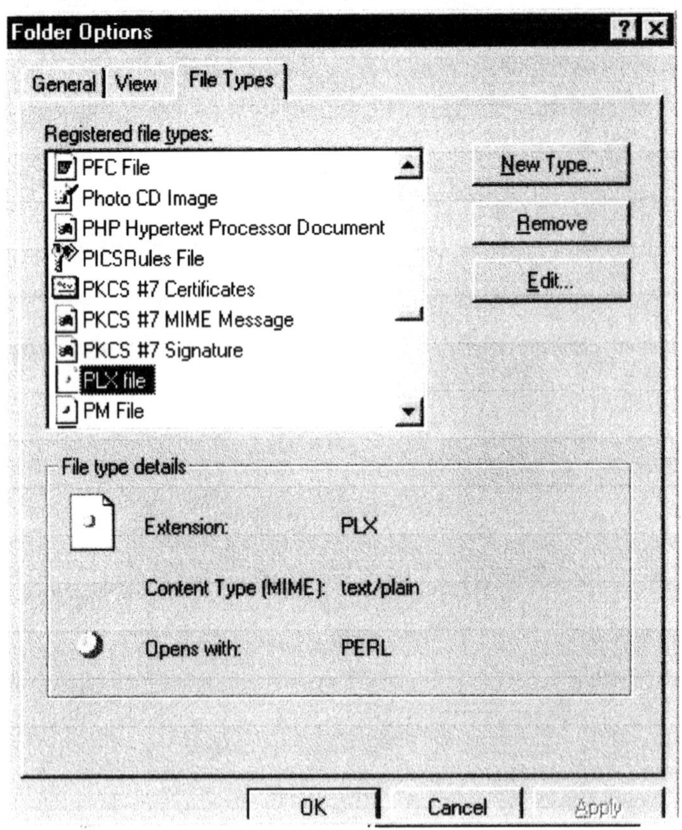

Illustration 6

Security Problems

CGI scripts are the biggest sources of security holes in Web servers. A poorly written script can cause serious problems. In fact, some ISP companies do not allow all their clients to use CGI scripts which can let the crackers gain access to the Web server. It should be carefully noted that the 'mailto' method is the least secure, though it is the easiest method of submitting forms. Do not use it, as it is the biggest security risk.

Chapter 12

Frames

The prime aims of this chapter are as follows:-

- to enable you to understand the basic structure of frames
- to enable you to design frames with a view to including them in your Web documents.

By reading and practising techniques that are demonstrated in this chapter, you should be able :-

- to create some simple frames in order to understand how your browser or any other user agent window can be divided into its sub – windows or a number of frames
- to make a distinction between simple frames and nested frames
- to construct a nested frame
- to create some frames in order to understand how your browser or any other user agent interprets dynamic frames
- to include hyperlinks in your dynamic frames so that the user can navigate frames
- to make use of <noframes> element so that Web pages can be viewed by different user age

• What is a frame?

A section of a browser window or a section of any other user agent window is a frame. Thus, if you divide your browser window into four parts, you will get four frames. These frames can have either the same size or different sizes. You can design these frames in such a way that you can either restrict the viewer to have some degree of control over these windows or no control at all . Nevertheless, each frame is independent. Frames can be drawn either horizontally or vertically or both. Thus, the technique of framing enables you to divide the browser window into a number of sub- windows or frames. Frame techniques were developed at Netscape. At a later stage, W3C recommended for HTML 4. It must be noted that officially frames are not part (deprecated) of XHTML. Therefore, only **Frameset DTD** applies to frames.

• Static and dynamic frames

Furthermore, you can design either **static** or **dynamic frames**. Static frames are created for things which must remain visible and the content does not change. For instance, static frame is a good idea for a table of contents. A static frame is always visible. On the other hand, a dynamic frame responds to user's simple actions. Therefore, the user can change the content of a dynamic frame. For example, your action of clicking the hyperlink in a Web page can change the content of a frame.

• Should you include frames in your Web pages?

- The inclusion of frames in your Web pages can be invaluable. However, frames should be used with some care and discretion. **Why?**

The straightforward reason is that the application of frames involves more than one page, and thus it can be both time consuming and rather expensive when loading pages on the Internet. Generally speaking, pages containing frames take a comparatively longer time loading than pages without frames. Therefore, if you are loading such pages, with a dial up Internet connection, you will end up with a big bill.

- The big advantage of having frames is that they can let you display several pages within one window. On the other hand, the drawback is that if you include too many frames, you will not have a big enough working area which may defeat the purpose of frames. Therefore, it requires careful laying out of frames.

- The display of several frames at a time can lead to smaller frames, which may not be user-friendly. Furthermore, the effectiveness of the document may be hindered by their presence.

- Frames which look good on a larger screen do not impress the viewers who have smaller screens. One should remember this at the time of designing documents with frames.

- Frames can add some stylish presentation to your Web pages.

- It may be that frames are highly desirable as layout and navigation tools for some specific tasks.

I would suggest the inclusion of frames in Web pages as it is an efficient information communication method, as long as you do not over do it.

• How can you create frames ?

Firstly, it is desirable that you understand the basic frames terminology so that it becomes easier for you to follow how to construct frames.

- The purpose of **<frameset>** element is to enable the Webmaster to define how many frames or sections of the browsers' window are needed for the task to be carried out. Once you have defined a frameset, it is then a <frameset> container. The frameset definition can include:-

    - the size and shape of each frame
    - the division of window into rows and columns

  In fact, the <frameset> element plays the role similar to that of <body> element. In a framed document, there is no <body> element, instead it contains <frameset> element.

- This is then followed by <frame> element, which allows the Webmaster to decide what should be the content of each frame.

This can be illustrated as follows:-

- **<frameset cols = "50% , 50%"** > - this frameset container divides the browser window into two equal sub –windows or just call it frames. Here, the division of the browser window is into two equal vertical sections, which are, indeed, columns. The abbreviation **cols** is an attribute. It is for creating columns.

- Having divided the browser window, the next step is to place something in them. This is done by applying the <frame> element. For instance, you can display in each column an XHTML document, namely **page1.xhtml** and **page2.html**. The required code for it is :-

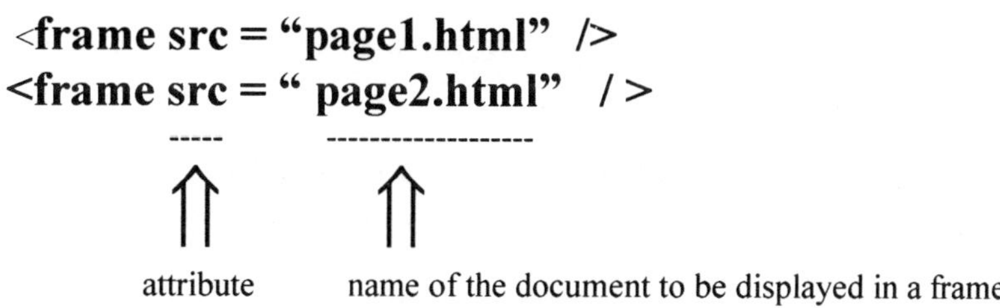

Note that <frame> element is an empty element, and thus, you must end it with "/ " before closing it with " > ". Since the browser window is divided into two frames, you need two Web pages to display in them.

. Different ways of dividing the browser window

The above illustration shows that you can divide the browser window into a number of columns. Yes, indeed, you can also divide it into several rows. Furthermore, it may be necessary to divide a row or a column into rows or columns of their own. The following 4 examples are devised to demonstrate how you can create the required divisions of the browser window into some rows and columns.

• Example 1

The purpose of this example is to illustrate the method of creating four equal size frames by dividing the browser window into four columns, and display some information in each frame.

• Explanation

In order to create four frames and display some information, you have to create and store documents listed in Illustration 1 below. The top file in this structure is the document in which the code for setting up the required four frames is stored.

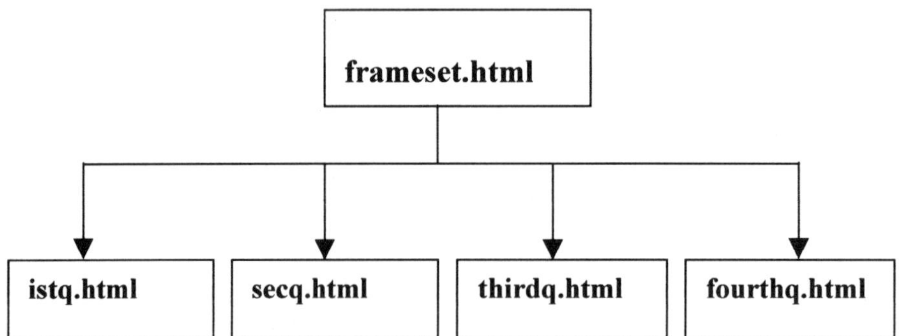

Illustration 1

All these documents were submitted to W3C Validation Service for validation. frameset.html validated as frameset as "XHTML 1.0 Frameset!" The other 4 documents were validated as "XHTML 1.0 Transitional!"

• frameset.html

• In Diagram 1, you can examine the XHTML code for **frameset.html** document. It must be noted that:-

• this document is written under Frameset.DTD

• No need to include <body> element, because it is written under Frameset DTD. Thus, instead of <body> element you must implement <frameset> element, just below the <head> element. It is written as :-

<frameset cols = "*, * , *, *" >

- Here, the **col attribute** defines four columns in this set of frames. These four columns are then the required four frames. How is the size of each column decided?

- The size of each column is also controlled by the **col attribute**. In the above segment of the code, you can find dimensions of four columns listed as values. The attribute **col** uses these values in order to divide the browser window in four frames. In fact, you can specify values or dimensions of each row as well as each column in a number of ways. See rows and columns attributes in Tables 1 & 1A. At this stage, it is worth knowing how the wildcard operator - * is used. Each wildcard operator is for each quarter of space of a browser window, and thus it creates four equal quadrants or frames. In the above code construction, a comma is inserted between wildcard operators. Thus, the size of each individual frame is controlled by the **cols** attribute.

Division of browser window into frames – cols attribute applied

top left section = first frame	second section = second frame
third section = third frame	fourth section = fourth frame

- The next step is to define the content of each frame, which has to be displayed. To achieve this, there are four segments of the code. The following segment of the code defines/names the document whose content is to be displayed in the first frame. The first frame is the top left section of the divided browser window.

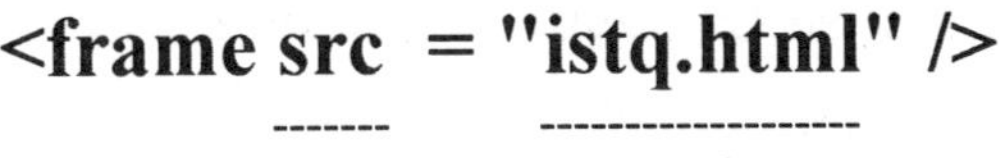

<frame src = "istq.html" />

attribute — src is an abbreviation for source

the document which contains the information for displaying in the first frame

You may be asking yourself the reason for displaying the content of this file in the first frame. The reason is that this segment of the code is the first item in the list of frames that are given within the <frame > element. The segment of the code for defining the content of each frame follows the above pattern, as given in Diagram 1. Thus, the content of each document will be displayed in frames 2,3, 4 in the same order in which they are listed.

- The <frameset> element must have its closing tag, which comes at the end of a list of frames within the <frame> element. The document should end with </html> tag.

. istq.html, secq.html, thirdq.html and fourthq.html

These are separate XHTML 1.0 Transitional documents. You should examine these in Diagrams 2, 3 and 4 and 5 respectively. They are simple enough to follow.

- Once these documents were successfully validated by W3C Validation Service, I previewed the frameset page in the IE 5. 5. You can see the screen capture of this page in Diagram 6. It shows that the browser window was divided as planned. The diagram is self-explanatory.

The XHTML code for dividing up screen into four equal windows – frameset.html

```
<?xml version= "1.0" encoding = "UTF-8"?>
<!DOCTYPE html
        PUBLIC "- //w3C//DTD XHTML 1.0 Frameset//EN"
 "http://www.w3.org/TR/xhtml1/DTD/xhtml1- frameset.dtd">
<html xmlns="http://www.w3.org/1999/xhtml" xml:lang="en" lang= "en">
<head>
<title>Frame set</title>
</head>
<frameset cols = "*, * , *, *"  >
<frame src  = "istq.html" />
<frame src =  "secq.html" />
<frame src =  "thirdq.html" />
<frame src =  "fourthq.html" />
</frameset></html>
```

Diagram 1

The XHTML code for the first frame – istq.html

```
<?xml version= "1.0" encoding = "UTF-8"?>
<!DOCTYPE html
        PUBLIC "- //w3C//DTD XHTML 1.0 Transitional//EN"
 "http://www.w3.org/TR/xhtml1/DTD/xhtml1- Transitional.dtd">
<html xmlns="http://www.w3.org/1999/xhtml" xml:lang="en" lang= "en">
<head>
<title>Frame set</title>
</head>
<body>
<p>   First Frame <br>
    This is 25% space of
    your browser window</p>
</body></html>
```

Diagram 2

The XHTML code for the second frame – secq.html

```
<?xml version= "1.0" encoding = "UTF-8"?>
<!DOCTYPE html
        PUBLIC "- //w3C//DTD XHTML 1.0 Transitional//EN"
 "http://www.w3.org/TR/xhtml1/DTD/xhtml1- Transitional.dtd">
<html xmlns="http://www.w3.org/1999/xhtml" xml:lang="en" lang= "en">

<head>
<title>Frame set</title>
</head>
<body>

<p>   Second Frame <br>
    This is 25% space of
    your browser window</p>
</body>
</html>
```

Diagram 3

The XHTML code for the third frame – thirdq.html

```
<?xml version= "1.0" encoding = "UTF-8"?>
<!DOCTYPE html
        PUBLIC "- //w3C//DTD XHTML 1.0 Transitional//EN"
 "http://www.w3.org/TR/xhtml1/DTD/xhtml1- Transitional.dtd">
<html xmlns="http://www.w3.org/1999/xhtml" xml:lang="en" lang= "en">

<head>
<title>Frame set</title>
</head>
<body>

<p>   Third Frame <br>
    This is 25% space of
    your browser window</p>
</body>
</html>
```

Diagram 4

The XHTML code for the fourth frame – fourthq.html

```
<?xml version= "1.0" encoding = "UTF-8"?>
<!DOCTYPE html
        PUBLIC "- //w3C//DTD XHTML 1.0 Transitional//EN"
 "http://www.w3.org/TR/xhtml1/DTD/xhtml1- Transitional.dtd">
<html xmlns="http://www.w3.org/1999/xhtml" xml:lang="en" lang= "en">
<head>
<title>Frame set</title>
</head>
<body>
<p>   Fourth Frame <br>
   This is 25% space of
   your browser window</p>
</body>
</html>
```

Diagram 5

The document for example 1 previewed in IE 5.5

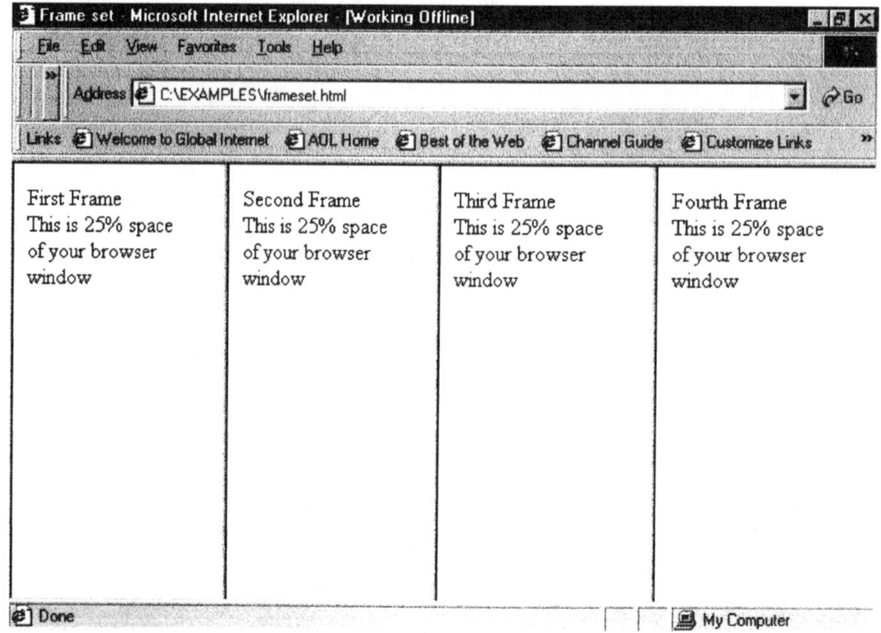

Diagram 6

Methods for specifying values for cols & rows attributes (cont. in Table 1A)

Method	Format	Outcome & when to apply
• **Percentages**	• <frameset rows = "25%,50%,25%">	• Useful if you want to specify as values as quarter, or half ... • Height for each row is set as 25%,50%, &25% • All percentages should add up to 100%
• **Relative**	• < frameset rows = " 200, *">	• It is used when the Webmaster wants to make one frame of x–size, and allocate the remaining space to the other frame. • The dimension for the second frame is set by *
	• <frameset cols = " 100, 200, *">	• The width of three columns will be set as 100, 200 pixels, and the remaining space will be allocated for setting the width of the third column • It is essential that one frame size is marked by *, irrespective of the number of frames to be created. It simply means that in a frameset not all dimensions can be specified as absolute sizes – one must be with * or open - (* means open size)
• **Wildcard operator**		• A wildcard operator (*) fills up any space available. • Often use it with some other units, such as an absolute value, say 100. Use it when you want • X numbers of wildcard operators divide the window into x numbers of frames.
	• <frameset rows = "*,*" >	• This code will generate two frames, each of which will be a row of equal height

Table 1

Methods for specifying values for cols & rows attributes (cont from Table 1)

Method	format	Outcome & when to apply
	• <frameset cols =" 100, *">	• It will generate two columns. The left column will have 100 pixels width, and the right column will occupy whatever is the remaining window space
• **Pixels**	•<frameset rows = "100, *" >	• The size given in absolute x number of pixels will have the advantage over other methods, because it is the same size on all screens irrespective of their different resolutions or types of systems • The absolute size implies that it does not change, and thus, for instance 200 pixels wide column should have the same appearance on all screens, but it is not always the case. Why? It depends on current monitor resolution settings of a sys where the document is being viewed. • For example, frames on a screen which has a 640x 480 pixels resolution setting, do not have same appearance when they are shown on a screen with 1024x 768 pixels. • Its use is usually with wildcard value - *

Table 1A

. Frame attributes

In Table 2, I have listed some frame attributes together with their respective values and the outcome of using these in your Web pages. These attributes are applied to <frame> element. Attributes namely, **src** and **id** are often used. You have already learnt the application of src attribute.

Attributes applied to <frame> element(cont. in Table 2A)

Attribute	Value	Outcome
. frameborder	. "o " or . "1"	. "0" will switch off the default border . "1" is the default value. If you use this value, it simply means that you are explicitly asking for a border. . It should be noted that this attribute results in placing all adjoining frames in a border, when its value is "1" or default. When it is set to "0" all adjoining frames will not have a border.
. scrolling	. "yes" or . "no"	. "yes" will add a scrolling bar to a frame- it means that if a page or writing in a page is too large to fit in a frame, a scrolling bar is added to the frame. A scrolling bar allows the user to see the content of the page in a frame. . "0" results in no scrolling bar. . In fact, if a page is too large to fit in a frame, a scrolling bar will be automatically added to the frame by default. If no scrolling bar is wanted, implement <scrolling = "no">.
. src	. a textfile such as my.html"	. It stands for source of the document, which can be a text file , the URL of a document, or any other type of file which is supported by a a particular browser or a user agent.
. id	. frame name such as front_view	. It is useful to name a frame. This attribute lets you identify a frame by naming it. Here, the name of a frame is front_view.

Table 2

Attributes applied to <frame> element(cont. from Table 2)

Attribute	Value	Outcome
• **marginheight**	• x number of pixels	• It is used to define a margin on top and bottom sides of the frame. Thus, it creates a space/margin between the top and bottom sides of the frame, which is equivalent to x number of pixels specified.
• **marginwidth**	• x number of pixels	• It takes x number of pixels as value, and sets a margin on the left and right sides of a frame.
• **noresize**	• noresize	• Its purpose is to instruct the browser to refrain the user from re-sizing the frame • A word of warning – if the user has a smaller screen or the monitor has a low resolution, it is likely that the application of this attribute can be to your disadvantage, as the user may not be the content of your frame. Think!!!

Table 2A

. Nesting framesets: frames within frames

• How can you use only one frame to display the contents of several <frame> elements?

In order to achieve this requirement, you have to apply the technique of nesting frames, which is discussed and demonstrated by means of solved example in this section. The following skeleton code generalises the technique of nesting frames. The nested frames will be created by the segment of the code shown on a white background in Illustration 2 below. Here, it does show how a frameset is nested within another frameset.

Skeleton code for nesting framesets

```
<frameset ------- >                          ⇐ first frameset element – opening tag
<frame ---------- / > ⇐ frame element
          <frameset …….. />                  ⇐ second frameset element inside the first –opening
tag
         <frame ….. / >
         <frame ….. / >

            •

            •

            •

          < / frameset >                     ⇐ second frameset element inside the first – closing tag
<frame…….. />
</ frameset >                                ⇐ first frameset element – closing tag
```

Illustration 2

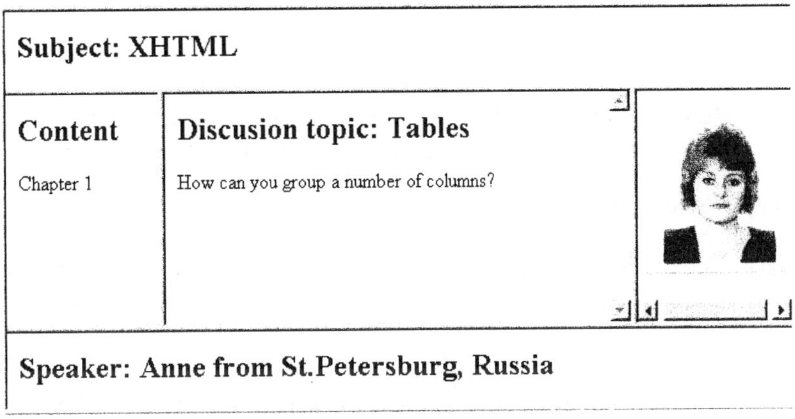

Subject: XHTML

Content

Chapter 1

Discusion topic: Tables

How can you group a number of columns?

Speaker: Anne from St.Petersburg, Russia

Illustration 3

- **Example 2**
- **nested frames** – see next page.

Your task is to design a Web page which should appear on a screen as shown above. This Web page has five sections. In one section of this page is an image. Prior to previewing this Web page on your system (locally), use W3C Validation Service to validate five documents for XML well-formedness and validity. One of these documents should be validated as XHTML 1.0 Frameset.

The sixth document is **.gif** type, as it contains an image/photo. No need to submit to W3C. Display the validated document containing frames into IE 5.5 or any other user agent to make sure that it has met all requirements.

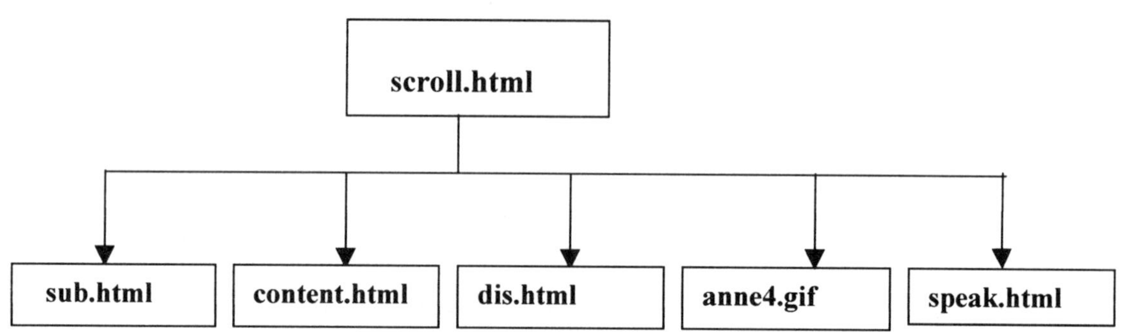

Illustration 4

• Explanation

• The document shown above contains altogether five frames. For the completion of this task, you need to design six different files altogether. These files are listed below in Illustration 4.

scroll.html – this is listed in Diagram 7.

• Here, by means of our first <frameset> element, the aim is to create a set of three frames by dividing the browser window into three rows. The top (first row) frame is given a unique name as shown below.

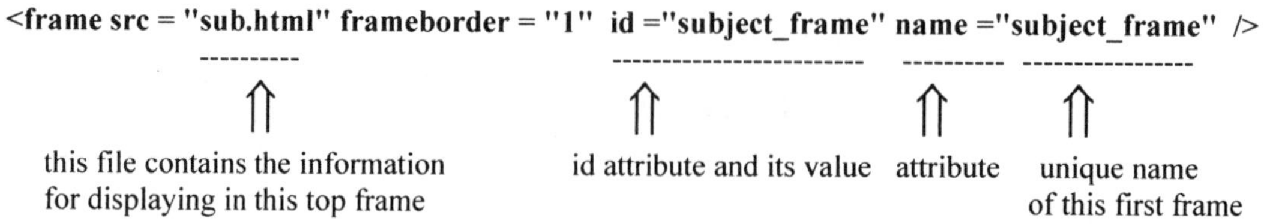

The name attribute is not included in the XHTML 1.0 Strict, and therefore your document cannot be validated as XHTML 1.0 Strict. However, it can still be validated as XHTML 1.0 Transitional.

- The second row is in the middle of the browser window, but it contains another set of three frames. In fact, this is no longer defined as a row, but as a set of three columns. These columns are within the second <frameset>, and thus nested within the first <frameset>. The documents which have to be displayed in each column are laid out by the following segment of the code:-

```
<frameset cols = "20%, 60%, 20% ">
<frame src = "content.html" frameborder ="1"  id = "content_frame" name ="content_frame"  />
 <frame src = "dis.html" frameborder ="1" scrolling ="yes" id ="discuss_frame" name
="discuss_frame" />
 <frame src ="anne4.gif" frameborder ="1" id ="anne_frame" name= "anne_frame" />
</ frameset>
```

- For creating each of these documents, you can find XHTML codes in Diagrams 8,9,10 and 12.

- The first <frameset rows = "20%, 60%, * " > has created three sections, one of which is at the bottom part of the browser window. This is equivalent in size to the remaining space allocated by the wildcard (*). In this row, you must also place a document for its display in this area. To do so, the following segment of the code is essential:-

```
<frame src = "speak.html" frameborder = "1" id ="speaker_frame" name ="speaker_frame" />
```

- </frameset /> closes the first <frameset> - as the rule states: an opening tag must have a closing tag.

- In Diagram 7, there is only one following line of code which contains scrolling.

```
<frame src = "dis.html" frameborder ="1" scrolling ="yes" id ="discuss_frame"
                    name="discuss_frame" />
```

The above segment of the code is for a frame named "discuss_frame", but in Diagram 13, you can see a frame named "anne_frame" which also has a scrolling bar added to it.

. How has it happened?

If there is not enough space in a frame for its content the browser automatically provides a scrolling bar.

- Prior to previewing this document, it was validated by W3C as XHTML 1.0 Frameset! You should examine its screen capture in Diagram 13 in order to check that it matches completely with that of the original format given in the example at the beginning.

Diagram 7: The XHTML code for setting up frames for example 2 - scroll.html

```
<?xml version= "1.0" encoding = "UTF-8"?>
<!DOCTYPE html
        PUBLIC "- //w3C//DTD XHTML 1.0 Frameset//EN"
 "http://www.w3.org/TR/xhtml1/DTD/xhtml1- frameset.dtd">
<html xmlns="http://www.w3.org/1999/xhtml" xml:lang="en" lang= "en">
<head>
<title> Nested frames</title>
</head>
<frameset rows = "20%, 60%, * " >
  <frame src = "sub.html" frameborder = "1"
   id="subject_frame" name ="subject_frame"  />

   <frameset cols = "20%, 60%, 20% ">
   <frame src = "content.html" frameborder ="1"
    id = "content_frame" name ="content_frame"  />
   <frame src = "dis.html" frameborder ="1" scrolling ="yes"
    id ="discuss_frame" name ="discuss_frame" />
   <frame src ="anne4.gif" frameborder ="1"
     id ="anne_frame" name= "anne_frame" />
   </frameset>
 <frame src = "speak.html" frameborder = "1"
 id ="speaker_frame" name ="speaker_frame" />
</frameset></html>
```

Diagram 8: The XHTML code for 'Subject' – sub.html

```
<?xml version= "1.0" encoding = "UTF-8"?>
<!DOCTYPE html
        PUBLIC "- //w3C//DTD XHTML 1.0 Strict//EN"
 "http://www.w3.org/TR/xhtml1/DTD/xhtml1- strict.dtd">
<html xmlns="http://www.w3.org/1999/xhtml" xml:lang="en" lang= "en">
<head>
<title> Subject</title>
</head>
<body>
<h2> Subject: XHTML  </h2>  </body></html>
```

Diagram 9: The XHHTML code for 'Contents' – content.html

```
<?xml version= "1.0" encoding = "UTF-8"?>
<!DOCTYPE html
        PUBLIC "- //w3C//DTD XHTML 1.0 Strict//EN"
 "http://www.w3.org/TR/xhtml1/DTD/xhtml1- strict.dtd">
<html xmlns="http://www.w3.org/1999/xhtml" xml:lang="en" lang= "en">
<head>
<title> Table of contents  </title>
</head>
<body>
<h2>Content</h2>
 <p> Chapter 1 </p></body></html>
```

Diagram 10: The XHHTML code for 'Contents' – speaker.html

```
<?xml version= "1.0" encoding = "UTF-8"?>
<!DOCTYPE html
        PUBLIC "- //w3C//DTD XHTML 1.0 Strict//EN"
 "http://www.w3.org/TR/xhtml1/DTD/xhtml1- strict.dtd">
<html xmlns="http://www.w3.org/1999/xhtml" xml:lang="en" lang= "en">
<head>
<title> Speaker</title>
</head>
<body>
<h2>
   Speaker: Anne from St .Petersburg, Russia </h2>
</body></html>
```

Diagram 11: The .gif file for 'anne frame' – anne4.gif

Diagram 12: The XHTML code for 'Discussion – dis.html

```
<?xml version= "1.0" encoding = "UTF-8"?>
<!DOCTYPE html
        PUBLIC "- //w3C//DTD XHTML 1.0 Strict//EN"
 "http://www.w3.org/TR/xhtml1/DTD/xhtml1- strict.dtd">
<html xmlns="http://www.w3.org/1999/xhtml" xml:lang="en" lang= "en">
<head>
<title> Discussion </title>
</head>
<body>
<h2>
   Discussion topic: Tables </h2>
 <p> How can you group a number of columns?  </p>
</body></html>
```

Diagram 13: The Web page previewed locally in IE 5.5 – scroll.html

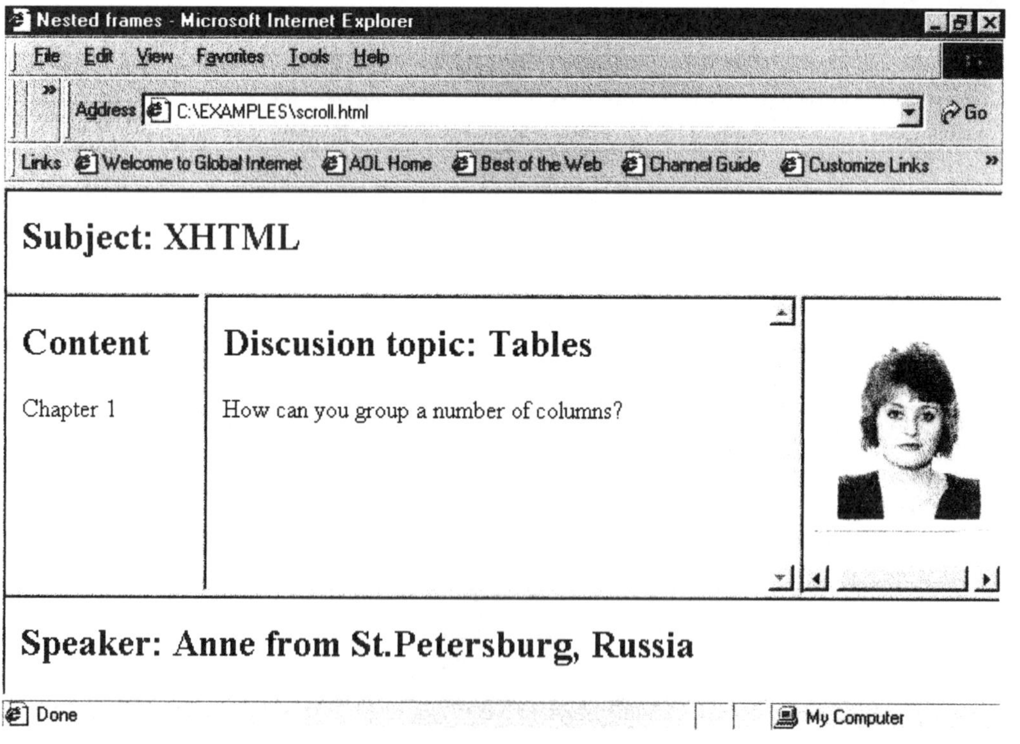

. Dynamic Frames

The idea is to give the user the opportunity to select information by clicking the hyperlink, or just for simplicity, say, the link which is provided in the Web page. Unlike the static frames, the content of a dynamic frame can change in response to a user's action. The following solved examples are aimed at demonstrating the knowledge and skills that are essential for handling these frames efficiently.

. Example 3

The task is to create two equal sized frames for displaying the content of two documents, so that each frame has its own document for displaying it, in accordance with the following actions:-

In **frame 1**, the text "Group picture – click here" has to be shown. When the user clicks it, a group picture should be displayed in this frame. The information/picture should be loaded only in the current window in which the link is made.

In **frame 2**, the text "single picture – click here" has to be displayed. When it is clicked, a single picture in this frame must be displayed. This picture should be loaded only in the current window, which is frame 2, in which the link is made.

If the user makes a link by clicking in both frames, then each frame should display the content of the document aimed for displaying it in each frame. Also submit your documents to W3C Validation Service so that these can be validated for XML well-formedness and validity, prior to previewing these on your PC.

. Explanation

For the completion of this task, you need to create five documents, which are listed in Illustration 4.

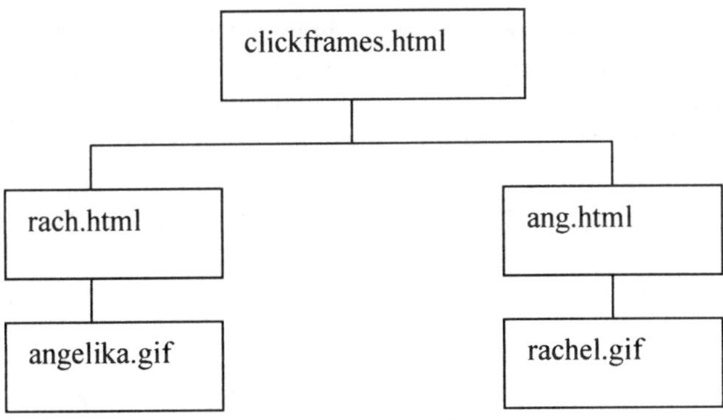

Illustration 4

- **'clickframes.html'**

• How does it relate to the other four documents?

It is explained below:-

- The browser first reads clickframes.html, which contains the XHTML code for setting up the frames. This is listed in Diagram 14. This code is written under XHTML Tramsitional 1.0 Frameset
- It finds the <frameset> element, which contains column definition. In accordance with this definition, it divides the browser window in to two equal parts, and thus two frames are set up.
- In the same file, it reaches the next line, where it finds the <frame> element together with its src attribute pointing to an external source namely: rach.html. This is another document. It is listed in Diagram 15. It is an XHTML 1.0 Strict document. This document contains <a> link element, which is for linking one document to another document. The segment of the code that creates the hyperlink is shown below:-

```
<a href = "rachel.gif"> Group picture - click here</a>
```

This document contains group picture — Hyperlink is printed in blue colour. When it is clicked it loads the group picture in first frame

- When this document is loaded, at that time, only the hyperlink is displayed in frame 1. It waits for the user to click it. The group picture appears only when the hyperlink is activated. The **'rachel.gif'** document contains the group picture. It is shown in Diagram 17.
- The next line of code in clickframes.html file is another <frame> element. This time, the attribute points to another external source file, which is **ang.html** document. This file has the same structure and the purpose as rach.html. See Diagram 16. It has the following segment of the code for the hyperlink and the single picture to be displayed when the hyperlink is invoked:-

```
<a href = " angelika.gif"> single picture - click here</a></h2>
```

I have also shown **'angelika.gif'** in Diagram 18, whose content will be displayed when the user clicks the hyperlink in frame 2.

- By this procedure, both frames are set up, and in both frames relevant hyperlinks are also displayed. This way, both frames are made to act as dynamic, ready to respond to the user's appropriate click.

The XHTML code for creating two frames – clickframe.html

```
<?xml version= "1.0" encoding = "UTF-8"?>
<!DOCTYPE html
        PUBLIC "- //w3C//DTD XHTML 1.0 Frameset//EN"
 "http://www.w3.org/TR/xhtml1/DTD/xhtml1- frameset.dtd">
<html xmlns="http://www.w3.org/1999/xhtml" xml:lang="en" lang= "en">
<head>
<title>Frame set</title>
</head>

<frameset cols = "50%, 50%"  >
<frame src  = "rach.html" />
<frame src =  "ang.html" />
</frameset>
</html>
```

Diagram 14

The XHTML code for first frame – rach.html

```
<?xml version= "1.0" encoding = "UTF-8"?>
<!DOCTYPE html
        PUBLIC "- //w3C//DTD XHTML 1.0 Strict//EN"
 "http://www.w3.org/TR/xhtml1/DTD/xhtml1- strict.dtd">
<html xmlns="http://www.w3.org/1999/xhtml" xml:lang="en" lang= "en">
<head>
<title>Frame set</title>
</head>
<body>
<h2>
<a href = "rachel.gif"> Group picture - click here</a></h2>
</body>
</html>
```

Diagram 15

The XHTML code for second frame – ang.html

```
<?xml version= "1.0" encoding = "UTF-8"?>
<!DOCTYPE html
        PUBLIC "- //w3C//DTD XHTML 1.0 Strict//EN"
 "http://www.w3.org/TR/xhtml1/DTD/xhtml1- strict.dtd">
<html xmlns="http://www.w3.org/1999/xhtml" xml:lang="en" lang= "en">
<head>
<title>Frame set</title>
</head>
<body>
<h2>
<a href = " angelika.gif"> single picture - click here</a></h2>
<body></html>
```

Diagram 16

rach.gif

Diagram 17

angelika.gif

Diagram 18

When frames are loaded for the first time

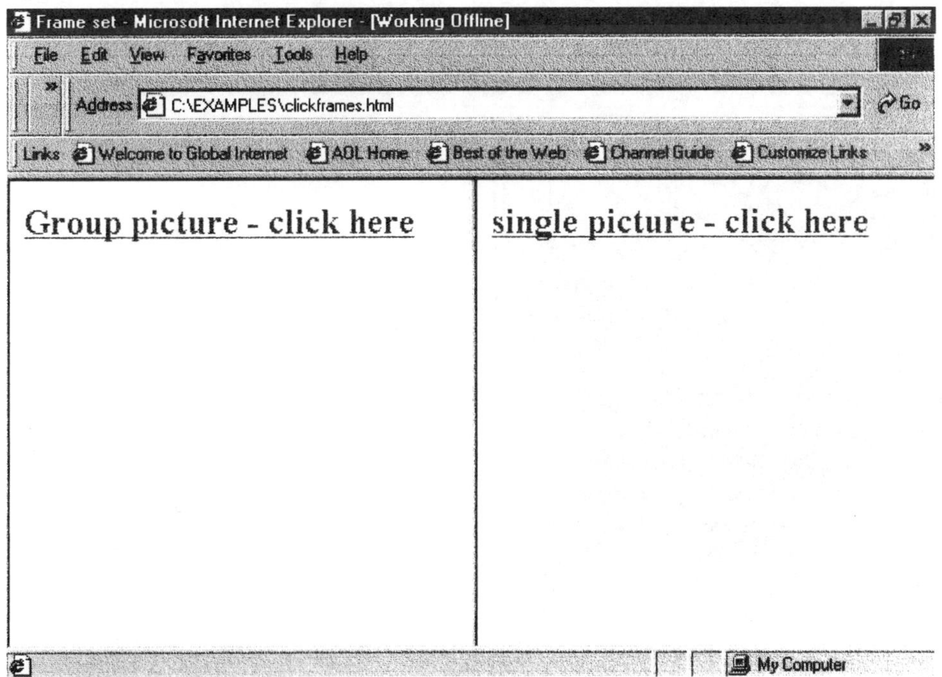

Diagram 19

• Previewing the document

Prior to previewing the document locally in the IE 505, all **. html** documents were checked for XML well-formedness and validity by W3C.

- When you load the document for the first time, in the IE5.5, the browser window is filled with two frames, each showing the hyperlink for each frame created. See Diagram 19. Now, the user has an opportunity to click any of these two hyperlinks.
- Firstly, I clicked the hyperlink in the first frame (top left frame). In response to my action, the browser removed the hyperlink from this frame, and filled it with the required group picture. So, the hyperlink worked well as the correct picture was displayed. See Diagram 20.

Result of clicking in first frame – group picture displayed

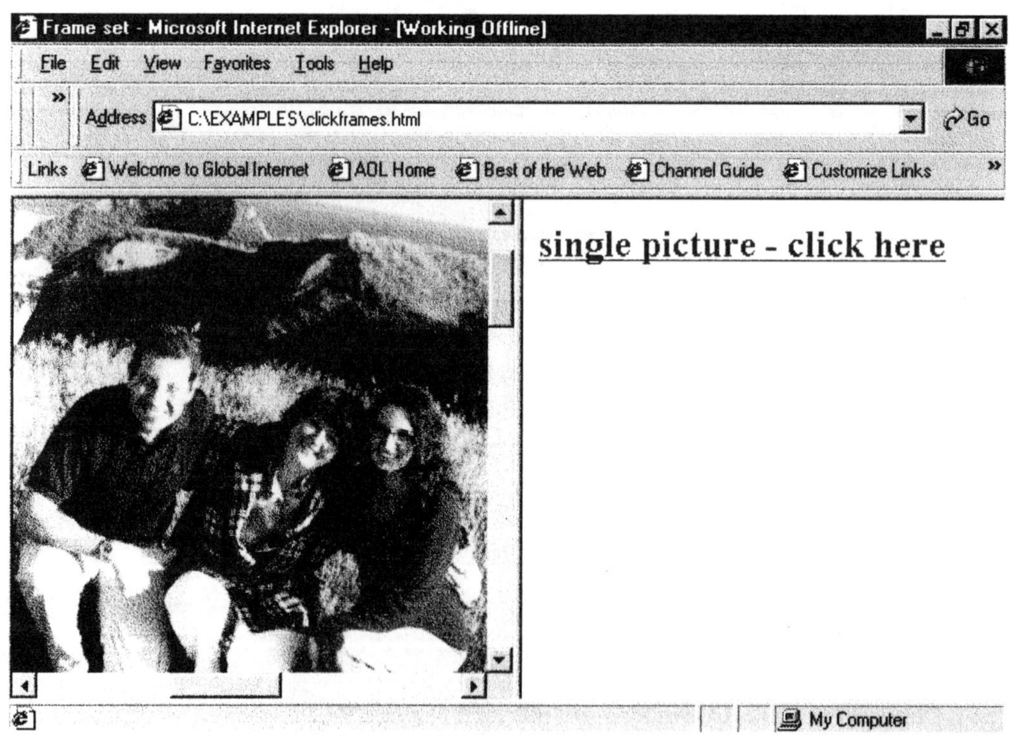

Diagram 20

- Secondly, I clicked the hyperlink in the second frame. The browser wiped out the hyperlink from the second frame, and displayed in it the single picture. It is in the correct frame, as shown in Diagram 21.

Result of clicking in second frame –single picture displayed

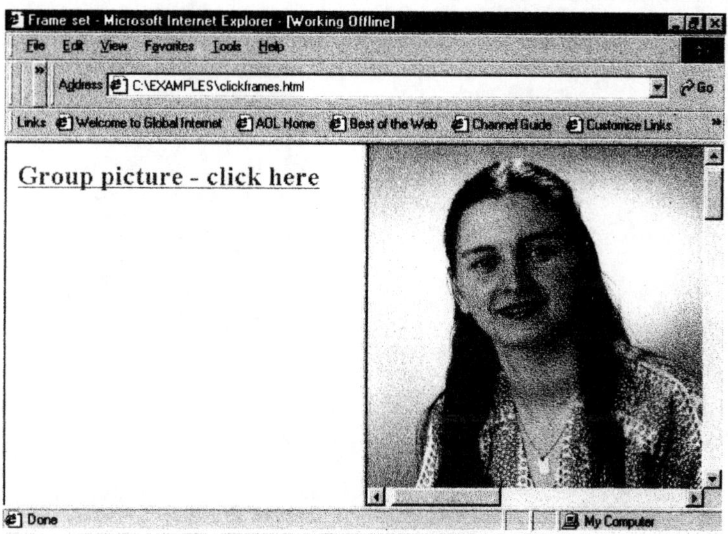

Diagram 21

- Thirdly, I loaded clickframes.html document in IE 5.5. This time, I clicked both hyperlinks. As a result of it, both frames displayed documents containing pictures. These pictures/photos are, once again, displayed in the current frames, where hyperlinks were clicked. See Diagram 22.

• Are there any pros and cons of loading pages into current windows as demonstrated by the above example?

As long as only one hyperlink is needed in each current window, this method is suitable. On the other hand, the problem is that as soon as you click the hyperlink, the page is loaded for displaying its contents in the current frame in which the link is invoked, but the clicked link has disappeared from the screen. Thus, you cannot select it again. The only way you can re-select is to load all pages again. For instance, if you have three frames, you must re-load three pages for interacting with them again, despite the fact that you clicked only on link. Furthermore, if a current page, has more than one link facility, you can only activate one of them. The reason for this drawback is apparent from the above explanation.

Result of clicking in both frames

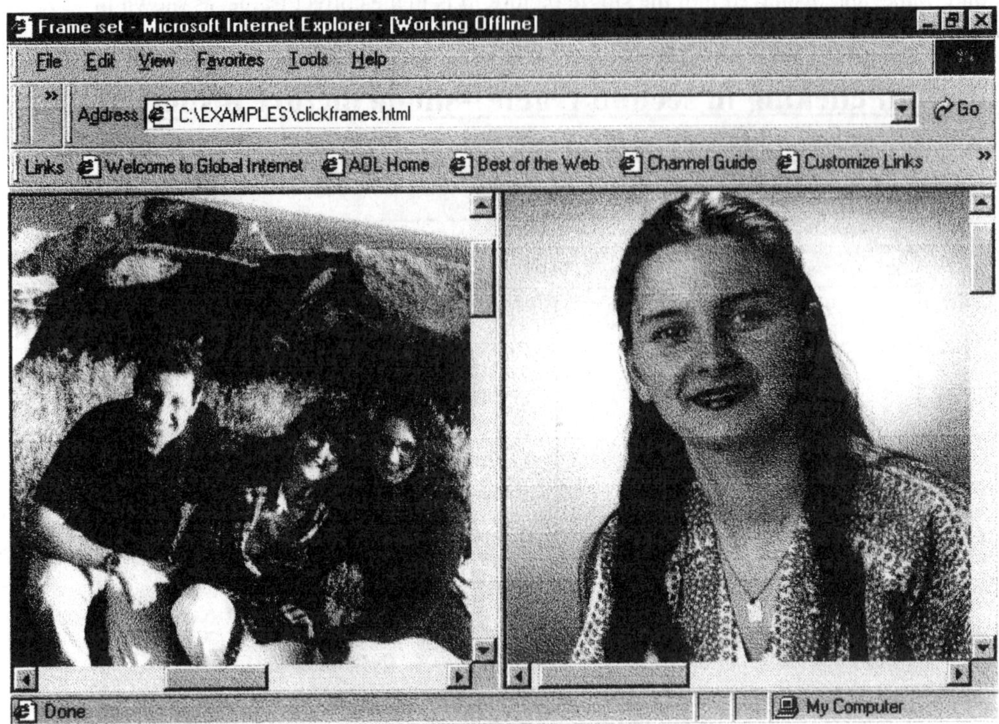

Diagram 22

• How can we improve the linking of pages so that hyperlinks are still visible?

Indeed, you can load pages into different windows. This way, your hyperlinks remain visible at all times. You can select any of these links in any order from the given list of hyperlinks. By applying this technique, your pages on the Net can be selected for viewing, and re-selected as many times as the viewer wishes. This is achieved by implementing the target attribute. The target attribute lets the new page be loaded into another frame – target. So, you target another frame. This targeting works with the name attribute. You name a frame where you want the page to be loaded. Note that the name of the frame is invisible in the window.

• Example 4

The task is to design a simple Web site to be previewed locally in order to demonstrate how to load a that the hyperlink is still visible, and that the current page can also be replaced by another page, when another hyperlink is clicked. The task requires the designing of seven different documents, and creating both static and dynamic frames. You should read carefully the following description so that you can appreciate more the working of this Web site.

• Illustration 5

It shows the structure in which your browser window is to be divided into two rows of 35% and 65% ratios of the browser window's space. The first frame (35%) should be of a static nature, which implies that no changes can be made to the page displayed in this frame.

- The bigger row is to be divided into two columns whose sizes are 30% and 70% of the total space allocated to the second frame (row). The first column must have an index in which hyperlinks are listed.
- One page is to be displayed permanently in the top window. There should be three other pages whose relevant content is to be displayed when an appropriate hyperlink is clicked.
- The task is to design all documents required for setting up a simple Web site to be previewed locally. You should also check your documents for XML well-formedness and validity like other documents.

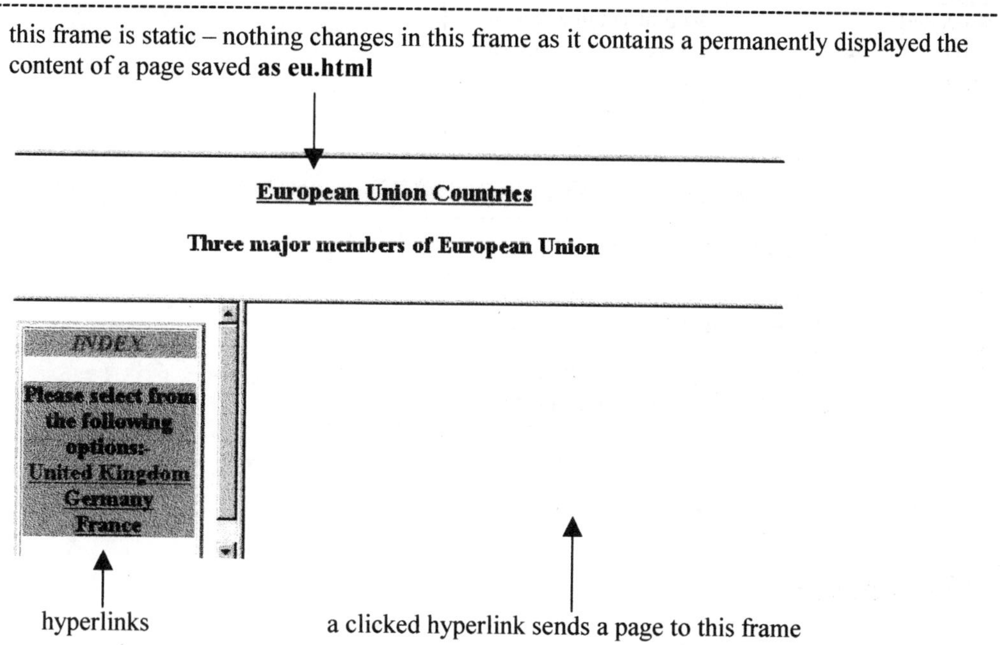

---

this frame is static – nothing changes in this frame as it contains a permanently displayed the content of a page saved **as eu.html**

European Union Countries

Three major members of European Union

INDEX

Please select from the following options:-
United Kingdom
Germany
France

hyperlinks

a clicked hyperlink sends a page to this frame

Illustration 5

Documents for example 4 – the top document contains framesets

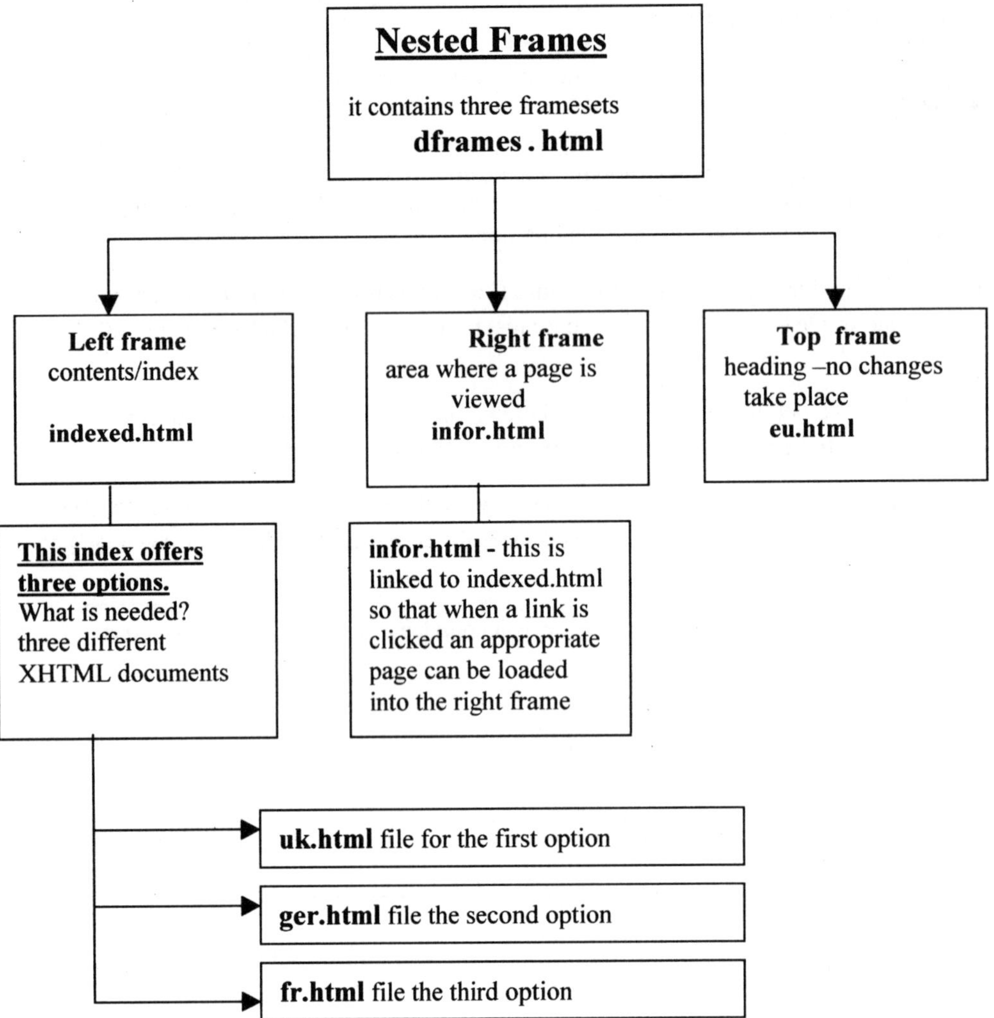

Illustration 6

• Explanation

For the completion of this example, you have to design and save eight documents. In Illustration 6 above, I have listed these documents.

- In the top box of this Illustration, **dframes.html** document is shown. The XHTML code for this document is in Diagram 23. It is suggested that you read this file in order to relate it to the requirement set up above. If you study it carefully, you will agree that it is similar to the code of the last example, and some other examples in the last chapter. You can assume that this file sets the whole scene as without it, there will not be any frames to place information in them. Here, frames are also named by means of **name attribute**. This document is written as XHTML 1.0 Frameset DTD. Why? You should check it for XML well formedness and validity by submitting it to W3C Service. I have done so.

- Having divided up the browser window and frames set up, the next thing is to design the document, whose content is to be displayed in the top row/frame. The XHTML code for this document is saved as **eu.html**, which is listed in Diagram 11. Here, the markup code includes the application of CSS rules for text formatting and presentation of text. The text on the first line is on a yellow background, in the centre of a line, and underlined. The CSS rule also places the second line in the centre of the line. See Diagram 24.

- The next requirement is to set up in the first column of the second row, the index table for selecting any of the three hyperlinks to three individual documents. You can see the link between these documents in Illustration 6. The XHTML document for **indexed. html** is listed in Diagram 25. Here, the following segment of the code sets up links, and sends each document for display it into a named frame.

```
<a href ="uk.html" target ="infor_frame" > United Kingdom</a><br />
 <a href ="ger.html" target ="infor_frame"> Germany</a><br />
 <a href ="fr.html" target ="infor_frame"> France</a>
```

One of these lines can be analysed for your ease of learning as follows:-

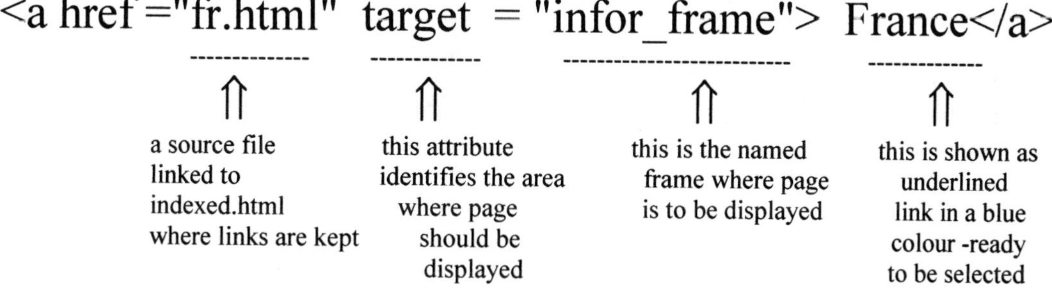
<a href ="fr.html" target = "infor_frame"> France</a>
a source file linked to indexed.html where links are kept
this attribute identifies the area where page should be displayed
this is the named frame where page is to be displayed
this is shown as underlined link in a blue colour -ready to be selected

- There are three source documents stored as **uk.html**, **ger.html**, and **fr.html**. These are simple XHTML markup codes, which are listed in Diagram 23-29.

- When any of these hyperlinks in the index box is clicked, a correct Web page has to be loaded to the right frame (the second column of the second row). This frame is named as **infor_frame**, which is the targeted frame. This frame can only be a Web page, providing you create a link between the frame called **infor_frame** and the **indexed.html** file, where hyperlinks are stored. For this reason, there is a need to create another document. The code for this document is in Diagram 26. It is another XHTML simple file, but contains an important following segment of the code:-

<a href =" indexed.html" target ="infor_frame"></a>

Without this segment of the code, no Web page will be displayed in the right frame – target infor_frame, where information about each country is displayed.

- In diagram 30, you can see the screen capture of the preview in IE5.55. It shows all required frames set up. In the top box/frame the content of **eu.html** is displayed, and within the left frame, a table is placed within which the index is shown. This is the content of document saved as **indexed.html**. There is nothing in the left frame (the second column within the second row). It is created by **infor.html** , and patiently waiting to receive a page when any of the three hyperlinks is clicked.

- Finally, the user clicked 'United Kingdom' in **index table**, as shown in Diagram 31. The browser placed a boxed around this hyperlink in order to indicate that it is currently clicked, and also sent the correct document to an empty frame, where it is displayed.

• How long will it be displayed in this frame?

When a user clicks another hyperlink, the content of the newly clicked document will replace the current display in this frame with that of the newly clicked document. The process can be repeated many times.

The XHTML code for setting up nested frameset - dframes.html

```
<?xml version= "1.0" encoding = "UTF-8"?>
<!DOCTYPE html
        PUBLIC "- //w3C//DTD XHTML 1.0 Frameset//EN"
 "http://www.w3.org/TR/xhtml1/DTD/xhtml1- frameset.dtd">
<html xmlns="http://www.w3.org/1999/xhtml" xml:lang="en" lang= "en">
<head>
<title>Nested Dynamic frames</title>
</head>
<frameset rows = "35%,65% ">
<frame  src = "eu.html" name ="eu_frame" />
 <frameset  cols = "30%,70% ">
  <frame src = "indexed.html" id ="indexed_frame" name ="indexed_frame" />
<frame src =  "infor.html" id ="infor_frame"  name ="infor_frame"  />
</frameset>
</frameset></html>
```

Diagram 23

Diagram 24 is on page 286 due to lack of space.

The XHTML code for the index table (hyperlinks) - indexed.html

```
<?xml version= "1.0" encoding = "UTF-8"?>
<!DOCTYPE html
        PUBLIC "- //w3C//DTD XHTML 1.0 Transitional//EN"
 "http://www.w3.org/TR/xhtml1/DTD/xhtml1- transitional.dtd">
<html xmlns="http://www.w3.org/1999/xhtml" xml:lang="en" lang= "en">
<head>
<title>Index</title>
<style type ="text/css">
h2
   {
    font-size = 110%;
    font-style:italic;
    color:#ff0000;                  /* red */
    background = #00ffff;              /*aqua */
    text-align:center;
   }
h3
   {
    font-size = 120%
    font-style:normal;
    color:#000000;                  /*black */
    background:#00ffff;
    text-align:center;
   }
</style>
</head>
<body>
<table border = "3">
<tr>
  <td>
        <h2> INDEX</h2>
        <h3> Please select from the following options:-<br />
 <a href ="uk.html" target ="infor_frame" > United Kingdom</a><br />
 <a href ="ger.html" target ="infor_frame"> Germany</a><br />
 <a href ="fr.html" target ="infor_frame"> France</a>
</h3>
 </td></tr>
 </body></html>
```

Diagram 25

The XHTML code for a Web Page Europe - eu.html

```
<?xml version= "1.0" encoding = "UTF-8"?>
<!DOCTYPE html
        PUBLIC "- //w3C//DTD XHTML 1.0 Strict//EN"
 "http://www.w3.org/TR/xhtml1/DTD/xhtml1- strict.dtd">
<html xmlns="http://www.w3.org/1999/xhtml" xml:lang="en" lang= "en">
<head>
<title>EU Union Countries </title>
<style type ="text/css">
h1
   {
    font-size = 120%; font-style= normal;  color: #000000;                    /* black */
    text-align:center; text-decoration: underline;  background = #ffff00;        /* yellow */ }
h2 { font-size = 110%; text-align:center; }
</style>
</head>
<body>
         <h1> European Union Countries </h1>
          <h2> Three major members of European Union</h2>
</body></html>
```

Diagram 24

The XHTML code for the frame in which each document is to be displayed - infor.html

```
<?xml version= "1.0" encoding = "UTF-8"?>
<!DOCTYPE html
        PUBLIC "- //w3C//DTD XHTML 1.0 Transitional//EN"
 "http://www.w3.org/TR/xhtml1/DTD/xhtml1- transitional.dtd">
<html xmlns="http://www.w3.org/1999/xhtml" xml:lang="en" lang= "en">
<head>
<title> This is view area</title>
</head>
<body>
<a href =" indexed.html" target ="infor_frame"></a>
  </body>
</html>
```

Diagram 26

The XHTML code for a page containing information on Uk –uk.html

```
<?xml version= "1.0" encoding = "UTF-8"?>
<!DOCTYPE html
        PUBLIC "- //w3C//DTD XHTML 1.0 Strict//EN"
 "http://www.w3.org/TR/xhtml1/DTD/xhtml1- strict.dtd">
<html xmlns="http://www.w3.org/1999/xhtml" xml:lang="en" lang= "en">
<head>
<title>EU Countries </title>
</head>
<body>
<h1> United Kingdom</h1>
<p> United Kingdom of Great Britain and Northern Ireland.
   Its capital is London.
   <br />
   Population: 58,258, 000 (in 1995 est). <br />
   Life expectancy: 73(men), 79 (women)<br />
   GDP per capita (PPP) (US$) 18,360 (1995)
</p>
</body></html>
```

Diagram 27

The XHTML code for a page containing information on Germany ger.html

```
<?xml version= "1.0" encoding = "UTF-8"?>
<!DOCTYPE html
        PUBLIC "- //w3C//DTD XHTML 1.0 Strict//EN"
 "http://www.w3.org/TR/xhtml1/DTD/xhtml1- strict.dtd">
<html xmlns="http://www.w3.org/1999/xhtml" xml:lang="en" lang= "en">
<head>
<title>EU Countries </title>
</head>
<body>
<h1> Germany</h1>
<p> Federal Republic of Germany in central Europe. Its capital is Berlin.
     Population: 81,591 000 (in 1995). <br />
     Life expectancy: 72(men), 78 (women)<br />
    GDP per capita (PPP) (US$) 20,370 (1995)
</p>  </body></html>
```

Diagram 28

Diagram 29 is on page 299 due to lack of space.

A preview in IE 5.5 shows all aspects of the required simple Web site set up

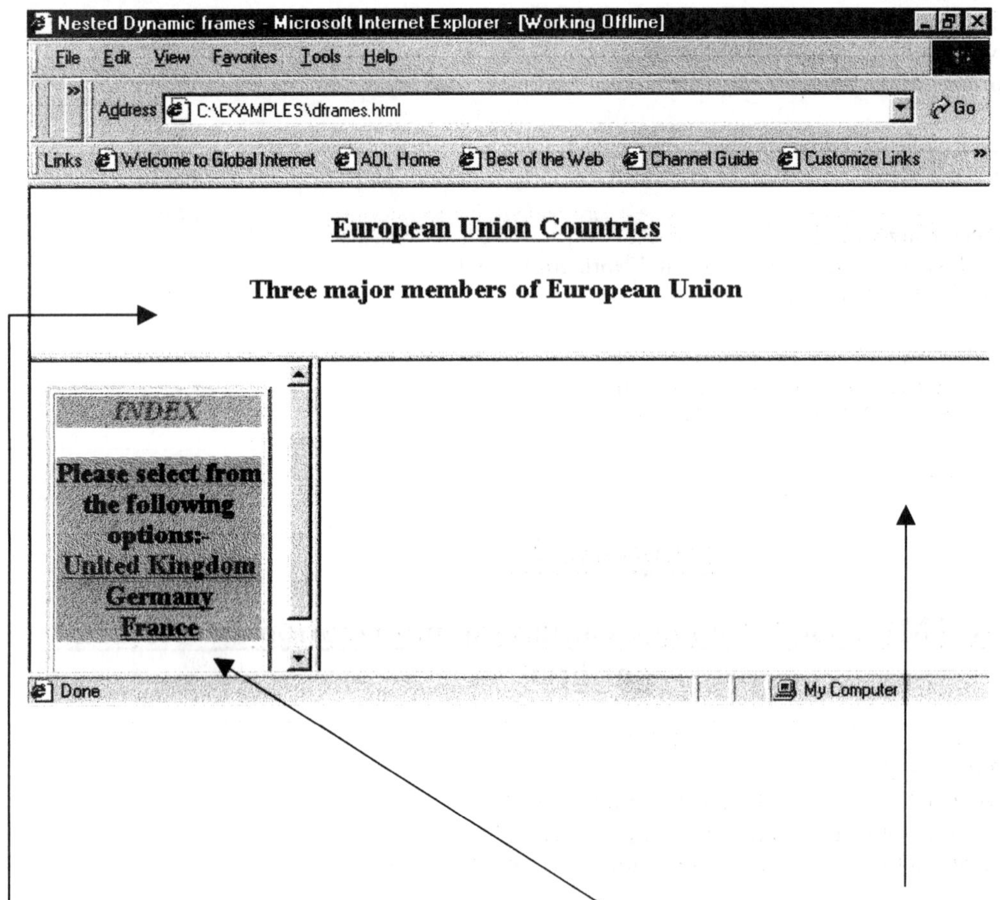

This is a permanent area. Here, no interaction takes place. You can display things such as topic, or subject matter or any other material for setting up headings

This is the area where some interaction takes place between the user and the system set up for making choices

The result of the interaction is shown in this area. Each time the user makes a choice the system responds by sending the page to this area

Diagram 30

The XHTML code for a page containing information on France fr.html

```
<?xml version= "1.0" encoding = "UTF-8"?>
<!DOCTYPE html
        PUBLIC "- //w3C//DTD XHTML 1.0 Strict//EN"
 "http://www.w3.org/TR/xhtml1/DTD/xhtml1- strict.dtd">
<html xmlns="http://www.w3.org/1999/xhtml" xml:lang="en" lang= "en">
<head>
<title>EU Countries </title>
</head>
<body
<h1>France</h1>
<p> French Republic. Its capital is Paris.<br />
   Population: 57,981 000 (in 1995 est). <br />
   Life expectancy: 73(men), 81 (women)<br />
   GDP per capita (PPP) (US$) 19,995 (1995)
</p>  </body></html>
```

Diagram 29

A preview in IE 5.5 shows a response to a click action in the right frame

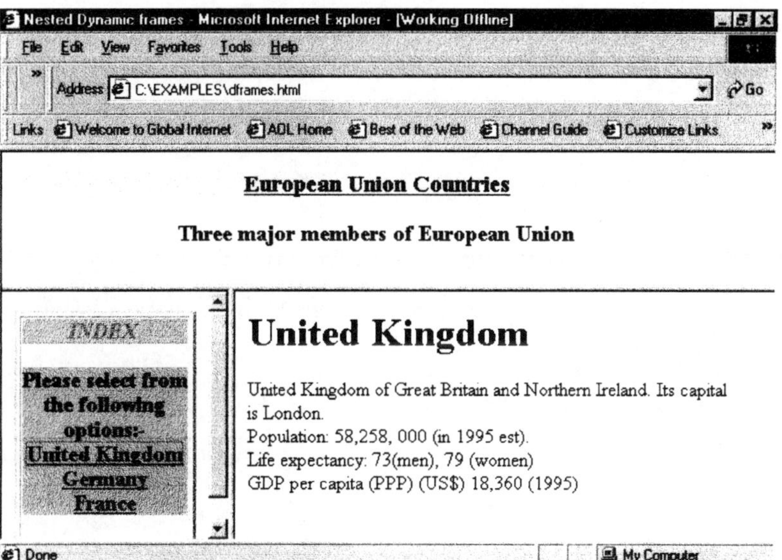

Diagram 31

. The <noframes> element

. What facility can you include in your Web pages for a variety of user agents which cannot interpret frames?

You can make use of an element called **<noframes>**.

This can enable you to design Web pages containing frames in such a way that the viewer can still get some sort of display. It may not be as efficient and work as smoothly as frames do for frame lovers, but your Web pages can be viewed. However, the **<nonframe>** element's inclusion in a Web page is really useful, as you can create your Web site for all viewers. Your documents can be visible to those whose browser can read frames, as well as to other users whose browser or any other user agent cannot understand frames. It is explained below by making some amendments to Example 2.

. Example 4 A

The idea is to make all necessary amendments to all or some of the documents created for example 2, so that documents can be viewed by all Web site visitors.

. Explanation

You should insert the following piece of XHTML code in your document which contains **frameset(s)** . In this case, it is the document saved as **dframes.html**.

```
<noframes>
<body>

<p> This browser does not support frames. Still you can select any of the following hyperlinks :-</p>
 <ul>                         ← creates an unordered list of hyperlinks shown below
<li> <a href= "eu.html"> Europe </a></li>
<li> <a href = "uk.html"> United Kingdom </a></li>
<li> <a href ="ger.html"> Germany </a></li>
<li> <a href ="fr.html"> France</a></li>
</ul>
</body>
</noframes>
```

- This whole code should be inserted between </frameset> and </html> in the XHTML code shown in Diagram 23.

- Resave it as **dframes.html**.

. <u>Caution!</u>

- If you run this in the IE 5.5, or any other user agent that supports frames, you will still get the same effects, and the display of documents in the same way as you have already seen in the last example. The reason for this happening is that the browser that can interpret frames will do so, before reaching this segment of the code for <noframes> element.

- Any other user agents, which cannot read frames, will go on to reading the above segment of the code, and display the text and hyperlinks for selecting any of the hyperlinks. If you click on one of the hyperlinks, the relevant document will appear on the screen, and at the same time all hyperlinks will become invisible. This means you cannot make any further selections, until you load **dframe.html** again, and start all over the process of selecting any of the hyperlinks. **<u>This is a serious drawback!</u>**

. Can you overcome this problem by adding in each document a return link to dframe.html?

Yes, you should also add the following segment of the code to each of the above four **.html** files, which contain XHTML markup codes for documents to be displayed, when a hyperlink is activated by the user.

```
<a href ="dframe.html" > To return to the selection list -click here</a>
```

- This segment of the code should be placed on the line just above the **</body>** tag in each file of the following documents/files:-

  - eu.html - containing information on Europe - Diagram 24
  - uk.html - containing information on UK - Diagram 27
  - ger.html - containing information on Germany - Diagram 28
  - fr.html - containing information on France - Diagram 29

- Having added this line of code to each of these files, you must save them under the same name as **. html** files. <u>No more adjustments are needed</u>.

• When you load your **dframes.html** in any browser which does not support frames, you should get the following display on your screen:-

This browser does not support frames. Still you can select from the following hyperlinks:-

- Europe
- United Kingdom
- Germany
- France

From this list, any of the hyperlinks can be selected, repeatedly, if necessary. Note that this will work only on any system which does not support frames.

• Inline frames

There is another type of frames known as inline frames, which are created by means of **<iframe> element**. An inline frame can be included in an XHTML page. In reality, an inline frame is a floating box, which you can use for whatever purpose it is useful. The <iframe> element can take a number of values, of which **height**, **width** and **src** are commonly used.

In case, your Web page containing inline frame is viewed by any of these browsers, it is a good idea to create and store a backup file. This file should contain the same information which is intended for displaying in the inline frame.

• Example 5

The purpose of this example is to demonstrate the application <iframe> element, and its important attributes namely, 'height', 'width' and 'src'. In order to do so, the following two documents are to be designed.

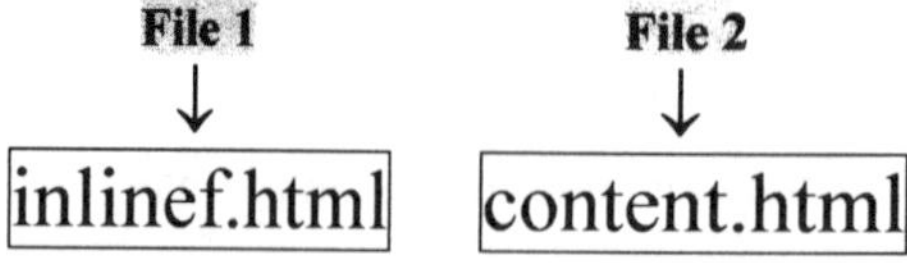

• **File 1** – When the Web page is viewed locally, it must have the following information together with a box/inline frame for inserting in it the information listed below for File 2:-

My Home Page
You can see below a table of contents.

- **File 2** – When the Web page is viewed, the following information should also be shown in the same Web page (see File 1), but must it be inserted in the inline frame:-

A Table of Contents

. Inline Frames
. Importing Frames
. Tables

. Explanation

The required XHTML codes for these two files are simple enough. In fact, organising files and identifying the correct information for these files deserve careful planning. You should pay attention to the following points:-

. **In Diagram 32**, you should study the code which is for creating a Web page containing the implementation of the <iframe> element.

<iframe src ="content.html" height ="200" width = "200" >

attribute points to the source file containing the information to be displayed in an inline frame within " " is the source file

the height of the inline box in pixels

width of the inline box in pixels

height + width = size of an inline frame

- The code in Diagram 32 is written under XHTML 1.0 Transitional. You can only write it under this DTD. It was validated for XML well-formedness as XHTML 1.0 Transitional by W3C Validation Service.

- The code in Diagram 33 is simple enough to follow. It is written under XHTML 1.0 Strict, validated as such by the same W3C Service.

The XHTML code for inline frame – inlinef.html

```
<?xml version= "1.0" encoding = "UTF-8"?>
<!DOCTYPE html
        PUBLIC "- //w3C//DTD XHTML 1.0 Frameset//EN"
 "http://www.w3.org/TR/xhtml1/DTD/xhtml1- frameset.dtd">
<html xmlns="http://www.w3.org/1999/xhtml" xml:lang="en" lang= "en">
<head>
<title> Setting up Inline frames</title>
</head>
<body>
<h1>
   My Home Page</h1>
<p> You can see below a table of contents.</p>
<iframe src ="content.html" height ="200" width ="200" >
</iframe>
</body>
</html>
```

Diagram 32

The XHTML code for text to be displayed in inline frame - cotent.html

```
<?xml version= "1.0" encoding = "UTF-8"?>
<!DOCTYPE html
        PUBLIC "- //w3C//DTD XHTML 1.0 Strict//EN"
 "http://www.w3.org/TR/xhtml1/DTD/xhtml1- strict.dtd">
<html xmlns="http://www.w3.org/1999/xhtml" xml:lang="en" lang= "en">
<head>
<title> Setting up Inline frames</title>
</head>
<body>
<h1> A Table of Contents</h1>
<p>. Inline Frames  <br>
   . Importing Frames<br>
   . Tables </p>
</body>
</html>
```

Diagram 33

A preview of inline document in IE 5.5 –example 3

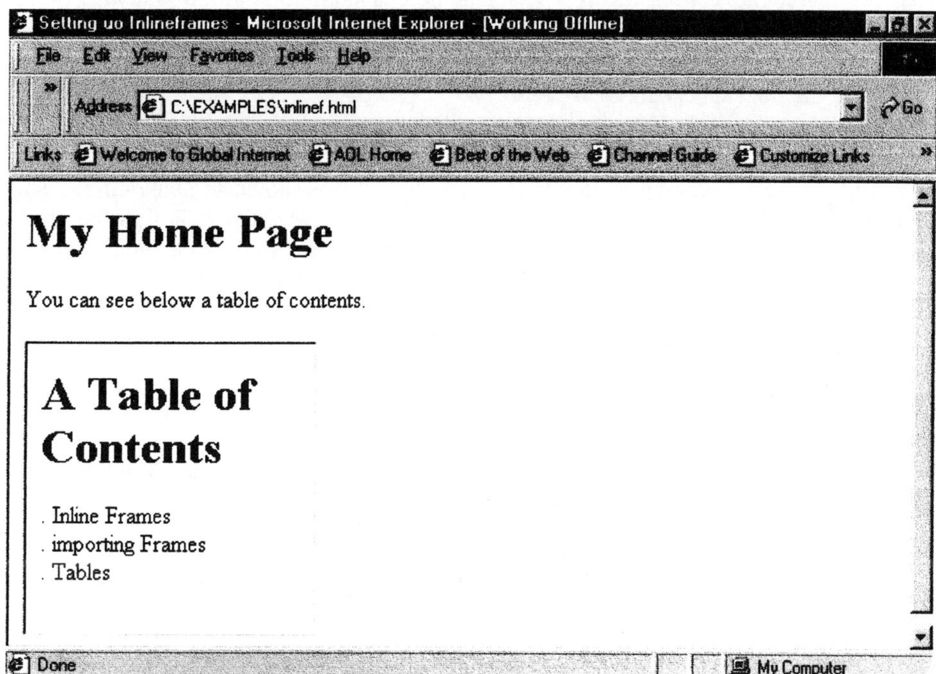

Diagram 34

The above screen capture illustrates that frames including inline frames are well supported by IE 5.5. In fact, I have previewed all frames in this browser. This version of IE is excellent.

• Example 6

- Suppose your Web page containing an inline frame has to be viewed by a browser which does not support frames at all.

• How can you make the whole content which is within the inline frame available to all Web page viewers?

. Explanation

You can set up another backup document which contains both the line frame and a reference to the source document in which the text for this inline frame is kept.

In order to illustrate the operation of a backup file/document, I have made use of both documents which are for example 3. The amendment has to be made to the code for inlinef.html, so that it also contains a reference to the source file: **content.html**. The amendment is in the form of the following piece of code added to **inlinef.html**:-

```
<p>Your browser does not support online frames.<br>
 Below you can see what you would have seen in a box. <a href ="content.html"> </a></p>
```

This piece of code is placed between < iframe > and </iframe>, as shown in Diagram 35. This is an additional code, which lists some text and then by means of <a> element points to the source file, which can be invoked by the browser, providing it does not read the <iframe> element. Thus, the following two documents are essential for the correct working of this backup document.

- You have to preview it in a browser which does not support frames. The IE 5.5 will not invoke this additional piece of code, as it can read the <iframe> element.

The XHTML code for the backup file – inlineback.html

```
<?xml version= "1.0" encoding = "UTF-8"?>
<!DOCTYPE html
        PUBLIC "- //w3C//DTD XHTML 1.0 Frameset//EN"
 "http://www.w3.org/TR/xhtml1/DTD/xhtml1- frameset.dtd">
<html xmlns="http://www.w3.org/1999/xhtml" xml:lang="en" lang= "en">
<head>
<title> Setting up Inline frames</title>
</head>
<body>
<h1>
  My Home Page</h1>
<p> You can see below a table of contents.</p>
<iframe src ="content.html" height ="200" width ="200" >
<p>
  Your browser does not support online frames.<br>
 Below you can see what you would have seen in a box.
  <a href ="content.html"> </a>
</p>
</iframe> </body></html>
```

Diagram 35

Use frames with care and moderation in order to benefit from this invaluable technique.

Chapter 13

Setting Up a Web Site

The prime aims of this chapter are as follows:-

- to assist you to understand that setting up a Web site requires careful planning in the light of the objective/s for publishing your documents for public viewing on-line
- to enable you to know the steps that are essential for setting up your Web site
- to provide you with some relevant information for submitting your site to search engines, directories or other automated systems

At the end of the chapter, you should be able:-

- to know some popular search engines and directories
- to explain the difference between a directory and a search engine
- to explain the meaning of meta-data (meta information)
- to describe the reason for using the meta-data in an XHTML document
- to construct some meta tags with 'name' attribute
- to explain the need for keywords, keyword phrases, and descriptions in a meta tag used with the name attribute
- to construct some meta tags with 'http-equiv' attribute
- to write some meta tags with Expires, Content- Script-Type
- to make a distinction between linear and hierarchical Web site structure designs
- to explain the need for uploading pages with the aid of FTP browser to ISP's computer system

- to know from where to acquire some resources in relation to setting up the Web site, and promoting it
- to be able to maintain a Web site on a regular basis

. Introduction

If you have followed this book from the start, and practised using all the solved examples, by now you should be in a position to setting up of a Web site or take a part as a member of a team to set up a sizeable Web site. It is not the size which matters most, but the successful setting of a Web site. A Web site does not have to be complex, because a simple and straightforward Web site is more appealing and successful, as a means of communication. By now, you have acquired sufficient knowledge, skills, and confidence in using XHTML. The next stage is to put it into practice. Of course, you can design XHTML documents, but to put them together as a Web site, you require some more information which is the subject of this chapter.

Some Popular Search Engines

Engine	ULR
. AltaVista	http:// www.altavisat.com
. AOL	http://www.aol.com
. Excite	http://www. excite.com
. Google	http://www.google.com
. HotBot	http://www.hotbot.com
. Lycos	http://lycos.com
. WebCrawler	http://www.webcrawler.com
. Yahoo	http://www. yahoo.com

Table 1

. What is a search engine?

A search engine is an indexing software. It is often called robot or spider. These programs are designed to crawl the Web non-stop, day and night in search of new or updated Web pages. Their search goes on URL to URL, until they have visited every Web site on the Internet. There are thousands of search engines constantly searching the Web. The number of search engines is growing every day. Some popular search engines are listed below in table 1.

Search engines find information from the URL , Web pages, and record the full text from all pages of a site. Search engines also follow all external links. This way, they can find your Web site, even if you do not submit your site to them directly. The same way, they also find any amendments made to Web pages. Therefore, in reality, you do not have to submit your site to search engines, as eventually they can find your site from your Web address. On the other hand, if you submit your site for registration to some search engines of your preference, the great advantage is that your site can be considered by them for registration and storing it in their databases. Anyway, many search engines take a considerably long time (1-8 weeks) to register a site. A submission of a Web site is not a guarantee of its registration. No registration means your site is not in the database of a search engine which has not registered your site.

If you wish to speed up the process of registering your site with a lot of search engines, it is suggested that you use Microsoft Submit Service for this purpose. It costs $59 for a year (at the time of writing). It is worth investing this money. They can submit your site to some 400 search engines and directories.

You can find Microsoft Submit Service at:- **http://www.submit-it.com**

. What is a directory?

A Web directory is something akin to a huge reference library. The directory is hierarchically arranged by subject – from broad to specific. Unlike the search engines, a directory will only register your URL, if you submit your URL to it. Since directories do not use an indexing software, you have to provide on-line information by filling in a form. You must choose the most relevant category for listing your site for each directory of your choice. If you use Microsoft Submit It! Service, you will be given the opportunity to submit your site to dozens of directories, which include:

- Big Bang
- Info Links
- Scrub The Web
- PepeSearch
- GeneralSearch
- MallPark
- InfoHiway

. Regional directories

On the Net, you will find directories for different regions of the world. Some of the UK directories are listed below:-

- BritIndex
- Excite UK
- Lycos UK
- SearchUK
- ShopGuide
- Yahoo! UK & Ireland

• Meta-data

Most printed books have a table of contents. This table of contents is all about the book in such a way that it lists the title of each chapter and page number where the chapter begins. Of course, sometimes, a table of contents may have chapters, which are divided into their sections, and against each section a page number is listed, where it begins. In fact, in both these cases, the principle is the same, which is to give information about the book in advance of someone reading the whole book.

This information can be considered as a summary of information about the book itself. Indeed, a book gives information about a major topic on which it is written. On the other hand, the table of contents is also information about the whole book. In XHTML and the Internet jargon, this summary information about the book is **meta-data**. In fact, meta-data is descriptive information about the Web documents. In XHTML, the **<meta> element** is used for including this descriptive information. You can include this optional element in each of your Web documents, but it must be included in your **index.html** document, which is the home page.

. Why is there a need for meta-data for documents on a Web site?

- Usually, a Web site has a number of documents. Each document contains some information about some specific topic(s). Meta-data can summarise the essence of the document in a few phrases.
- Meta-data helps search engines to locate a particular document or a Web site. Not all search engines make use of <meta> tags. The inclusion of <meta> tags in Web pages makes them more accessible to those engines, which make use of <meta> tags.
- Meta–data gives extra information about your Web pages to the search engine. This extra information is not visible to the reader. Most search engines do take these keywords into account when indexing your Web pages.
- Meta-data helps browsers and other user agents to know the type of the document being dealt with.

• How can you include meta-data in your document?

The <meta> tags are inserted within the <head></head> tags. The general format of the syntax is as follows:-

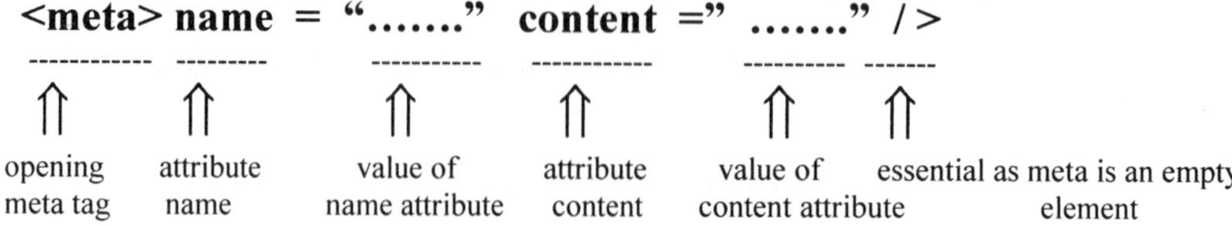

• Example 1

```
<head>
<title> Computer Bookshop - Internet and computer printed Books</title>
<meta name ="keywords" content ="computer bookshop, XHTML, HTML, JavaScript, Perl,
            Java, C++, C, Python, Web design , programming" />
 <meta name ="description" content ="ADR London publishers and booksellers. Students simplified
text series. Web site development, and practical books for serious readers." />
</head>
```

• You can use more than one <meta> element within the <head> section of your document.

• The interpretation of meta-data

• The majority of search engines find the requested Web page by comparing the search keywords typed by the user with the information which is stored about the required Web page/Web site in its database. Often, the information stored in the search engine's database is a list of keywords found in a Web page.

• If you include these two <meta> elements shown in the above example, in your **index.html** file, both keywords and description will become the summary of your home page. These will be displayed after the title of your document in the index listing by a search engine.

• The content of 'Keywords' gives some additional information about your Web page to the search engine. It is an indication that the content will be having a comma separating lists of some keywords. In fact, this information is invisible to the reader.

Usually, search engines index the entire content of a Web page. You can still include some keywords which are unlikely to be derived from your Web page, when a robot/search engine or any other automated system visits your site. For instance, there is no need to include 'Computer', and 'Internet' words in your keywords, as the robot will index them when it finds these words as part of your Web page <title> during the indexing process.

• It is important to remember that 'the content of the description' should be worded in such a precise manner that it conveys what one can expect to find when visiting your site.

• Both 'keywords' and 'description' are indexed by robots. Therefore, these are searchable words. If someone keyed in "C++" or "ADR", your Web page should be found, if it is in the search engine's database.

• Try to use both singular and plural words. Also, if possible try to include active and passive verbs. The idea is that your meta-data should be designed in such a way that your site will come up on all keywords.

• Repeat of keywords

Some search engines may not register your site if you continually repeat keywords. They may completely ignore your meta-data and simply extract keywords from your pages. In fact, this is often the case, that is extracting keywords from the content of your Web page, but not all search engines do so.

• What is a keyword phrase?

A keyword phrase consists of a few words. It is often about three words long, which are truly relevant to your site. For instance for XHTML, the keyword phrase could be "XHTML Web language" or " XHTML Web technology". Keywords or keyword phrases which are well thought out and most relevant to your site can lead to the inclusion of your site in the databases of some search engines. You have to decide which are the most likely keyword phrases your prospective visitors are likely to submit to a search engine, when searching a site which should be your own site. You can include keyword phrases in your meta –data, or title. It should be remembered that too many keyword phrases does not necessarily mean producing better results.

• Can you use any value for the name attribute in the <meta> element?

You can use any name value in the <meta>element. However, keywords' description are well-recognised, and defined by search engine spiders, browsers, or other automated systems. You can also use in the <meta> element any of the following values of the name attribute:-

• summary • author • classification • copyright • generator • rating and • some other values

• Example 2

```
<meta name = "author" content = " Rachel Webster" />
<meta  name = "copyright" content = "September 2001, ADR " />
```

• The 'hhtp-equiv' attribute

The <meta> element can also be used to give information about the document. These are mainly for the benefit of search engines, browsers or any other automated systems.

• Example 3

```
<meta http-equiv = "Expires" content = "Mon , 3 1December 2001:00:00:00 GMT " />
```

The 'Expires' attribute informs the browser when it should retrieve a new/fresh copy of the page from the server. It is indicated by the date, and time given in the above segment of the code. In this case, the document will expire on 31 December 2001, at midnight. This way, the browser knows when to retrieve a saved copy (copy stored in cache).

• Example 4

```
<meta http-equiv = "Content-Script.Type"  content =" text/JavaScript"  />
```

It is used for identifying a scripting language, and makes it available for use. (see if there is any restriction placed by your ISP for using any scripting language, and which language is available for you.)

• **PICS** - You can also include in **'http-equiv'** a PICS label. What is PICS?

PICS is an acronym for **P**latform for **I**nternet **C**ontent **S**election. The idea is to prevent objectionable material from publication on the Web. This is also known as content rating system.

• How can you use this content ratings system?

It is suggested that you seek the advice of your ISP company. They should be able to tell you if it is possible to use such material in your documents. If your site is going to be for children, you must include a PICS rating label. For further advice on this topic, you must seek expert advice at:-

http://www.w3.org/PICS

• Tools for developing meta-data

When you use Microsoft Submit IT service, you will be given the opportunity to use their Meta Tag Builder for the construction of meta tags to be inserted between the <head> and </head> tags. Meta tag

Builder builds meta tags on the basis of information you will provide when completing an on-line form. It is important to develop effective meta elements. In fact, this service is also offered by some search engines when you submit your Web site directly to them. For instance, the CGI design team at:-

http://www.scrubtheweb.com/abs/meta-check.html

This is a free 'Meta Tag Analyzer'. Scrub The Web -the search engine has a robot called scrubby, which maintains this search engine.

. Web site design

Of course individual page design is an important aspect of a Web site, as these individual pages collectively become a Web site. A Web page is an important component, because it has some specific information for visitors. So, the beginning of a good Web site design, in fact, lies in the design of each individual page. The overall design of a Web site should be given careful consideration. There are many examples of poor designs of Web sites on the Net. Often a poorly designed site takes a long time to download. In such cases, the top page/home page is full of information, tables, graphic images, and is thus really confusing. Such sites are discouraging, due to problems of navigation. For end users, a poorly designed site is expensive, as it costs money to be on-line. In addition, a poorly designed site is also difficult to maintain.

. Are there any recommended rules for creating an overall structure of a Web site?

I can strongly emphasise the 'simplicity' rule of designing a Web site. According to this rule, a Web site must be easy to navigate, and reasonably fast to download. The Web designers/Webmasters must plan a Web site in accordance with this rule. What is really important is to apply common sense, so that the final design should be based on the precise **purpose of a proposed Web site**.

Once the purpose has been established, you should consider the type of **visitors** who are likely to read your pages. For instance, a small businessman looking for a product to buy is least interested in listening to music, watching a display of some visual presentation, or reading some personal profiles of some key employees of a company.

Your well planned design of both individual pages and the home page, **motivate the visitor**, because of the ease of navigation, instead of discouraging him/her through an annoying presentational style, and difficulty in finding the required information. The **time factor** for downloading the home page and the required information must be given serious consideration.

The Web has been here for sometime, and experience shows that Web sites do **grow in size**. Therefore, irrespective of the size of a site, whether it is for personal use, for a small business or for a large business, at the design stage, you must consider future growth. With the growth comes the problem of **maintenance**, and thus this point should also be born in mind.

. Structuring your Web site

In accordance with this rule, it is suggested that you devise a structure of your site which reflects the line of file linkage and flow of information stored within them. So, how do you go about it ?

The whole idea is to link pages together. Well, there are a number of ways to achieve it. However, by no means is it recommended that any of these methods is most suited for your personal or business needs. You make your own decisions. You are the boss!

- **Linear structure -** here the idea is to place your pages one after the other as a series of documents in one folder. Where are links in this structure?

- Each page has a forward link to the ⟹ next page, until the last page is reached.
- Each page also has a backward ⟸ link which takes the viewer back to the first page in this series.

This method is limited to the extent that it gives no choices to the visitor. He/she must follow these links to locate the required information. It is suitable for guiding viewers, say, through a shopping mall on the Net.

- **Hierarchical structure -** This is like an organisational structure which looks like the structure of an Egyptian pyramid. See Illustration 1.

The underlining principle for this method is analysed as follows:-

- The top page is the home page – top of the pyramid. It contains summary information/ index and links to pages. The user can select a document from the given list.
- In Illustration 1, you can see its general format.
- Arrows ⇓ ⇑ indicate that the viewer has the opportunity to go down the hierarchy from the top page to the lowest page and also return to the home page in this hierarchy.
- Try not to have too many levels and too many pages for each parent level of the hierarchy.
- Of course, how many levels you should have, will depend on the information and how you have organised it in your pages.
- More than seven levels of hierarchy and seven pages for each level is not a good idea. Why? It will prove difficult to navigate.
- Is it possible to have links across the hierarchy? You can have links with other relevant pages. See Illustration 2.

A skeleton of hierarchical site design structure

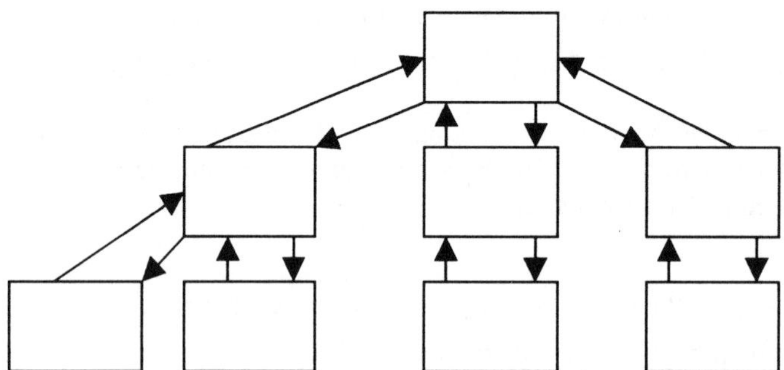

Illustration 1

- It is highly likely that in many situations, the **combination of these two methods** will be the only possible solution to the required Web site design.
- In Illustration 2, Order Form can be clicked from any product page. So, it is across the Web site, in this hierarchical structure. Of, course, from Order Form, you can also return to the home page. A user can easily navigate the Web site without any confusion.
- Of course, it is better to keep links simple. This can be done, if you somehow avoid creating up and down links. If you have a small number of documents, say 25, you can store these in one folder and manage these without any problems.
- Consult your ISP company for advice on any requirements for uploading files, storing files, home page, CGI script, security aspects, PICS or whatever your specific needs may be at the time of launching your Web site.

• Copying your pages to a Web server

Since you have developed your Web pages without using any text editor and any Web site management package such as FrontPage Microsoft package, you have to use FTP (File Transfer Protocol) to copy the pages yourself to your ISP's server or Web-serving computer. Indeed, this is an established method of transferring files across the Internet.

Your ISP firm should advise you on the precise method of how to achieve this objective without any serious problems arising during the transfer of files. You should also get from your ISP any passwords which are required for your use. It is highly likely that your ISP firm will include in their service package uploading of pages via FTP or some other software such as Microsoft FrontPage publishing wizard.

Hierarchical Structure

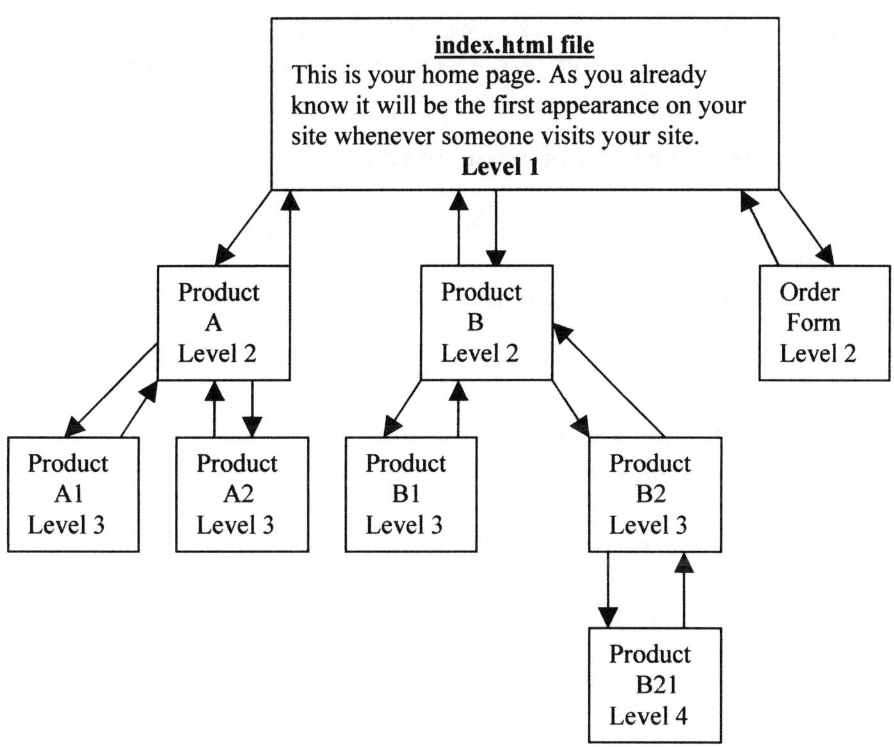

Illustration 2

. Can I upload Web pages via the browser?

The answer is no. A browser can download a file using FTP. For uploading files to an HTTP server, it is suggested that you obtain a copy of Terrapin FTP Browser V2.2 or the latest version. It is an excellent piece of software, which I enjoy using. It has graphical interface, and thus it is easy to use. It can be installed on your machine within a few minutes by following the accompanyng information. You can obtain it at **http://www.terra-net.com**

It is excellent software, It costs only $ 34.99 at the time of writing. Terrapin comes with a few examples of Site Maps in order to illustrate the concept. I suggest that before you invest any money, you should ask your ISP if they have a FTP software on their server for you to use it for copying your file onto their system. My guess is that it is most likely that your ISP firm have a package for uploading files and have included its use in their service contract. If you have a copy of Terrapin on your system, you can always use it, whenever there is a need to amend a file or add a new page, and so on.

. Further Web promotional information

. Banner Women is a banner network to help Web sites set up mainly for women with a limited or no advertising budget. If you have any products for women, and want to reach a target audience on-line, contact them at:-

http://www.bannerwomen.com/

. International Small Business Consortium is a useful contact. They have some 33000+ members in 140 countries. Contact them at:-

http://www.isbc.com/

. You can enter your web site free of charge in Yellow Pages in your country.

For UK at: **http://www/ukpages.co.uk/**
For USA at : **http://www.bigyellow.com**

. For international trade, find information at : **http://www.tradezone.com**

. For your personal Web site, free of charge, try Yahoo! at : **http://yahoo.com/**

. If you are a business, you have to pay Yahoo! for using their services. It is not cheap for a small business.

. Web site maintenance

Once your pages have been uploaded on the server of your ISP, and you have successfully submitted your site to some search engines and directories, you hope that, if not all, some of these will register your site. I say so, as the problem is that not all search engines and directories accept a commercial site free of charge. Often, some of them try to interest you in their own paid services or products. Even so, you should expect some good results to follow which will start attracting visitors to your site.

No system is for ever. Systems change, break down, and thus require some regular maintenance. From the feedback which you will receive from your visitors, you can learn a great deal about your Web site. It may be that there are some areas which need to be considered again. It is expected that most readers of this book are either small business owners, managers or individuals who fall within the definition of students in this book, and thus their Web sites are small. Therefore, there is no need to buy any Web management tools. Such tools are rather costly and unnecessary for your present requirements. Web Management tools are for large sites.

Since you have designed your own Web site and you know it well, you should be able to learn more about it by experience and be able to maintain it to the desired level of efficiency. You may find it helpful, if you record the following information:-

- visitors' negative comments on your Web site
- visitors' suggestions, if any, on your site and its contents
- technical problems such as links disappeared - check them on a regular basis.
- record number of visitors to your Web site. Your ISP can help you in this matter

It is highly likely that your ISP firm will include Hit counter, guest book , Perl or JavaScript script for logging visitors to your Web site and access to the server logs. If not, shop around until you find an ISP who includes these facilities. These facilities can assist you in knowing which pages get the most hits and which are least popular. Furthermore, such information can help you decide if it is big enough for your requirements or not. You may soon require more space. Thus, a record of visitors is important for the evaluation of your Web site success.

If you have such a record, you should be able to take appropriate action accordingly, when it is convenient. It does not mean that you leave problems unsolved for a long time as you have no time for solving Web site problems during your business hours. Since the Web site is part of your business, it is desirable that it receives regular attention to up-date it. Some problems, such as the links are missing in your pages will require prompt attention. It may be that one of your pages needs to be updated. If you leave it too late, it will not please your prospective clients/visitors.

On a regular basis, say, monthly, analyse objectively your record of the feedback received. It may be that you have to take some actions to remedy the situation. It will help your business if your site is always up-to-date in terms of its contents. If for some reasons, you decide to move your site to another ISP firm, make sure that you leave a referral page in place for some time. It is a good strategy and one that will endear you to potential customers.

• Addendum

Indeed, you can include in your Web pages some graphic images such as photos and logos which you have already seen in this book. In addition, you can also include audio and video objects. The term multimedia covers the inclusion of graphics, audio, video into Web pages. There are two types of audio files. These are **audio** and **streaming audio**. Audio files are simple files. These include Microsoft Windows Plug-ins. Streaming audio files are rather complex files. The browser or any other user agent downloads the whole file first before it starts playing the audio. The <object> element is used to put the document containing audio objects into an XHTML documents. In the case of **streaming audio files**, the browser/user agent downloads only a portion of the file before it begins playing the file. For instance, a radio on the Internet makes use of streaming audio file, as something is being recorded and played back at the same time.

Similarly, video files are of two types, namely **video** files and **streaming video** files. Your PC will have some video plug-ins which can be embedded in your Web page. There are a number of video formats for both the Internet Explorer and Netscape. For further information, you should contact W3C at: **http://www.w3.org/**

Glossary

Address

The electronic equivalent of a postal address of the Webmaster. See also URL

Address Element

The address of a Webmaster is written within <address> and </address> tags. This will be displayed in ***italics***. For instance:- < address> famous @ famous.com</address>

ASCII (or Ascii)

Acronym for American Standard Code for Information Interchange. It has been widely used since it was introduced in 1963. It has 128 different character values in the range 0-127.

ASCII text file

It does not have any special characters, such as **boldfaced** text.

Attributes

An additional piece of information which extends an HXTML basic tag. For instance:

```
<ol  type ="a">
---  ---------    ----
 ⇑      ⇑          ⇑
element attribute attribute's value
```

Browser

It is a piece of software that allows a user to interact with Web pages, such as to locate and retrieve information. There are many browsers on the market. Browsers differ in their features. Microsoft Internet Explorer and Netscape are the most popular browsers. Microsoft Internet Explorer 5.5 is the latest version. The other famous browser is Netscape 6.1 – the latest version of Netscape browser.

Cascading Style Sheets (CSS)

It is a language for adding style (e.g. fonts, colours, spacing) to Web documents. CSS1 became a W3C Recommendation in December 1996. CSS2 became a W3C Recommendation in May 1998. It is built on CSS1 and adds support for media-specific style sheets (e.g. printers and aural devices), downloadable fonts, element positioning and tables.

Case-sensitive

It means that all characters must match exactly. For instance: c++ and C++ are unmatched, as c and C are lower and upper case letters, and thus two different letters. It should be c++ = c++ or C++ = C++.

Child Element

An element which is nested within another element is called child element. For instance:-

<grandfather><father></father> </grandfather>

In this segment of code element<father> is the child element of the <grandfather> element.

Common Gateway Interface (CGI)

The simplest description of CGI is that it is an interface between the Web server and the computer on which the Web server is stored. It communicates user requests in the form of scripts (see scripts) to an interpreter program on the same computer for processing user requests.

Container Element

The container element is known as <html> element. It is the container of the XHTML document. It is vitally important that its end tag </html> is the last tag, marking the end of the entire document

Content

. The text between opening and closing tags is an element content, as illustrated below:-

< h1> This is element content</h1>

. The content can also be the content of an attribute, as shown below:-

<meta name = “author” content = “Rachel Webster” >
Here, content is an attribute, and its content is within “ ”

. The content can also mean document content. The document content is further classified as:-

1. the **actual information**, text or whatever, for which the document is designed;
2. the markup structures that make the document well-formed; and
3. the **meta information** – the information about the document itself.

CSS

See Cascading Style Sheets.

Document

A document contain some information. In XHTML, it also contains information. This information is its content. See content for its meaning.

Document Type Definition (DTD)

It defines how a browser or any other user agent will display the content of an XHTML document. XHTML 1.0 document can be written under three different DTD,s. These are:-

Strict DTD

```
<!DOCTYPE html PUBLIC "- //w3C//DTD XHTML 1.0 Strict//EN"
                    "http://www.w3.org/TR/xhtml1/DTD/xhtml1- strict.dtd">
```

Transitional DTD

```
<!DOCTYPE html PUBLIC "- //w3C//DTD XHTML 1.0 Transitional//EN"
                    "http://www.w3.org/TR/xhtml1/DTD/xhtml1- Transitional.dtd">
```

Frame DTD

```
<!DOCTYPE html PUBLIC "- //w3C//DTD XHTML 1.0 Frameset//EN"
                    "http://www.w3.org/TR/xhtml1/DTD/xhtml1- frameset.dtd">
```

Domain (Domain name)

It is that part of the Internet address which identifies the computer where the address is located. It can be the computer of your ISP or your chosen name followed by one of the domain names endings allocated to your country. For instance: sales@ MyName.co.uk In this case, the required country code is **.co.uk** - the domain name ending.

It can also be: Anne@ adrlondon.ltd.uk. In this example, **ltd.uk** is the country code. You must know your own country code, which is the domain name ending.

Download

When you copy files from the network or any other computer on to your own computer it is known as download. When you are copying files this way, then you are downloading files on to your computer.

E-Commerce

If you start selling your goods or services on-line, you will be involved in E-Commerce.

Element

A logical unit of information in XHTML. For instance:-

< b> bold typeface</b>

This structure of opening tag, text content, and closing tag is a logical unit of information. It is, therefore, an element in XHTML.

Empty Element

An empty element has only one tag, and also does not enclose any content. The following is an example of an empty element.

```
<input type = "text"  name = "ML" size = "25"  />
```

Extensible Markup Language (XML)

It is a standard developed by W3C which is not fixed like HTML. It allows users to create their own tags, or use any other tags developed elsewhere. It is more flexible and simpler than HTML.

External DTD

You can have an external DTD, which is not stored as a component of a document, but kept separately. An external DTD has the advantage of availability to multiple documents. This way, many documents can share the same DTD.

File Format

The way in which information in a file is encoded is called file format. There are many file formats. See GIF file.

Frameset

It is a set of more than one frame. A frameset by itself contains no information. It requires content. The content of a frame is XHTML document. The browser window can be divided into a number of frames, each containing its own separate information. This is then a frame. A typical set of frames has an index frame, which has navigation links, the top, where you can have your company logo, or banner, and body frame for the text.

Freeware

Software packages can be obtained free of charge from the Internet or through some Internet magazines. See also Shareware.

Front page

This is the first page which appears on your site when someone visits it. See Home page.

FTP

You cannot upload files by means of the browser. Thus you have to do so by means of a program which uses the File Transfer Protocol. Also note that there are FTP sites which are also on the Net.

Generalised Markup Language (GML)

It was developed at IBM in the late 1960s. GML was the first language to use “<” ,” >”, and “/” for markup. It is still in use for document application.

GIF file

This is an image file. For instance, ADRLogo.gif in which ADR company logo is stored. The file extension is **.gif**. GIF format is most commonly used for viewing images on the World Wide Web.

Graphical user interface

The components such as buttons, text fields and the like help the user to interact with the computer by using the mouse or the keyboard. For short GUI is often used.

Hits

It is a record of the number of visitors to your site. It is very useful for an evaluation of your site.

Home page

It is the index page (index.html file) of an individual or a business on the Internet. Here links to relevant pages are stored. It may also have links stored to some other related sites.

Host or host

It is a computer at the Internet Service Provider which is primarily for the purpose of offering a service to users commercially. If you are a big company, you can have your own host computer.

‘hotbot’

One of the popular search engines at: **htp:// www.hotbot.com**

HyperText Markup Language (HTML - Or html)

HTML became the most popular markup language, and one of the foundations of the World Wide Web. Its own success has contributed much to its eventual replacement by XHTML.

HyperText Transfer Protocol (HTTP)

It is the protocol spoken and understood by Web servers, browsers and other user agents. It is the first thing you write when you describe a Web address. The format is **http://.....**

With the aid of this protocol, clients can send requests to Web servers which send back the required information, or an error message.

Internet

Broadly speaking, it is a network of computer networks across the world.

Internet Explorer

It is one of the World Wide Web browsers on the market. This piece of software from Microsoft is really good for XHTML, and CSS application. The latest version is 5.5. You can use CSS and XHTML efficiently with this browser.

Internet Service Provider (ISP)

A business enterprise specialising in providing internet access across the Web. Many ISPs provide a variety of other related services, such as developing a Web site for a client. In the UK, there is a trade organisation called Internet Services Providers in the UK. Some ISPs firms are members of this organisation. Contact them at: **http://www.ispa.org.uk**

ISO

It stands for the International Organisation for Standardisation. It was founded in 1946, and its members are national standards bodies all over the world. It sets international data processing standards and many others.

Java

Java is an object-oriented programming language. It was developed in the 1990s at Sun Microsystems. It is especially applicable to the world Wide Web.

JavaScript - see next page

It is a scripting language. JavaScripts are small programs which may be embedded in a Web page. The JavaScript is used to facilitate some interaction between the user and the Web page such as an inquiry form. Java Scripts can also be an external Web page.

Links (or hyperlinks)

A link is highlighted text or an image that can connect you to another site, or another page on the same site or on the same computer locally. Links appear in different colours in accordance with their status(eg. visited link...) and are underlined. Without links in your XHTML documents, your documents would just be another display system and no internet communication would take place.

Lycos

A popular search engine at: **http// www.lycos.com**

Mailing List

A group of people with similar interests communicate with each other by E-mail through a central E-mail. There are a large number of such mailing lists across the Web. Surely, you will be able to find many such lists of interest to yourself. You can start your own mailing list. For instance, make a list of all your customers and send them information from your own computer system. In this case, you are the owner of the list and you control it centrally (it is a traditional list).

Markup

Formatting or structural information which is also stored in the Web page but is not displayed. It is defined with tags. Your XHTML file includes the markup information and the actual information to be displayed.

Meta- information

The meta-information is about the document itself. It is also in your Web page. The title of your Web page which appears in the browser title bar is meta-information.

Meta tag

This information within the pair of meta tags is needed so that a visiting search engine can recognise your site. It does not appear in your pages when pages are viewed by visitors. It actually describes your site and is thus invisible to users. It is also referred as meta-data. See Appendix A.

'name'

It is an attribute. It must always begin with a lower case n, and must not contain any other characters.

namespace

It is a mechanism devised in XML, and also used in XHTML. This mechanism allows you to use elements from one document type and combine them with elements in another document type. In XHTML, all elements have names. Collectively, all XHTML elements belong to XHTML namescape. For instance:

<html xmlns = "http://www.w3.org/1999/xhtml" xml:lang ="en" lang ="en">

```
          --------      ----------------------------------------
             ⇑                          ⇑
it is an attribute of <html>      this is XHTML namespace
```

Netscape

The company's latest browser is Netscape 6.1. In accordance with their e-mail message on my PC, it is described by Netscape as, "the most powerful, efficient, and reliable browser for your PC today." You can obtain a free copy at:- **http://wwww.netscape.com/**

Newsgroups

There are many thousands of international discussion groups on the Internet. They form a special area on the Net and are sometimes known as **usenet**.

Nominet UK

It is the Registry for all **.uk** Internet Domain Names. It is equivalent to the DVLA for driving licences in the UK. It maintains the database of **.uk** registered Internet names. It is not a governing body but provides a public service for the **.uk**.

Parent Element

Within the parent element, another element is nested. For instance:-

<grandfather><father></father> </grandfather> - here <grandfather> is the parent element.

Parser

A parser is a piece of software which is used with all XML applications. It takes an XML document, and converts it into its structure and content accessible to an application, via a standard interface, such as DOM. There are two types of parsers, namely, Validating and non-validating. Parsers have been given a great deal of publicity. There are scores of parsers on the Internet which you can copy free of charge or shareware at:-

http://www.xmlsoftware.com/parsers/

Perl

It is a scripting language developed at Unix. It is very popular for developing CGI scripts.

Pixel

A pixel is the smallest fine-grained mosaic which makes up the screen display. There are different sizes of monitors. The standard VGA display is 640x 480 pixels. If you invest freely, you can get a super VGA. It is 800 pixels wide by 600 pixels high.

PoP

It stands for point of presence. If your ISP firm does not use PoP or the local-dial telephone number, your telephone bill can be pretty high. Therefore, prior to entering a legally binding contract find out about it first. You will find that larger ISPs have local numbers throughout the UK. It is better to look around for a better ISP.

Processing Instruction (PI)

The XML declaration is a processing instruction itself. Furthermore, PI allows the insertion of non-XML statements in the XML document. The processing instruction is written where dots are in this illustration: **<? ....?>**

Prolog

In XML , prolog includes both the XML declaration and document type declarations.

Protocol

It is a legal agreement between parties that exchange information between computer systems. It governs the rules and procedures for data communication between two computers. The World Wide Web uses a number of protocols. HTTP is the most common. FTP is also used for transferring FTP type files.

Python

This is a scripting language. It is popular with XML, as it has an XML parser.

Root Element

Root element is the first element in a document. The only thing which is listed above the root element is the prolog or the DOCTYPE declaration. In XHTML, the root element is html. Why ? The reason is that XHTML is an extensible, and thus it is still a hypertext markup language. For this reason alone, html is its root element.

Search engine

It is an indexing site. It tracks down useful interesting information from other sites. A visitor can search for sites that mention particular words. There are Meta search engines as well. They are so powerful that instead of using one search engine at a time, they can start a search by using a number of search engines simultaneously. You can get a list of meta search engines at:

http://www.yahoo.com/computers_and_internet/internet/world_wide_web/searching_the_web/all_in_one_search_pages

Shareware

Software packages or programs which you can load from the Internet or get with a magazine, and where a small charge is required, are called shareware.

Sibling

When some elements have the same parent element, each element which shares the same parent element is called a sibling element. For instance:

<p><b> <tt> This is an example of sibling elements</tt></b></p>

In this code, <b> and <tt> are sibling elements, because both share the same parent element, <p>.

Standalone document

When a document does not contain any references to any external document, which can affect its processing then it is called a standalone document. A standalone document is more efficient because there is only one file to be downloaded.

Standard RGB Values

The standard colours are red, green and blue. All other colours are specified by giving the percentage of red, green and blue.

Style Sheet

A style sheet contains instructions for formatting and presenting/displaying a document. A style sheet may be part of the Web page, or an external style sheet stored under its own name, but linked to the Web page. For an external style sheet, you must include a reference within the <head> section of your Web page by using the <link> element. For instance:- <link rel = "stylesheet" href = "first.link.css" />

⇑

this is the external style sheet file saved under **.css** extension

Tag

It is XHTML element. <p> for example is a basic paragraph tag. Within the tag, you can include some attributes. Most XHTML tags are in pairs. The closing tag is written as </p>. It has a forward slash in front of the tag name. For instance: <html>.......</html> . You can use only lower case letters within the angle brackets.

TCP/IP

Transmission Control Protocol/Internet Protocol. It is a communication system which transfers information between computers

Text area - It is one of the user interface components in the GUI system. It allows you to enter more than one line of text. See Forms.

Text editor

XHTML documents are prepared by using a text editor, such as WordPad. It is a kind of word processor.

Text Field

It is a user interface component. It can allow you to enter only one line of text.

Unicode

Unicode is a recent major development for international character encoding. The idea is to include all spoken languages on the planet Earth, as well as scientific and mathematical symbols. For further information, visit the Unicode Consortium at :- http:// www.unicode.org

Usenet

Seen **newsgroups**.

Upload

Your XHTML pages are stored on your computer hard disc. These files must be transferred to your ISP server. Once they are on your ISP's server, they constitute your Web site. The server is regarded as at a higher level than your own computer. This is the reason for calling the transfer of your files to the server as upload. When you are copying your pages on to the server then you are uploading your files on to your ISP's computer system.

URL

An abbreviation for Uniform(or universal)Resource Locator. It is the address system which is used to specify the location of a document in the WWW. For instance: http://www.you.com

UTF-8

The UTF-8 encoding uses 8 bits for English characters. This encoding provides access to the Unicode character set. For further infrmation, visit: http://www.w3.org/International

Valid

A document is valid if it meets the requirements of the DTD under which it is written, and satisfies the conditions for well-formedness.

W3C

The World Wide Web Consortium is the organisation that sets many standards for the success of WWW. Find out more about it at: http://www.w3.org/

W3C Validation Service

It is a free service which can check XHTML 1.0 documents under all three DTDs, namely, Strict, Transitional, and Frameset. It is the best service in the world for this purpose at: http://validator.W3.org

Web page

It means a single page that appears on your screen when you are connected to a site.

Web rings

These are Web sites, mainly for consumers.

Web server

A computer which has a special software for holding Web pages and passing them to another Web server over the Internet which in turn passes to the computer visiting the site where Web pages are stored. For instance, if you are searching using your PC, you have to communicate with the site where Web pages are kept via the Web server of your ISP firm.

Web site

A Web site consists of Web pages. It is just like this book, but on -line. A collection of whatever you wish to communicate to the world.

W W W

Interconnected networks of computer networks make up WWW.

Yahoo! - It is an internet directory and search engine. It is a very popular site in the world.

Appendix A

XHTML Elements & Associated Attributes

• Introduction

You have been shown the application of as many XHTML elements, and associated attributes as was possible within the space of this book. In this chapter, a comprehensive list of current XHTML elements is drawn with a view to providing you with a set of both elements and their associated attributes for reference purposes. The list covers the requirements for developing XHTML 1.0 Strict and Transitional type documents. Where any element allows the use of attributes which are specifically implemented in XHTML 1.0 Transitional type documents, this fact is stated in bold text, in the Description & Attributes column of the list. This way, it covers both Strict and Transitional DTDs. The list is in alphabetical order. A brief description of each element is an indication of its purpose. No claim is made for the inclusion of all current attributes, and elements, despite the fact that these are the known current XHTML 1.0 elements.

XHTML 1.0 Elements

Element	Description & Attributes
<a>	It creates hyperlinks. *href, name, rel, type, hreflang, lang, xml:lang* are some of the attributes it takes.In **Transitional type document** - it can accept *target.*
<abbr>	It is used to mark up abbreviations. It takes attributes including:- *dir, id, style, title, lang xml:lang.*
<acronym>	It is for marking up acronym. Among other attributes, it can take: *dir, id, lang, xml:lang, style* and *title.*
<address>	The Web document author can use it to give contact information. *style, title, dir, id,lang, xml:lang* are some of the common attributes it takes.

XHTML 1.0 Elements (cont.)

Element	Description & Attributes
<area>	The purpose of this element is to define the hyperlink region of a client image map. *nohref, shape, href, alt,onblur,onfocus,tabindex,id,style,title* are some of the attributes it takes. In **Transitional type document** - it can accept *target.*
<b>	It displays text in bold font. Some of the attributes which it can take are :- *dir, id, lang, xml:lang, style* and *title.*
<base>	It defines the location of a Web page. It is the document's base URL. It takes *href.* In **Transitional type document** - it can accept *target* attribute.
<bdo>	It is a useful element, if you want to override the text flow from left to right or from right to left. Attribute *dir* is needed with it. It can also take some other attributes including:- *onclick, ondblclick, onmousedown onmouseup, onmousemove,onmouseout, lang and xml:lang.*
<big>	You can apply it in order to use bigger text characters. It takes attributes including:- *dir, id, style, title, lang xml:lang.*
<blockquote>	It indents text. Some of the attributes which it can take are *cite,dir id, style, title,lang and xml:lang.*
<body>	It is the document body element. It takes attributes including: *dir, title, lang , xml:lang and style*. In **Transitional type document** - it allows: *bgcolor, text,link,vlink, alink* and *background* attributes.
 	It is an empty element. It creates a line break. Some attributes which it takes are:- *id, style and title*. In **Transitional type document** - it can accept *clear* attribute.
<button>	It is used for creating buttons. Some of the attributes which go with it are:- *name, value, disabled, type, id, style, title, accesskey, onfocus, onblur, tabindex*
<caption>	It is used for creating a caption for a table. It can take these attributes:- *dir, id, lang, xml:lang, style, title.* In **Transitional type document** - it can accept *align.*
<cite>	It is used for citation of some text which is someone's speech or work. Some of the attributes, which it takes are:-*dir, id, lang xml:lang, style,* and *title.*

XHTML 1.0 Elements (cont.)

Element	Description & Attributes
<code>	It allows you to insert a programming code in your document. Some of the attributes which it takes are:-*dir, id, lang xml:lang style,* and *title.*
<col>	It is used with the creation of tables. 'col' means column. Among other attributes, it can take are:- *align, valign, width, span, dir, id, lang ,xml:lang, style* and *title.*
<colgroup>	It is for making a group of some columns of a table. Among other attributes, it can take are:- *align, valign, width, span, dir, id, lang, xml:lang, style* and *title.*
<dd>	A definition description element for definition lists of a table. some of the attributes it takes are:- *dir, id, lang,xml:lang, style* and *title.*
<del>	This element marks deleted text. some of the attributes it takes are:- *id, dir, cite, lang,xml:lang, datetime, style, and title.*
<dfn>	It is used for defining terms/phrases. Among other attributes, it allows *dir, id, lang, xml:lang, style and title.*
<div>	It is a block level element. It is suited for use with Cascading Style Sheets. Among other attributes, it also takes *dir, id, lang, style, title lang* and *xml:lang* In **Transitional type document** - it can accept *align.*
<dl>	You can use it for defining a 'definition list'. Some of the common attributes, which are allowed are:- *id, dir, lang, xml:lang, style*, and *title.* In **Transitional type document** - it can accept *compact.*
<dt>	It is used for defining each list item within <dl> element. Some of the attributes one can use with it are:-*dir, id, lang, style,lang,xml:lang* and *xml.*
<em>	It is used for emphasising some text. It renders text in italics with regular emphasis. It can take any of these attributes:- *dir, id, lang, style, lang* and *xml:lang*
<fieldset>	It sets up a group of fields in order to group related items on a form. Some of the attributes, it can take are:- *dir, id, lang, xml:lang, style* and *title.*
<form>	It is used for creating a form. Some of the attributes it can take are:- *method, action, onsubmit,onreset, accept, acceptcharset ,enctype, dir, id, lang, xml:lang, style* and *title.* In **Transitional type document** - it can accept *target*

XHTML 1.0 Elements (cont.)

Element	Description & Attributes
<h1>,<h2>, <h3>, <h4>,<h5> and <h6>	These six elements are used to create headings from the largest to the smallest. Among other attributes, they can take are:- *dir, id, lang, xml:lang, style* and *title*. In **Transitional type document** - they can accept *align attribute.*
<head>	This element contains the title element and any other content that will be stored in meta tags. Meta-data is not displayed. It can take these attributes:- *dir, lang, xml:lang* and *profile.*
<hr />	This is an empty element whose function is to display a horizontal rule. Among other attributes, they can take are:- *dir, id, lang, xml:lang, style* and *title*. In **Transitional type document** - it can accept *align, size, width and noshade.*
<html>	This is the root element. Note that you <u>do not</u> begin it with x for XHTML. But in the document type definition, it must be written as:- <html xmlns= "http://www.w3.org/1999/xhtml" xml:lang = "en" lang = "en"> ------ ⇑ here **x** is essential *xmlns, xml:lang,* and *lang* are attributes. It can also take *dir* as attribute.
<i>	It generates *italic* font. Some of the attributes you can use with it are:- *dir, id, lang, xml:lang, style* and *title.*
<image>	Its application allows you to include an image/graphic in your Web page. You can use any of these attributes with this element:- *src,* and *alt* (essential), *height, widh, id, dir, lang, xml:lang, style* and *title.* In **Transitional type document** - it can accept *align, name, border, hspac and vspace*
<input>	It is used with forms in order to specify any of the 10 different input controls *(buttons, text boxes, text areas, password, checkboxes, radio buttons, select groups, file loadup controls, image controls* and *hidden controls).* You can use any of these attributes with it:- *name, type, checked, disabled, accept, src, alt, tabindex, accesskey, onfocus, onblur, onselect, value, onchange, readonly, dir, id, lang, xml:lang, style, title,* and *maxlength.* In **Transitional type document** - it can accept *align.*

XHTML 1.0 Elements (cont.)

Element	Description & Attributes
<ins>	The element is used in tandem with <del> element. Its purpose is to insert some other text alongside the text which has been crossed off in order to show the crossed off and inserted text side by side. This is the reason why <del> and <ins> have to be implemented in tandem. These two elements are not currently supported by Netscape Navigator. It is suggested that you avoid their application, and instead use <s> and <strike> elements to achieve the same effect. You can use any of these attributes:- *datetime, dir, id, lang, xml:lang and cite.*
<kbd>	Its purpose is to let you define the text to be input in a monospaced font. Among other attributes, it can take are:- *dir, id, lang, xml:lang, style* and *title.*
<label>	Its purpose is to let you label a form field. Among other attributes, it can take are *dir, id, for, accesskey, onfocus, onblur, lang, xml:lang, style* and *title.*
<legend>	It is a form's field group caption. Some of the attributes it can take are:- *accesskey, dir, id, lang, xml:lang, style and title.* In **Transitional type document** - it can accept *align relative to <fieldset>.*
<li>	Its function is to let you define each item in any ordered or unordered list. Some of the attributes it can take are: *dir id, lang, xml:lang, style and title.* In **Transitional type document** - it can accept *type and value.*
<link>	It is used to link documents, such as Cascading Style sheet file to the document concerned. It can take these attributes:- *href, hreflang, type, rel, rev, lang, xml:lang, charset, id, dir, style and title.* In **Transitional type document** - it can accept *target.*
<map>	It specifies client-side image map. Among other attributes, it can take are :- *name,style, title, id, lang, xml:lang, onmousemove, onmouseout, onmouseup, onmousedown, onkeypress, onkeydown, onkeyup, onclick, ondblclick, dir.*
<meta>	The function of this element is to let you specify information about the document (meta-data).it can take any of these attributes:- *content* (it is essential), *dir, name, lang, xml:lang, http-equiv*, and *scheme.*
<noscript>	It is a very useful element as it can provide an alternative content to browsers, which cannot run any script. It can work with these attributes:- *dir, id, lang, xml:lang, style* and *title.*

XHTML 1.0 Elements (cont.)

Element	Description & Attributes
<object>	It allows you to embed objects such as images, multimedia, and so on in a Web page. Among the attributes it takes, these are also allowed:- *data, declare, id, dir, height, width, name, tabindex, type, standby, archive, style, title, lang, xml:lang and, codetype.* In **Transitional type document** - it can take these attributes:- *align, border, hspace* and *vspace.*
<ol>	It is used to define an ordered list, which is a 'numbered' list. It can take these attributes:- *dir, id, lang, xml:lang, style* and *title.* In **Transitional type document** - it can take these attributes:- *compact, start* and *type.*
<optgroup>	It is used to define 'choice groups' in order to create a list of options. You must use the *label* attribute with this element. It can also take the following attributes:- *disabled, dir, id, lang, xml:lang,* style and *title.*
<option>	It is the menu options in the <select> element. It can enable you to define each option in <select> element. Use it with pull-down menus and scrollboxes for multiple choices. You can use any of these attributes with this element:- *dir, id, selected, disabled, label, value, lang, xml:lang, style and title.*
<p>	It starts a new paragraph. It is the main text block element. You can implement any of the following attributes with this element:- *dir, id, lang, xml:lang, style* and *title.* In **Transitional type document** - it can take align attribute.
<param>	It is an object-parameter element used with <applet> and <object> to supply a named property value. The following attributes can be used with this element:- *id, name, type, value and valuetype.* In **Transitional type document,** *'name'* is an essential attribute.
<pre>	It is used to preserve the formatting of text. For instance, it can preserve white spaces. If you use this element for displaying the text, the text will be displayed in mono-space font. It can take these attributes:- *dir, id, lang, xml:lang, space, style,* and *title.* In **Transitional type document,** it takes *width.*
<q>	It is used for including quotations in a document. It can take any of the following attributes:- *cite, dir, id, lang, xml:lang, style* and *title.*
<samp>	It is a program and sample output element which displays output in monospaced font. It takes:- *dir, id, lang, xml:lang, style* and *title.*

XHTML 1.0 Elements (cont.)

Element	Description & Attributes
<script>	This element is used to embed scripting statements in XHTML document. The scripting segment is written within <ascript>........</script> in <head> section of a document. When a document containing a script is displayed, the actual script is hidden. For instance, scripted Web authors, and dates do not appear on screen. It can take *type, defer, src, charset* and *xml:space* attributes. In **Transitional type document,** it takes *language* attribute.
<select>	It is for making a selection from multiple choices offered as a menu on a form. It can take any of the following attributes:- *dir, id, disabled, lang, xml:lang, name, multiple, onfocus, onblur, onchange, style,* and *title.*
<small>	If you want to display some text in a smaller font then use it. You can also apply any of these attributes with it:- *dir, id, lang, xml:lang, style* and *title.* In **Transitional type document,** it takes *lang* attribute.
<span>	It is a generic inline element. It is primarily used for Cascading Style Sheets application. It can take these attributes:- *dir, id, lang, xml:lang, style* and *title.*
<strong>	It is used for placing strong emphasis in a bold font on some text. It can take these attributes:- *dir, id, lang, xml:lang, style* and *title.*
<style>	It is an embedded style sheet element, which is used to include style sheet rules in a Web document. It is placed in the <head> section of the document. You can use any of these attributes with it:- *type, lang, xml:lang, xml:space, media,* and *title.*
<sub>	It is used for containing subscripts. It can take these attributes:- *dir, id, lang, xml:lang, style* and *title.*
<sup>	It is used for containing superscripts. It can take these attributes:- *dir, id, lang, xml:lang, style* and *title.*
<table>	The purpose of this element is to let you create a table with rows and columns. In the table body, you can place both text and images. Among other attributes, it can also take these attributes:- *dir, id, lang, xml:lang, border, width, frame, rules,summary, cellspacing, cellpadding, style* and *title.* In **Transitional type document,** it can take *align* and *bgcolor* attributes.

XHTML 1.0 Elements (cont.)

Element	Description & Attributes
<tbody>	A table can only have one head, and one footer. On the other hand, it can have a number of separately defined **bodies**. They are just like new groups, and to start these new groups/bodies, you must use <tbody> element. You can use any of these attributes:- *align, valign, char, charfoo dir, id, lang, xml:lang, style and title.*
<td>	Its function is to define a table data cell. It can take these attributes:- *abbr, axis, align, valign, char, caroff, colspan, rowspan, dir, id, headers, scope, lang, xml:lang, style and title.* In **Transitional type document,** it can take *bgcolor, height and width* attributes.
<textarea>	Its purpose is to enable you to create a multi-line text field for data input in a 'form application'. It can accept these attributes:- *cols, rows, disabled, name, accesskey,onblur, onfocus, onselect, onchange,tabindex,readonly, id, dir, lang, xml:lang, style and title.*
<tfoot>	A table can have only one footer which is created by this element. You can use any of these attributes:- *align, valign, char, charfoo dir, id, lang, xml:lang, style and title.*
<th>	It defines a table header cell. It can take these attributes:- *abbr, axis, align, valign, char, caroff, colspan, rowspan, dir, id, headers, scope, lang, xml:lang, style and title.* In **Transitional type document,** it can take *bgcolor, height and width* attributes.
<thead>	Its function is to define a group of rows which make up the table head. It can take any of these attributes:- :- *align, valign, char, charfoo dir, id, lang, xml:lang, style and title.*
<title>	This element is used to create the title of the document, This title appears in the title bar of the browser. It takes *dir, lang, xml:lang* attributes.
<tr>	It is used to define a row of a table. It can take any of these attributes:- *align, valign, char, charfoo dir, id, lang, xml:lang, style and title.* In **Transitional type document,** it can take *bgcolor* attribute.

XHTML 1.0 Elements (cont.)

Element	Description & Attributes
<tt>	It is a teletype-text element which uses a fixed width font. It can take any of these attributes:- *dir, id, lang, xml:lang, style* and *title.*
<ul>	It is used to define an unordered (bulleted) list. It can take any of these attributes:- *dir, id, lang, xml:lang, style* and *title.* In **Transitional type document,** it can take *compact and* attributes.
<var>	It is a variable-content element in order to specify a variable. It accepts these attributes:- *dir, id, lang, xml:lang, style* and *title.*

The following list includes only those elements and their associated attributes that can only perform their relevant function in XHTML Transitional Document Type Definition -DTD. These are not recognised(deprecated) in XHTL 1.0 Strict DTD

- If you use any of these elements and their associated attributes in a document written under Strict DTD, you will get a long list of errors, when a document is submitted to W3C Validation Service for checking the document for xml well-formedness and validity. You have been warned!
- Try not to create your documents with these elements and their attributes, as eventually modern browsers will be for **core** XHTML which is strict type DTD.

Transitional XHTML 1.0 Elements(cont.)

Element	Description & Attributes
<applet>	It enables the running of interactive Java applets in a Web page. Java applets are mini programs written in Java programming language. It can take these attributes:- *align, alt, archive, code, codebase, object, id, height, width, name, hspace, vspace, style and title.*
<basefont>	It is used to set the default font size for the whole page, but it could be reset when there is a need for doing so. It uses 1-7 range. It can take *size, face, color* and *id* attributes.

Transitional XHTML 1.0 Elements(cont.)

Element	Description & Attributes
<center>	It is used for centre alignment on a web page. It can take any of these attributes:- *id, dir, lang, xml:lang, style* and *title.*
<dir>	It is a directory list element that is used for defining a listing of directories. It can take any of these attributes:- *compact, dir, id, lang, xml:lang, style* and *title.*
<font>	It defines the font size for the text to follow. Any of these attributes can be used with it:- *color, face, size, dir, id, lang, xml:lang, style* and *title.*
<iframe>	This is inline floating element which creates a floating box. It can take any of these attributes:- *align, src, height, width, name, frameborder, scrolling ,marginheight, marginwidth, id, style* and *title.*
<isindex>	It is a single line text input control element. It accepts these attributes:- *dir, id, lang, xml:lang, style* and *title.*
<menu>	Its purpose is to define a menu list. It accepts these attributes:- *compact, dir, id lang, xml:lang, style* and *title.*
<noframes>	Its function is to provide an alternative content/text when the browser cannot handle frames. Associated attributes are:- *dir, id lang, xml:lang, style* and *title.*
<s> and <strike>	Both of these elements have the same function which is to strike-through some text. They can take these attributes:- *dir, id lang, xml:lang, style* and *title.*
<u>	It is a presentational element for the underlining of some text. It can take attributes:- *dir, id lang, xml:lang, style*, and *style.*

FRAMES

If you include frames in your XHTML documents, in this case, you must use the correct **doctype declaration**, before the actual content of the Web document is written. It is listed below:-

```
<!DOCTYPE html
      PUBLIC "- //w3C//DTD XHTML 1.0 Frameset//EN"
 "http://www.w3.org/TR/xhtml1/DTD/xhtml1- frameset.dtd">
```

Appendix B
CSS2 Properties Digest

• Introduction

Cascading Style Sheets (CSS) is a simple mechanism for adding style (e.g. fonts, colours, spacing) to Web documents. If you want to learn about Cascading Style Sheets Versions 1 and 2 in greater depth, you should visit W3C Web site at:- **http://www.w3.org/Style/CSS/**

At this site, you will find the latest information on all aspects of both CSS1 and CSS2 versions. The current version is CSS2 which also includes all properties of CSS1. When you visit this site, you can learn all about browsers which support this W3C technology, and comprehensive information on other related resources, and CSS. Here, most CSS2 current properties are listed in order to assist you to use these in your Web documents or develop external cascading style sheet rules, and link these to your own documents. For your ease of reference, the list has organised these properties under **7 sections**, so that you can refer to this list quickly when needed.

CSS2 Properties (cont.)

Section 1. Box/Border and Tables Properties

Property	inherited	values	operates with
border/box	no	<border-width>,<border-style>,<color>	all elements
border-top	no	<border-width>,<border-style>,<color>	all elements
border-bottom	no	<border-width>,<border-style>,<color>	all elements
border-left	no	<border-width>,<border-style>,<color>	all elements
border-right	no	<border-width>,<border-style>,<color>	all elements
border-width	no	thin, medium, thick <length>	all elements
border-top-width	no	thin, medium, thick <length>	all elements

CSS2 Properties (cont.)

Property	inherited	values	operates with
border-bottom-width	no	thin, medium, thick <length>	all elements
border –left-width	no	thin, medium, thick <length>	all elements
border-right-width	no	thin, medium, thick <length>	all elements
border-style	no	none, dashed, dotted, double, groove, ridge, inset, solid, outset	all elements
border-top-style	no	none, dashed, dotted, double, groove, ridge, inset, solid, outset	all elements
border-bottom-style	no	none, dashed, dotted, double, groove, ridge, inset, solid, outset	all elements
border-left-style	no	none, dashed, dotted, double, groove, ridge, inset, solid, outset	all elements
border-right-style	no	none, dashed, dotted, double, groove, ridge, inset, solid, outset	all elements
border-color	no	<color>	all elements
border-top-color	no	<color>	all elements
border-bottom-color	no	<color>	all elements
border-left-color	no	<color>	all elements
border-right-color	no	<color>	all elements
border –spacing	yes	<length>	inline tables and tables
caption-side	yes	top, bottom, left, right	table caption elements
clear	no	none, left, right, both	all elements
display	no	if you set " " – the element is rendered if you set **none** - the element is rendered	all elements
empty-cells	yes	show, hide	table cell elements

CSS2 Properties (cont.)

Property	inherited	values	operates with
float	no	none, left, right	all elements, but not with content and positioned elements
height	no	<length>, auto, <percentage>	replaced, DIV, and SPAN elements
left	no	auto, <length>, <percentage>	all elements
margin	no	<length>, <percentage> auto	all elements
margin-top	no	<length>, <percentage> auto	all elements
margin-bottom	no	<length>, <percentage> auto	all elements
margin –left	no	<length>, <percentage> auto	all elements
margin-right	no	<length>, <percentage> auto	all elements
overflow	no	scroll, clip, none	all elements
padding	no	auto, <length>, <percentage>	all elements
padding-top	no	auto, <length>, <percentage>	all elements
padding-bottom	no	auto, <length>, <percentage>	all elements
padding-left	no	auto, <length>, <percentage>	all elements
padding-right	no	auto, <length>, <percentage>	all elements
position	no	static, relative, absolute	all elements
table-layout	no	auto, fixed	inline and table elements
top	no	auto, <length>, <percentage>	all elements
visibility	no	visible, hidden, inherit	all elements
white-space	no	<length>, <percentage>	block level elements
width elements	no	auto,<length>,<percentage>	block and replaced

CSS2 Properties (cont.)

Property	inherited	values	operates with
Section 2. 'color' and background Properties			
background	no	<color>,<repeat>,<position>, <scroll>, <url>	all elements
background-attachment	no	scroll, fixed, inherit	all elements
background-color	no	<color>, transparent	all elements
background-image	no	none, <url>	all elements
background-position	no	left, right, centre, top, bottom	all elements
bacground-repeat	no	repeat, repeat-x, repeat-y, no-repeat	all elements
color	yes	RGB value or color name	all elements
Section 3. Font Properties			
font	yes	<font-size>,<font-family>, [/ <line-height>]? <font-variant>	all elements
font-family	yes	serif, sans-serif, monospace, and some other font-family names	all elements
font-size	yes	small, smaller medium, large, larger, and some other values including <percentage> value of the parent font	all elements
font-style	yes	normal, italic, oblique	all elements
font-variant	yes	normal, small-cape, inherit	all elements
font-weight	yes	normal, bold, bolder, light. you can also declare numeric values: 100,200,300,400,500,600,700,800, 900	all elements
Section 4. Interactive style and control Properties			
cursor	yes	auto, crosshair, default, pointer, move, text, wait, and some other values connected with re-size	all elements
outline	no	'outline-color', 'outline-width', 'outline-style'	all elements

CSS2 Properties (cont.)

Section 5. Page and Printing Properties

page	yes	auto,<identifier>	block elements
page-break-after	no	auto, left, right, always, avoid	block elements
page-break-before	no	auto, left, right, always, avoid	block elements
page-break-inside	yes	auto, avoid	block elements

Section 6. Text Properties

letter-spacing	yes	normal, <length>	all elements
line-height	yes	normal, <number>, <length>, <percentage>	all elements
text-align	yes	left, right, centre, justify	block elements
text-decoration	no	none, underline, overline, line-through, blink	all elements
text-indent	yes	<percentage>,<length>	block elements
text-show	no	none,<color>	block elements
text-transform	yes	none, capitalise, uppercase, lowercase	all elements
vertical-align	no	baseline, sub, super, top, top-text, middle, text-bottom, <percentage>	inline elements
word-spacing	yes	normal, <length>	all elements

Section 7. visual presentation handling position Properties

clip	no	auto, <shape>	block & replacement element
display	no	block, inline, compact, none and some other values	all elements
left elements	no	auto, <length> <percentage	positioned
marker-offset	no	auto, <length>	only with elements 'display: marker'
overflow	no	auto, hidden, visible, scroll	block and replaced elements
right	no	auto, <length>,<percentage>	positioned elements
visibility	no	visible, hidden, collapse	all elements

Appendix C

W3C Validation

• Introduction

Undoubtedly, the best validator in the world is W3C's validator. For validating your documents saved with **.html** extension, the location is at:-

http://validator.w3.org/

• For validating Cascading Style Sheets (CSS), the location is at:-

http://jigsaw. w3.org/css-validator

• A method of document validation

• You must make sure that the document you wish to validate is uploaded to your Web site. This may be your personal Web site or any other Web site where your documents are stored. When your page is accessible via a Web site, it is then on the Internet and thus it is http accessible. At present, W3C accepts documents by means of http protocol.

• Open the IE or any other browser in order to enter in the address bar one (URL) from the above list.

• Once you are connected to W3C, enter the URL of the document you wish to submit to W3C Validation Service. This should be entered in the address bar of W3C window as shown in Diagram 1 below.

• Next step is to select 'Document type' in the W3C window. This is achieved by opening the pop-up menu in the same W3C window. This is indicated by an arrow pointing to the opened pop-up menu.

• Now, click on one of the document types which is the correct type for the document you wish to validate.

• There are four more options available to you to choose from as shown in Diagram 1. If you do not wish to select any of these options then click on the button labelled " Validate this page". At this stage, the system will start validating your document. Soon, on your screen some text will appear.

- If you have made any mistakes in entering your document's URL, then you will get an error message informing you about this occurrence. Your document will not be checked at all.

- If your document has met all the requirements, you will get :-

  " Below are the results of checking this document for XML well-formedness and validity---------
  No errors found! --- Congratulations ...."

- If your document has failed to meet XML well-formedness and validity conditions under the selected DTD, you will get an error list. For instance, Page 85 contains a full error list generated by this validation service. You can examine it now. You may find some of the reasons for reported errors unclear. In fact, after reading a few error lists, in my opinion, you will soon become familiar with finding out where things have gone wrong. Sometimes, due to one minor error, the validator points to a number of mistakes. If you can correct this particular mistake, all other mistakes automatically will disappear. Submit it again. If no mistakes are found, you will get a message: "No errors found !" message.

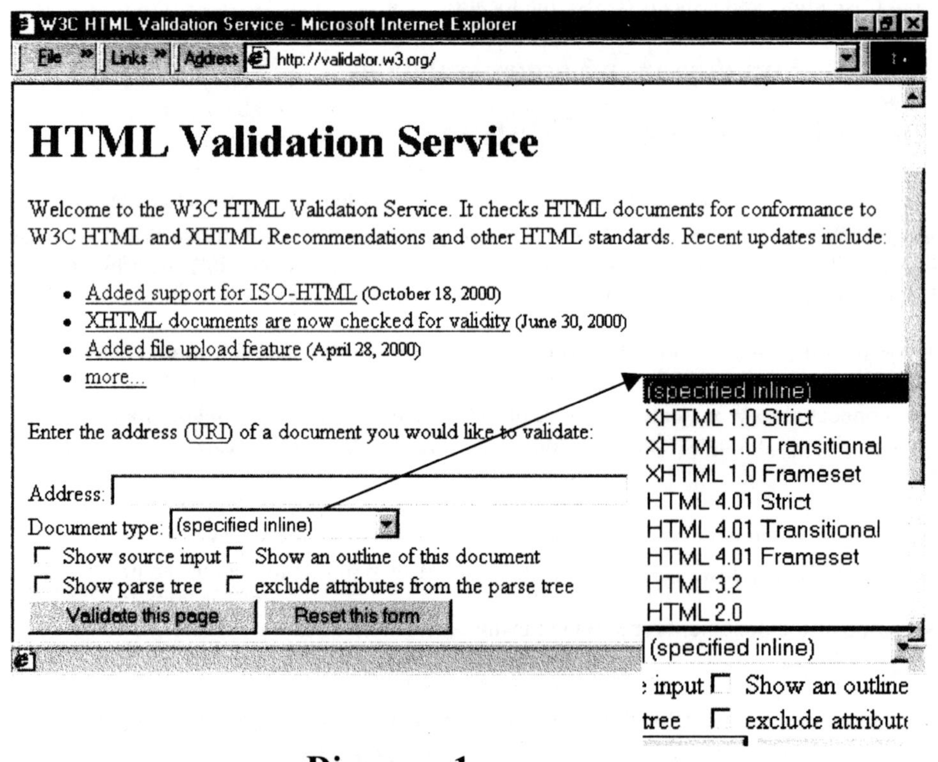

Diagram 1

Index

F

G

H

I

J

K-L